Alg
Lool
Wars

Alger Hiss's Looking-Glass Wars

Wars

The Covert Life of a Soviet Spy

G. EDWARD WHITE

OXFORD
UNIVERSITY PRESS
2004

OXFORD

UNIVERSITY PRESS

Oxford New York

Auckland Bangkok Buenos Aires Cape Town Chennai
Dar es Salaam Delhi Hong Kong Istanbul Karachi Kolkata
Kuala Lumpur Madrid Melbourne Mexico City Mumbai Nairobi
São Paulo Shanghai Taipei Tokyo Toronto

Copyright © 2004 by G. Edward White

Published by Oxford University Press, Inc.
198 Madison Avenue, New York, New York 10016

www.oup.com

Oxford is a registered trademark of Oxford University Press

Library of Congress Cataloging-in-Publication Data

White, G. Edward.
Alger Hiss's looking-glass wars: the covert life of a Soviet spy / by G. Edward White.
p. cm.
ISBN 0-19-515345-6
1. Hiss, Alger.
2. Spies—United States—Biography.
3. Communists—United States—Biography.
4. United States. Dept. of State—Officials and employees—Biography.
5. Subversive activities—United States—History—20th century.
6. Espionage, Soviet—United States—History—20th century.
I. Title.
E743.5.H55 W47 2004
364.1'31—dc22   2003015933

10 9 8 7 6 5 4 3 2 1
Printed in the United States of America
on acid-free paper

For Susan Davis White

Also by G. Edward White

The Eastern Establishment and the Western Experience (1968)
The American Judicial Tradition (1976, 2d. ed. 1988)
Patterns of American Legal Thought (1978)
Tort Law in America: An Intellectual History (1980, 2d. ed. 2003)
Earl Warren: A Public Life (1982)
The Marshall Court and Cultural Change (1988, 2d. ed. 1991)
Justice Oliver Wendell Holmes: Law and the Inner Self (1993)
Intervention and Detachment: Essays in Legal History and Jurisprudence (1994)
Creating The National Pastime: Baseball Transforms Itself, 1903–1953 (1996)
Oliver Wendell Holmes: Sage of the Supreme Court (2000)
The Constitution and the New Deal (2000)

CONTENTS

LIST OF ILLUSTRATIONS

PREFACE

Readers of my previous books might wonder why I came to write on Alger Hiss. My work in twentieth-century American history has centered on legal topics, with a particular emphasis on constitutional law and judges. Hiss was a lawyer, but this book does not focus on him in that capacity. It is about his far better known lives as accused Communist and Soviet spy, convicted perjurer, defender of his innocence, and tireless campaigner in pursuit of his vindication. It is also about the changing reaction of sectors of the American public to Hiss, and to the domestic and international issues with which he was identified.

My interest in Hiss did not derive from any of my former scholarly interests. It originated when I learned, in the late 1960s, that my father-in-law, John F. Davis, had provided legal representation for Alger Hiss in 1948. John Davis had been Hiss's counsel at an August 25, 1948, hearing in which Hiss appeared before the House of Representatives's Committee on Un-American Activities to deny accusations made about him by Whittaker Chambers. John continued to work with the Hiss defense team for the remainder of 1948, in which Hiss filed a libel suit against Chambers and appeared before a New York grand jury that eventually indicted him for perjury, and throughout Hiss's 1949 and 1950 perjury trials. John was not among the counsel of record in the libel suit, nor did he represent Hiss in court during either of the trials. He was nowhere near as closely involved with the Hiss defense efforts as Edward McLean, William Marbury, or Harold Rosenwald, who coordinated them and, along with Hiss, developed the principal defense strategies. But John was nonetheless an active member of the Hiss defense between August 1948 and January 1950, corresponding frequently with McLean and Marbury.

John played no part in any of Hiss's legal proceedings after his 1950 conviction, which consisted of retrial motions, appeals, petitions to the United States Supreme Court, and a 1978 petition to vacate Hiss's 1950 perjury conviction. He never discussed privileged information about the Hiss case with me; much of what I learned about his role in the case came from published sources. Between 1966, when I first met John, and 1978, our discussions of the Hiss case were infrequent, and John's contributions tended to be laconic.

In August 1974 John Davis was interviewed by Allen Weinstein as part of Weinstein's research for his book on the Hiss case, *Perjury*, which was published in 1978. John did not mention the interview until after *Perjury* appeared. In fact he expressed no interest in reading *Perjury*, and only discussed the interview after I read it, sometime in 1979, and asked him about it. After reading *Perjury* I was inclined to take a different view on the Hiss case. To the extent that I had a position on the case before reading *Perjury*, it was sympathetic to Hiss, but my sympathy was not based on much knowledge of the details of Hiss's career. Had I been asked for a candid assessment of the basis of my sympathy, I would have said that it was grounded on my admiration for John Davis, the fact that he, I, and Hiss were graduates of Harvard Law School, and the fact that when I attended that law school in the late 1960s, many students and faculty were inclined to think that Hiss had been wrongly convicted.

After reading *Perjury* I began to talk to John Davis in earnest about the Hiss case. John was born in 1907, graduated from Harvard Law School in 1932, and died in 2000. He moved to the Washington, D.C. area in the early 1930s, returned there in 1946, and stayed for the rest of his life. He was in private practice at the time he represented Hiss. In 1950, the year of Hiss's conviction, John joined the staff of the Solicitor General's Office, remaining there until 1961, when he became Clerk of the Supreme Court of the United States. After retiring from that position in 1970, he taught at Georgetown and Maryland law schools until 1988.[1] John's friends and professional associates knew him to be a conspicuously honest and fair-minded person. He was not at all inclined to make impulsive assessments of the behavior and temperament of others. He did not covet success or attention, and he was not swayed by the opinions of people with whom he came in contact. He valued character in others, and, to use one of his favorite expressions, he was independent as a hog on ice.

When John eventually read *Perjury*, he was not persuaded by the evidence that Weinstein assembled in support of his conclusion that the second Hiss jury had been correct in convicting Hiss. John did not believe that Hiss had engaged in espionage. He found Weinstein's evidence against Hiss far shakier than Weinstein claimed, being subject to alternative interpretations that favored Hiss. He also felt that some of the principal antagonists of Hiss—Whittaker Chambers, a former Communist who admitted to having committed perjury himself, J. Edgar Hoover, the head of the FBI, whose files Weinstein drew heavily upon in presenting evidence incriminating

Hiss, and Richard Nixon, who almost single-handedly kept Chambers's initial accusations against Hiss from being discredited—were not trustworthy sources. In contrast, he thought that Alger Hiss was a person of good character—honest, thoughtful of others, straightforward, and cooperative with his lawyers—and that, having been successful and prominent in his public career, Hiss had no motive to spy for the Soviets and lie about it.

The summer John died I was asked to write a short essay on the Hiss case. The essay was mainly about the testimony of Justices Felix Frankfurter and Stanley Reed, who appeared as character witnesses for Hiss in his first trial.[2] In preparation for the essay I read some additional sources about Hiss, and became intrigued by what I now saw as a historical and personal puzzle. Why have so many people over the years believed, and why do they continue to believe, in Hiss's innocence, or at least to believe that the Hiss case was one of those intractably ambiguous historical episodes, when the evidence of his guilt was so plain? And why, if Hiss had been a Communist and a Soviet agent all along, had he mounted so prominent a campaign to, as he put it, "vindicate" himself by convincing the public that he had not been? Why had he enlisted close friends and members of his family in that campaign? Why, in short, had he become a spy, and resolved to lie about his covert life, to as broad an audience as he could, for more than 60 years?

I will subsequently acknowledge the contributions of many other people who helped with this book. But the book would not have been written had I not come to conclude that John Davis's continued belief in the innocence of Alger Hiss, coupled with my understanding of the sort of person John was, revealed something elemental in coming to grips with Hiss as a person and as a historical figure. A close study of Hiss's life can help us understand why he was a gifted spy and successful publicizer of his innocence. It can also help us understand how the story of Hiss is a story, in part, about others, such as John, who found Hiss an admirable and sympathetic figure, and wanted to believe in him.

INTRODUCTION

On March 17, 1976, Alger Hiss was in Boston to give a public lecture at Boston University. He was 72 years old at the time, and in good health, as slim and erect a figure as when, 38 years earlier, he appeared before the House Un-American Activities Committee (HUAC), to deny categorically the claims of Whittaker Chambers that he and Hiss had been members of an underground group of Communists in Washington, D.C. in the 1930s. Hiss had ultimately been sent to jail for perjuring himself about a more serious accusation Chambers made about him, that in 1938 Hiss had passed copies of stolen classified State Department papers, typed on a Hiss family typewriter, a Woodstock, to Chambers so that they could be transmitted to Soviet military intelligence. By 1976, however, Hiss had been out of prison for 22 years, had regained his license to practice law, and, as his Boston University appearance suggested, had become something of a fixture on college and university campuses.

Hiss had lost some of his hair by 1976, but otherwise looked much as he had when he was first confronted by Chambers. He was a tall, graceful-looking man with angular, regular features, somewhat prominent ears, and the rangy build of an athlete. His impression of grace was accentuated by his height, his wiry frame, the ease with which he moved, and his calm demeanor. His voice was cultivated, with no trace of a regional accent. As a public speaker he was exceptionally articulate, if somewhat measured and occasionally wooden. In more informal exchanges with his audiences, now composed mainly of college and university students, he was approachable and animated. For someone who had been widely branded a "convicted traitor" in the 1950s, and identified as one of the most notorious American Communists and Soviet spies of his time, Alger Hiss seemed to be doing rather well. As he prepared to give his Boston lecture, he could look forward to participating in a celebratory press conference in New York the following day. The press conference, at the Overseas

Press Club, was to launch the publication of a book written by the journalist John Chabot Smith, and published by Holt, Rinehart, and Winston. The book, entitled *Alger Hiss: The True Story,* would conclude that Hiss had been innocent of the charges Chambers made against him, and that he had very likely been the victim of a frame-up instituted by Chambers, with possible help from the FBI and members of HUAC.

Although the appearance of Smith's book represented a high point in what Hiss had come to call his campaign for vindication, there was a slight cloud on his horizon as he anticipated the March 18 press conference. A week earlier a professor in the history department at Smith College, Allen Weinstein, had met with Hiss to inform him that Weinstein's forthcoming book on the Hiss case would conclude that the jury that convicted Hiss on two counts of perjury in 1950 had been correct. Weinstein's meeting with Hiss had been awkward for both men because Weinstein had previously suspected that Hiss had been framed. In the early 1970s, with that hypothesis in mind, he had asked Hiss for access to his lawyers' files on the Hiss case. Hiss had granted Weinstein, as well as John Chabot Smith, that access. Now Weinstein was telling Hiss that his research in the files, as well as in other sources, had led him to conclude that Hiss had not been framed, and that Chambers's charges against him were essentially correct.

Weinstein's book was not close to completion when he met with Hiss, and Smith's was due out very soon. In the spring of 1976 Hiss was still profiting from the fact that his leading antagonists in the case had been Richard Nixon, in disgrace after resigning the presidency in the summer of 1974, J. Edgar Hoover, who had been exposed, after his death in 1972, as having run the Federal Bureau of Investigation in a partisan and sometimes malevolent manner, and Chambers, whose death in 1961, under obscure circumstances, was thought by some to have been a suicide connected to mental instability. In the wake of Vietnam and Watergate, McCarthyism had become a pejorative label, and more Americans were coming to see Alger Hiss as the victim of Cold War excesses.

So when Tony Hiss, Alger's son, called his father in Boston on the evening of March 17 to say that a story with the headline "Professor Says Alger Hiss Lied About his Links With Chambers," had appeared that morning in *The New York Times,* Hiss may not have been prepared for that news—the professor was Weinstein himself—becoming public so soon. But he responded with his usual aplomb. He relayed a comment to *The Times* calling Weinstein's claims "terribly thin stuff," and "childish," and Tony added that a week ago his father had accused Weinstein of having "biased views" on the Hiss case. And the next day, before a packed audience of journalists at the Overseas Press Club, Hiss defiantly proclaimed his innocence.

When Whittaker Chambers had first accused Hiss of being a Communist in testimony before HUAC on August 4, 1948, Hiss had responded by appearing before the Committee two days later and stating that he had never been a member of the Communist Party or involved in any of its activities. Now, nearly 28 years later, after have been convicted of lying about activities that Chambers had associated with Hiss's being a Communist, Hiss again made a sweeping denial of the charges against him. He began his remarks at the March 18 press conference by repeating that he had never had any connection with the Communist Party of the United States or participated in any of its work. He then added that he had "never handed Whittaker Chambers any State Department documents," and that he had "never engaged in espionage." Hiss had said the same thing at his perjury trials, and the jury at his second trial had concluded that he had not told the truth. His comments at the Overseas Press Club indicated that he was continuing to treat the jury's finding as a gross injustice.

Hiss concluded his remarks at the launching of Smith's book by stating that he had sued for access to FBI files on the Hiss case under the Freedom of Information Act, that after a long delay some files had been released to him, and that those files tended to exonerate him from the charge of having passed typed copies of stolen State Department documents to Chambers (documents Chambers had produced at Hiss's trials). *The New York Times,* reporting on the occasion, ran a front-page story on March 19, headlined "Hiss Says FBI Files Support Some of his Claims of Innocence."[1]

The events just described captured the state of the Alger Hiss case in the mid-1970s. That state of affairs would endure, with only slight modifications, until Hiss's death in 1996. Now, nearly a decade later, three central features of the case have become established. The first is that although the question of Alger Hiss's innocence was still being debated when he died in 1996, nearly 50 years after Chambers first accused him, the principal evidence that convicted Hiss in 1950 remained largely uncontroverted. Hiss's lawyers, in several appeal proceedings and a 1978 effort to have Hiss's conviction vacated, claimed that the technology to "forge" typewriter faces existed at the time of Hiss's trials. But they were never able to introduce any evidence that Chambers, or anyone else, had access to a machine that could duplicate the typeface of the Hisses's Woodstock. Hiss's lawyers also charged that when the Hiss defense introduced a Woodstock typewriter at Hiss's trials, the FBI knew that the Woodstock being introduced could not have been the one owned by the Hisses. But the only possible basis for that charge was an internal FBI memorandum suggesting that the serial number on the Woodstock might not have been consistent with its being in existence when Priscilla Hiss's father reportedly bought it. Further, the actual identity of the typewriter produced in court was not crucial to the charge that someone in the Hiss household had typed copies of stolen documents: what was crucial was the match between Chambers's documents and Hiss family correspondence, whatever typewriter was used.

The second central feature of the Hiss case is that since he was convicted, a good deal more evidence corroborating and authenticating Whittaker Chambers's version of events, and undermining Alger Hiss's version, has come to light. I review that evidence in this book. Even if one assumes that the Hiss case can be reduced to a question of the comparative credibility of Chambers and Hiss—an assumption that I will argue is faulty—Chambers's credibility has increased, and that of Hiss diminished, with time.

The last central feature of the Hiss case lies in an uneasy coexistence with the one just described. In 1996, when Alger Hiss died, at least one American television network reported that he had been cleared of any suspicion of being an agent for the Soviet Union by Russian president Boris Yeltsin. The report was false—Hiss had not been cleared of that suspicion, and Yeltsin had not cleared him—but it revealed the great change in public perceptions of Hiss that had taken place since his perjury conviction. From the moment that Whittaker Chambers accused him of being a Communist, and subsequently becoming an agent for Soviet military intelligence, Alger Hiss strenuously and persistently denied being either, and made extensive efforts to enlist the public in support of his claims of innocence.

Between 1954 and 1996 Alger Hiss's campaign for vindication managed to reverse the state of public perceptions about him. For several years after his release from prison he continued to be thought of as a "convicted traitor," a notorious figure who had difficulty finding a job and was not welcome in public settings. But by the late 1960s he had begun to lecture on college campuses, and books suggesting that he had been an innocent victim of the McCarthy era had appeared, including a profile of the relationship between Hiss and Chambers that claimed Chambers may have had a "psychopathic personality," and had framed Hiss because Hiss had rebuffed his friendship.

By the early 1970s *The New York Times* had invited Hiss to write an op-ed column comparing the political dimensions of his trials to the "six crises" of Richard Nixon, heading for disgrace in the wake of the Watergate scandal. Later in that decade two more books declaring Hiss to be innocent were published, including one by his son Tony, *Laughing Last,* in which Alger's coming vindication was predicted. Hiss had his government pension restored, and his license to practice law in

Massachusetts reinstated, in the same time interval. In 1976 a survey among intellectuals and other public figures, which asked whether respondents found Hiss guilty or innocent, reported that "the new Hiss jury split down the middle."

Hiss's campaign for vindication received a major setback in 1978, when Allen Weinstein's *Perjury*, concluded that Hiss had been both a Communist and a Soviet agent. But Hiss's reputation survived even that assault. His supporters rallied to his cause, attacking Weinstein's research and enticing him into partisan skirmishes. The Hiss case came increasingly to be seen as a politically charged symbol of the Cold War era, precipitating ideological reactions that made recovery of the truth increasingly difficult. In 1986 a *Washington Post* reporter, interviewing Hiss in seclusion on Long Island, concluded that the Hiss case would remain intrinsically ambiguous.

That assessment appeared to be correct on Hiss's death, even though the collapse of the Soviet Union in the early 1990s precipitated the release of previously classified information about Hiss, from both Soviet and United States government archives. In 1992 a former Soviet general who had served as a custodian of Stalin-era archives announced, after a request from Hiss, that he had found no evidence in any Soviet records suggesting that Hiss was a Communist or a Soviet agent. Hiss and his family members rejoiced at the news and widely publicized it, but subsequently the general said that he had been misunderstood. He had only spent two days looking in one archive, that of the KGB, which was concerned with civilian intelligence, and Chambers had testified that Hiss worked for Soviet military intelligence, which had its own archives.

In 1995 a collection of essays on the case of Julius and Ethel Rosenberg, who had been executed in 1953 for passing atomic secrets to the Soviet Union, contained two evaluative references to the Hiss case. One commentator stated that it "remains unsolved," and the other declared that Hiss had "finally [been] cleared of conspiracy charges in 1992." And in 1996 former presidential candidate George McGovern wrote that "I've always believed that Hiss was a victim of the 'red scare' and of Nixon's political rapacity. It is a national outrage that this essentially decent and patriotic American went to prison as a consequence of the demagoguery of Nixon and the ignominious House Committee on Un-American Activities."[3]

Those comments, however, have turned out to be mistaken. Subsequent documents from Soviet and United States archives, taken together with other evidence assembled by Weinstein and other scholars, have demonstrated, as conclusively as any fragmentary historical records can, that Whittaker Chambers's charges against Hiss were correct. The cumulative evidence on Alger Hiss has removed any ambiguity about Hiss's guilt or innocence, and, consequently, any ambiguity about Hiss's protestations of innocence and lifelong campaign for vindication. Those were efforts to enlist others in a grand deception.[2]

This book begins by reviewing the evidence demonstrating that Alger Hiss was a committed Communist, and an agent for Soviet military intelligence, from the mid-1930s until 1946, when he was forced to resign from the State Department and was no longer in a position to supply the Soviets with classified information. It then asks two questions about Hiss's motivation. The first has previously been raised: Why, if Hiss was guilty, and knew it, did he devote so much of his life to an extensive public campaign to persuade others he was not, a campaign that invited close scrutiny of his life and career? It is one thing to proclaim innocence when one has legally been found guilty: convicted persons regularly do so. It is another to encourage the world to scrutinize one's public and private lives, so that innocence may be established, when one knows innocence to be an illusion.

The other asks how Hiss, without producing any new evidence supporting his innocence, was able to convince many people that he was innocent. That question requires an extended analysis of Hiss's campaign for vindication. In that campaign Hiss seized every opportunity to publicize his innocence; he sought to take advantage of any development in American intellectual or political culture that might play to his advantage; he attempted to enlist his entire family in the campaign, helping to destroy his first marriage in the process. He gave sympathetic biographers unrestricted access to his defense files and made himself available for lengthy interviews; he encouraged lawyers to challenge his conviction for a period of more than 30 years; he wrote two books defending himself and contributed heavily to a third. He engaged in all those activities knowing that his professions of innocence were not true, and that his vindication, if it ever came, would be a confidence game. And at the time of his death he had persuaded influential sectors of the American public that he might well have been framed.

One of my goals in the book is thus to put the ambiguity about Hiss's guilt or innocence to rest by marshaling the evidence for his guilt and demonstrating the weaknesses of arguments for his innocence. Although there has been a longstanding perception of the Hiss case as intractably ambiguous, I suggest that that perception needs to be seen as the residue of Hiss's remarkably successful campaign to promote his innocence rather than an accurate rendition of historical reality.

Another of my goals is to better understand why Hiss became a spy, why he chose to continue spying after Chambers defected, why the Soviets continued to regard him as one of their prize assets, and why, after being exposed, he proceeded to

deny, for nearly 50 years, that he had any connections with Communism or the Soviets. Finally, I have sought to gain a clearer sense of why Hiss's campaign to vindicate himself was so successful. In order for him to reach a position where at the
time of his death many Americans believed that he had been retroactively cleared
for the charges of being a Communist and spying for the Soviets, he needed to make
himself into a resonant, rather than a distasteful, public figure. To do that he needed
a fair number of persons in the American population who *wanted* to see him in that
capacity. How was he able to find such persons, and why did their number tend to
increase in the latter years of his life?

The title of this book is drawn from one of John le Carré's novels about persons
engaged in underground intelligence work during the Cold War period. Spies,
le Carré suggests, engage in looking-glass wars. Le Carré had in mind Lewis Carroll's *Through the Looking Glass* in using the phrase. In Carroll's *Alice in Wonderland*
books characters from the real world pass back and forth—through the looking
glass—between that world and a secret world inhabited by figures who are not what
they seem. In le Carré's hands, the looking-glass metaphor takes on an additional
meaning. It not only signifies the passage between the overt "ordinary" world and
the covert secret world, but the illusions—the images in the glass—that spies need
to create as they make the passage. Looking-glass wars are thus efforts, on the part
of the spy, to gain an understanding of potential adversaries in the spy trade, and,
simultaneously, to keep them, and others, from discovering the spy's secrets.

Every spy, le Carré suggests, has an existence he or she keeps behind the looking
glass. The glass purportedly reflects the likeness of the spy, but that likeness is partially an illusion; there are other sides hidden away. All humans have this quality of
not being quite what they seem, and many humans may try to keep something of
themselves hidden from the world. But spies are in the profession of doing so.
Le Carré's protagonists struggle with the duplicity of their profession and the cor-
rosive effects of that duplicity. Alger Hiss practiced his version of duplicity for
more than 60 years. He did so, to many observers, with unfailing graciousness and
self-composure, or with what some saw as an inner peace. That image of Hiss was
his public likeness. I am interested in the relationship of that likeness to Hiss's other
sides, the ones he strove to keep behind the looking glass.

Alger Hiss and the Hiss case remain important to us for two reasons. First, over
time, with almost no new helpful evidence, he managed to transform the attitudes
of a segment of American public opinion toward him. In the 1950s that segment, a
group of educated, cultured, "liberal" professionals of which Hiss was himself a
member, was decidedly unambiguous about his being a "convicted traitor." By
Hiss's death many members of that segment were inclined to think that he was

innocent of perjury and espionage, a victim of the rabid anti-Communism of the Cold War. Since Hiss's campaign for vindication had primarily served to keep him and his protestations of innocence in the public eye, rather than to introduce any significant evidence exculpating him, the shift in attitudes is a powerful testament to the capacity of changing public perceptions to affect, even to distort, our understanding of historical personages and events. Alger Hiss fooled a large number of people for many years, and it is worth reflecting on how that happened.

The other reason Hiss remains important is that he exemplifies a comparatively unusual type of human that continues to inhabit our world. Hiss was one of those rare individuals whose traits and characteristics were complemented by, rather than conflicting with, the secret world of a professional spy. Far from finding the norms of duplicity that mark the secret world disquieting, Hiss appears to have taken pleasure in the pursuit of covert goals and in the creation of devices to shield that pursuit from others. And Hiss was remarkably skillful and effective in those tasks. He operated as a high-level undercover Soviet agent in the federal government for 11 years, and his career in the federal government thrived during that period, so that by 1945 he was one of the most important officials in the State Department, a possible future secretary of state. He was only exposed because of his fortuitous interaction with Chambers. After being released from prison, he launched and publicized an elaborate cover story portraying himself as an innocent scapegoat framed for partisan reasons, and over the years he convinced a large number of Americans that the story was true.

Hiss spent over 60 years of his life promoting a deception. By all accounts, he was energized by the process. He represents the rare example of someone who thrived on living a secret life of betrayal and deceit. It may be that those who rise to the higher echelons of the spy trade are such persons. Since the spy trade, and its consummate practitioners, are just as common a feature of the first decade of the twenty-first century as they were in the 1930s, when Hiss launched his secret career, we may learn something from a close look into the mind and temperament of a quite successful spy. It is time to understand Alger Hiss as an example of that species rather than as a victim of the Cold War. To do that it will be necessary to penetrate Hiss's inner life.

Alger Hiss's Looking-Glass Wars

Alger Hiss, at the age of 14, standing with a group of his contemporaries in Baltimore. He is in the back row, third from the right.

CHAPTER ONE

Family and Marriage

In a 1978 column in the *New York Post*, the journalist Murray Kempton revealed that he, Alger Hiss, and an unnamed third person had grown up in "circumstances of shabby gentility" in Baltimore. "[All] three of us," Kempton went on to say, "shared the condition of having had our fathers die when we were infants." And two of the three publicly admitted to having joined the Communist Party of the United States in the 1930s. The third, Hiss, denied having done so, but Kempton assumed that he had joined as well. None of the three came from impoverished circumstances, Kempton noted, but "[t]he theory that deprivation produces Communists" might nonetheless have been applicable to them. "[D]eprivation," he felt, "is not always . . . only economic deprivation."[1]

Twenty-three years earlier, in an essay on Hiss and his relationship with Whittaker Chambers, Kempton had also emphasized the circumstances of "shabby gentility" in which Hiss had grown up. As Kempton put it,

> The Hisses were not a distinguished family run down. In his final tragedy, his friends and enemies would join in exaggerating the nobility of his origins. When disaster came to him, he was listed in the Washington *Social Register*, but his mother was not in its Baltimore edition.
>
> Alger Hiss's father was a wholesale grocer; he committed suicide when Alger was nine. His older brother was a bohemian who died young. They lived near Lanville Street, which is the heart of shabby gentility in Baltimore.

> As he grew up, more substantial families around him were moving out into the suburbs. The Hisses stayed there in a neighborhood slowly running down. They were not a family of special social prestige, but the Baltimore in which Alger Hiss grew up [had] its own corner for the sort of family that . . . rested on that border between respectability and assured position. In the circumstances of her life, society felt a particular sympathy for Alger Hiss's mother. . . . In a family like this one, . . . it was better to be a boy than a girl, if only because Baltimore needed more boys than girls at debutante parties.[2]

Kempton's description of the Hiss family was not quite accurate. Alger was two and a half when his father, Charles Alger Hiss, committed suicide. There is not much evidence that Baltimore "society" was particularly solicitous of the Hiss family, or particularly sympathetic to the plight of Mary Lavinia (Minnie) Hiss, his mother, after her husband's demise in 1907. Minnie relied primarily on family members for financial support and help in raising her five children, Anna, born in 1893, Mary Ann, in 1895, Bosley, in 1900, Alger, in 1904, and Donald, in 1906. Alger Hiss described the economic circumstances in which he grew up as "modest," but "not particularly shabby." Life insurance policies held at the time of Charles Hiss's death resulted in an income to Minnie Hiss of approximately $5,000 a year through the 1920s, and provided a $10,000 bequest to each of the Hiss children.[3]

Nonetheless Kempton's description of "the young man of shabby gentility" as one who is constantly reminded "that he has been put into the world to better his family, and that the price of fortune is unrelenting effort, and that he cannot be too careful" captures some themes of Alger Hiss's adolescence and young adulthood. Minnie Hiss, Alger recalled, was a woman of considerable energy, good organizational abilities, high ambitions for her children, and a tendency to be didactic and moralizing rather than affectionate. Her children found her company somewhat trying, Alger once describing her as "the family magistrate." "When I went to my mother for solace of a hurt," he recalled in his memoirs, "I was likely to receive a homily on how best to get on in the world." Minnie Hiss's "favorite admonition," Alger said, was "Put your best foot forward," which had the effect of making him "suspicious of the bitch-goddess Success."[4]

Minnie Hiss was determined that her sons should achieve professional success and that her daughters should marry well. Her aspirations were only partially achieved. Her eldest child, Anna, began a career in physical education after attending Hollins College. She was one of the first women in American higher education to do so, eventually becoming head of the Women's Department of Physical Education at the

University of Texas. She never married, and had limited, if friendly, relations with other Hiss family members after moving away from the Baltimore area. Minnie's second daughter, Mary Ann, seemed content to follow a more conventional path. She attended the Bryn Mawr School, a private girls' school in the Baltimore area, and from there went to Smith College.

After college Mary Ann married Elliot Emerson, a Boston stockbroker with an upper-class background, but her life began to disintegrate shortly after her marriage. Elliot Emerson, who was 17 years older than Mary Ann when they married in 1920, suffered financial reverses, and at one point had to borrow money from Hiss family members to avoid taking bankruptcy. As the Emersons' financial situation remained unstable for the next several years, Mary Ann began having emotional difficulties, and had to be hospitalized on two occasions. The Hiss family did not tell Alger, who was attending high school and college at the time, about her hospitalization.

Alger had been comparatively close to Mary Ann as young man, despite the nine years difference in their ages. He had spent the fall semester of 1921 at Powder Point Academy, a private school in Duxbury, Massachusetts, where the Emersons had a country house. Alger had graduated from Baltimore City College, a boy's public high school, in the spring of 1921, but did not go on to college that fall. "My family thought I was young for college," Alger told Meyer Zeligs, one of his biographers, and "for financial reasons" he needed to go to Johns Hopkins University, in Baltimore, and live at home. "[U]nder all the circumstances," he recalled, "it was decided that a year away from home . . . would be good for me." Then, after graduating from Johns Hopkins in the spring of 1926, he enrolled in Harvard Law School and renewed acquaintances with the Emersons, who also had a home in Boston.[5]

In May 1929, a month before he was scheduled to graduate from law school, Alger learned from Minnie that Mary Ann, after a late-night altercation with Elliott Emerson, had swallowed a bottle of Lysol, killing herself. She had previously expressed fears that she might commit suicide, but Alger was not aware that she had suffered from emotional distress. He described himself as "shocked and uncomprehending" when hearing the news of Mary Ann's death, which he believed to be a "sudden, irrational act."[6]

Thus Minnie Hiss's expectations for her daughters were thwarted. So were those for Bosley, her third child. Bosley Hiss was born in 1900, and after Charles Hiss's death was treated by Minnie with special solicitude as "the man of the house." Despite that treatment, or because of it, he was the most conspicuous rebel of the Hiss children, running away from home several times between the ages of 13 and 15. He nonetheless managed to retain Minnie Hiss's affection, and was given considerable freedom to indulge his interests, which included literature, music, and the outdoors. Bosley was "was largely on his own . . . and did not stay around the house" during Alger's youth, and his independent, adventurous life served as a contrast to that of Alger. Even after enrolling at Johns Hopkins in 1918, Bosley, who spent summers working in camps in New England or traveling in Europe, was not much in Alger's company. But he was admired by his younger brother, who shared his interests in culture and the arts. Contemporaries of Bosley described him as a "delightful conversationalist," "in constant demand for dinners and parties," and something of a rake.

After graduating from Johns Hopkins, Bosley took a job as a reporter with the *Baltimore Sun*, hoping to launch a career as a writer. But a year after joining the *Sun* he suddenly became ill, and was diagnosed with Bright's disease, an often-fatal impairment of the kidneys. He was forced to live at home, with Minnie supervising his care. He chafed under the arrangement, and eventually left Baltimore for New York, where he renewed a relationship with an interior decorator, Margaret Owen, who was 20 years his senior. Owen and Bosley traveled to Florida for what was hoped to be a rest cure, but Bosley's condition did not improve. In the spring of 1926, about two years after the disease had first been diagnosed, Bosley and Margaret Owen took up residence in her house in Rye, New York. Subsequently, with Bosley "reduced to a state of physical dependency and almost complete immobility," he and Margaret Owen married.[7]

In June 1926 after his graduation from Johns Hopkins, Alger was dispatched to Rye to serve as "the family's . . . representative" and "a steward or manager" of Margaret Owen's household while she commuted to New York for her business. He handled the grocery shopping, drove Bosley to hospital visits in New York, and served as a companion to his older brother. "Bosley was largely bedridden," Alger recalled, "but his mind and spirit were as vital and dynamic as ever." As Alger read books and played phonograph records for Bosley, and the two talked, "I certainly recognized with grief and sorrow that he was dying," but "I'm not sure I accepted fully the nearness of his death." Alger remained in Rye from June through the middle of September, when he began law school at Harvard. Six weeks later he was hastily summoned to Rye, and shortly after he arrived Bosley died.[8]

Alger subsequently gave an assessment of Bosley's impact on him:

> I have long thought that Bosley was romantically elevated . . . within the family. His charm and precocious talents were enhanced and frozen by his lingering illness and early death. . . . After his death, I heard for a number of years constant references . . . about his magnetism, wit, and scintillating bon mots deflating pompous and self-important people. . . . He had a some-

what willful, romantic vanity that showed itself in scorn for complacency and hypocrisy . . . and was carried to the extreme of liking to shock. . . . This quality I did not admire in Bosley.[9]

One can glimpse some tension beneath the surface of these comments. Later in his life Alger said that "Bosley's spontaneity and ability to relate warmly to many kinds of people struck me as a good in itself," but that it was at the same time a form of "quixotic, impulsive self-expression." Far more introverted than his elder brother, Alger found being spontaneous, and relating warmly to others, qualities he valued but that did not come naturally to him. In his comment on Bosley he associated those qualities with impulsive, even flighty behavior. At Johns Hopkins, Alger was regarded as popular as well as intellectually talented, the yearbook describing him as "the epitome of success," and "a nice chappie, in spite of his attainments." But in contrast to Bosley, self-control was high on his list of priorities.[10]

Sexual relations was one example. Although premarital sexual intimacy among "eligible" young men and women in the social circles frequented by the Hiss brothers was comparatively uncommon in the early 1920s, Bosley had had numerous intimate relations with women by the time he graduated from college. Alger, in contrast, was to first experience intimate sexuality on his wedding night. "I learned . . . from Bosley's mistakes in the area of emotional judgment," Alger later said. "He was undisciplined in habits of sleep, diet, and drink and was . . . too casual in sexual matters. His close cronies were . . . glaring examples of frivolous and destructively living young men." Alger associated self-control with the "practical" survivor skills he thought he possessed, again in contrast to Bosley. When Bosley fell ill, Alger noted, his assuming the role of Bosley's steward was inevitable, because the role required "the kind of practical aid I was qualified to supply." Practical skills came naturally to Alger as a young man; romance, despite its attraction for him, remained more comfortable in idealized, abstract forms.[11]

By 1929 two of the three elder children of Minnie Hiss were dead, and the third was in pursuit of a career that would take her far from the path on which Minnie had hoped to set her. The younger children seemed in better shape. Donald Hiss, two years younger than Alger, had also gone to Johns Hopkins, graduating in the spring of that year and following Alger to Harvard Law School in the fall. Donald and Alger would remain close friends and have remarkably parallel early careers. Both entered government service in the 1930s, briefly worked for the Justice Department, and went from there to the State Department, where Donald served from 1938 to 1945 as an assistant to the legal adviser of the Philippines. After the Second World War, Donald entered private law practice with Covington and Burling in Washington, D.C.[12]

Alger, even more so than Donald, appeared to be on a track toward the kind of professional and social success that his mother had envisaged. He also seemed, at least on the surface, to be a more tractable, less adventurous personality than Bosley. He recalled that he "liked to go to [grammar] school," and "did [my] homework with pleasure and pride," and that he and a friend were among the very few students who did not cheat on homework exercises or examinations in high school. His outstanding characteristic, as a grammar and high school student, seems to have been a sunny disposition. His high school yearbook described him as "[a] witty, happy, optimistic person," whose "happy habits" made him "irresistible" to his contemporaries. A student at Hopkins remembered him as "gracious, friendly, dependable, and admirable." As a boy he had struck one of his cousins as having "an unusual genial and happy nature," and another as "having inherited . . . unselfishness, tolerance, and [a] broad outlook" from his father. And "everyone who knew him" as a youth, Meyer Zeligs concluded after interviewing a number of Baltimore residents who encountered Hiss in the years after the First World War, "seems to share a picture of Alger as a model of good manners." He was, "in any conventional sense of the phrase, a 'good boy.'" He "seems hardly ever to have expressed . . . any hostility" toward his surroundings or his acquaintances.[13]

The young Alger Hiss's apparent cheerfulness and amiability, given the family atmosphere in which he grew up, invites comment. The circumstances of the Hiss household were by no means easy. Alger's father, the sole wage earner in a household that included five children, had died when the oldest of those children was fourteen and two were under the age of three. Minnie Hiss, for all her energy and organizational capacities, did not have a college education or any job skills. It was apparent that if Minnie's goal of steering her children toward professional and social prominence was to be attained, the Hiss family would need some form of financial help. Although Charles's insurance policies would keep the Hisses out of poverty, Minnie's aspirations were more exalted.

The result was that Anna was sent to an institution for southern women with social and intellectual ambitions, Mary Ann to a private day school and Smith College, and Bosley, for a time, to the Blair Academy in New Jersey. That form of education was not inexpensive, and although George Hiss, a brother of Charles's who made a considerable amount of money in the cotton business in North Carolina, regularly provided financial assistance to Minnie, it was clear to all the Hiss children that family resources were not plentiful. Bosley returned to Baltimore to attend Johns Hopkins on a scholarship, and Alger applied for, and was granted, scholarship aid his last three years at Hopkins. Although he was able to travel by steamship to Europe in 1924, it was on a student tour, with a four dollar a day spending limit, and a friend recalled that he and Hiss "were both pretty hard up." When Alger decided to go to Harvard Law School after graduating from college, it was on the understanding that he could get a scholarship.[14]

All but two of the first 25 years of Alger Hiss's life were thus lived in an environment without a father, with an emotionally distant mother, without substantial resources, and with significant demands placed upon him by his family situation, such as having to serve as the family's designated steward to Bosley in the last stages of his illness. Alger Hiss grew up under strong pressure to focus his intellectual talents on professional success and support for his family. Despite those disadvantages and pressures, by all appearances Alger not only survived but thrived, doing conspicuously well academically at both Johns Hopkins and Harvard, gaining popularity with his teachers and fellow students at both institutions, and all the while exhibiting the endearing, infectious amiability his contemporaries remarked upon.

Was that amiability a pose? Although there were surely some dark themes in Alger's childhood, he had been, especially given the Hisses's diminished financial circumstances, favored. Charles Hiss had had an insurance policy, and had been able to bequeath a legacy of $10,000 to each of his children. The Hisses's financial and social situation did not prevent Alger from participating in the usual round of activities enjoyed by affluent college students of his time. Bosley had clashed with his mother repeatedly as an adolescent and young man, whereas Alger had been less openly defiant. Although the Hiss boys were required to attend Johns Hopkins and live at home, Johns Hopkins was an elite university, both socially and academically. Academic work and social approval seemed to come almost effortlessly to Alger. He doubtless found aspects of Minnie's personality irritating; he may have resented being the family custodian; and he surely felt the loss of a father, and a brother, as he grew up. But there is very little outward impression of his being, as he entered law school in 1926, an unhappy young man.

By the time he graduated from Harvard, at the age of 25, Alger had added another component to the social image he projected. This was an aura of distinction, the product of a somewhat reserved but impeccably polite manner, a fastidious appearance, and an impressive carriage. Lee Pressman, one of his classmates at Harvard Law School, gave a description to Murray Kempton of Hiss at the time:

> I remember Alger Hiss best of all for a kind of distinction that had to be seen to be believed. If he were standing at the bar with the British ambassador and you were told to give a package to the ambassador's valet, you would give it to the ambassador before you gave it to Alger.
>
> He gave you a sense of absolute command and absolute grace.[15]

Pressman's portrait of Hiss as a law student should be seen as more than the re-actions of a young Jewish contemporary, from a comparatively impoverished back-ground, who was conscious of Hiss's upper-class persona in a world in which social standing, ethnicity, and professional success were still closely linked. His comment also attributed to Hiss the qualities of "command" and "grace." Given the eco-nomically and socially marginal position of the Hiss family, to what extent was Hiss's aura of distinction natural, and to what extent self-fashioned?[16]

Hiss was, on the one hand, tall and lithe and good-looking, with well-developed aesthetic and sartorial tastes. He had been, on the other, dependent on scholarship aid for his education, required to live at home during his college years, and been able to travel to Europe (in third-class accommodations) only through the contributions of family friends. If he was not quite "shabby gentility" because of Charles Hiss's legacy and other family members' contributions, he was not quite "gentility" either, despite Minnie's social ambitions. He nonetheless appeared to most of the people who encountered him from the late 1920s through the late 1940s as the personifica-tion of established wealth, breeding, and cultivation. Whittaker Chambers and Richard Nixon, who thought of themselves as social outsiders, would both see him in that role, and as a burgeoning administrator in the State Department he main-tained the persona. Hiss's "distinction" traded on some of his natural qualities, but it was also an aura that Minnie had encouraged, and he had readily constructed. Here was one of the early examples of Hiss's powers of self-control and self-fashioning. Those powers, coupled with his intellectual gifts, had helped him to emerge, at least on the surface, unscathed from the convulsions of his early life. They had the additional advantage of allowing him to shield, from those who encountered him, some portions of his life that he preferred to keep from public view.

When Alger Hiss entered Harvard Law School in the fall of 1926, Minnie may have felt that his matriculation was one of the few promising developments in a family that seemed on the verge of disintegration. Bosley was dead. Anna was pursuing a career that was sufficiently controversial to smack of notoriety. Although Mary Ann appeared to have made the sort of marriage Minnie had planned for her, Minnie was well aware of Eliott Emerson's financial troubles and the devastating effect they were having on Mary Ann's marriage and her emotional health. Minnie hoped, in the midst of these troubles, that Alger would become the family "steward." Just as he had lent support to Bosley in his debilitating illness and unfortunate marriage, and kept the Hiss family apprised lest the situation become scandalous as well as tragic,

Alger might emerge from Harvard Law School prepared to assume his father's role as family breadwinner and source of stability. From the first, it was taken for granted that Alger would return to Baltimore for law practice.

That did not happen, and by the early 1930s Alger had become the center of support for another household. He had not come back to Baltimore to practice law, and he had made a marriage, of which Minnie publicly disapproved, with a divorcée who had a young son. By rejecting the family steward role that Minnie had projected for him, Alger was clearly distancing himself from his troubled family. His years as the "good boy" in the Hiss household had taken their toll.

The trail that had led Alger away from the role of Hiss family steward to that of head of a family that included Priscilla Fansler and her young son Timothy had been a long and roundabout one. It began in 1924, when Alger, then 19, met Priscilla, then 20, on one of the first European steamship passages designed for students. Priscilla, who had just graduated from Bryn Mawr, was the youngest child of an insurance executive from the Philadelphia suburbs. She had majored in literature and philosophy at Bryn Mawr, and was entering a master's degree program in literature at Yale in the fall. She appeared to Alger as a prototypically "modern" young woman, independent, politically "advanced," and comfortable in mixed company. She was planning on traveling by herself in England, and Alger felt sufficiently concerned about her welfare to rent a room at the first boardinghouse where Priscilla stayed in London so that he could assure himself that she could manage on her own. Although he was smitten with Priscilla after the voyage, she simply regarded him as one of the college men she had met.[17]

In the late summer of 1924 Alger met Priscilla again in London, and escorted her to the ship she took back to America (he was booked on a different ship). Although he and Priscilla exchanged addresses, and corresponded after she arrived in New Haven, she had no particular interest in him. In April 1925, when Priscilla was on spring break from Yale, she visited a friend in Baltimore, and they subsequently joined a group of young men, including Hiss, who were attending a dance. Priscilla sat on Alger's lap as the group rode to the dance in a taxi, and Alger thought that romance might be in the offing. But during the same taxi ride Priscilla announced to the group that she had become engaged to another Yale graduate student, Thayer Hobson. That summer she and Hobson married.[18]

Alger and Priscilla went their separate ways for the next few years. Hobson was independently wealthy, and for a time he and Priscilla lived in Paris, and then in New York. In the fall of 1926 the Hobsons had a son, Timothy, but shortly thereafter they separated, and eventually, in January 1929, divorced. After the separation, which seems to have been precipitated by Thayer Hobson's infidelity, Priscilla took a job with *Time* as a copy editor and office manager. In 1928 she renewed her graduate studies at Columbia, receiving an M.A. in the spring of 1929. Although she had managed to support herself and Timothy from a divorce settlement and income from her job with *Time*, her financial condition was precarious. She had also begun an affair with a newspaperman, William Brown Meloney, whom she hoped to marry.[19]

There matters stood in the spring of 1929, when Alger learned that Priscilla, with whom he had lost contact, was divorced from Hobson and living in New York with Timothy. The years since his last meeting with Priscilla in the spring of 1925 had been eventful ones for Alger, with Bosley's death, his graduation from Johns Hopkins, and his entering Harvard Law School. After not succeeding with Priscilla, Alger had developed a relationship during his senior year at Hopkins with a woman from New Orleans who was attending school in Baltimore. They became engaged, and the relationship continued during his first year at Harvard. But after Alger visited the woman's family in New Orleans during the summer of 1927, he decided to break off the engagement. Marriage, he later told his son Tony, "stood in a man's way and restricted his freedom," and "had not been much use in making his parents happy."[20]

Although he had had no other romantic attachments in the four-year interval since Priscilla had told him of her engagement to Hobson, Hiss's intellectual achievements had been considerable. He was Phi Beta Kappa at Johns Hopkins, and his grades at Harvard Law School put him on the law review, which brought him to the attention of Professor Felix Frankfurter. In the same conversation in which Lee Pressman spoke of Hiss's "distinction" as a law student, he said that Frankfurter "felt [Hiss's] sense of absolute command and absolute grace . . . more than anyone. He seemed to have a kind of awe of Alger."

Hiss had met Frankfurter shortly after coming to Cambridge, armed with a letter of introduction from William Marbury, a Baltimore friend who had graduated from Harvard. The Frankfurters had Sunday teas for students and other guests, at which Hiss became a regular. The teas amounted to seminars on whatever topics were on Frankfurter's mind. Frankfurter was keenly interested in students and in their future careers, but he tended to have close relationships with and to promote the careers of only those students who had conspicuously good grades. Moreover, as Pressman's comments suggested, Frankfurter sometimes had a particular attraction for persons whose bearing suggested they came from families of established wealth and status. Two years after Hiss's graduation from law school Frankfurter would describe him, in a job recommendation to John Lord O'Brian of the Justice

Department's Anti-Trust Division, as "a man of unusual cultivation, charm, and prematurely solid judgment."[21]

From 1915 on Frankfurter was responsible for selecting legal secretaries for Justice Oliver Wendell Holmes of the Supreme Court of the United States. Holmes used his secretaries, invariably Harvard Law School graduates, as intellectual and social companions more than as legal assistants. Holmes's social habits were comparatively reclusive in his older age, and he wanted "presentable" secretaries who could "represent him in society." Frankfurter almost invariably chose WASP candidates for the position. Despite Holmes's idiosyncratic requirements for his secretaryship, the job was a coveted one, significantly increasing the holder's marketability among law firms.[22]

In the early spring of 1929 Frankfurter recommended Hiss to be Holmes's legal secretary for a period of 12 months, beginning in October 1929.[23] Alger thus renewed acquaintances with Priscilla with a much clearer sense of his academic achievements and professional aspirations than he had had when she sat on his lap and dropped the news of her engagement in 1925. But he had not gained much more experience in his relationships with women. Other than the woman to whom he had been engaged, a relationship that seems to have made so little an impact on him that he never mentioned her by name in any of his reminiscences, he had had no romantic attachments with women during his years at Johns Hopkins and Harvard. "It wasn't that I was saving myself for a good woman," he told his son Tony in the 1970s, "it was a matter of the accidents of opportunity . . . I made passes—they just didn't work." But his "passes" were apparently far from indiscriminate. "Promiscuity," he said to Tony, "has always seemed to me a sign of confusion. . . . One is likely to be exploiting another person."[24]

When a law school friend invited Hiss to accompany him and a date to New York to see the opera *Parsifal* in the spring of 1929, however, Alger decided that Priscilla Fansler Hobson, a divorcée, might be somewhat more available to him sexually than the recipients of his unsuccessful "passes." Although Priscilla agreed to go to the opera, and invited Alger to stay at her apartment, she once again met him with news of her attachment to another man. Although Alger and Priscilla continued in contact with one another before Alger sailed to Europe with his brother Donald in June 1929, the relationship seemed, at least on her side, a platonic one.[25]

Shortly after the Hiss brothers arrived in Paris. Donald, who was poised to enter Harvard Law School that fall, was stricken with what was diagnosed as a severe bout of stomach ulcers. The doctors recommended that he return to the United States and have an operation. Unfortunately, one of the transatlantic liners in operation at the time had had a fire on board and was out of service, and the resultant pressure on the other ships made it impossible for the Hisses to get a prompt booking. With no other options, Alger decided that they would abandon their plans for a general tour of Europe and seek some place in the French countryside where Donald could rest and drink fresh milk, which was then thought a remedy for ulcers. The town of Giverny, in the southeast corner of Normandy, was recommended. The painter Claude Monet had been a longtime resident of Giverny, and the town, had become something of a tourist attraction during Monet's lifetime. It had a hotel, where the Hiss brothers found rooms, a tennis court, a river that could accommodate swimmers, and at least one cow for the use of guests.[26]

Even though Donald's condition rapidly improved in Giverny, restoring him to full health and making a quick return passage unnecessary, the Hisses decided not to attempt the tour of Europe they had planned. One reason was a desire to have Donald rest and recuperate in relatively tranquil surroundings. Another may have been the presence of two young Frenchwomen, students at the Sorbonne, one of whose parents owned a summer house in Giverny. The women were generally restricted from male company in the evenings, but most days were able to accompany Alger and Donald on outdoor excursions. They also made the acquaintance of Jimmy Butler, Monet's grandson, who lived with his father, an American artist, in a "peasant cottage," once occupied by Monet, in which a number of his paintings were scattered about. In his memoirs Hiss, aware of the "resurgence of [Monet's] influence" and the restoration of Monet's cottage that accompanied it, predicted that "Giverny . . . will no longer . . . be the magical setting of a summer vacation for two young foreigners . . . thirsty for direct contact with the ancient daily rounds of the French countryside."[27]

Alger and Donald stayed the summer in Giverny, returning to the United States in late August. As he waited to begin his secretaryship with Holmes, his relationship with Priscilla suddenly blossomed. She met the ship when Alger arrived, and told him that she was about to enter the hospital for an operation. Priscilla's relationship with William Brown Meloney had dissolved, and unbeknownst to Alger, Priscilla was pregnant with Meloney's child. Although Meloney was married when the affair with Priscilla began, he was apparently considering leaving his wife and marrying Priscilla when, over the summer of 1929, his wife also became pregnant. Meloney then broke off his relationship with Priscilla, who elected to have an abortion. She apparently did not tell Alger about the nature of her hospitalization until many years later. At the same time she encouraged Alger to visit her in New York, and, after he began work for Holmes, Alger spent most weekends in her company. At this time, however, Alger had no plans to marry. For one thing, Justice Holmes had a rule forbidding his secretaries from marrying during the term of their employment.

Hiss and Justice Oliver Wendell Holmes, taken in July 1930, at Holmes's
summer house in Beverly Farms, Massachusetts. The photograph was
taken by John Knox, another graduate of Harvard Law School who would
subsequently become legal secretary to Justice James McReynolds.

Holmes was 88 by the time Hiss went to work for him, and the justice's secretaryships had assumed a familiar character. Holmes's secretaries helped him with a few
comparatively routine legal tasks, and some other matters that occupied Holmes at
that stage of his life. Their most extensive legal work involved assisting Holmes with
the evaluation of petitions for certiorari filed with the Court. Since the passage of the
Judiciary Act of 1925, most of the Supreme Court's jurisdiction had become discretionary. The Court's docket was primarily composed of cases that four justices
of the Court had agreed to hear after entertaining petitions urging them to do so. A
writ of certiorari—the technical procedure signaling that the Court had decided to
review a case from a lower federal court—was granted in comparatively few cases,
but those cases made up most of the Court's business. The bulk of the certiorari petitions came in during the summer, and were forwarded to the justices in their re-
spective summer residences, but other petitions were filed while the Court was in
session in Washington. In his memoirs Hiss said that his "chief job" among his
"legal duties" for Holmes was "the almost daily delivery of oral reports on the numerous petitions for review." "In reporting on those cases," he recalled, "I stood behind the Justice's big desk." While Holmes made notes, "I gave the facts of each
case, summarized the decision of the lower court and the arguments of counsel,

and offered my comments on what I thought was the adequacy or inadequacy of the petition." Holmes would invariably "leaf . . . through the record himself to check the accuracy of my summary."[28]

Hiss performed few other legal tasks for Holmes. Holmes's duties as a Supreme Court justice included listening to oral arguments, participating in conferences where the justices discussed and voted on cases that had been argued, writing opinions in cases that had been decided, and for which he had been assigned responsibility for producing the opinion of a majority of the Court, and reading draft opinions circulated by his colleagues as part of the process by which the Court rendered decisions. Sometimes Holmes's decision not to join an opinion circulated by another justice would result in his writing a dissenting opinion. None of the work was particularly arduous for Holmes, even in his 88th and 89th years. He wrote opinions with astonishing swiftness, partly because he was quick to make up his mind, and partly because he favored terse, pungent opinions that featured vivid language more than elaborate reasoning. Holmes needed little help from a secretary. He wrote all of his own opinions, only asking secretaries to occasionally locate sources supporting legal propositions he wanted to advance. Often he knew the source, and sometimes even its location. "[H]e seldom called on me for discussion or research," Hiss recalled.[29]

Attending arguments and conferences took up a fair amount of Holmes's day when the Court was in session, but the Court did not hear arguments every week, nor did it invariably hold weekly conferences. Holmes could typically complete two opinions a week if he was assigned them, a pace so fast that some Chief Justices who worked with him deliberately delayed giving him assignments lest he embarrass his colleagues. He did not ask secretaries to supply him with memoranda summarizing the briefs filed to accompany oral arguments, only to organize the briefs so that he had easy access to them during the arguments. Nor did he ask them to attend the arguments. In short, Holmes did not expect his secretaries to assist him with most of the legal work of a justice of the Supreme Court.

Nonetheless there was plenty for Holmes's secretaries to do. He expected them to work in his house up to seven days a week, including, the year that Hiss worked for him, some evenings. This was because Holmes spent the majority of his time away from court on pursuits other than those directly connected to his legal duties. After the combination of age and a prostate operation resulted in Holmes's sharply curtailing his social life once he entered his 80s, he spent much of his time at home, and the bulk of that time reading or writing. He had a very large number of correspondence friendships, and insisted on "improving his mind" by reading books on philosophy, history, political theory, and literature. He also read light, and not so light, fiction. He liked to converse about books and ideas in his correspondence and with anyone else who came within his purview.[30]

A secretary was expected to participate in these pursuits, and to engage in some others not obviously connected to Holmes's work as a judge. Regularly Holmes would complete an opinion, or come to a stopping place in it, and turn to his reading, breaking off from time to time to discuss issues that the reading suggested. Sometimes he would use his correspondence to discuss those issues, while at the same time asking his secretary to answer more routine correspondence. As Holmes became a more visible figure as he aged and remained on the Court, he received an increased volume of letters from the general public, and he felt obligated to answer most of them. He also asked a secretary to pay routine household bills and to balance his checkbook. Sometimes secretaries accompanied him to the bank to serve as witnesses to transactions. Secretaries were also expected to involve themselves with callers or others who sought access to Holmes. Finally, they were expected to attend some functions to which Holmes was invited. As a consequence, a secretary's work, although not often intellectually demanding, was constant.[31]

In April 1929 Fanny Holmes died from complications after breaking her hip. Wendell Holmes and Fanny Dixwell had been married for 57 years, beginning in 1872. They were childless, and some observers have wondered, in light of Holmes's reputation as a flirt for much of his life and his infatuation with Clare Castletown, the wife of an Irish peer, in the late 1890s, how much romance they had in their marriage. Nonetheless they were undoubtedly close, affectionate companions, and after Fanny's death Justice Louis Brandeis wrote Frankfurter that Holmes's current secretary was "needed as no secretary has ever been."[32]

Alger Hiss's year with Holmes thus marked something of a transition period in the Holmes secretaryship, where the secretary's role had the potential to take on some functions, including that of companion, previously performed by Fanny. Hiss responded to the situation in a way that might seem unusual for an unmarried man of 25. Far from chafing under the increased informal duties that resulted from Holmes's loss of Fanny's company, Hiss welcomed them, and tried to increase the amount of time he and Holmes spent on nonlegal pursuits. Even though he was courting Priscilla in the early months he spent working for Holmes, and journeying to New York to do so, Hiss intimated to Holmes that he was available to provide companionship for the justice whenever needed. As Holmes put it after Hiss had left his employ, Hiss expressed an interest in "doing extras that are not within his strict duties." Holmes so enjoyed the "extras" that they became an expectation for future secretaries.[33]

One long-established ritual of Fanny and Wendell Holmes was after-dinner readings, in which Fanny read aloud to Wendell as he played solitaire. It had apparently begun in the early years of the Holmeses's marriage, when Wendell was doing a great deal of close reading and editing of scholarly works in the daytime, and wanted to give his eyes a respite in the evening. The Holmeses had continued the ritual for over 50 years. It was an elemental feature of their life together.[34]

Hiss had had his own experience of reading aloud. After Charles Hiss killed himself, his unmarried sister, Eliza Millemon (Lila) Hiss, moved in with Minnie and her children to assist in child-rearing and household duties. Alger was not yet three at the time, and Lila would continue to live in the house until he was fourteen. Lila loved the theatre, performing in public, and reading aloud, and nearly every weekday afternoon, until Alger was ten, she would read to the Hiss children, and then instruct them in the art of reading aloud. The sessions with Lila were Hiss's "favorite diversion" as a young child, he recalled, and he learned how to read aloud effectively. With the experience in mind, he proposed to Holmes that he assume Fanny's role of reading aloud to him whenever Holmes "had a period of leisure."[35]

Holmes "refused summarily, almost brusquely," to let Hiss attempt the task. He told Hiss that it "wouldn't work" because "it was too personal." The common ground for Holmes and his secretaries, these comments indicated, was the legal and other intellectual issues that came before Holmes as a judge, whereas reading aloud was a ritual associated with domestic life and marriage.

Yet Hiss persisted in urging Holmes to let him attempt some reading aloud sessions, and Holmes eventually acquiesced. In his memoirs Hiss gave an account of the process. As Hiss described it, he was not deterred after proposing that he read aloud to the judge and being rebuffed. Rather than giving up, he sought to persuade Holmes in a roundabout, somewhat deceptive fashion. Having learned that "one of the justice's favorite visitors, Sir Esme Howard, the British Ambassador, was read to by his secretary," Hiss resolved to acquaint Holmes with Howard's practice. The secretary who read to Howard, however, was his son. Hiss did not disclose that fact to Holmes when he mentioned Howard's being read to, and went so far as to enlist Howard himself in his campaign to persuade Holmes. "I urged [Howard]," Hiss recalled, "to tell the Justice how relaxing and pleasant he found the reading to be." Eventually "the Justice asked if I was still willing to try reading aloud."[36]

Hiss told the story in a tone of triumph in his memoirs. The reading aloud was a marked success. "I read to Holmes almost every weekday. . . . [R]eading aloud became a normal part of the duties of his secretaries from then on. I was also able to see to it that the reading aloud continued even during the Court's summer recess." And the increased intimacy produced by the reading aloud ritual, Hiss suggested, resulted in his having greater access to other "personal" dimensions of Holmes's life.[37]

An example was Holmes's "Black Book," a notebook in which he kept lists of the books he read and made occasional jottings. After a time Hiss was allowed to fetch the "Black Book" so that Holmes could record the dates he had completed books and their titles; later secretaries were allowed to record the entries for him. "My adequate fulfillment of . . . chores that he had previously regarded either as too personal or too menial to be delegated," Hiss felt, had "made me eligible for the far more intimate task of taking part in the ritual of his entering authors and titles in the Black Book." Hiss took on other "personal" tasks as well, he recalled.

> Before I came to work for him, Justice Holmes had made it his practice personally to acknowledge all letters . . . and had done so by hand. Similarly, he had himself drawn all his own checks and personally clipped the internal coupons from the bonds in his safe-deposit box. At about the same time that I began to read aloud to him, Holmes consented to my answering letters of no particular importance from strangers. I was also permitted to fill out the checks for household bills and keep a running account in his checkbook, plus accompany him on trips to the bank, where, under his watchful Yankee eye, I would clip the coupons.[38]

This passage, and Hiss's earlier comments, overstate the extent to which the tasks that Hiss identified himself as performing for Holmes were intensely "personal" ones, or novel ones for a secretary of Holmes. In a 1925 letter to Felix Frankfurter, Holmes had indicated that "a condition" of his secretaryship was that the secretary "be able to keep my simple accounts." Holmes's secretary for the 1927 Term, Arthur Sutherland, recalled having access to Holmes's black book. The practice of Holmes's secretaries making "Black Book" entries for him was not a tacit recognition by Holmes of the "personal" nature of the task. It was the result of Holmes's losing the ability to grip a pen after suffering a mild stroke in the later summer of 1931. Hiss was incorrect in suggesting that he was the first of Holmes's secretaries to keep accounts for him, and there is no reason to conclude that he was the first to answer letters, or to help Holmes "clip coupons" from his portfolio. And it is significant that Hiss thought the act of fetching a copy of Holmes's "Black Book" so he could enter the titles of books he had read an "intimate . . . ritual."[39]

Hiss's eagerness to read aloud to Holmes seems worth pondering. Reading books aloud is an inefficient way of conveying the information in them, and can distract the reader, who needs to focus on communicating material effectively, from the substance of what is being read. At the same time it can subtly change the relationship of the two people who are being exposed to a book from one of relative equals (the relationship that would exist if the two were reading the same book simultaneously) to one more resembling that of a caretaker and a patient. Not only does the reader control the pace at which the book is digested, the reader's linguistic and vocal skills can affect the listener's understanding of the book. Hiss, aware of his long experience with reading aloud, seemed particularly eager to serve as Holmes's reader.

It is understandable that a man recalling, in his eighties, the "enchanted year" he had spent with Holmes, whom he called "the most profound influence in my life," might have been inclined to exaggerate the novelty or significance of his relationship with the justice. Hiss's being the first secretary to read aloud to Holmes may not have had the transformative effect on Holmes's future secretaryships that Hiss implied. But it certainly had an effect on Hiss. Reading aloud to Holmes was sufficiently important to Hiss that he was prepared to enlist the British ambassador to the United States in a deception whose purpose was to overcome Holmes's misgivings about Hiss's proposal. The strategy could well have backfired. Holmes might well have been offended at Hiss's mentioning a private matter involving him and his secretary to the British ambassador, let alone at Hiss's conniving with that official to override Holmes's position on that matter. Hiss was prepared to take the risk, and later to publicize his deception.[40]

Holmes did not, on the whole, appear to invest a good deal of his time or energy in scrutinizing the personalities of his secretaries. By the time Hiss joined him, he called most of them "sonny," or "idiot boy" when they failed to perform a task adequately, and he assumed they would be capable of undertaking the usual duties of their position. After retiring from the Court, he defined the position of his secretary as that of an "intelligent valet," and the work as mostly consisting of "letters, accounts, etc., a good deal of reading aloud and taking a drive with me." His secretaryship at that point, he felt, was "not a place for a young lawyer who wants to rise," and one in which "a young lawyer [would] waste his time." But even after giving up his judicial duties, he told Frankfurter that "I very much wish to have a young man." He assumed, by then, that Frankfurter would know the sort of young man he wanted.[41]

Holmes's secretaries had some characteristics in common. As noted, they were almost universally graduates of Harvard Law School, and with one (or possibly two) exceptions, they were white Anglo-Saxon Protestants. They were also, with just two exceptions, neither of which pleased Holmes, unmarried men. In 1915, when Frankfurter succeeded John Chipman Gray (who died that year) in selecting

Holmes's secretaries, Holmes wrote him that he did not want a married secretary "till you tell me that is the only possibility." He had "put the case of the married man to my wife," Holmes added, and Fanny "had reinforced my unwillingness as it means a major interest outside his work."[42]

Nine years later Frankfurter recommended Barton Leach, then a third-year student at Harvard Law School, for the position, and Holmes agreed with the recommendation, as he invariably did. But by the time Leach came to work he had married. Holmes was irritated, writing Frankfurter that he would not have taken Leach "had I known earlier that he was married." "I want a free man," he added, "who may be a contribution to society." Two years later, after Frankfurter had recommend Arthur Sutherland for the position, Holmes discovered, in July of 1927, that Sutherland was planning to get married before starting work with him. He was furious, and asked Frankfurter whether, at so late a date, he could get another person for the position. "I am a good deal annoyed at the situation," he told Frankfurter: "I don't suppose you could get me another young man as good as you . . . have depicted Sutherland. I think therefore that I shall take him. . . . [B]ut before a final decision I should like to know whether you have in mind anyone who will stay single and whom you think fairly equal to the work." Frankfurter persisted in recommending Sutherland, and Holmes "waive[d] [his] objections," but added that "I shall fear preoccupation and a wish to get back to the beloved one in place of the general availability of a bachelor."[43]

Hiss began his secretaryship with Holmes in October 1929. By that time his relationship with Priscilla was changing. Having had an abortion, and having terminated her relationship with Meloney, Priscilla found herself alone in New York with a small son. From her perspective, Alger Hiss may have seemed a more attractive prospect for marriage. He was holding down a very prestigious job, with a decent salary, and he was likely to have a bright future in the legal profession. His continuing to court her, after she had twice rebuffed him for other men, suggested that his attitude to her approached devotion. He had already shown himself to be gifted at helping people in distress. He was a prospective father for her son Timothy.

Hiss began "going to New York Saturday afternoon all fall" to visit Priscilla. Holmes knew about his trips, and knew that a young woman was involved: Hiss later reported that Holmes showed "apparent amusement" at the situation, and "often chaffed me about the 'dangers' I was headed for." But when those "dangers" came to a head, probably sometime in November, Holmes was not informed. Priscilla apparently gave Hiss something of an ultimatum: if he wanted to marry her, she was available, but they needed to get married as soon as possible. With Timothy and

finances to consider, she obviously did not want to continue very long in a relationship that did not lead to marriage. Hiss agreed, and they decided to get married
in December, in an unobtrusive civil ceremony.[44]

Very little has emerged about the process that lead to Alger's and Priscilla's getting married on the evening of Wednesday, December 11, 1929. Apparently the
couple initially decided that because of Alger's obligations to Holmes, they needed
to be married by a justice of the peace, with no one attending the ceremony. Alger's
close friend William Marbury persuaded them to have a Presbyterian minister perform the ceremony and to invite a few friends and members of their families. They
limited the persons in attendance to a small number of Hiss's male friends, all from
Baltimore except Hiss's Harvard Law classmate Richard Field, and Priscilla's parents. Donald Hiss attended the wedding, and Minnie and Anna Hiss were invited,
but Minnie was visiting Anna in Texas at the time. Not only did neither choose to
travel to the Washington area, where the wedding took place, Minnie sent Alger a
telegram, on the day of the wedding, that read "Do Not Take This Fatal Step."
Priscilla was not enamoured of Alger's Baltimore friends, and they may have reciprocated the sentiment. One told Meyer Zeligs that "[w]hen the minister got to the
part, 'speak now or forever hold your peace,' I can remember Alger gently waving
his hand behind the back as though to quiet his few friends who were present."[45]

William Marbury, who also attended the wedding, later wrote that Alger and
Priscilla had initially thought of getting married before a justice of the peace because
Alger "knew that he had to go back to work for Justice Holmes immediately, since
in getting married during his [secretary]ship he was violating one of the conditions
of his employment." This suggests that either Hiss had known of Holmes's no-
marriage rule when he began the secretaryship, or he had learned it by the time
Priscilla and he decided to marry in December.[46]

But after getting married, Hiss took pains to give the impression that he was unaware of Holmes's rule. In a December 13, 1929, letter to Felix Frankfurter, Hiss discussed the circumstances of his marriage as follows:

> I learned some ten hours before my marriage [from a comment of
> Holmes's] that the justice had definitely stipulated that his secretaries be un-
> married. Of course, I had appreciated what must be [at] the bottom of this
> rule—the secretary's personal affairs must never impinge upon a "scintilla"
> of the justice's time or energy, and I—rather we—laid meticulous plans
> until the last moment. As part of these plans the justice was not informed
> until the last moment (the evening before the wedding). . . . It never oc-
> curred to me that he had a definite "rule of law" on the point. . . . I in no

wise sensed any fiat negative to marriage qua marriage—of inconsiderateness which might reasonably grow out of a secretary's marrying he did gently complain, I suppose.[47]

Hiss told his authorized biographer John Chabot Smith a slightly different version of the story. "It was on the morning of the wedding day," John Chabot Smith wrote, "that Dick Field happened to mention to Alger that Justice Holmes's secretary wasn't supposed to marry during his term of office." Smith then added:

> Horrified at the idea of offending the justice, Alger hurried to him and broke the news, apologizing profusely but explaining that it was too late for him to back out now. Holmes graciously accepted the apology . . . and forgave the transgression. He told him to take two weeks off for a honeymoon.[48]

Hiss's subsequent explanations to Frankfurter, and to Smith, were at odds and internally inconsistent. Smith's account suggested that Hiss had intended to get married without even mentioning that fact to Holmes. But in Hiss's letter to Frankfurter, he said that he had understood Holmes's disinclination to have married secretaries, because "the secretary's personal affairs must never impinge upon a 'scintilla' of the justice's time or energy." The context of the letter, written only two days after Hiss's marriage, indicates that Hiss wanted Frankfurter to know that he "had appreciated" the reason for Holmes's rule, and consequently had "laid meticulous plans" to spare Holmes any "time or energy" thinking about his forthcoming wedding. He had even said that "as part of these plans the justice was not informed until the last moment [the evening before the wedding]."

If Hiss had not known about the rule, what was he laying "meticulous plans" about? When had he come to "appreciate what must be [at] the bottom of [the] rule," as he wrote to Frankfurter, if not before he told Holmes he was getting married? And when had he "sensed . . . inconsiderateness which might reasonably grow out of a secretary's marrying," if not when Holmes had "gently complain[ed]" about that inconsiderateness during his discussions with Hiss about his trips to New York in the fall?[49]

In sum, the best explanation for Hiss's puzzling statements to Frankfurter about when he learned about Holmes's no-marriage rule, and to Smith about how and when he had learned about it, is that were they were false and self-serving. Hiss was less concerned with shielding Holmes from knowledge of his personal affairs than he was concerned about shielding him from the knowledge that he planned to get married during his secretarial year. The latter concern would seem to be the basis for Alger's and Priscilla's "meticulous plans," which included keeping Holmes in the dark about their wedding "until the last moment."

Hiss may well not have known, when Frankfurter selected him to be Holmes's secretary, or when he first took up the job, that a criterion of Holmes's secretaryship was that his secretary be unmarried. It seems unlikely that had Frankfurter clearly informed Hiss of the no-marriage rule, Hiss would have written Frankfurter in December 1929 that he knew nothing about it. But it seems clear that Hiss had learned about the rule sometime in the fall of 1929, and, when he decided to marry Priscilla in December, had resolved not to let Holmes know about his marriage until he could present that information when the event was imminent. The obvious inference is that Hiss's "meticulous plans" were designed to put Holmes in a position where if he objected to Hiss's marrying, he would be asking Hiss to renege on a commitment he had already made and was on the verge of carrying out. Hiss knew that Holmes was very unlikely to object under those circumstances.

Even though Holmes acquiesced in Hiss's marrying during the secretaryship, he was not pleased by it. His reaction can be illustrated by a story told by Donald Hiss, who was Holmes's secretary during the 1932 Term, after Holmes had retired from the bench. A frequent visitor to Holmes was William Hicks, a federal judge who worked in Texas but called on Holmes when he came to Washington. On one of Hicks's visits during Donald Hiss's secretarial year, Hicks told Donald that "the subject of my brother Alger's marriage during his year with Holmes was taboo." The fact that Hicks cautioned Donald that it was "taboo" suggests that the circumstances of Hiss's marriage still rankled with Holmes. The probable reason was that Holmes felt that Hiss had violated one of the conditions of his job, and put Holmes in a position where he could not honorably object to the violation.[50]

Hiss's desire to read aloud to Holmes might not, on first impression, seem all that similar to his desire to marry Priscilla Fansler in the midst of his secretaryship. Yet Hiss's calibration of the risks and benefits in both incidents is striking. Once confronted with what surely seemed formidable obstacles in the way of his reading aloud to Holmes or getting married during the secretarial year—Holmes expressly declined to be read to, and forbade his secretaries from marrying—Hiss could have abandoned his goals at apparently little cost. He could have continued a working relationship with Holmes that he found pleasant and stimulating, and over time he might have found other opportunities to expand his personal contacts with the judge.

He could also have postponed his marriage to Priscilla until his year with Holmes came to an end.

Instead, Hiss maneuvered to evade the obstacles. The tactics he employed, in both cases, were predicated on a belief that once Holmes became aware that Hiss was seeking to get around edicts laid down by Holmes, no negative consequences for Hiss would result. If Esme Howard told Holmes that Hiss had tried to enlist him, Holmes would only think that Hiss was trying to do some "extra duties." If Hiss had taken the awkward step of planning a wedding without first seeking Holmes's approval, it was because he had not been aware of Holmes's insistence that his secretaries remain unmarried. Hiss's tactics assumed that Holmes would not take another view of the incidents: that in both cases Hiss had refused to take Holmes's "no" for an answer, and was maneuvering to get around it.

In both incidents, then, Hiss believed that he could fool Holmes and get away with it, and that he was willing to risk the consequences if he could not. Hiss, at 25, was a person with a strong belief in his ability to manipulate others, and perhaps with an underdeveloped appreciation of the risks of being exposed. Even if one associates those characteristics with many males in Hiss's age group, when one compares the relatively low costs of abandoning the project of reading to Holmes, or of postponing his marriage, against the quite significant consequences that might have ensued if Holmes took a more negative view of Hiss's conduct, the choices Hiss made seem unusual, and revealing.

The incidents reveal Alger Hiss as a young man used to getting his own way and confident in his ability to achieve goals indirectly when they could not be secured directly. They also demonstrate the significance he placed on opportunities to expand his intimacy with Holmes, as if intimacy with an older man was a particularly important need at the time. They suggest that he regarded getting married to Priscilla as so high a priority that he was unwilling to postpone the event even if it cost him his position with Holmes. Finally, they suggest that however much Hiss may have admired Holmes and loved being in his company, he was not intimidated or awed by the venerable justice. On the contrary, he thought that he could manipulate Holmes and that Holmes would either not discover the manipulations or not think less of Hiss for them. And, by all appearances, Hiss was correct in this belief. After his marriage he remained with Holmes through the rest of the 1929 Term and the summer of 1930; he and Holmes maintained affectionate relations throughout that time; and when Felix Frankfurter recommended Donald Hiss to serve as secretary for Holmes four years later, Holmes acquiesced in the recommendation. In summing up his year with Holmes, Hiss could have told himself that he had gotten everything he wanted out of the experience.

When Priscilla Fansler Hobson married Alger Hiss in December 1929, their relationship, if one relies on the reactions of close friends and family members at the time, had already taken on a certain tenor. Priscilla was someone to whom Alger tended to cater, in whose company he seemed to lose some of his upbeat qualities. She did not approve of Alger's Baltimore friends, and found Alger "disloyal" on one occasion when he left her alone at a party in Baltimore. Alger's friends, for their part, were on the whole not fond of Priscilla. Meanwhile Minnie Hiss had formed the impression that Priscilla was a flirt, and when she was invited to the wedding she responded by sending a telegram to Alger that precipitated a strongly negative reaction from Priscilla. Alger, for his part, seemed to welcome Priscilla's strong-mindedness, and subsequently described his marriage as making him feel "independent."[51]

Two themes seemed to have combined to establish the framework from which Alger viewed the prospect of marrying Priscilla Fansler Hobson. One was his instinctive desire to help persons in distress. He had tended to Bosley in his weakened condition; he had secured a restful environment for Donald in Giverny; more fundamentally, he had been Minnie Hiss's "good boy," her surcease against familial deterioration. In the fall of 1929, Priscilla was a person in distress. Already a divorced single mother, she was enduring the breakup of a love affair and the aftermath of an abortion. Faced with limited resources and a young son to take care of, she represented someone whom Alger could help. And Alger was, for the first time in his life, in a financial position to do so. He was earning $3,600 a year from his position with Holmes, enough to afford an apartment with a cook and maid in Washington. And, despite the worsening economic times that would surface in the 1930s, he could expect to find a potentially lucrative position with a law firm. He could thus take satisfaction from being able to rescue Priscilla from straitened financial and personal circumstances.

The other theme was Hiss's desire for personal independence. The troubles of his brothers and sisters, coupled with his success and his willingness to help out, had resulted in his having to spend a fair amount of time in his young adulthood responding to his mother's explicit or implicit calls for aid. He had had to spend one summer tending to Bosley, and another providing support for Donald. He had had to attend college in the Baltimore area, and live at home, because of the family's limited resources, even though Minnie Hiss contributed no income to the family. Through no choice of his own, he had emerged as a family factotum, one whose sacrifices helped prevent difficulties from turning into calamities. And all the while Minnie Hiss, although not sparing in her didacticisms, was sparing in her affection. By turning to Priscilla and Timothy, in the face of Minnie's disapproval, Alger was turning quite decisively away from Minnie and the Hiss family circle in Baltimore.

Whittaker Chambers once reported Alger's describing Baltimore as a "city . . . so backward that it still lights its streets by gas . . . a city of dying old men and women." When Chambers had responded by describing Baltimore's senior population as "pleasant and harmless old people," Hiss had countered, "Yes, the horrible old women of Baltimore!," with a "dry laugh that . . . made me feel that I had touched depths which I had not suspected."[52]

After marrying Priscilla, Alger abandoned his plans to return to Baltimore to practice law, accepting a job with Choate, Hall, and Stewart, a Boston firm, after leaving Holmes in the fall of 1930. The major decisions of the Hisses in the early years of their marriage, in fact, were made by Priscilla. She had pressed Alger to marry her in the fall of 1929; she had encouraged him to seek a position in Boston; a year after their arrival she was once again encouraging him to accommodate her wishes. For by the fall of 1931 Priscilla wanted to move back to New York, where her brother Thomas and her sister-in-law Roberta Fansler lived. She made arrangements for herself and Timothy, taking an apartment in the same building in Morningside Heights as the Fanslers, and she and Roberta Fansler applied, successfully, for a research grant from the Carnegie Foundation to study the state of fine arts in American colleges and universities. These developments made it clear that Priscilla, after her marriage to Alger, remained capable of pursuing a career and supporting herself. When she urged Alger to follow her to New York, he agreed. In the spring of 1932, having wound up his commitments to Choate, Hall, and Gordon, he took a job with the New York firm of Cotton, Franklin, Wright, and Gordon, and he, Priscilla, and Timothy moved to an apartment on Central Park West.[53]

It was in New York, in the early 1930s, that Alger Hiss was to make his first acquaintance with groups engaged in radical politics. Priscilla very likely provided the catalyst for Alger's participation in causes such as the plight of labor workers or farmers in a depressed economy. As early as 1930 Priscilla, along with Thomas Fansler, had joined the Morningside Heights branch of the Socialist Party. Her involvement consisted primarily of working at soup kitchens set up by the Morningside Socialists for the numerous unemployed persons who lived in the Upper West Side of Manhattan. She may have first called Alger's attention to "the growing breadlines and soup kitchens, the shanty towns in parks and vacant lots, the beggars [that] gave sharp reality to accounts of similar and even worse conditions throughout the country." He resolved to "offer my legal skills to a small group of young and similarly motivated New York lawyers who had come together to issue a journal for labor lawyers and those representing hard-pressed farmers."[54]

The group called itself the International Juridical Association (IJA). Its members digested cases for the benefit of workers and farmers who sought potential legal remedies against the economic hardship they were encountering in the early 1930s. Alger "became responsible for reading the decisions that dealt with agricultural issues," and through his work gained "a sense of identification with members of . . . farm associations who . . . were actively trying to help themselves weather the Depression." Although Alger subsequently described his work for the International Juridical Association as *"pro bono publico* work that is part of a lawyer's social responsibility," the experience was part of a transformation in his political perspective. Throughout Johns Hopkins and Harvard Law School he had been largely apolitical, his primary interests being in avant-garde literature and the arts. By the time he joined the International Juridical Association he had come to feel that "the Depression . . . was the result of decrepit social structures, of mismanagement and greed."[55]

Among the lawyers that participated in the International Juridical Association's activities was his Harvard classmate Lee Pressman. Later Pressman was to admit to joining the Communist Party in the 1930s, although he denied being a Communist when he and Hiss worked with the IJA. Another member of the IJA later indicated, however, that the IJA's membership included Joseph Brodsky, who was then attorney for the Communist Party of the United States. The IJA was an example of a 1930s "popular-front" organization, dedicated to the proposition that a broad coalition of liberals and collectivists could secure the political reforms necessary to alleviate economic conditions and promote the rights of disadvantaged groups. Although Alger Hiss was probably neither a Communist nor a Socialist when he worked for the IJA, he was very likely sympathetic to "popular-front" politics, and the contacts he made there would be important for his future reform efforts.[56]

In the spring of 1933 Alger's growing interest in political reform translated itself into a career change.[57] In the wake of Franklin Roosevelt's electoral victory in 1932, an expansion of the federal government was taking place, and a new agency, the Agricultural Adjustment Administration, was created to oversee programs designed to alleviate the economic plight of farmers. Hiss was offered a position in the general counsel's office of the AAA. After being urged to accept the position by Felix Frankfurter "on [the] basis [of the] national emergency," Hiss eventually resolved to leave his New York practice and move with Priscilla and Timothy to Washington. There he became involved in drafting contracts between the Department of Agriculture and farmers that were designed to secure a restriction of crop production in order to raise prices. At the same time he, Lee Pressman, and some other former members of the IJA, who had also relocated to Washington, joined a "discussion group," organized by Harold Ware, a member of the Communist Party who served as a consultant to the Department of Agriculture. The Ware Group was to form the base for Hiss's entry into secret intelligence work for the Soviet Union.[58]

In retrospect, Hiss's metamorphosis from a follower of avant-garde culture to a committed political reformer was remarkably swift. But at another level it was not altogether unexpected. Hiss had entered the employment market at the very time that the first effects of the economic turmoil of the 1930s were beginning to take shape. Even before moving from Boston to New York, Priscilla had exhibited an attraction to collectivist politics. Once Alger came to the conclusion that the Depression was a result of moral and political failure on the part of "decrepit social structures," popular-front collectivism seemed an attractive alternative. The Soviet Union, which the United States government was officially to recognize in 1933, had yet to begin its Stalinist purges, and the darker side of Fascist collectivism was not yet visible. The International Juridical Association itself seemed an example of how liberals and collectivists of different stripes could join in work designed to help casualties of the Depression.

Alger's commitment to political reform may have seemed all the more attractive because it took him down a path that served to separate him and Priscilla more decisively from the network of his family. No one in the Hiss household had participated in politics. The engagement of Alger and Priscilla with reformist political programs served to give their household an identity quite distinct from that of the Baltimore Hisses. Further, Alger for the first time had become the center of his household's pursuits. He had left Baltimore and Boston on Priscilla's urging, accommodating her personal and professional needs. Now it was she who followed him to Washington, where he became simultaneously involved as a New Dealer and a member of Harold Ware's group.

By as early as 1934 Hiss had begun intelligence work for the Soviets. There are hints of what may have made him take that step. A combination of frustrations he encountered at the AAA and during his years as a designated custodian and "good boy" in the Hiss family made achieving a position of independence and mastery, that would boost his self-esteem, even more important. Although his marriage to Priscilla had been an act of defiance to Minnie and the accumulated weight of family responsibilities, it had at the same time been a taking on of a new set of burdens. Alger continued to search for something that would set him apart and allow him to exercise his unique talents. Participating in the New Deal, even if it had been the culmination of a new political awareness Priscilla's interests may have engendered, was something he, and not Priscilla, was qualified to do. Priscilla may have helped out at soup kitchens, but it was Alger's legal skills that had enabled him to join the IJA. And it was Alger who had been asked to join the Ware Group; he had emerged as a person who might possibly influence governmental policy.

The Ware Group's discussions and activities started with the premise that the existing policies of New Deal agencies were inadequate to achieve the reforms its members supported, and that the members should try to promote radical alternatives. Hiss had quickly learned, at the AAA, that some of the reforms he was seeking to implement were meeting resistance. As part of the effort to decrease crop production, the AAA was drafting contracts paying various types of farmers to curtail their outputs. In the cotton industry, tenant farming was the norm, with plantation owners hiring tenants and sharecroppers to harvest cotton on their plantations. Hiss and his AAA contemporaries drafted contracts that made direct payments to tenant farmers and sharecroppers, rather than paying benefits to plantation owners who allegedly would distribute some of the proceeds to their employees. After resistance from large cotton interests, the Department of Agriculture intervened, and eventually most of the staff in the AAA general counsel's office, including its head, Jerome Frank, were fired. This did not take place until 1935, and Hiss, who was on leave from the AAA at the time, was not terminated. But Hiss was aware from the time that he joined the AAA that Chester Davis, the AAA's administrator in charge of farm programs, was opposed to direct payments to persons who harvested cotton.[59]

It seems to have been no coincidence that the first government officials recruited by Harold Ware for his discussion group were from the AAA. They included Lee Pressman, Nathan Witt, another graduate of Harvard Law School, and Hiss. Ware had access to the AAA in his capacity as a consultant to the Department of Agriculture, and had reason to know of the opposition to the cotton contracts being drafted by Hiss and others. He also knew that Pressman, Witt, and Hiss had all worked for the IJA. According to later testimony by Pressman, two other members of the group, Ware and Charles Kramer, were members of the Communist Party of the United States at the time, and encouraged the others to join that organization.[60] Hiss, already familiar with popular-front discussion groups, may have felt that the resistance to his office's cotton contracts was symptomatic of the difficulties reformers would encounter in the existing political structure. According to Whittaker Chambers, Alger Hiss also brought his brother Donald, who had joined the Department of Interior's Office of Subsistence Homesteads in 1934, into the Ware Group.[61]

Thus a number of factors coalesced in the years between 1933 and 1935 to transform Alger Hiss from a political liberal with a sympathy for casualties of the Depression to a popular-front collectivist who had become dissatisfied with the pace and scope of reform in the New Deal. In 1935 three more factors combined to facilitate Hiss's crossing the line from Communist Party member to active Soviet agent. First, Harold Ware died in a car crash, and Joszef Peter, a professional recruiter for Soviet intelligence, assumed control of the Ware Group. Next, Hiss took leave from the AAA to join a Senate committee, under the chairmanship of Gerald Nye from North Dakota, investigating the role of the munitions industry in World War I. The Nye Committee, which reflected the isolationist views of its chairman, had access to some confidential government documents detailing negotiations on sales of munitions between the United States and foreign nations. Hiss was now in a position where he could gain information that was valuable to Soviet military officials and could be covertly passed on to them. Peter asked him to do that. Peter had identified Hiss as someone with a bright future in government, who might rise to a high position in one of the "old-line" agencies, such as the Treasury or State Departments, which Peter believed were at the heart of American foreign and domestic policymaking.[62]

The final factor was psychological. Here, as with most speculation about the inner basis of Hiss's motivation, corroborating evidence is thin. Hiss quite naturally left no candid record about why he chose to become a Communist or an agent for Soviet military intelligence, leaving, instead, a well-constructed record of why he had not followed those paths. With very few exceptions, such as Whittaker Chambers and a few other former Soviet agents who renounced their affiliations and "defected" to Western intelligence services, those who knew the truth about Hiss's ideological affiliations and espionage activity, including Priscilla and Donald Hiss, had strong incentives not to come forward. Priscilla and Donald might themselves have been vulnerable to criminal prosecution, and the others were either also in that category or were members of the Soviet intelligence community. So there is no evidentiary smoking gun revealing Alger Hiss's motivation for choosing to spy for the Soviets in the 1930s.

What does exist, however, is enough of a consistent pyschological pattern in Hiss's behavior as to form the basis of an explanation that makes better sense of his decision to spy, and to lie about it, than any other. One can begin to glimpse the early stages of that pattern in the events highlighted in this chapter. Hiss had a superficially fulfilling but deeply scarring early life. He lost his father and his older brother, both under gruesome circumstances; his mother was emotionally distant and controlling; he was placed under considerable pressure to be the personal and professional caretaker of the Hiss family. He was directed toward elite social and professional worlds, but his immediate family lacked the financial resources to participate in the world of wealthy members of the upper class. He appeared to be the very personification of a cultured, affluent upbringing, but he knew that he was not quite that. He also knew, however, that he was intellectually gifted, handsome, and capable of charming, even manipulating, others.

By the time he married Priscilla Fansler, Alger Hiss sensed that a world of large professional opportunities was opening to him. But at the same time he remained, reflexively, a "good boy," instinctively inclined to cater to his mother, to his perceived family obligations, and to Priscilla herself. Although there is no reason to doubt that he shared Priscilla's growing involvement with the economic plight of disadvantaged persons in the early 1930s, and that he came to share her ideological enthusiasm for collectivist alternatives to capitalism as well, he may have chafed at her insistence that he choose his law firm affiliations on the basis of her preference to live in particular cities. He may have relished the fact that in 1933, when the Hisses left New York for Washington, it was his job choice that dictated their move. He may have also taken some satisfaction in knowing that as a trained lawyer, a potentially high-ranking government official, and a formidable intellect, he was a far more valuable commodity for the Communist Party and Soviet intelligence than Priscilla was.

But, above all, Alger Hiss, as he turned 30, may have been attracted to the secret life of an underground espionage agent. The life of an agent offered opportunities to exercise one's intellect, which could be directed not only toward the details of covert spying, but the details of constructing a carapace of misinformation, half-truths, and lies to cover one's espionage activities. Part of that carapace required one to be charming, and seem reliable and authentic, in one's overt roles. Hiss was to learn that he was not only very good at spying, he was also very good at keeping others away from his secret life. So, over time, Hiss found out that by being a spy, and keeping others from knowing that, he could find a deep sense of satisfaction, even a kind of inner peace. In the early 1930s he was quite far from that realization: he was fired with the enthusiasm of helping Soviet Communism make a better world. Later, after his secret life was partially exposed and he had opportunity to reflect upon it, his journey toward satisfaction and peace would begin in earnest.

By the mid-1930s Alger Hiss had traveled very far from the world in which he had grown up. He had left Minnie Hiss's household to start his own, with its defining personal relations and political inclinations. Without any conscious effort to do so, he had become a potentially valuable asset to the apparatus of Soviet intelligence that was seeking to expand its operations in America. In the process Hiss had developed a distinctive orientation and a distinctive style of pursuing his goals. He had learned that he was instinctively attracted to altruistic endeavors, could perform custodial or caretaker roles successfully, and relished the feelings of power and self-esteem he associated with helping others. He had also learned that he was good at ingratiating himself with people, and at manipulating them in the pursuit of his goals. When he wanted something, he could be quite persistent, even single-minded, in his efforts to get it. And he had usually gotten what he wanted. He had the ability to project a unique self-confidence without appearing arrogant or overbearing.

At the same time his reflexive desire to help people in distress meant that he regularly subsumed his goals in the agendas of others, and he had found that posture chafing. But his role as the selfless steward of others had begun to diminish by the mid-1930s. He was now a government official of some influence, on the track to a distinguished career in public service. He was someone whom the Soviets could identify as a potentially valuable agent. To him the Soviets could offer the prospect of participating in yet another altruistic activity—in this case nothing less than the eventual betterment of humankind in some classless, international future utopia—coupled with the sense of power and mastery associated with a secret, controlled life. They could offer him a way to pursue idealistic, selfless goals and be independent of Minnie and Priscilla at the same time.

As Alger Hiss began the process of taking up the Soviets on their explicit and implicit offers, Whittaker Chambers entered his life.

Alger and Priscilla Hiss, standing facing the camera in front
of a car in August 1935 at a time when they were having
regular social contacts with Whittaker Chambers.

CHAPTER TWO

Exposure

The exposure of Alger Hiss as a Communist and a Soviet agent began with a story about Hiss told by his accuser Whittaker Chambers. In 1952 Chambers produced a long, polished version of that story in his memoirs, *Witness*. He was at that time a celebrity, the star prosecution witness at the 1949 and 1950 perjury trials of Hiss, whom Chambers had accused of being in a Communist cell with him, and passing him stolen government documents, in the 1930s. Chambers admitted to having been a member of the Communist Party of the United States and an undercover Soviet agent, but stated that he had broken with the Soviets in 1938 and become a rabid anti-Communist.

When the story began, in 1934, Hiss was in his second year at the Agricultural Adjustment Administration, frustrated with what he regarded as the slow pace of efforts to alleviate the plight of economically deprived agricultural workers. He was an active member of the Ware Group and, Chambers said, an enthusiastic, dues-paying member of the Communist Party of the United States. When Chambers first met Hiss, he did not know what had prompted Hiss to become a Communist Party member. Hiss, for his part, never acknowledged being in the Ware Group, let alone the Communist Party.

One can only speculate about why Hiss concluded, sometime shortly after he arrived in Washington in 1933, that his career could only be fulfilled if he combined being a government official with being a secret member of the Communist Party. Harold Ware, who asked Hiss to join his discussion group, was a fervent Communist, a tireless recruiter of party members, and a charismatic figure: Hiss may have been impressed with Ware's convictions or his presence. Alternatively, Hiss may have been influenced by Lee Pressman, who had encouraged him to join the International Juridical Association in New York and had preceded Hiss at both the AAA and the Ware Group: Pressman was a Communist by 1934. Or Hiss may have been inspired by Priscilla's commitment to leftist politics and humanitarian causes. Or he may simply have decided that only the Communist Party could offer a version of popular-front collectivism that would precipitate the massive economic reforms he thought the Depression required. In any event, Whittaker Chambers felt, Hiss was already a passionate Communist when he first met him.

Chambers recalled that he entered Hiss's life when he received an assignment from Joszef Peter, the "head of the underground section of the American Communist Party." Peter, together with Harold Ware, had organized a group of government employees into a cell that met regularly in Washington, ostensibly for the purpose of discussing Marxist ideas. Peter's design for the group was to encourage its members, who were placed in various government agencies, to "influence policy at several levels" as their careers progressed.[1]

Following standard intelligence practice, Chambers said, Peter resolved to separate the members of the Ware Group, several of whom worked in the Agricultural Adjustment Administration, into discrete intelligence cells, and eventually to funnel them into the "old-line" government agencies, such as the Treasury and State Departments, where they might have greater access to information useful to the Soviet intelligence services. In 1934 Peter learned that one of the members of the Ware Group was about to be transferred from the AAA to a position that might give him access to confidential State Department documents of particular interest to Soviet military intelligence. The member was Alger Hiss. By 1934 Hiss had been appointed chief counsel to the Nye Committee, which, in the course of its investigations of the munitions industry, had access to correspondence that discussed military policies of the United States government. Accordingly, Peter asked Chambers, who had been working in New York as an information courier for the Communist Party of the United States, to come to Washington to oversee the formation of a special "parallel apparatus" whose members would report directly to the GRU (Glavnoye Razvedyvatelnoye Upravlenie, or Chief Intelligence Administration), the Soviet agency in charge of military intelligence. Hiss was to be the center of that apparatus.[2]

On coming to Washington, Chambers recalled, he met Harold Ware at a "Childs restaurant near the Union Station." Ware had been in New York the week before, where Peter had introduced him to Chambers and the meeting had been planned.

Ware and Chambers drove around Washington and then separated. Chambers went to meet Peter, who had taken a separate train from New York, at Union Station. Peter and Chambers then reconnoitered with Ware, and the three drove in his car "to a basement cafeteria on Wisconsin Avenue in Georgetown." At the meeting Chambers was briefed by Ware and Peter about Alger Hiss. "I learned," Chambers wrote in his memoirs,

> that he was an American, a lawyer, an exceptional Communist for whom [Peter] had an unusual regard, and that he was a member of the Ware Group. He was about to leave, or had just left, the AAA, where he had been assistant general counsel, for the Senate munitions investigating committee. This change made it important that he should be separated from the Ware Group at once. He would be the first man in the new apparatus which I was to organize.[3]

Later that day Chambers met Hiss for the first time "at a downtown cafeteria . . . on Pennsylvania Avenue." The meeting was brief, and Chambers did not see Hiss again for over a month. On that occasion he was invited to Hiss's apartment, then on 29th Street, "about nine o'clock" on a "hot, sticky Washington night." Priscilla Hiss was present, but she "took almost no part in a conversation which was rather pawing and aimless." Feeling awkward, Chambers "wondered rather desperately how I give the conversation some point." Believing "that intellectual Communists, especially those who are most fastidious, are usually fascinated by the image of . . . proletarian experience," Chambers told the Hisses of his experience, in 1919, of helping lay rails for subway trains in Washington. The story apparently fell flat. "There was a polite but complete short circuit," Chambers recalled. "I left shortly after feeling that it had been pretty awful."[4]

After first thinking that he would have to secure the help of Ware or Peter to develop a relationship with Hiss, Chambers resolved to try an additional visit to Hiss's apartment. This time things went better. Hiss explained that "he had not known what to make of" Chambers on the first visit, since "I was obviously not a proletarian," and "was not like any American he had ever known." Eventually Hiss had concluded that Chambers was a European of some sort, probably a Russian. The fact that Chambers insisted that he was an American only made Hiss believe that he was trying to conceal his identity to stay "one jump ahead of the police." When Chambers consulted Peter about Hiss's erroneous impression of him, Peter urged Chambers to let Hiss think he was a Russian.[5]

The original purpose of the Ware Group, Chambers said, had not been espionage, although he added that "it is axiomatic that any Communist . . . will always steal for the party anything that can possibly be of interest or use to it." The group's purpose was "to influence, from the most strategic positions, the policies of the United States Government." In his memoirs Chambers gave a list of members of the Ware Group "and the posts that mark their progress through the Federal government." If Chambers was accurate, members of the Ware Group, from 1934 through 1948, were on the staffs of the National Labor Relations Board, the Agricultural Adjustment Administration, the Works Progress Administration, the Securities and Exchange Commission, the Department of Justice, the Department of Agriculture, the National Recovery Administration, the State Department, and the Treasury Department. He could "imagine no better way to convey the secret power of the Communist Party in the domestic policies of the United States Government," Chambers noted, than to list the number of Ware Group members who held responsible positions with government agencies in the 1930s and 1940s.[6]

Chambers then described how, in the mid-1930s, pressure came to be placed on Ware Group members to include espionage among their functions. The reason was related to Stalin's inauguration of the second "Five-Year Plan," an economic retrenchment directive. Previously the Communist International had subsidized foreign Communist parties, including the Communist Party of the United States. The second Five-Year Plan required resources to be directed elsewhere, and parties in other nations were asked to become self-sufficient. Joszef Peter, in response to the situation, decided to make use of the Ware Group connections with government agencies to sell stolen documents to the Soviets. He asked Chambers to photograph documents, using a camera he bought for him, and to convey them to New York, where "Bill," the Soviet military intelligence officer in charge of overseeing American operations, would peruse them. On one occasion Alger Hiss, then with the Nye Committee, proposed that he request confidential documents from the State Department and give them to Chambers to photograph for "Bill." One set of documents was sent to Hiss by the State Department, and Chambers passed them on, but the State Department declined to comply with any more of Hiss's requests, and "Bill" was not impressed with the documents.[7]

Thus, in the context of the Ware Group and its growing contacts with Soviet intelligence in the 1930s, the paths of Alger Hiss and Whittaker Chambers first crossed. Alger's participation in the Ware Group, and his first forays into intelligence work for the Soviets, had been the culmination of a progression that had begun with his pro bono work for the International Juridical Association. Friends in that organization had joined him in New Deal agencies in the 1930s, and through them he had met Ware. When Chambers first met Hiss, his impression was that Hiss was a dedicated Communist, happy to participate in the dual goals of influencing policy in his overt work and engaging in covert espionage. Chambers's path toward intelligence work for the Soviets in the 1930s had been more tortuous. After working on the Washington subways as a teenager, he had enrolled in Williams College and Columbia University, leaving the latter to travel for a brief time in Russia. By 1925 he was a member of the Communist Party of the United States, and for most of the 1920s worked for the *Daily Worker*. In the early 1930s he joined the staff of the *New Masses* magazine, to which he contributed fiction and essays, and had begun to make contacts with Soviet intelligence sources in the United States. Through them he was to meet Joszef Peter and end up as the Ware Group's courier, and, soon thereafter, Alger Hiss's friend.[8]

That was the polished version of Whittaker Chambers's story as to how he had met Alger Hiss. He had told other versions of it since 1939, but for many years had had trouble getting anyone to take it seriously. When Chambers told the story again at Hiss's two perjury trials in 1949 and 1950, Hiss denied almost all of it. He denied any connection with the Ware Group, the Communist Party, or Soviet intelligence. By the outset of his first trial, however, he had acknowledged an acquaintanceship with Whittaker Chambers. Hiss's concession that he had known Chambers in Washington in the 1930s remained grudging; he stated that he had known him as "George Crosley," a journalist covering the Nye Committee, and nothing more. Confronted with evidence that Crosley had lived for a time in an apartment rented by the Hisses on 29th Street in Washington, Hiss remembered the episode, but suggested that he had resisted contacts with Crosley, finding him something of a sponge. The relationship between Hiss and Chambers, however, was far more extensive.

In his memoirs Chambers described his relationship with Hiss as existing on "two incongruous levels." One was "the level of conspiracy," with Hiss and Chambers, whose public alias was "Lloyd Cantwell," and who was known within underground circles as "Carl," participating in the process of conveying information from United States government sources to the Soviets. The other was "the easy, gay, carefree association of two literate . . . middle-class families." Although Hiss and Chambers occasionally talked "about underground activity," most of the communications involved Priscilla Hiss and Esther (Lise) Chambers as well as their husbands. Chambers found Priscilla to be a "brittle and tense" person who warmed to the "transparently sincere, forthright, gentle, warm" nature of Lise. The two couples engaged in the "spontaneous surface talk of people among whom there exist . . . intangible compatibilities of temperament."[9]

The friendship between the Hisses and the Chamberses was precipitated by the latter's move to Baltimore in the summer of 1934. At that time Chambers was acting as courier for the Ware Group, and Hiss was working for the Nye Committee and had been reassigned to his own "parallel apparatus," also serviced by Chambers. Despite Joszef Peter's belief in the potential usefulness of the Ware Group and Hiss's cell, the resident agent for Soviet military intelligence, whom Chambers called "Bill," planned to reassign Chambers to a courier position in London. The projected cover for Chambers was that of a literary agent, working in connection with Maxim Lieber, a New York-based literary agent whom Peter had recruited for the Soviets. Efforts were made to secure cover identities for Chambers, Lise, and their infant daughter, and to create a process where information Chambers secured in England could be funneled to Soviet authorities. That project was occupying "Bill" and Peter during the summer of 1934, and when it was completed Chambers was to go abroad.[10]

The fact that Chambers saw himself as a temporary resident of Baltimore, and that Hiss, once segregated from the Ware Group, was operating in "isolation," contributed to the social interactions of the Hisses and the Chamberses, which were in violation of "underground procedures." And as the friendship between the two families developed, Chambers's transfer to London was delayed. The Chamberses would remain in the Baltimore-Washington area for most of 1934 and 1935. For part of that time they lived, rent-free, in the 29th Street apartment rented by the Hisses, which was vacant for two months after the Hisses moved, in the spring of 1935, to a furnished house on P Street. They also lived briefly with the Hisses, occupying the third floor of the P Street house for about a month. Eventually they moved back to Baltimore, to an apartment on Eutaw Place, not far from Minnie Hiss's house. Their frequent changes of location were dictated by the fact that they believed that any moment they might be dispatched to England and thus chose places with short-term rentals.[11]

Meanwhile, changes were taking place in Hiss's and Chambers's underground work. A purge of the GRU had begun in 1936, and "Bill" was dispatched to Moscow and never heard from again. Bill's last contact with Chambers consisted of a penciled note warning him not to trust Bill's successor, Colonel Boris Bykov. Bykov had arrived in New York in the fall of 1936 with a different agenda for the Ware Group and Hiss's cell. Chambers's London assignment was canceled, with Bykov instructing him to increase the espionage activity of his Washington sources. He was particularly interested in securing government documents that could be sent on to Soviet intelligence sources in Moscow. Four of Chambers's sources had access to documents: Abel Gross, an employee of the Bureau of Standards, Julian Wadleigh at the State Department, Harry Dexter White of Treasury, whose documents were conveyed by another Treasury Department employee, George Silverman, and Hiss. When Bykov expressed an interest in gaining expanded access to stolen documents, Chambers's role in underground operations changed.[12]

Beginning in the fall of 1936, the Soviets established a photographic workshop in Baltimore. Sources would bring documents home from work, where they would be transferred to Chambers, who would take them to Baltimore to be photographed. Chambers would then return the documents to his sources the same night, or by the next morning. Once a week Chambers would journey to New York with photographed copies for Bykov.[13]

By that time Hiss had moved from the Nye Committee to the Justice Department, where he had worked on the case of *United States v. Butler,* in which the government made an effort to salvage the legislation that created the AAA, only to have it declared unconstitutional by the Supreme Court in January 1936. After the *Butler* case came down, Hiss continued to work at the Justice Department until September 1936, when he accepted a position in the office of the Assistant Secretary in the State Department. The job offered a salary of $5,600 a year, and Hiss had been making $7,500 in the Justice Department. Although Hiss later claimed that he was attracted to the State Department because of his long-term interest in the field of international relations, the State Department was an unlikely choice for a young man dedicated to the goals of the early New Deal, which were largely domestic in their orientation. In addition, the State Department was thought to be among the more hide-bound and less progressive of the federal government's old-line agencies. But one member of the assistant secretary's office in the State Department described it as being, in the 1930s, "the best possible place to work" for someone interested in gaining access to confidential diplomatic and military documents.[14]

Bykov's arrival, and the new procedures he instituted for photographing stolen government documents, coincided with Hiss's occupying a position that would expand his opportunities for espionage. Before long Hiss's brief case was "well filled," as Chambers put it, with documents he thought of interest to the Soviets. Hiss was so productive in bringing home documents that he precipitated a further change in the Soviets's methods for obtaining them. As Chambers recalled,

It was Alger Hiss's custom to bring home documents from the State Department approximately once a week or once in ten days. He would bring
out only the documents that happened to cross his desk on that day, and a
few that on one pretext or another he had been able to retain on his desk.
Bykov wanted more complete coverage. He proposed that the *Advokat*
["Lawyer," the Soviets's code name for Hiss at the time] should bring home
a briefcase of documents every night.

Chambers, however, only visited Hiss about once a week, since his practice was to
round up documents from his sources, have them photocopied and returned, and
take the photocopies to New York only at weekly intervals. In order to continue this
practice, but protect Hiss, Bykov instructed Hiss to type copies of the documents
himself and retain them for Chambers. "When I next visited him," Chambers noted,
"Alger would turn over to me the typed copies, covering a week's documents, as well
as the briefcase of original documents that he had brought home that night. The
original documents would be photographed and returned to Alger Hiss. The typed
copies would be photographed and then returned to me . . . I would destroy them."[15]

In recollecting his espionage activities Chambers gave no indication that the procedure employed for documents Hiss supplied was replicated by any other of his
sources. Hiss may have been the only agent who produced enough documents to
merit bringing them home on a daily basis, or he may have been the only one whose
household was capable of supplying typed copies. One thing remains clear: when
Whittaker Chambers broke with the Soviets, virtually all the copies of stolen government documents that he retained were documents that had been typed on a typewriter from the household of Alger Hiss. This may have been an entirely fortuitous
choice on Chambers's part. The Hiss documents might have been the only typed
copies Chambers had available to him to use as part of a "life preserver" he was seeking to create against the possibility of reprisals once the Soviets learned of his defection. In any event, the decision on Alger Hiss's part to acquiesce in Bykov's new
procedure, and to supply typed copies as well as originals to Chambers, would
change Hiss's life.[16]

"Sometimes important documents passed through Alger's hand," Chambers recalled, "but he was able to keep them only for a short time, often only long enough
to read them." In such cases Hiss made penciled copies of the documents, or notes
summarizing their main points, which "he wrote down hastily on State Department
memo pads." He gave his handwritten summaries to Chambers as well. Some of
those summaries were included in the batch of documents Chambers, after resolving to leave the employ of the Soviets, chose to retain rather than to destroy. Al-

though the handwritten summaries Chambers retained were cryptic, Hiss was forced to concede, when confronted with them, that they were in his handwriting.[17]

For most of the period between 1934 and 1937, Alger Hiss and Whittaker Chambers were forming a close friendship and participating in espionage together. Chambers shared Hiss's dedication to the ideological goals of the Soviet Union: he had, in fact, a much longer record of service to those goals. But in 1937 he began to have second thoughts. He heard of the growing purges in the Soviet Union and noted that two American Soviet agents had recently disappeared. He himself was twice asked to go to the Soviet Union, ostensibly to supervise other agents, and avoided being sent, claiming that his intelligence work in Washington was too pressing. He later wrote that Hiss had not shared his apprehensions. Hiss "observ[ed] admiringly to me," Chambers recalled, "Stalin . . . always plays for keeps." By the fall of 1937 Chambers had resolved to defect from the Soviets. He encouraged Bykov to provide him with a car, insisted on having an actual government job (Joszef Peter found him one with the Bureau of Standards), rented rooms in a house in Baltimore as a hideaway, and began secreting away copies of stolen government documents to use as bargaining chips with the Soviets once they discovered his defection. By December 1937 he had told two friends, former Communists who had become disillusioned with the Soviets, that he was considering defecting, and asked for their help.[18]

Chambers's plan for defection came to a head in the first three months of 1938. In that period he continued to work, ostensibly, with his sources and Bykov, but at the same time he made arrangements to take his children out of school, move briefly to his hideaway apartment, and then move to Florida. Through friends he secured a translating job with Oxford University Press to bring in some income, and he assembled his life preserver of stolen documents. By April 1938 he was ready to put the plan into operation. Before moving out of his Baltimore apartment, and taking his elder child out of school, he secreted his documents with his wife's nephew in New York. He then took his family to Florida, where he remained for a month, completing the translation.

While in Florida the Chamberses concluded that the only way in which they could survive reprisals from the Soviets was for Whittaker to surface from hiding and publicize his defection so that the Soviets might be constrained from attacking him openly. With that in mind, they returned to Baltimore and bought a house. In the fall of 1938 Chambers began to call on his principal contacts in the Washington underground, to let them know that he had surreptitiously broken with the Soviets, but was not about to publicly denounce them. He encouraged his contacts to do so as well. In conversations with Julian Wadleigh, Harry Dexter White, and George Silverman, Chambers warned his contacts that if they did not defect as well, he might have to reveal their identities to authorities. But only Silverman seemed to have learned of Chambers's earlier defection, and none followed his advice.[19]

The final conversation Chambers had with a contact took place in December 1938 when he called on Alger and Priscilla Hiss, now living in a house on Volta Place in Washington. The visit, Chambers reported, went badly. The Hisses were aware of Chambers's defection, and Alger urged him to reconsider. Chambers then launched into a denunciation of the Soviets, citing their cooperation with the Nazis, their betrayal of the Republicans in the Spanish Civil War, and Stalin's purges. He concluded by urging Alger Hiss to defect along with him. Hiss's response, as Chambers later recalled it, was to describe Chambers's comments as "mental masturbation," and to ignore his advice. As Chambers prepared to leave, Priscilla handed him a small Christmas present for his daughter, a "little wooden rolling pin such as could be bought at the dime store for a nickel." Chambers's first reaction was to be offended by the gesture, and on returning home he threw the present into the furnace. Later he concluded that the present "had been given in spontaneous kindness," and that he should not have destroyed it.[20]

In the decade that followed Chambers's defection, Alger Hiss continued his career as a government employee and a Soviet agent, and Chambers's efforts to alert authorities about him and other underground agents had little success. After transferring from the Justice Department to the State Department in 1936, Hiss continued at State for the next ten years, working his way up to the position of director of the Office of Special Political Affairs, the last position he held before accepting the presidency of the Carnegie Endowment for International Peace in 1946. He had been an assistant to Francis Sayre, the assistant secretary of state, to Stanley Hornbeck, political adviser to the Far Eastern Division of the State Department, and, in 1944, to Leo Pasvolsky, the first head of the Office of Special Political Affairs. In the last capacity he worked closely with Secretary of State Edward Stettinius in planning for conferences designed to create the United Nations. He also attended, along with Stettinius, the Yalta Conference in 1945, in which the Soviet Union, Great Britain, and the United States attempted to define geographic boundaries for postwar Europe. His rise to influence culminated in his being named temporary secretary-general for the April 1945 San Francisco conference in which the U.N. came into being.[21]

Alger, Priscilla, and Donald Hiss continued to function as a separate cell affiliated with Soviet military intelligence during this period, but it is not clear what work Priscilla and Donald did for the Soviets. After Alger's and Priscilla's first child, Anthony (Tony) Hiss, was born in 1941, Priscilla did not hold an outside job. Once Donald secured a position in the State Department, Bykov proposed that he begin to procure stolen documents for the Soviets as well, but Alger rejected the idea, telling Bykov that Donald was "not ready" for that task. Alger was, we will see, reflexively protective of family members, and he may have wanted to safeguard Donald from the risks of espionage. He was also aware that Donald was not as intellectually gifted as he, and may have adopted a paternalistic attitude toward his younger brother. Finally, Alger may have wanted the truly significant work of the cell to revolve around himself. In any event, although Donald worked with the State Department's legal advisor to the Philippines from 1938 to 1945, and might have been in a position to pass on confidential documents related to Japan's interest in southeast Asia—information in which the Soviet military was strongly interested— there is no evidence that he did so.[22]

Alger Hiss's work, however, was substantial, its importance accentuated by Hiss's rise up the State Department ladder. Hiss's increased access to confidential sources, especially after he became an assistant to Secretary of State Edward Stettinius, made it possible for him to funnel intelligence information of considerable value to the Soviets. For example, Hiss's placement, coupled with that of the British Soviet agent Donald Maclean, who held a high-level post in the British Embassy in Washington from 1944 to 1949, meant that Stalin had a firm grasp of the postwar goals of the United States and Great Britain before the Yalta Conference. A recent study, in highlighting Soviet intelligence success in the 1940s, singled out the contributions of Hiss, Maclean, and other British-based Soviet agents in "providing a regular flow of classified intelligence or [confidential] documents in the run-up to [Yalta.]" "Some sense of how Moscow felt that good intelligence had contributed to Stalin's success at Yalta," the study concluded, "is conveyed by Moscow's congratulations to Hiss."[23] The reference was to a secret meeting in Moscow, just after the Yalta Conference, at which Hiss was personally thanked for his efforts by Deputy Soviet Premier Andrei Vyshinki.[24] Although there is clear evidence that Maclean and Hiss knew each other comparatively well, and were in a position to consult with one another publicly about postwar planning measures involving the Soviets, Hiss regularly denied any memory of even having met Maclean.[25]

Hiss's access to information also meant that the Soviets could use him to learn a good deal about prospective United States policy toward the Far East, because Hiss had been privy to internal deliberations about postwar goals in that region as an adviser to Hornbeck. In addition, State Department records show that Hiss, when affiliated with the Office of Special Political Affairs, had made requests for confidential information from the Office of Strategic Services on postwar atomic energy policy and the internal security of Britain, France, China, and the Soviet Union. In this period Hiss had the sponsorship, within the State Department, of Hornbeck, Pasvolsky, Stettinius, and Assistant Secretary of State Dean Acheson.[26]

Meanwhile Chambers had had some success in creating a post-underground career for himself. A friend, Robert Cantwell, told him in 1939 about an opening on the staff of *Time* magazine, and Chambers was hired as a "third-string book reviewer." He remained with *Time* for the next nine years, working his way up to senior editor. Although Chambers encountered some internal opposition at *Time*, centering on his desire to "reverse . . . the magazine's policy toward Russia," which he regarded as "not a friend, but an enemy," his years with *Time* gave him financial stability and a voice for his militantly anti-Communist views. "My debt and my gratitude to *Time* cannot be measured," he wrote in his memoirs. "At a critical moment, *Time* gave me back my life." In the same time period the Chamberses bought a farm in Westminster, Maryland, and Chambers became a Quaker. "I returned to the land," he wrote, as "a way of bringing up my children in close touch with the soil and hard work, and apart from what I consider the false standards and vitiating influence of the cities."[27]

Chambers's efforts to denounce his former colleagues in Soviet intelligence, however, proved less successful. His first attempt came in August 1939 when he had an interview with Adolf Berle, then assistant secretary of state and adviser to the Roosevelt White House on internal security matters. The interview was arranged by Chambers's friend Isaac Don Levine, an anti-Communist journalist. It was precipitated by the announcement of the Nazi-Soviet pact, which had radically altered the attitudes of Great Britain and the United States toward the Soviet Union, which had previously been thought of as a firm opponent of Hitler's Germany. Chambers had initially been concerned about the consequences of revealing to government authorities that he had been a Soviet agent, a necessary step in any disclosures about others. He told Levine that he would only provide information directly to Roosevelt, and asked for a promise of immunity. The Nazi-Soviet pact made him feel that the Roosevelt administration might be more receptive to that offer, and when Levine informed him that Roosevelt could not meet with him but Berle could, Chambers decided to risk the meeting.

Chambers attached some conditions to disclosing information to Berle. He did not give his real name, identifying himself only as "Carl." Although he stressed the importance of taking action against Communists in place in the government, he indicated that before being formally asked to provide evidence, he would insist on immunity from prosecution. And although he indicated that the persons he identified were more than simply ideological sympathizers of the Soviets, he did not furnish any details of particular espionage activities. He was particularly careful not to mention his own role in transferring purloined government secrets to the Soviets.

Berle took notes at the end of a rambling conversation between himself, Chambers, and Levine that lasted for more than two hours. The result of his notes was a memorandum entitled "Underground Espionage Agent," which contained a list of names of governmental officials associated with "underground" activity. Comments accompanying the names, such as "leader of British Underground C.," "head of the underground group," and "Underground connections," indicated that Chambers had not merely identified the individuals as Communists. The list included Lee Pressman, Harold Ware, Nathan Witt, and Julian Wadleigh. It described Joszef Peter as "responsible for Washington Sector." It identified the State and Treasury Departments as containing several "underground" participants. And it concluded by listing Donald and Alger Hiss as involved persons. Donald was described as a "[m]ember of CP with Pressman & Witt," and as "[b]rought along by brother." Alger was described as "Ass't to [Francis] Sayre," "CP," and "Member of the Underground Com.—Active." Priscilla Hiss was also mentioned, described as a "Socialist."[28]

Chambers left the meeting with the impression that Berle was going to follow up immediately with the White House, and that he would arrange to secure Chambers immunity from prosecution. But although Berle's conversion of his talk with Chambers to a memorandum suggested a prompt follow-up, nothing came of the meeting between Berle and Chambers for several years. Chambers later wrote that Levine had told him that Berle, on taking his information to Roosevelt, had been laughed off. Berle wrote, in a memoir, that he had delayed checking on the Hiss brothers until 1941, when he had asked Dean Acheson and Felix Frankfurter about Alger, and had been assured that he was above suspicion. Chambers, who was not prepared to say anything more specific about Hiss without an assurance of immunity, waited for Berle to get back to him, but heard nothing. Finally, in 1941 he contacted Berle again. Berle reassured him of the government's interest, but did not mention immunity.

Meanwhile Hiss's name had appeared on a long list of "Communists, fellow travelers, and Communist sympathizers" in the federal government sent to Attorney General Francis Biddle by Congressman Martin Dies of Texas in October 1941. Hiss, along with Donald Hiss, had appeared on the list because Dies believed they were members of the Washington Committee for Democratic Action, a group with allegedly radical political sympathies. The report on Alger and Donald was erroneous, although Priscilla Hiss had briefly been a member of the group. Biddle passed Dies's list on to the FBI, and in February 1942 an agent interviewed Alger Hiss and asked him if he had been or was a member of the Communist Party. Hiss denied being such, adding that the only government he wanted to overthrow was Hitler's.[29]

The FBI did not pursue the matter, even though in 1943 it requested a copy of Berle's "Underground Espionage Agent" memorandum, and even though Isaac Don Levine had circulated the gist of that memorandum to various sources in the government, hoping they would pass it on to Roosevelt, little had happened. An illustration of the FBI's general indifference to both Chambers and Hiss had come in 1942, when Chambers learned, after being interviewed by two FBI agents, that the Bureau was unaware of Berle's memorandum. The result was that Chambers, who had heard nothing about the immunity he sought, was cautious with the agents, and J. Edgar Hoover concluded, after being briefed on the interview, that Chambers had little specific information. Hoover recommended that the FBI take no further action to follow up Chambers's disclosures, and Chambers himself, absorbed with his work for *Time* and suffering from angina, resolved not to pursue the matter any further.[30]

For the next five years Chambers continued to work for *Time*, confining his anti-Communist activities to writings in that magazine. In that time frame, however, other sources had emerged to identify Alger Hiss as a potential Soviet agent. Two of those sources had come to the attention of the FBI by 1945: Elizabeth Bentley and Igor Guzenko. In August 1945 Bentley walked into an FBI office and announced that she was a former Soviet agent. She had joined the Communist Party in the 1930s and had been recruited into espionage by Jacob Golos, her lover and employer at United States Service and Shipping Corporation, a cover for Soviet espionage activities. Bentley became a courier for networks organized by Golos, and when he died in 1943 she took over the network organization. Among her networks were two in the Washington area: one centered in the War Production Board, the other in the Treasury Department. The networks included two of the most highly placed Soviet agents in the government, Harry Dexter White in Treasury and Laughlin Currie, an administrative assistant in the White House.

By 1945 Soviet intelligence operations in the United States were being controlled by two agencies. One was the NKGB (Narodny Kommissariat Gosudarstvennoye Bezopasnosti, or People's Commissariat for State Security). The NKGB was the successor of the NKVD (Narodny Kommissariat Vnutrennikh Del, or People's Commissariat of Internal Affairs), which was in existence from 1922 to 1943. The NKGB would later become the KGB, the more familiar acronym to Americans. Its jurisdiction extended to all foreign and domestic intelligence matters that were not military in nature. The other agency was the GRU, originally a division of the General Staff of the Soviet Red Army. The two agencies had overlapping functions and tended to compete with one another. By the end of the Second World War the GRU, which had initially been the elite Soviet intelligence agency, had come to be overshadowed by the NKGB, primarily because Stalin became persuaded that the GRU bore some responsibility for the Soviets's military difficulties in the war.

In the 1930s and 1940s, most of the American-based Soviet agents reported to the NKVD or NKGB rather than the GRU. But the most important agents, those involved in atomic espionage and other military matters, reported to the GRU. Hiss had been assigned to the GRU originally because of his affiliation with the Nye Committee, and the Soviets continued to hope that he would gain access to top-secret military plans through his State Department affiliations. Nonetheless the NKGB, as it began to outrank the GRU in the 1940s, felt free to demand access to any GRU agents, including Hiss.

After Golos's death, Iskhak Akhmerov, the NKVD-NKGB controller of Soviet intelligence agents in America, concluded that the Soviets should acquire more direct control over Bentley's networks. Beginning in 1944, they began to do so, and soon Bentley was stripped of all her responsibilities, including, by 1945, her overt work for the United States Service and Shipping Corporation. Depressed by Golos's death, and increasingly fearful that the FBI was investigating her, she decided to preempt matters by defecting. In the fall of 1945, in interviews with the FBI, she gave a list of Soviet agents operating in the United States. Among those was Alger Hiss, whom she identified as "in the State Department," and the head of a Washington-based Soviet network different from the ones she had organized.[31]

As the FBI was receiving this information, it was also getting some from Igor Guzenko, a clerk in the Soviet Embassy in Ottawa, who defected to Canadian authorities in September 1945, bringing with him a number of documents detailing the existence of a large Soviet military intelligence network in Canada. Guzenko revealed, in one interview with the FBI, that a Canadian-based Soviet military intelligence officer had told him that "the Soviets had an agent in the United States in May 1945 who was an assistant to the then secretary of state, Edward R. Stettinius." Hiss was Stettinius's assistant at the time.[32]

The FBI's posture toward Hiss had begun to change by the time this information became available. When Hiss was named to organize the San Francisco conference to plan the composition of the United Nations in early 1945, the decision apparently precipitated a routine security inquiry, and the FBI sent a copy of Chambers's 1942 interview with them to State Department security officials. One of them, Raymond

Murphy, interviewed Chambers in March 1945 and Chambers gave more detailed information about Hiss, naming him as both a Communist and an underground intelligence agent. Murphy produced a March 26 report on Chambers's accusations, which he circulated to the FBI, and the FBI followed up with a May 1945 interview of Chambers, who this time was more forthcoming about Hiss's activities. By November 1945 the FBI, taking this information and that supplied by Bentley and Guzenko into account, had concluded that Hiss was a potential Soviet agent, and submitted its conclusion to Secretary of State James Byrnes and Attorney General Tom C. Clark. As a result, in the spring of 1946, Hiss was placed on a "pending list" of State Department employees, which meant that he would be given no further consideration for promotion.[33]

At the same time Hiss was told by Byrnes that sources in Congress were suggesting that he had Communist affiliations, and that he should schedule an interview with the FBI to clarify matters. Hiss received an interview on March 25, 1946, with D. M. Ladd, the FBI's Assistant Director, and denied any associations with Communism. Ladd did not tell Hiss about the charges made against him by Bentley, Guzenko, and Chambers, not wanting to compromise those sources. Hiss may have consequently felt reassured by the interview, but the FBI and the State Department had begun to act as if he were a security risk. State Department security officials monitored his desk calendar and restricted his access to confidential documents, and the FBI wiretapped his office and home phones and scrutinized his business appointments.[34]

By the fall of 1946 pressure was mounting on Hiss to resign from the State Department. Through Dean Acheson, he made contact with John Foster Dulles, who was on the board of directors of the Carnegie Endowment, and by December Hiss had received an offer to succeed Nicholas Murray Butler as president of that organization.[35] Hiss had a conversation with Acheson in which he expressed concern about leaving the State Department before the question of his Communist affiliations had been decisively put to rest. Acheson suggested that "[t]his is the kind of thing which rarely, if ever, gets cleared up," and advised Hiss to accept the Carnegie position. By February 1947 Hiss, Priscilla, Timothy, and six-year-old Tony had moved to New York, and Hiss had begun work at Carnegie.[36]

The circumstances of Chambers's 1938 break with the Soviets, the initially lukewarm reception of United States government authorities to Chambers's charges about Hiss, and the process by which Hiss came under suspicion by the State Department and the FBI in 1945 and 1946 were each to contribute to shaping Hiss's response to Chambers's eventual claim, in the fall of 1948, that Hiss had been a Soviet agent as well as a Communist.

Although the FBI and the State Department had begun to be very concerned, by the mid-1940s, about the potential infiltration of government agencies by Communists, that issue was not a high priority in the 1930s. Chambers's 1938 defection, considered in the context of the Cold War years, seems strikingly casual. Chambers did not "defect" to American security officials at all, nor did he attempt, after his brief interval in Florida, to conceal his whereabouts or change his identity. He simply approached some of his left-wing acquaintances in New York and informed them that he had become an anti-Communist. He did not contact any government official for 16 months after his initial break, and he did not publicize his defection outside the limited circle of his acquaintances. Hiss of course knew of Chambers's break with the Soviets, but he had no reason to think, initially, that United States government officials knew.

The response of the Roosevelt administration to Chambers's interview with Berle was in keeping with the low-key nature of Chambers's defection. Chambers did not single out Hiss in the Berle interview, and when Berle informed members of the Roosevelt administration about his informant's revelations (Berle did not even know Chambers's name), their response was to dismiss the incident. That reaction, given the fact that World War II had begun, that Nazi Germany had emerged as the principal threat to world security, and that the United States was still hoping to become allied with the Soviets against the Axis powers, was understandable. Even if some officials of the federal government were suspected Communists, dealing with them was hardly a priority. In retrospect, Berle's failure to supply the FBI with the notes of his Chambers interview until the FBI requested them in 1943 may appear grossly negligent, but Berle had not received any support from higher-placed Roosevelt officials for pursuing Chambers's information, and two people he respected had dismissed the charges against Hiss out of hand.

The relatively unobtrusive nature of Chambers's defection, and the apparent indifference of United States security officials to information about Communists employed by government agencies, may have served to reassure Hiss, in the period between 1939 and 1945, that his status as a Soviet agent would not be endangered by Chambers. And when rumors that Hiss was a Communist began surfacing in 1945, Hiss had no reason to think they were coming from Chambers. Clearly some of them were, but no one in the FBI or the State Department security apparatus was about to publicize that fact.

Because the government was reluctant to reveal the sources implicating Hiss in 1945 and 1946, Hiss had the illusion that suspicion of him was based solely on rumors. He had made an effort to lay those rumors to rest in his 1946 FBI interview, and, as far as he knew, had forestalled any action to remove him from the State Department. When Chambers's charges surfaced, two years later, Hiss still did not know that other incriminating information about him was in the possession of government authorities. Chambers had disappeared from Hiss's life for a decade, his charges related to events in the past and he had had his own checkered career. Although Hiss had known Chambers comparatively well in the 1930s, he may not have even known his real name. So when Chambers surfaced in 1948 with claims that Hiss had been a Communist in the 1930s, Hiss's first impulse was to launch a reputational defense. He simply denied any such affiliations, and asked the House Un-American Activities Committee who they were inclined to believe, a highly credentialed government official with an impressive demeanor, or a fat, rumpled, ex-Communist with bad teeth. Hiss's reputational defense required him to assume the posture of an outraged innocent, scapegoated by an unstable accuser for personal and political reasons. That was the posture he was to adopt for the remainder of his life.

The House of Representatives's Committee on Un-American activities was the product of World War II and the Cold War. It had first come into existence as a temporary committee in 1938, under the chairmanship of Martin Dies. Initially it functioned as a watchdog on potential Nazi collaborators in the United States, and a forum for groups deploring the alleged tendency of American culture to become more heterogenous and less religious. But, as the list Dies sent to Francis Biddle in 1941 suggested, HUAC was becoming increasingly interested in Communist infiltration of the federal government by the outbreak of World War II, and by 1945, when John Rankin of Mississippi assumed the chairmanship and the Committee was made permanent, its principal focus was the threat of Communism to postwar America. In 1947 it began an investigation of Communist propaganda in the movie industry, which resulted in a number of prominent screen writers, producers, and directors being ostracized and deprived of economic opportunities. Although the Truman administration initially disassociated itself from HUAC, by 1947 Truman had signed an executive order establishing a loyalty and security program for all federal employees, and the hunt for Communists in government had begun.[37]

HUAC was nonetheless controversial: its investigations of the motion picture industry had received some sharp criticism in the press, and President Harry Truman's staff had drafted a bill to abolish it should the Democrats control Congress after the

1948 election. It was partly to buttress its credibility, therefore, that the Committee decided to hold hearings, in July 1948, featuring the testimony of Elizabeth Bentley about the infiltration of Communists into the federal government. Bentley had previously testified before a Senate subcommittee to the same effect, but in her HUAC testimony she was more specific, giving the names of several government officials who had funneled stolen documents to her to pass on to the Soviets. Bentley's appearance galvanized the press, but she produced no corroborating evidence for her charges, and the Truman administration labeled them as false.[38]

With its credibility at stake, HUAC sought witnesses who might support Bentley's testimony. One who came to mind was Whittaker Chambers. Chambers, who had been interviewed by HUAC in March 1948 had grudgingly given some information about his past role as a Communist and Soviet agent. After Bentley's July 31 testimony, HUAC subpoenaed Chambers. He had heard of Bentley's defection earlier that year and knew of her July testimony. He anticipated that he might be subpoenaed, and had resolved to accept the subpoena, having been encouraged by Henry Luce of *Time* to do so. On Monday, August 2, he was served, and his appearance before HUAC was scheduled for the following day.

Chambers appeared before HUAC on August 3, 1948, with a prepared statement. The Committee ignored it and began questioning him about his knowledge of Communists in the federal government. As Chambers began to discuss the Ware Group, one Committee member suggested that the hearings move out of executive session in a hearing room to the Ways and Means Committee, where a public session could be held. After microphones, newsreel cameras, and lights were installed, Chambers was called as a witness. He gave his name and date of birth, and then stated that prior to going to work for *Time* he had been "a member of the Communist Party and a paid functionary of that party."[39]

After his introductory comments, Chambers asked if he could read his prepared statement. After being granted permission, he stated that he had joined the Communist Party in 1924, had broken with it in 1937, and had "reported to the authorities what I knew" shortly after the announcement of the Hitler-Stalin pact in 1939. He then described the "apparatus to which I was attached" as an underground agent, the Ware Group, and named some of its members. Those included "Alger Hiss, who, as a member of the State Department, later organized . . . the United States side of the Yalta Conference." Chambers added that the Ware Group's "original purpose" was "not primarily espionage," but "the Communist infiltration of the American government." "I had tried to shield those who were most deeply involved," he wrote in his memoirs, "from the darker charge of espionage."[40]

The news of Chambers's accusations broke in the August 3 afternoon papers, with his charges against Hiss being the lead story. Hiss already knew the gist of Chambers's testimony, having been called, the evening before Chambers's appearance, by a reporter who had learned the substance of Chambers's remarks from a source on the Committee. Chambers had no sooner completed his testimony when Hiss sent a telegram to Parnell Thomas, HUAC's acting chairman. "I do not know Mr. Chambers," the telegram read, "and, so far as I am aware, have never laid eyes on him. There is no basis for the statements about me made to your committee." Hiss asked for an opportunity to "appear . . . before your committee to make these statements formally and under oath." He stated that he would be in Washington on Thursday, August 5. He also sent a copy of the telegram to Dulles, in his capacity of chairman of the board of trustees of the Carnegie Endowment.

As the news of Chambers's testimony was breaking, Priscilla Hiss and Tony were in Peacham, Vermont, where the Hisses had a summer house. Priscilla, a neighbor remembered, was unaware of the events in Washington until the neighbor, who had happened to be in New York on August 5, picked up a paper with a story about Chambers's allegations and a picture of him. When the neighbor showed the story to Priscilla, she recalled "a dreadful man named Crosley or something like that . . . we knew once." In a 1975 interview, however, Alger Hiss remembered calling Priscilla the afternoon of Chambers's testimony, August 3, and reassuring her that he would be refuting the testimony before HUAC and "[t]his will all blow over." If Hiss's recollection of the timing of his call to Priscilla is accurate, it is possible that she already suspected, when she saw the newspaper story, that Whittaker Chambers was the man she and Alger had known as "Carl" or "George Crosley."[41]

On August 5 Hiss appeared before the Committee with a statement he had drafted and shown, that morning, to his brother Donald, Dean Acheson, and William Marbury. The statement was an unequivocal denial of any affiliation with the Communist Party. As Hiss put it,

> I am not and never have been a member of the Communist Party. I do not and never have adhered to the tenets of the Communist Party. I am not and never have been a member of any Communist-front organization. I have never followed the Communist Party line, directly or indirectly. To the best of my knowledge, none of my friends is a Communist. . . .
>
> To the best of my knowledge, I never heard of Whittaker Chambers until 1947, when two representatives of the Federal Bureau of Investigation asked me if I knew him . . . I said I did not know Chambers. So far as I know, I have never laid eyes on him, and I should like to have the opportunity to do so.[42]

Given Hiss's affiliations with the Ware Group, "Carl," Joszef Peter, Boris Bykov, and Soviet intelligence since the 1930s, this was an extraordinarily bold, even reckless, series of lies. If Chambers is to be believed, Hiss began paying Communist Party dues as soon as he joined the Ware Group in 1934. The Ware Group was a prototypical "Communist-front" organization, serving, on the surface, as an intellectual discussion group but actually consisting of an espionage cell. All of the members of the Ware Group were Communists, and Hiss had known, and been on friendly terms, with several other Communists. And although Hiss may not have known a Whittaker Chambers, he had clearly known the man whose testimony he was choosing to rebut.

By his categorical disassociation of himself from even the slightest connection with Communism or Communist-front activities, Hiss set in motion a narrative of his career that he would devote the rest of his life to telling and retelling. In that narrative Hiss was simply a young lawyer who had gone to Washington and became committed to the policies of the New Deal and international peace. His career had been a consistent effort to promote those ideals. He had never been a Communist, and those who were accusing him of being such were seeking to scapegoat him for partisan purposes. They were a pack of liars, and he was their intended victim.

Hiss's choice meant that each time some additional evidence associating him with Communism or the Soviets surfaced, he would be required to fashion an additional cover story to account for that evidence. It meant that he would be constantly preoccupied, for the rest of his life, with strategies to keep the public from entering his secret world. In the period between the 1948 HUAC hearings and his 1950 conviction for perjury, those strategies sought to buttress the wall of denials that his August 5 statement before the Committee had thrown up.

Hiss would first say, of his relationship with Chambers, that he did not know Chambers at all. He then amended that statement, admitting that he known Chambers briefly as "George Crosley." He subsequently was to deny that he had allowed Crosley to live rent-free in an apartment the Hisses owned, that he had loaned Crosley money for a car, and that he and Priscilla had taken trips with Crosley and visited him in summers. Hiss would also say that he knew nothing of any Soviet underground intelligence cell; that he had known the alleged participants in the Ware Group only as fellow government workers; that he had never been a Communist; that he had no friends who were Communists. He would say that the typed copies of stolen government documents Chambers produced at his perjury trials, which appeared to have typed on a Hiss family typewriter, had been typed by someone else. All those denials were designed to promote the view that, given his successful and promising career, Alger Hiss had no reason to be an undercover Soviet agent, and Whittaker Chambers was an unreliable witness with a checkered past.

Hiss's August 5 response to Chambers's charges was sufficiently effective that several members of HUAC believed that the Committee's credibility had been tarnished. Some proposed that the Committee investigate some other issue "which would . . . take the minds of the public off of the Hiss case"; others suggested sending Chambers's and Hiss's testimony to the Attorney General "to determine who was lying." At this point Richard Nixon, a junior Congressman from California who had been appointed to the Committee when he was first elected to Congress in 1947, made an alternative proposal. Nixon argued that "while it would be virtually impossible to prove that Hiss was or was not a Communist," HUAC "should be able to establish by corroborative testimony whether or not the two men knew each other." Nixon proposed that he be named head of a subcommittee to pursue that inquiry. His proposal was seconded by Robert Stripling, HUAC's chief investigator. The Committee agreed, and from that point on Nixon emerged as the architect of HUAC's probe of Hiss.[43]

Although Nixon would subsequently claim that he had only the barest impression of Hiss before his August 5 appearance, he was not being candid. In 1946 Nixon and another congressman had met with a Baltimore priest, John Cronin, who had written a report for the Bishops of the American Catholic Church, "The Problem of American Communism," in which Cronin had named Hiss as a suspected Communist. At the meeting with Nixon, Cronin gave him a copy of the report and repeated his charges against Hiss. Nixon did not disclose that he had that information about Hiss before Hiss's August 5 appearance. Nor did he suggest any personal antipathy toward Hiss. But Stripling later said that "Nixon had his hat set for Hiss" at the hearing. "It was a personal thing," Stripling told Allen Weinstein.[44]

Nixon decided that a face-to-face confrontation between Hiss and Chambers might clarify the question of their previous acquaintance. He first asked Chambers to come to New York on August 7 for an additional interview with the Committee. This time Committee members asked Chambers very specific questions about Hiss. Two of Chambers's answers provided the Committee with information they could use to clarify the extent to which Hiss and Chambers had known one another. The first was related to Hiss's interest in bird-watching. The second involved Hiss's efforts to give an old Ford car he owned to the Communist Party. The interview with Chambers ended with Nixon asking him if he would be prepared to take a lie detector test on his testimony, and Chambers agreeing to do so.[45]

HUAC called Hiss back for an executive session in New York on August 16. At that session Hiss suddenly concluded that he had known a man who resembled the photograph of Whittaker Chambers he had been shown. The man's name was George Crosley, and Hiss had "met him when I was working for the Nye committee." Crosley was "a writer" who "hoped to sell articles to magazines about the munitions industry." He then gave some additional details about Crosley. He had "[v]ery bad teeth." He had rented an apartment from Hiss in June 1935, and Hiss had given Crosley an old Ford car at the same time. Hiss had seen Crosley "several times" in the summer of 1935. Crosley had on one occasion given Hiss a rug as partial payment of rent on the apartment. Hiss had given Crosley "a couple of loans" until concluding that Crosley "was a sort of deadbeat," and ending his relationship with him.[46]

Congressman John McDowell asked Hiss about his hobbies. Hiss listed "[t]ennis and amateur ornithology." McDowell then asked whether Hiss had ever seen a prothonotary warbler, a bird rare in the region, and Hiss said that he had seen one while walking on the Potomac.[47] Unbeknownst to Hiss, Chambers had told HUAC on August 7 that Hiss was a very enthusiastic bird watcher, and that he had told Chambers about having sighted the prothonotary warbler.

Nixon concluded that Hiss was, for some reason, "tr[ying] . . . desperately to divert the Committee from questioning him on the facts Chambers had previously testified to." This conclusion was reinforced, at the end of the session, when Hiss stopped short of agreeing to take a lie detector test on his testimony. Nixon decided that by the time of Hiss's next appearance before the Committee, scheduled for August 25, Hiss, who knew Chambers would also appear at that session, would be better prepared to "make his story fit the facts." Nixon resolved to call an unscheduled meeting of the Committee the next day, August 17, and to confront Hiss with Chambers at that meeting.[48]

Hiss had not been accompanied by lawyers to any of his initial encounters with HUAC. Nor was he at the August 17 session, although Charles Dollard, on the staff of the Carnegie Endowment, joined him on that occasion as "a friend." After his August 17 hearing, however, Hiss would retain a number of lawyers to help him with the HUAC investigation and its long aftermath. His legal responses to the HUAC investigation, and to his perjury trials, were coordinated by his old friend William Marbury, of Marbury, Miller and Evans (subsequently Piper and Marbury) in Baltimore, and Edward McLean of Debevoise, Plimpton and McLean in New York. John F. Davis of Hilmer and Davis in Washington, D.C., and Harold Rosenwald of Beer, Richards, Lane and Haller, which had offices in Washington and New York, also participated in the Hiss defense through the perjury trials. Lloyd Stryker, a solo practitioner from New York City, defended him in court at the first perjury trial, and Claude Cross of the Boston firm of Withington, Cross, Park, and McCann did so at the second trial. Chester Lane and Robert Benjamin, also of Beer, Richards, Lane, and Haller, coordinated his appeal and his motion for a new trial, which took place between 1950 and 1953. Helen Buttenweiser, who had joined the Beer, Richards firm in 1956, was Hiss's personal lawyer from the time he went to prison in 1951 until her retirement in 1986. Victor Rabinowitz of Rabinowitz, Boudin, and Standard (New York) filed Hiss's writ of *coram nobis*, seeking to vacate his 1950 conviction, in 1978. And John Lowenthal, a New York City solo practitioner, performed legal services for Hiss from the perjury trials (when as a law student he did some research for the Hiss defense) until Hiss's death in 1996.[49]

In the August 17 session, however, Hiss continued to represent himself. Nixon would later described Hiss's attitude at the session "edgy, delaying, belligerent, fighting every inch of the way." After Hiss arrived at the meeting, he complained that he had made an appointment later that day and would need to telephone if the Committee intended to keep him more than 15 minutes. He also complained that "parts of his [August 16] testimony had been leaked to the press and implied that the Committee was responsible." After about ten minutes of sparring on these matters, Chambers was called in. On seeing Chambers, Hiss acted as if he were unsure whether he knew the man or not. He first asked Chambers to speak, and to open his mouth. He then said, "I think he is George Crosley, but I would like to hear him speak a little longer." He then asked Chambers, "Are you George Crosley?" "Not to my knowledge," Chambers replied.

Subsequently Hiss said that Chambers's voice "sounds a little less resonant than the voice that I recall of the man I knew as George Crosley," and that Chambers's teeth "look to me as though either they have been improved upon or that there has been considerable dental work done." He was still "not prepared without further checking to take an absolute oath that he must be George Crosley." Nixon then asked Chambers if he had had any work performed on his teeth since 1934, and Chambers responded that he had had some extractions and bridgework done. Hiss asked Nixon to ask Chambers the name of the dentist who had done the work. On being told the dentist's name, Hiss said that he would like to verify that Chambers had had dental work with him. At this point Nixon concluded that "the comedy had gone far enough," and asked Hiss whether he would need to speak to the dentist before he could identify Chambers.

Hiss then conceded that he felt "very strongly that [Chambers was] Crosley." Nixon thought Hiss's performance "incredible, and in some ways almost pitiful." It had "erased . . . our last lingering doubts that Hiss had known Chambers," Nixon concluded. Hiss had "a look of cold hatred in his eyes," and "fought like a caged animal as we tried to get him to make a positive identification for the record." Nixon took Hiss through some of the details of his testimony, such as his giving his car and making small loans to Crosley, and "the longer he testified, the more apparent it became that despite his original protestations, his acquaintance with Crosley was far from casual."

The session's most dramatic episode was an exchange between Chambers and Hiss. Hiss asked Chambers whether he had ever sublet an apartment on 29th Street in Washington from him, and Chambers said no. Hiss then asked whether Chambers, his wife, and his child had ever spent any time in that apartment after the Hisses had vacated it. When Chambers said yes, Hiss asked how he could reconcile his two answers. "Very easily, Alger," Chambers replied. "I was a Communist and you were a Communist. . . . [You] suggested that I live there, and I accepted it gratefully." After Hiss said that he was "now perfectly prepared to identify this man as George Crosley," Congressman John McDowell, who was chairing the session, asked Chambers, "Is this the man, Alger Hiss, who was also a member of the Communist Party, at whose house you stayed?" "Positive identification," said Chambers.[50]

At that point, Nixon recalled,

> These words were hardly out of Chambers's mouth when Hiss arose from his chair and strode over to him, shaking his fist and exclaiming, "'May I say for the record at this point that I would like to invite Mr. Whittaker Chambers to make those same statements out of the presence of this committee, without their being privileged for suit for libel. I challenge you to do it, and I hope you will do it damned quickly.'"[51]

One of HUAC's investigators, Louis Russell, "apparently thinking Hiss might strike Chambers," then approached Hiss and took him by the arm. "I am not going to touch him," Hiss exclaimed. "You are touching me." Eventually, after being asked to sit down by McDowell, Hiss continued to respond to questions from Stripling, who sought to pin Hiss down on the fact that he no longer required certification that Chambers had had dental work to identify him as "George Crosley." The session eventually ended with McDowell saying to Hiss, "Thank you very much." "I don't reciprocate," Hiss said in response.[52]

The surprise confrontation of Hiss and Chambers that Nixon had arranged changed the dynamics of Chambers's allegations about Hiss. Prior to the meeting only a handful of persons connected with the HUAC investigation were inclined to think that Chambers was telling the truth about his previous contacts with Hiss. Hiss's August 5 appearance before the Committee had been such a public relations success that without the confrontation, the whole matter might have been dropped. Now there was a public record of Hiss's admitting that he had known Chambers as George Crosley, and there had been an exchange that had gone badly for Hiss. Instead of HUAC members believing that they had better cut their losses on the Hiss inquiry, they were filled with renewed confidence that the investigation might lead to the revelation of some Communist infiltration of the federal government. Alger Hiss's "pitiful" response to Chambers had given them that confidence. From that point on Nixon, and others close to the Hiss investigation, believed that Hiss had probably known Chambers very well.[53]

The HUAC hearings resumed on August 25, and another piece of information damaging to Hiss was revealed. Chambers had told HUAC, on August 7, that in 1935 Hiss, after having bought a new car, had wanted to give his existing car, a Ford, to the Communist Party, and that although both he and Joszef Peter had tried to dissuade him, he had persisted. Peter had then arranged a transaction, the details of which Chambers was not aware, that enabled Hiss to make the gift covertly. Between August 17 and 25 HUAC investigators had frantically searched for evidence that Hiss had transferred a car, eventually finding a title transfer for a 1929 Ford in Hiss's name in 1936 (Chambers had misremembered the year of the transaction). The car had been transferred to William Rosen, a known member of the Communist Party of the United States. Rosen was called to testify at the August 25 hearing, but declined, on self-incrimination grounds, to testify about his membership in the Communist Party or about his ownership of the 1929 Ford.

Armed with this information, Nixon questioned Hiss about his transfer of the car. Hiss admitted that it was his signature on the title transfer, but denied any knowledge of a transaction with Rosen, claiming that to the best of his recollection he had made the car available to Crosley.[54] Once again Chambers had furnished details about Hiss that only someone in close contact with Hiss would have known, and once again Hiss's response to the information had been evasive. The HUAC members were sufficiently buoyed by the bird-watching and car transfer incidents to issue an interim Committee report, on August 27, in which they described Hiss's testimony at the hearings as "vague and evasive," and Chambers's as "forthright and emphatic." Newspaper reactions to the report, and to the Committee generally, were favorable. And after the August 25 hearing Chambers received an invitation to appear on the radio program "Meet the Press" on August 27.[55]

The program consisted of a panel of journalists putting questions to Chambers about his charges against Hiss and others. One panelist, Edward Fouillard of the *Washington Post*, asked Chambers whether he was "willing to say now that Alger Hiss is or ever was a Communist." Chambers responded, "Alger Hiss was a Communist and may be now." He added, "I do not think Mr. Hiss will sue me for slander or libel." On being asked whether Hiss had committed any espionage in his capacity as a Communist, Chambers sidestepped the question. "I am only prepared at this point to say he was a Communist," he told the panel.[56]

In making those remarks Chambers had acquiesced in Hiss's demand, in their exchange on August 17, that he repeat his allegedly libelous charges about Hiss outside of a privileged setting and that he do it "damned quickly." Chambers had repeated the charges within ten days. But Hiss did not respond with a libel suit as promptly. He did not file that suit until September 27, 1948, after lengthy discussions with the several lawyers who had agreed to help with any defense against Chambers's accusations. Some of those lawyers felt that Hiss should sue at once, since public opinion might draw adverse inferences from his delaying. Others felt that a suit should not be brought until the case was fully prepared, and raised concerns about the effect of a suit on Hiss's job with the Carnegie Endowment. Eventually the Endowment's Board of Trustees acquiesced in an arrangement in which Hiss nominally remained president of the Endowment while the suit was pending, but turned over the daily operations to James Shotwell, the Endowment's administrative director. Eventually, on September 27, 1948, a suit was filed in Baltimore, and Hiss's lawyers, headed by William Marbury, began depositions.[57]

Despite the setbacks Hiss had suffered at the August 17 and August 25 HUAC hearings, very few people knew that Hiss's and Chambers's relationship had included espionage. Chambers had not mentioned that in any of his earlier testimony, and had resolved not to mention it in connection with any of his revelations about Communists in the government. But Hiss's August 17 exchange with Chambers would, eventually, lead to the revelation of espionage as well. Once again Hiss had taken a significant risk as part of his reputational defense, and on this occasion the risk was to backfire.

Marbury's plan, in the defamation lawsuit, was to depose Chambers about "the entire history of his dealings with Alger." The strategy of the lawsuit was consistent with Hiss's reputational defense. Hiss's lawyers sought to present a number of witnesses testifying to Hiss's character and integrity, while portraying Chambers as emotionally unstable. Efforts were made to find out whether Chambers had ever been hospitalized for mental illness, and to probe into many other aspects of Chambers's life. In one deposition the subject of Chambers's Communist Party work with Hiss was raised, and Chambers testified that he had seen some government documents Hiss brought home, but that he had "never transmitted a government document from Mr. Hiss to the Communist Party."[58]

In connection with this line of questioning, Chambers was asked to produce any papers he might have received from Hiss or members of the Hiss family. Before his November 4 deposition, Chambers revealed to one of his lawyers, Richard Cleveland, that there was "something missing" in his testimony, and that he was "shielding Hiss." What was missing was evidence that Chambers and Hiss had not just known each other as Communists, but had committed espionage together. Upset by the Hiss defense team's detailed scrutiny of his life, which had included a plan to submit Esther Chambers to a searching examination, Chambers had resolved to respond to the demand for production of documents by digging up the life preserver of papers he had created in 1938. He contacted his nephew, Nathan Levine, a lawyer in New York, and retrieved a large envelope of documents he had previously entrusted to Levine. He then took the envelope to his Westminster farm. On November 17, Chambers's lawyers handed the contents of the envelope to Cleveland, who showed them to William Marbury.[59]

Chambers's release of the documents to Marbury was in response to a specific request made by Hiss's counsel in the libel suit. But in turning over the documents, Chambers was well aware that he was producing evidence that strongly suggested that Hiss had stolen government documents and passed them on to Chambers for transmission to the Soviets. He was also aware that he had previously testified that neither Hiss nor anyone in the Ware Group had committed espionage. He would now need to admit that his earlier testimony had been false, and he was aware that his credibility as a witness might be affected. Moreover, he was worried, given the date he released the documents, that if that information became known to the Justice Department, as it almost surely would, he might well be indicted for perjury.

In the November 1948 election, the Democrats had won control of the presidency and Congress, and the Justice Department, controlled by the Truman administration, was influential with the New York grand jury. Moreover, the Justice Department under Truman reflected Truman's hostility to HUAC. If the grand jury chose to believe Hiss's account of events rather than his, the Justice Department might well relish prosecuting Chambers for perjury. In taking advantage of Marbury's unwitting request to produce documents from Alger Hiss that might shed light on the Hiss-Chambers relationship, Chambers had dug up his life preserver to try to protect himself not only against a libel suit but against a perjury indictment. And although Chambers's gamble placed him in a very touchy situation, in the end it resulted in Hiss, not Chambers being indicted. Several of the documents that Chambers produced in response to Marbury's request, known as the "Baltimore documents" because the libel suit deposition was in that city, were typed copies of classified papers from the State Department, covering the period between late January and early April 1938. Hiss was an employee of the State Department at that time and would have had routine access to all of the documents.[60]

For some time after Chambers's lawyers turned copies of the life-preserver documents over to Marbury, things stood at a standstill. Marbury insisted, and Hiss agreed, that the Justice Department should be given copies of the documents, and on November 19 Alexander Campbell, the head of the Justice Department's criminal division, was given access to the documents. Both parties in the Hiss libel suit agreed to put it on hold for two weeks, and the Justice Department began an investigation. But it appeared, by the end of November, that the most likely outcome of that investigation would be a perjury indictment against Chambers for failing to reveal, in his previous HUAC testimony and in testimony before a New York grand jury investigating Communist activities, that he was aware that some of the persons he had accused of being Communists had committed espionage. The members of HUAC, including Nixon, knew nothing about Chambers's life-preserver documents, and Chambers was under a court order not to disclose their contents.[61]

On December 1, as he was planning to leave for a vacation to Panama, Nixon saw a newspaper article indicating that the Justice Department was planning to drop its investigation of the Hiss-Chambers case. On contacting Robert Stripling, Nixon learned that Stripling had heard rumors of new evidence circulating in the case. On a hunch, Nixon and Stripling decided to pay Chambers a visit at his Westminster farm, where they found him depressed by the news. Chambers admitted to having produced new evidence, but wouldn't disclose its contents. He also said that he had a second batch of evidence that he planned to release if no action was taken on the first batch. Nixon and Stripling urged him not to give that evidence to anyone except HUAC. To ensure this outcome Nixon, on Stripling's suggestion, drafted a HUAC subpoena for Chambers, including a demand for documents related to his charges against Hiss.

HUAC investigators then returned to Westminster with the subpoena, and an episode was staged in which Chambers retrieved two strips of developed microfilm, and three rolls of undeveloped film, from a hollowed-out pumpkin on his land. He had already told the investigators about the microfilm rolls, which he secreted in the pumpkin overnight for dramatic effect. The result was the association of Hiss and Chambers with the "Pumpkin Papers," and the erroneous impression that the microfilm rolls were the only source of information confirming that Hiss had passed stolen government documents to Chambers. Nixon and Stripling were subsequently photographed looking at the microfilm rolls with a magnifying class, and the

Pumpkin Papers became one of the symbols of the Hiss perjury trials. But the hollowed-out pumpkin did not contain any evidence that was more incriminating to Hiss than evidence that Chambers had already produced at the November libel suit depositions. The two developed microfilm rolls only contained copies of more stolen State Department documents, from the same time frame as the typed copies Chambers had disclosed in November. As for the three undeveloped rolls, one was blank, and the other two were copies of Navy documents, apparently secured from the Bureau of Standards, that could not be connected to Hiss.

Nonetheless the Pumpkin Papers episode resulted in HUAC, rather than the FBI or any other branch of the Justice Department, being able to control the release of information about the investigation of Hiss and Chambers. It also convinced Robert Stripling that sufficient evidence now existed to indict Hiss. He sent a telegram to Nixon in Panama that opened, "Case Clinched, Information Amazing," and on December 5 Nixon returned to the United States. On December 6, HUAC began a negotiation with the Justice Department about Hiss and Chambers. As Nixon recalled, he and his fellow Committee members "did not trust the Justice Department to prosecute the case with the vigor that we thought it deserved," and were afraid that if they gave the Pumpkin Papers to Justice Department officials, Chambers might be indicted, which would weaken any case against Hiss. Eventually they agreed to give the Justice Department copies of the documents they had received from Chambers, in exchange for being allowed to question Chambers, who was technically barred from discussing matters related to the Hiss libel suit.[62]

A lengthy interview with Chambers convinced Nixon that "the Chambers case was so airtight that the Justice Department had no choice but to ask for an indictment of Hiss." Chambers detailed for Nixon the procedures of the espionage ring that had resulted in Alger or Priscilla Hiss's copying stolen documents on a Hiss family typewriter. The copies of documents that he had held back in his life preserver, Chambers suggested, had been typed on that typewriter. Here, instead of incompatible stories by the chief protagonists, was compelling physical evidence, especially if other Hiss family documents typed on that typewriter could be retrieved. Only one hurdle, Nixon thought, remained. The term of the New York grand jury investigating Communism was scheduled to expire on December 15, and Nixon was not convinced that the grand jury was prepared to indict Hiss rather than Chambers. Nixon was concerned that if the grand jury indicted Chambers for previously lying to it, the chief witness in any prosecution of Hiss for perjury would have been discredited. At a December 8 public hearing of HUAC, Nixon announced that the Committee intended "to do everything we can to see that the [Justice] Department does not use the device of indicting Chambers as an excuse for not proceeding against Hiss."[63]

Nixon was correct in surmising that the grand jury was still contemplating indicting Chambers rather than Hiss. In a December 8 session, the grand jury had shown exasperation with Nathan Levine, who declined to confirm that Chambers had hidden documents and microfilm in Levine's apartment in 1938, citing attorney-client privilege, and claimed that if Chambers had left an envelope with him, he did not know his contents. The next day the grand jury grilled Chambers about the reasons why he had first lied to them about his and Hiss's involvement in espionage, and why, if he was so concerned with the Communist threat to the security of the United States, he had waited ten years to accuse Hiss. As late as December 14, Nixon, who testified before the grand jury that day, was still not convinced that Hiss, rather than Chambers, would be indicted.

Chambers became increasingly depressed, in this period, at the lengths he needed to go to convince even his staunchest supporters that he was telling the truth about his relationship with Hiss. He had withheld so many crucial details of that relationship for so long, and his career had been so checkered, that he knew that people who wanted to believe his story were having difficulty perceiving him as a credible figure, and there were many other people who had written him off as a liar. He was pressured to resign from his job at *Time*, which he did on December 9.

Chambers's depression culminated shortly after his resignation from *Time*, when he attempted suicide at the home of his mother in Lynbrook, New York. The suicide attempt consisted of an effort to asphyxiate himself, while he slept, with fumes from rat poison containers. He wrote several suicide notes that said he had told the truth about Hiss but was now "removing myself as a witness." The suicide failed. The next morning Chambers's mother found him vomiting, but alive, and, according to Chambers, made him a pot of coffee and lectured him for being "a quitter."[64]

Meanwhile the FBI and HUAC investigators had been encouraged to look closely into issues related to Hiss family typewriters. Between December 6 and December 13 the FBI had come up with two sets of correspondence that the Hiss defense conceded had been typed on a Hiss family typewriter. One, submitted by the Hiss defense lawyers, was correspondence in 1933 between the Hisses and an insurance company. The other was a three-page memorandum, entitled "Description of Personal Characteristics of Timothy Hobson," which had been sent to Paul Banfield, the headmaster of the Landon School in Bethesda, Maryland, in 1936. It was part of the school's admission procedure, and was accompanied by a handwritten cover letter from Alger Hiss. Now the Justice Department had a possible match between the typeface on those documents, which came to be known as the "Hiss standards," and that on the typed copies of State Department files among Chambers's Baltimore documents. On December 14 an FBI expert testified to the grand jury that the Hiss standards and the State Department papers in the Baltimore documents had identical typefaces.[65]

As for HUAC, on December 9 Stripling told the grand jury that its investigators planned to look for Hiss family typewriters or documents typed on them, and by December 13 Stripling had retained a typewriter expert, Ordway Hilton, to see if the Hiss's 1933 insurance policy correspondence seemed to have been typed on the same typewriter that had typed Chambers's Baltimore documents. By December 23 Hilton and another expert, Elbridge Stein, had examined both documents, and by December 30 Hilton had telephoned a HUAC investigator, and Stein had written Stripling, to the effect that the two sets of documents were a match. Hilton and Stein agreed with Freehan that the typewriter on which both the Hiss family correspondence and Chambers's documents had been typed was a Woodstock, and that the documents had an identical typeface.[66]

Prior to these findings by the experts retained by HUAC, the grand jury, on the morning of December 15, had asked Hiss two questions it had previously put to him. It asked him whether he had known Whittaker Chambers after 1936, and whether he had passed copies of any stolen government documents to Chambers. Consistently with his previous testimony, Hiss answered no to both questions. The grand jury then indicted him on two counts of perjury. It did not indict Chambers. Hiss was released on $5,000 bail. *The New York Times* reporter, who witnessed Hiss's arraignment, stated that he "appeared solemn, anxious, and unhappy," with "a grim and worried look." "To observers," *The Times* correspondent suggested, "it seemed obvious that he had not expected to be indicted."[67]

The perjury indictment of Alger Hiss had been a difficult struggle for those, such as Richard Nixon, Robert Stripling, and J. Edgar Hoover, who had become convinced that Hiss was also guilty of espionage. The difficulties centered in the fact that much of the evidence incriminating Hiss could not be released because the United States government was unwilling to compromise its sources. Bentley's accusations had been made public at HUAC hearings, but they had not been corroborated. Guzenko's revelations were known only to the FBI. There was an additional story about Hiss's seeking to recruit a State Department employee, Noel Field, for espionage in the 1930s, and the source of that story, a former NKVD network courier named Hedda Gumperz (known in the United States as Hede Manning) would tes-

The Woodstock typewriter used as an exhibit at both of Hiss's perjury trials. It was first produced by the Hiss defense.

tify at Hiss's second perjury trial. But that story was also not corroborated, and had been vigorously denied by both Hiss and Field.[68]

In light of the difficulties of proof, the Hiss perjury trials became exercises in the comparative credibility of Hiss and Chambers, even with respect to the batch of documents incriminating Hiss that Chambers produced. This was another reason why Hiss's defense was reputational. If he could convince a jury that Chambers was an unstable character with some motive for framing him, the small amount of corroborative evidence that Chambers could produce might be discounted. Even if Chambers were able to make a persuasive case that he had known Hiss far better than Hiss claimed, this did not mean that he and Hiss had engaged in espionage together. In fact the closeness of Hiss's and Chambers's relationship might have furnished a motive—jealousy, envy, or revenge—for Chambers to accuse Hiss of passing stolen documents to him. The more Hiss could draw a contrast between his credentialed, respectable career and Chambers's netherworld existence, the more likely he was to create a context in which the small amount of evidence against him could be undermined.

The defense team that Hiss assembled after being indicted in December 1948, led by Edward McLean in New York and William Marbury in Baltimore, with Lloyd Stryker as Hiss's chief trial lawyer, immediately decided on their strategy. "[Stryker] feels, as do I," Marbury wrote Dean Acheson in March 1949, "that the question of character is basic, and he intends to bend every effort to see that Alger has the full benefit of the unblemished reputation which was his prior to last August." Hiss's reputational defense sought to combine three strategies: the production of a list of very distinguished people as character witnesses for Hiss; Hiss's categorical denials of any affiliation with Communist activity, let alone espionage; and the production of information designed to suggest that Chambers was an unreliable, possibly even disturbed, witness. None of these strategies directly confronted the authenticity of Chambers's documents, but they were designed to suggest that Chambers might have obtained that information from other sources and used it to frame Hiss.[69]

By the time the trial opened, at the end of May 1949, the Hiss defense team had lined up a number of character witnesses, including some of Hiss's confederates, such as Dean Acheson, his colleague at the State Department, and John Foster Dulles, who had been the principal force securing him the Carnegie Endowment presidency. Some of his former employers, such as Jerome Frank at the AAA general counsel's office, Francis Sayre and James Byrnes at the State Department, and Stephen Raushenbush at the Nye Committee, declined to testify, but the list, which included Supreme Court Justices Felix Frankfurter and Stanley Reed, was impressive. The Hiss defense team had also, with the aid of a private detective, looked into Chambers's early life, hoping to find that he had had homosexual relationships or been hospitalized for mental illness. Hiss's lawyers had lined up two psychiatrists to speculate about Chambers's instability, his attachment to Hiss, and possible motives for taking revenge on his former friend. They had attempted to identify other candidates for the perpetrator of the document stealing, notably the self-confessed Soviet agent Julian Wadleigh, who had also worked in the State Department. Finally, Hiss's defense team had prepared the way for Hiss to renew his denials of ever having been a Communist and ever having passed stolen papers to Chambers.[70]

In the months after the indictment both sides searched for the Hiss family typewriter on which the documents known as the Hiss standards had been produced. The typewriter was a Woodstock previously owned by Thomas Fansler, Priscilla's father. It was no longer in the Hiss household, and Alger and Priscilla claimed that they did not know what had happened to it. In an interview with the FBI on December 4, 1948, Alger Hiss said that "Mrs. Hiss disposed of [the] typewriter to either a secondhand typewriter concern or a secondhand dealer in Washington. . . . The whereabouts of this typewriter is presently unknown to me." At the same time two of Hiss's lawyers interviewed Priscilla, who said she "did not know where she disposed of the Fansler typewriter. She thought she must have sold it for a few dollars to some dealer in secondhand typewriters in Washington. She had no names of any of them."[71]

In fact Alger and Priscilla knew exactly what they had done with the typewriter. They had given it to Perry ("Pat") and Raymond ("Mike") Catlett, the sons of

Claudia ("Clytie") Catlett, a long-term maid for the Hisses, probably in April 1938. Their concern about the typewriter had heightened after Hiss's lead counsel Edward McLean, on December 6, 1948, remembered that Hiss had turned over some old family letters to him in early September, when he was preparing the libel suit against Chambers. McLean showed one of the letters, which had been written in 1933, to the defense's documents examiner, Howard Haring, who felt that it had been typed on the same typewriter as the copied documents Chambers had produced. Faced with this information, Alger and Priscilla Hiss redoubled their efforts to conceal the whereabouts of the Fansler typewriter.[72]

On December 7 Alger called John F. Davis, who had represented him at the August 16 HUAC hearing, and asked Davis "to check on an old machine which he remembers he gave to Pat [Catlett]." In summarizing the conversation to McLean, Davis added that Donald Hiss believed that he knew Pat Catlett's Washington address, and that Pat "can be located without too much difficulty." He offered to find Pat and ask him about the Fansler typewriter, but added that he believed that McLean preferred to check on the machine himself. McLean received Davis's summary of the December 7 conversation at the end of the month, but the Hiss defense took no action to find the typewriter.

Much would subsequently be made of Hiss's phone call to Davis, since in the same time interval Hiss was denying to the grand jury that he had any knowledge of the typewriter's whereabouts. But if Hiss did not want the typewriter found, why would he have given Davis information about its possible location? He had done so because by early December Hiss knew that not only HUAC but the Justice Department were aware that Chambers had produced copies of documents that looked like they had been typed on a Hiss family typewriter. This meant that even if Chambers rather than himself was ultimately indicted for perjury, that typewriter would be vital evidence, and thus the FBI and HUAC investigators would be searching for it. If either the FBI or HUAC found the typewriter, and it could be traced back to the Hisses, there was a distinct possibility that Hiss would be subject to a charge of obstructing justice. It was far better for Hiss to have his lawyers find the typewriter than to have it discovered by his prospective adversaries.

In late January 1949, Mike Catlett called on Donald Hiss, and told him that the FBI had interviewed him several times that month, asking him each time if he knew the whereabouts of the Fansler typewriter. Although Catlett had denied knowing anything about it, he told Donald that he had been given the typewriter by the Hisses, and that although he did not currently have it, he could probably find it. Shortly after this conversation Edward McLean decided to pursue the matter, and came to Washington to interview the Catletts. He learned that the Hisses had given the typewriter to the Catletts, probably in 1938; that Pat Catlett had given the type-writer to his sister, Burnetta. The sister lived with a "Dr. Easton" until his death in 1945, when she moved to Detroit. On Easton's death a man named Vernon Marlow had apparently taken the typewriter from the Easton's house. Mike Catlett contacted Vernon Marlow, who, for $50, agreed to help find the typewriter.

Mike apparently reached a dead end when Marlow indicated that he had given the typewriter to Ira Lockey, a mover and junk dealer, in part payment for helping him move the contents of his house. Lockey was unavailable when Mike looked for him, and Mike received some erroneous information that Lockey had junked the type-writer. Mike did not follow up for another two months, and Donald Hiss, who had driven Mike to Ira Lockey's house, did not inform any of the Hiss defense lawyers about Lockey's connection with the typewriter. Nothing transpired until McLean re-turned to Washington in April, again on the hunt for the typewriter.

Although Vernon Marlow was on this occasion uncooperative, his wife, Louise Marlow, confirmed that Lockey had received the typewriter from the Marlows in 1945 as part payment for his help with moving furniture. At this point Mike Catlett took McLean to see Lockey, who sold McLean the typewriter for $15 on April 16, 1949. Neither the Catletts, the Marlows, Ira Lockey, Donald Hiss, nor any of the Hiss lawyers were forthcoming with the FBI about their knowledge of the typewriter's whereabouts. The evidence suggests that the Catletts did not want to help anyone (except the Hisses) find the typewriter; that the Marlows and Ira Lockey did not want to be identified with it; and that although the Hiss defense lawyers felt that they had to appear to be making best efforts to find it, they were in no hurry to turn it up.[73]

The importance attached to the Woodstock typewriter was somewhat ironic. First, the prosecution would not have needed to produce it in order to gain a con-viction for perjury. It already had evidence of documents typed on *a* Hiss family typewriter and evidence of stolen government documents produced by Chambers. The typefaces on those documents appeared to match. The experts produced by both sides agreed that both sets of documents had been typed on the same machine. Given the state of information about typewriters at the time, the possibility that a typeface on one machine could be duplicated on another was not thought techno-logically feasible. So all the prosecution had to show was that Hiss-standard docu-ments and some of the Baltimore documents produced by Chambers had apparently identical typefaces.[74]

The secreted documents that Chambers produced at the Hiss trials, and the Woodstock typewriter eventually produced by the defense, were the most sensa-tional pieces of evidence. The documents were collectively given the name Pump-kin Papers by the press, even though only some of them had been hidden overnight in the hollowed-out pumpkin on Chambers's farm. They were sensational because they constituted apparent proof that Hiss had committed espionage. Hiss was not, of course, being tried for espionage. He could not be prosecuted for that crime because the only documents furnishing proof of his espionage were dated between January and April 1938, and the statute governing espionage at that time ("unlawfully disclosing information affecting national defense to a foreign government") had expired since, it was limited to three years except "in time of war." The United States was not at war in 1938. Had Chambers produced a personal letter from Hiss, dated in the spring of 1938, it would have been just as strong a piece of evidence that Hiss had committed perjury as the Pumpkin Papers and the other batch of stolen government documents.[75]

But the Woodstock typewriter has rightly been described as a leading symbol of the Hiss case. This was because although Hiss was on trial for perjury, the prosecution was after bigger game. Had the only evidence that Hiss had committed perjury been about whether he had known a former Communist better than he claimed, that would hardly have been worth a perjury indictment and two lengthy federal trials. It was the evidence that Hiss had conspired with Chambers to commit espionage that made him potentially notorious, and thus worthy of an indictment and a high-profile prosecution. And the Woodstock typewriter, for all of its technical irrelevance to the perjury prosecution, came to be seen as a tangible reminder of Hiss's espionage.

The posture of the trials placed a burden on Hiss. He needed to convince a jury that just about everything Chambers said about him was untrue or exaggerated. This was in keeping with his reputational defense, which included an attack on Chambers's credibility and a categorical denial of any affiliations with Communist or Communist-front organizations. It would have been easier for Hiss if he could have admitted to knowing Chambers tolerably well, and for a longer period than he had first said. He might have been forgiven, as a public official, for downplaying his acquaintance with a person with as disreputable a past as Chambers admitted to having had. But Hiss's reputational defense rested on his own credibility being thought of as very high. He had, from the outset, acted as if he had only the barest recollection of Chambers.

As Hiss's first perjury trial unfolded, he was consistently confronted with evidence that he knew Chambers better than he had said. The first piece of evidence involved the incident, which Chambers had initially placed in the summer of 1935, in which Hiss attempted to give an old Ford car of his to the Communist Party.

Chambers had brought this incident up at the HUAC hearings, and Hiss had denied it, saying that he had "thrown in" the car at the time Chambers sublet an apartment from him. But at the first trial the prosecution produced a certificate of title for the car, signed by Hiss and notarized by a fellow employee of the Justice Department, where Hiss was working in the summer of 1936. The certificate, dated July 23, 1936, assigned the car to the Cherner Motor Company, and the company reassigned the car to William Rosen. Rosen was not available as a witness at the first trial, but the certificate clearly indicated that Hiss had not given the car to Chambers. At Hiss's second trial Rosen was subpoenaed, and asked whether he was a member of the Communist Party, and whether he had any connection with the car. He declined to answer, citing the Fifth Amendment's provision against self-incrimination.

This incident did not by itself demonstrate that Hiss knew Chambers better than he said he did: on its face it had nothing to do with Chambers. But in light of Hiss's previous explanation for his disposal of the Ford, it undermined his credibility. The second piece of evidence was even more damaging.

In late 1936, Chambers testified, the Soviet handler of the military intelligence network for which he and Hiss worked, Boris Bykov, gave Chambers money to purchase Oriental rugs for Hiss and three other Washington-based agents. In his memoirs Chambers indicated that Bykov had felt that by giving Hiss and the others "some costly present," they would "know that they are dealing with big, important people." Chambers protested that the gesture would be offensive to agents who were "Communists on principle." But he nonetheless arranged, through his friend the Columbia University art historian Meyer Schapiro, to have four rugs purchased and shipped to one of the Washington agents, George Silverman. When the rugs arrived, Chambers picked the one designated for Hiss up from Silverman (Hiss and Silverman were each unaware that the other was a Soviet agent) and delivered it to Hiss. The Hisses apparently did not like the rug given to them, and kept it in a closet.[76]

Chambers's story of the rug presented problems for Hiss. The prosecution produced a shipping form for the rugs, dated December 29, 1936. This was consistent with Chambers's claim that Bykov had made the decision to give the rugs as presents around Christmas of that year. Hiss admitted to owning a rug that matched the description of one on the shipping form. But he claimed that Chambers himself had given him the rug as a partial payment for rent on a Washington apartment. However, Chambers had sublet an apartment from Hiss in 1935, not 1936. Moreover, if Chambers's account of the rug gifts was accurate, Hiss and Chambers had remained in contact after the summer of 1936, the last time Hiss claimed to have seen "George Crosley." Thus the rug testimony not only undermined Hiss's credibility, it was directly relevant to one of the perjury charges.

The third piece of damaging evidence that surfaced at Hiss's first perjury trial involved an alleged loan from the Hisses to Chambers to purchase a car in the fall of 1937. In his memoirs Chambers disclosed how he came to ask the Hisses for a car loan. He was planning his defection from the Soviets, he recalled, and needed a new car, because the one he owned had been bought by the Communist Party and could easily be traced if he deserted. Bykov, however, was not inclined to finance a new car for Chambers, even though Chambers "urged its importance in the work." Finally Chambers told Hiss about his predicament.

> Alger . . . quickly grew serious and agreed that a car was a necessity of the work. . . . He offered to lend me four hundred dollars to use as part payment on a car . . . I used Alger's offer in my campaign with Bykov, who, to my surprise, one night suddenly capitulated. . . . [H]e authorized me to accept the money from Hiss, add it to whatever apparatus funds I might have on hand, and buy a car. He said he would give me the money for Hiss the next time I saw him. He always managed to forget it.[77]

Chambers bought the new car in Randallstown, Maryland. The prosecution was able to show that he paid $486.75 to a Randallstown car dealer on November 23, 1937. It also produced evidence that on November 19 the Hisses had withdrawn $400 from their joint savings account. At the first trial Hiss claimed that the $400 was to buy furniture for a new house. But the Hisses had not signed a lease on any house at that time, and could produce no receipts for the furniture. Further, they had existing checking and charge accounts at the time, so that there seemed no need for them to pay cash for the furniture. The incident was particularly damaging to Hiss's claim that he had lost contact with Chambers in 1936, because if Chambers's version of events was correct, he was in a position to borrow $400 from the Hisses late in 1937.

None of the incidents furnished proof that Hiss had passed stolen government documents to Chambers. Moreover, Chambers's memory for events was sometimes faulty, and the versions of events he narrated in *Witness* were not subject to cross-examination. Still the incidents, taken together, suggested a closer relationship between Hiss and Chambers than Hiss acknowledged, and each of them bore a connection to Communist activity or to the Soviet underground. They not only undermined Hiss's credibility, they made it more likely that in the spring of 1938 Hiss and Chambers maintained a relationship that was consistent with Hiss's transmitting documents to Chambers.[78]

The key to Hiss's conviction for perjury, however, remained the fact that some of the documents Chambers produced were typed copies of stolen State Department papers, and the typeface on those papers matched that on Hiss family correspondence. Even though some of the material that Chambers had retained in his life preserver included summaries of State Department transmissions written in Hiss's own hand—Hiss confirmed the writing on the summaries was his—the typed documents were more damaging. Hiss provided an explanation for the handwritten summaries: he had occasionally been asked to prepare them for the use of Stanley Hornbeck and Francis Sayre, his superiors in the State Department. Hornbeck was called as a witness at both trials, and Sayre at the second. Both testified that Hiss sometimes provided them with handwritten summaries of documents, although neither recognized the summaries Chambers produced, and both indicated that some of those, which included a handwritten version of an entire cable, were more extensive than Hiss's typical notes to them.[79]

Still, Hiss had produced an explanation for why notes in his hand might have existed, if not for how they had ended up in Chambers's possession. But he was hardpressed to account for the existence of copies of documents typed on one of his typewriters. None of his duties with the State Department included copying documents that already existed in files. In particular, there seemed no satisfactory explanation for why an employee of the State Department would copy files on a home typewriter, and the copies would end up in the possession of a person without any connections to the Department. Hiss was forced to claim that Chambers, or a confederate, had somehow gained access to a Hiss family typewriter, or copied the documents on a typewriter designed to duplicate the typeface of Hiss's. The first claim seemed implausible, especially in light of the fact that Hiss had denied having any contact with Chambers after 1936, and the second claim, in 1948, seemed technologically infeasible.[80]

The prosecution struggled to obtain a conviction in the Hiss trials. In the first trial prosecutor Thomas Murphy stated that if the jury did not believe Chambers, the government had no case, and, at the end, four jurors remained unconvinced that Chambers had been telling the truth about how he had obtained the typed copies of documents. They thought that somehow Chambers, or someone in league with him, had gained access to a Hiss typewriter and copied the documents. This resulted in their resisting finding Hiss guilty, and the first trial ended with the jury unable to render a verdict. The government immediately moved for a new trial, which began four months later, in November 1949.[81]

The two trials differed in their emphasis. Judge Samuel Kaufman, who presided over the first trial, interpreted the relevance of evidence strictly, so that a fair amount of testimony related to Hiss's and Chambers's past activities was excluded from that trial, including Hedda Gumperz's account of Hiss attempting to recruit Noel Field for Soviet intelligence in the 1930s. The Hiss defense strategy remained the same in both trials: a long list of character witnesses, emphasizing Hiss's reputation for competence and integrity, Hiss's categorical denials of any affiliation with Communists or the Soviets, and efforts to suggest that Chambers was an unreliable, even unstable witness, possibly with a grudge against Hiss. As part of the last effort, the defense attempted to put Dr. Carl Binger, a psychiatrist, on the stand, but Judge Kaufman refused to permit Binger to testify.[82]

The defense put Pat and Mike Catlett on the stand in an effort to show that the Hisses had given them the Woodstock typewriter in 1937, but the prosecution confused Pat by informing him that the typewriter repair shop to which he had taken the machine after receiving it had not opened until September 1938. Both Pat's and Mike's testimony was inconsistent and evasive, and they gave the impression of being primarily concerned with helping the Hisses. The defense also called Alger Hiss to deny several charges made by Chambers, including the loan for the car and the purpose of the rug gift. Priscilla Hiss was called to deny having extensive contacts with Whittaker or Esther Chambers, and in the process contradicted earlier testimony that she had given to HUAC.[83] All in all, none of the defense witnesses was able to undermine the essentials of Chambers's narrative about his contacts with Hiss. A great bulk of that narrative was based on uncorroborated testimony, but if one tended to believe Hiss's account rather than Chambers's, there was an explanation for the copied documents in Chambers's possession—Chambers had typed the copies himself. Hiss may well have expected to have been acquitted. But the fact that eight jurors had been prepared to believe Chambers meant that his reputational defense had not fully succeeded.

In the second trial Judge Henry Goddard gave both sides more leeway in introducing testimony whose relevance to the precise counts of perjury with which Hiss was charged was less direct. This meant that Hedda Gumperz was able to tell her story about encountering Hiss in the 1930s, and his intention to recruit Noel Field for his network. It also meant that the defense was able to introduce two psychiatrists, Binger and Dr. Henry Murray, whose testimony was designed to show that Chambers was a "psychopathic personality," capable of "pathological lying." The prosecution sought to ridicule this testimony, at one point informing Binger, after he had noted that one of Chambers's "psychopathic" characteristics was frequently staring at the ceiling when responding to questions, that Binger himself had stared at the ceiling 50 times during his 59 minutes on the witness stand.[84]

The two principal changes in the second trial were the subtle shift of evidentiary emphasis by the prosecution and the effort by Claude Cross, who had replaced Stryker as chief counsel for the defense, to introduce a potential source for the purloined State Department documents, self-confessed agent Julian Wadleigh. Thomas Murphy, who prosecuted both trials, had told the first Hiss jury that the government's case was dependent on their believing Chambers's account of events rather than Hiss's. He now abandoned this strategy, emphasizing that, with the aid of "immutable" documents, he would prove that Hiss's testimony included lies. This was an effort to deemphasize Chambers's admission that on several previous occasions he had lied to HUAC or the FBI about the Hiss case. When Cross, in his opening remarks, attempted to remind the jury that Murphy had previously said, "if you do not believe Whittaker Chambers the Government has no case," Murphy objected on the ground that the statement "[was] not evidence," and Goddard sustained the objection.[85]

Meanwhile Cross was seeking to shore up the weakest part of the Hiss defense, his claim that somehow Chambers had been able to secure copies of stolen State Department documents from a person other than Hiss. He called Julian Wadleigh to the stand. Wadleigh admitted having stolen documents for the Soviets, including some from the State Department. But when shown the typed copies of documents Chambers had produced, along with the memoranda in Hiss's handwriting, Wadleigh denied having ever seen them before. Moreover, there was still the problem that if Wadleigh had stolen the Baltimore documents, who had typed copies of them? Cross implied that Chambers had somehow managed to do this after defecting from the Soviets, but to do that he would have needed access to a Hiss family typewriter.[86]

Cross's summation, which took place on January 19, 1950, invited the jury to consider that Wadleigh may have been "the real thief" of the documents, that Chambers may have gained access to the Woodstock typewriter and copied documents to frame Hiss, and that Chambers had probably produced the documents out of desperation, once Hiss had sued him for libel. Cross added that if Hiss had known of the existence of the documents, he would have been "crazy" to deny any meaningful affiliation with Chambers. His denials could only be interpreted as the acts of an innocent man.

Murphy's summation reemphasized the importance of the documents Chambers had produced. No one had provided a credible explanation for how they happened to be typed on a Hiss family typewriter. They were illustrations of other "immutable" evidence in the case. Hiss had given a Ford to the Cherner Motor Company, not to Chambers: the car's certificate of title proved that. Hiss had been given a rug in 1937: a shipping form had identified the rug. Hiss had withdrawn $400 from a bank at the time Chambers said he had loaned him money to buy a car, and had not given any credible explanation for the withdrawal. Murphy even suggested an explanation for why the Hisses had given the Woodstock typewriter to the Catletts. "If they sold the typewriter," he said, "they might be traced." "[S]omebody might see them" if they "dropped it in the Potomac" or otherwise tried to dispose of it. "So they give it to their trusted maid's children, knowing full well . . . that it would . . . gradually disintegrate." Once again, Murphy invited the jury to "take the machine . . . with you to the jury room." The evidence of the Woodstock's typeface, he said, would "prove treason."[87]

The jury agreed. In the end the Woodstock typewriter—as a symbol of the allegedly identical typefaces on the Hiss standards and the Baltimore documents—convinced a jury that Alger Hiss had lied when he denied passing any stolen government documents to Whittaker Chambers. Had the prosecution not been able to demonstrate the similar typefaces on both sets of documents, Chambers might well not have succeeded in tying his Pumpkin Papers documents to Hiss. Anyone could have stolen State Department documents and passed them on to Chambers. Chambers was not authorized to have access to the documents, but he had already admitted having committed espionage.

Hiss's convictions, as Murphy suggested, branded him as a traitor. They represented the culmination of a process where, little by little, the veneer of Hiss's reputational defense was stripped away.[88]

In retrospect, Hiss's categorical denials of any affiliation with Communists, and of any close relationship with Chambers, seem hubristic. Perhaps a defense of confession and avoidance would have spared him the notoriety of having his life as Soviet agent exposed. Perhaps, had he admitted to HUAC that he had known Chambers, and had been a Communist in the 1930s (but had now repudiated his earlier views), he would not have been forced to sue Chambers for libel, and the two batches of life preserver documents would never have appeared. If so, he very probably would not have been brought to trial at all. HUAC was primarily interested in establishing that there had been Communists in the federal government in the 1930s. They were not a law enforcement agency, and few of the persons they investigated ended up being prosecuted. It was the espionage dimension of Hiss's activities that made him a candidate for prosecution, and Chambers, absent the libel suit, had no incentive to publicize Hiss's espionage. As he faced prison, Hiss might have been inclined to second-guess himself.

Once Hiss decided to stake out a position that categorically disassociated himself

from Chambers's allegations, he appeared very reluctant to abandon even a smidgen
of it. This produced a pattern of denials, and fall-back denials, that made him look
evasive. He first denied knowing Chambers at all. Then, after a charade of listening to Chambers's voice and examining his teeth, he admitted knowing him as
George Crosley, but denied having more than a cursory relationship with him.
Then, as Chambers continued to produce evidence of a closer relationship with the
Hisses, Hiss offered comparatively feeble efforts to minimize that evidence. Yes,
Chambers had occupied an apartment of Hiss's after Hiss had vacated it, but not rent
free, as Chambers suggested. Yes, Hiss had given a car to Chambers, but just the use
of the car, not the car itself. Yes, Chambers had given Hiss an Oriental rug, but in
part payment for rent. No, Hiss had not loaned Chambers $400, he had withdrawn
that amount from a bank account for other reasons.

No, Hiss did not know what had become of a typewriter first owned by Priscilla's
father. Priscilla had possibly sold the typewriter to a secondhand dealer.[89] On recollection, the Hisses may have given the typewriter to the Catletts. But they had done
so in 1937, so the documents Chambers had produced could not have been typed on
that typewriter. Well, perhaps the documents had been, but neither he nor Priscilla
had typed them. Chambers, or some associate of his, must have done so. The typist must have gained access to the typewriter while the Catletts had possession of it.
When successive pieces of incriminating information surfaced, Hiss sought to account for them in this manner. His approach only served to undermine the impression his reputational defense had sought to create. Instead of appearing as a person
whose innocence was the natural inference of his integrity and the absence of any
motive for him to commit espionage, Hiss appeared as someone who was doggedly
trying to keep others from learning about his secret past.

Thus, as Hiss prepared to enter prison, the shining reputation he offered at his trials had been replaced by another: that of "convicted traitor." Alger Hiss had lost the
first of his looking-glass wars. He had held up the image of himself that he had carefully fashioned from the time he first matriculated at Johns Hopkins in 1922, and,
under the scrutiny of the HUAC hearings and his perjury trials, it had shattered.
Now, once again, he was faced with the option of confession and avoidance. If he
survived prison—no sure thing, given his status as a "traitor" when he entered—
he could choose to live out his life in obscurity, possibly in another country. Priscilla
would propose that option.

Alternatively, Alger Hiss could defiantly reassert his innocence, repeating his
categorical disassociations with Communists or Communism in any form, claiming
that he had been scapegoated and framed by Chambers and others. He could mount
a campaign to vindicate his reputation, searching for evidence that might undermine

his opponents and discredit the narrative that Chambers had fashioned. Hiss elected that choice, even though he knew that he was not in fact innocent, and that his commitment to Communism and the Soviets had been far deeper, and far more enduring, than extant evidence suggested. By making it he assured that the rest of his life would be a series of additional looking-glass wars.

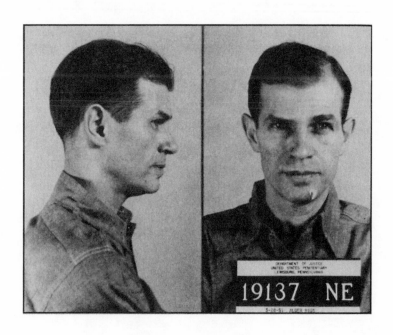

Hiss's "mug shots" on entering Lewisburg, Pennsylvania,
federal prison in March 1951.

CHAPTER THREE

Prison

O n March 22, 1951, Alger Hiss surrendered to federal marshals at the Foley Square courthouse in New York to begin a five-year jail sentence. His appeal from his January 1950 conviction on two counts of perjury had been unanimously denied by a three-judge panel of the United States Court of Appeals for the Second Circuit on December 7, 1950, and on March 12, 1951, the Supreme Court of the United States had denied his petition for certiorari.[1] Ten days later Hiss's tenure as a federal prisoner began. He had been sentenced to five years on both counts of perjury, with the prosecution recommending, and Judge Goddard agreeing, to have the counts run concurrently. A statute provided that if he maintained good behavior in prison he would be released in 44 months.[2]

Before Hiss went to prison, he had been informed that he was likely to be sent to a maximum security federal facility in Lewisburg, Pennsylvania, rather than the alternatives of Danbury, Connecticut, a prison with a "country-club" image, or Atlanta, one that tended to house prisoners sentenced to life or long terms of years. He also knew a good deal about the details of prison life, and had been given suggestions about how best to cope with those details. He had prepared for prison in the same assiduous manner that he prepared for his trials, and his goals of maintaining his innocence and assuming the persona of a "framed" scapegoat remained intact. But for the immediate future his constituency had sharply narrowed. He would no longer be dealing with potential supporters and opponents from the general public. He would be dealing with the population of a maximum security federal prison. He needed to survive at least 44 months in a world whose inhabitants were not likely to take kindly to spies for the Soviet Union.

His incarceration in Lewisburg federal prison meant that Hiss would be facing another looking-glass war. At first blush that conclusion may not seem apparent. Hiss's conviction had labeled him a Communist and a spy as well as a perjurer; how did the prison experience threaten to expose him any further? The answer comes from the fact that Hiss's principal constituency in Lewisburg was not the general public, nor the prison authorities, but the inmates. While in prison he had very little ability to influence how persons in the outside world perceived him. He could, and did, seek to influence the prison authorities in some minor respects, but he could hardly have anticipated convincing them that he had been wrongly convicted. Although Hiss spent some of his time in prison preparing himself for the life he expected to lead after being released, he spent most of it in the pursuit of helpful relationships with his fellow prisoners.

Successful relations with his inmate contemporaries was critical to Hiss's well-being in Lewisburg, and not merely to keep him alive. If too many members of the prison population concluded that he had been rightly convicted, and thus was a "Communist traitor," he could expect regular harassment and abuse, whether or not he survived. He needed to construct a persona for himself that would be well received by most of his fellow prisoners: the persona of a "knockabout guy," an average inmate who blended in with and subscribed to the general ethos of the prison population. By creating that persona, Hiss sought to foster an impression of himself that fit nicely with two suppositions about their contemporaries commonly made by persons who had been jailed in a moderate security facility. One was that Hiss, like several others in prison, had been framed, and was not guilty at all. The other was that, if he was guilty, he was "taking it like a man," serving his time in an uncomplaining, stoical fashion and not ratting on his fellow prisoners to the authorities. By appearing to be just a knockabout guy, Hiss sought to encourage those suppositions. He was remarkably successful in doing so.[3]

Once Hiss knew that he was going to jail, he sought, "like a traveler to an unfamiliar land," some information about "the customs and conditions of prison life." Through Dr. Viola Bernard, a psychiatrist who had assisted in his defense, he secured a contact with Austin MacCormick, who had been in the Federal Bureau of Prisons during the New Deal and during the 1950s served as the director of the Osborne Association, an organization dedicated to helping ex-convicts readjust to the outside world. MacCormick was thought to be a proponent of Hiss's innocence. His sister was the wife of Hubert James, the foreman at Hiss's first trial. The prosecution, in an effort to remove James, reported MacCormick's sister as having said that if "[i]t was up to [her husband], Hiss will get away with it." James remained, and Claude Cross, lead counsel for Hiss at the second trial, later speculated that "Austin MacCormick's brother-in-law was foreman of the jury, and he kept that jury hung."[4]

In a meeting early in 1951, MacCormick gave Hiss a forecast of what he might expect in prison. "[O]n all objective matters," Alger would write five months after arriving at Lewisburg, MacCormick's predictions were "crisply accurate." MacCormick told Alger that he would not be sent to Danbury, even though federal prisoners were typically placed in the facilities closest to their residences, because of Danbury's lenient reputation. Nor would he be sent to Atlanta, since his term was comparatively short and he was a first-time offender. He would go to Lewisburg, whose population was not primarily "white-collar" criminals, but whose inmates, for the most part, were serving short sentences.[5]

The United States Penitentiary in Lewisburg, Pennsylvania, as it is officially called, stands in the middle of 950 acres of federally owned land in the same township in central Pennsylvania where Bucknell University is located. The land is rolling, picturesque farmland, and the prison, when Hiss was an inmate, operated a farm. The prison itself is a massive brick structure, encircled by four concrete walls, 30 feet high and more than a thousand feet long, with brick watchtowers on each corner. Within the walls, in addition to the main building in which inmates are housed, are athletic fields and factory buildings. The main building, over 900 feet long, is two stories high with a tile roof. A huge brick smokestack rises from the center of the building, resembling an Italian Renaissance bell tower. The inmates are housed, in a combination of dormitories and cell blocks, on both floors: Hiss joined an inmate population that ranged between 1,500 and 2,000 men during the years of his incarceration. The housing arrangements at Lewisburg included an "honor block" of cells, set aside for inmates with good disciplinary records. Hiss was moved to the honor block, whose unlocked cells stood at the western end of the building, separated by locked doors from its other residential areas, after spending the first two years of his sentence in a second-floor dormitory.[6]

Before being sent to Lewisburg Hiss spent a week in a federal detention center on West Street in New York City, which was closed in 1975. That facility, he felt, "was really like a zoo, because it was made up of iron cages," with bars on the sides and top, containing double-decker bunks. The cages were designed to hold up to a dozen men. "Mostly there was a coming and going of newly convicted prisoners," Hiss recalled, "whose momentary stay at West Street was for the compiling of dossiers before their transfer to places of regular confinement." This meant that those detained at West Street "had no prescribed activities and little opportunity for recreation." Their time consisted mainly of "aimless, time-killing talk" in a "repellent" setting of "pandemonium." Naked bulbs burned day and night; prison intercoms blared constantly; the cages amounted to "holding pens." West Street was a place "of confusion and disorder," a "crowded and antiquated warehouse for unhappy men."[7]

Nonetheless Hiss had one fortunate, possibly life-saving, experience at West Street. He was thrown together with a man whose acquaintance was to have a significant effect on the quality of his stay at Lewisburg. In his memoirs Hiss referred to the man by the pseudonym "Danny F." He employed this practice of concealing the identities of many of his prison associates in his reminiscences, particularly those who were involved with organized crime. Danny F., a native of New York in his forties, was awaiting transfer to Atlanta for what he expected would be a long stay in that facility. He and Hiss apparently struck a bond because neither was particularly interested in "casual chatting with the numbers of confused and lonely men who approached anyone . . . who found himself alone." Danny never survived his Atlanta experience, dying in prison. But he felt comfortable enough with Hiss to tell him, when he found out Hiss was destined for Lewisburg, to "ask for his brother-in-law Mike M., and say that it was Danny who told me of him."[8]

Austin MacCormick had told Hiss about the groups of men he could expect to find in the prison population of Lewisburg in the early 1950s. Hiss's immediate contemporaries, MacCormick said, would all be Caucasians. Approximately 40 percent of Lewisburg's inmates were African Americans, but the facility was segregated on racial lines, and black and white prisoners were not allowed to mingle except during periods of outdoor exercise, where, Hiss noted, "a somewhat uneasy voluntary segregation" typically prevailed. Within the white population, MacCormick identified four groups, and predicted which representatives of the groups Hiss would find more or less congenial. A "tiny group of men charged with white collar crimes— chiefly businessmen guilty of tax evasions—" would be "boring" companions for Hiss, he thought. Hiss did not single out any members of that group in his reminiscences about Lewisburg.[9]

The other three groups were approximately equal in numbers. One group consisted of ex-soldiers in World War II who had been convicted of crimes against the civilian populations of Germany, Austria, or Italy. Members of that group tended to receive lengthy sentences by military tribunals that sought to foster good relations with the countries in which the crimes had occurred. MacCormick predicted that

Alger might find some of the incarcerated soldiers interesting, and Alger became closely acquainted with two, "Klaus H." and "Murph." Klaus had been imprisoned for a statutory rape that took place in Vienna, and Murph for participating in a brawl involving residents of Naples and American soldiers that resulted in the death of a Naples resident. Both felt that their sentences were excessive. Klaus claimed not to have known his partner was under age, and Murph that "he had been more onlooker than participant." Murph had become "mistrustful of all authority and of almost everyone" after initially being sentenced to death for the Naples brawl. Military review boards periodically reduced his sentence, and he was eventually paroled before Hiss was released. Klaus was a violinist, who shared with Hiss a love of classical music. Murph, a resident of New York City, coached Hiss in handball, and became sufficiently attached to Hiss that after being released he tried to ensure that he and Hiss would renew contact once Hiss reentered the outside world.[10]

A second group was "hillbillies," "kids from the small towns and hills of Kentucky and Tennessee, mostly inside for robbing banks and stealing cars for joy rides." Their presence in a federal prison was the result of their crimes having crossed state lines. They were for the most part without resources, and thus were unable to spend money in the prison commissary, whose cigarettes and sweets could be used, within the inmate and prison guard population, as a source of influence through barter. Hiss did not single out any member of this group as a particularly close acquaintance or memorable figure, although he did note that two participated in one of the "dramatic events" during his stay in Lewisburg. "[T]wo Appalachian brothers imprisoned for bank robbery," he recalled, "loosened a bar in a dormitory window, climbed down the traditional rope of sheets, and somehow got over the high brick wall without being discovered." They were eventually found, and shot to death by police, in New York City.[11]

The third group, because of Alger's fortuitous encounter with Danny F., became the source of Hiss's closest acquaintances in Lewisburg. It was "the 'racket guys,' or 'regular guys,' as they called themselves." MacCormick predicted that Hiss would find his "most companionable" associates in that group, and he was, Hiss recalled, "clairvoyant." Hiss described the racket guys as "[m]ostly Italian Americans from New York" whom MacCormick characterized as "affectionate family men," "quick-witted," and "loyally cohesive." Their "numbers, self-assurance, and natural intelligence," MacCormick told Alger, "would make them the dominant element in jail, pretty much setting the tone for the code of conduct adopted by the [white] prison population as a whole." Two participants in organized crime were

Alger's "closest friends at Lewisburg," Tony Hiss surmised. One was "Mike M.,"
whom Tony called "Vincenzo." The other Tony referred to as "Angelo."[12]

In a passage from his memoirs Hiss described the impression the "Italian Americans," as he called them, made upon him. "The Italian Americans' general attitude
toward their situation," he wrote, "reminded me of what I knew about the attitude
of prisoners of war. On release they would return to the same way of life as before.
Meanwhile, they made the best of it. Jail was an occupational hazard to be faced with
as much equanimity as one could muster. The restraint and loss of liberty were irk-
some in the extreme—painful, indeed—but a man of 'heart' endured them stoically. Constant complaining—'crying'—was scorned."

That attitude was precisely the one that Hiss hoped to assume in Lewisburg. A
"prisoner of war" was one who had yielded to superior force, but not surrendered
his convictions. He was determined to make the best of his time in prison, to be as
self-protective as he could. He was also determined to maintain the posture of his
innocence. In the racket-guys' code of prison behavior, however, one did not pros-
elytize excessively. One did not "cry" about one's current situation, nor did one defend one's profession, or describe oneself as a victim. This stoical approach was
consistent with the attitude Hiss wanted to take toward his prison experience. He was
mindful that his identification as a Communist and a spy might be provocative to
some of his peers. He did not want to draw attention to himself, either from inmates
or authorities.[13]

MacCormick had reinforced that attitude in his early 1951 conversation. "You'll
be the new boy in school," he told Alger, "and you'll have a lot to learn. The others will all be experienced upperclassmen. Listen and learn. That's the best advice I
can give you." In his memoirs Hiss stated that "[t]he men who best maintained their
sense of selfhood regarded their position much as do prisoners of war. They relied
on their own psychic resources to sustain them." He followed their example.[14]

Hiss employed three strategies to maintain his "sense of selfhood," which included the preservation of his posture of innocence, in Lewisburg. He took advantage of his previous acquaintance with Danny F. to ingratiate himself with the
representatives of organized crime in the Lewisburg population. In addition, he
acted as an unfailingly cooperative and well-behaved prisoner, not only to the authorities, but, more importantly, to his fellow inmates. He quickly absorbed the internal codes of prisoner conduct and was faithful to them. Finally, he scrupulously
avoided discussions of his case, and did not associate with other "political" prisoners, who included some persons convicted of subversive advocacy under the Smith
Act of 1940, which began to be applied against members of the Communist Party
after 1947. These strategies, taken together, amounted to a refurbished reputational

defense. By blending into the prison population, by never ruffling feathers, and by assuming the role, if not the identity, of a regular guy, Hiss managed to keep himself alive—a prospect that some might have bet against when he entered Lewisburg—and to convince some of his closer acquaintances that he was not the sort of man who could have been a spy. As one of them put it in a 1964 interview, "Hiss went about his own, had nothing to say to nobody, good or bad, about them and said very little about his own case. He seemed to just let it rest, 'Here I am, think what you want.' And that's what makes me say that this man is not guilty."[15]

On arriving at Lewisburg Hiss was placed in "quarantine," or semisolitary confinement, for a month. For the first ten days of the quarantine period, prisoners were not permitted to make purchases from the commissary or have any contact with the rest of the population. Approximately 50 men in Hiss's segment of the population were quarantined at any one time: they were marched in a unit to meals, exercise, and the library. After two weeks they were moved from isolated cells to a quarantine dormitory, and about two weeks later were moved into the general population. Hiss treated the quarantine period as the first test of his approach to Lewisburg. "For most of the men in my entering batch," he recalled, "the limited solitary confinement was harsh punishment." But he welcomed "the opportunity for uninterrupted reading," noting that the prison library contained books, such as the collected letters of Lenin's widow, that "would have outraged Senator Joseph McCarthy," and discovered "the efficiency of the grapevine," a means of communication among prisoners that served as a bonding device. During the period in which Hiss was denied access to the commissary, where prisoners could purchase cigarettes, he received a packet of cigarettes "from someone whose name I did not know." The grapevine passed along "[g]reetings, personal news, prison gossip, and cigarettes," and "the last transmitter" of its commodities to quarantined inmates would be "an inmate barber, hospital orderly, or clerk in the library." By the time Hiss entered the general population he was aware that "[p]rison society has devised its own customs to solace or protect its members." The positive effect of the grapevine on the morale of prisoners extended beyond the recipients of goods or information to those who had helped pass it along and even those who simply learned of the communications.[16]

The isolation of the quarantine period had "not incommoded" Hiss, and the interval had given him a sense of the powerful informal codes of conduct that marked prison life. Those codes of conduct, he concluded, were another reason why the inmates who most easily adapted to prison life had backgrounds in organized crime. They had a "sense of solidarity," he noted, that "antedated prison life," and was

ensured by "a marked sense of hierarchy" and a "code of . . . discipline." They were
well supported by their connections on the outside, receiving regular visits and financial help. Hiss perceived them as "the most stable group in prison," with "wonderful family relationships." In 1959 he told the historian C. Vann Woodward that
the racket guys were "the healthiest inmates in prison" because "[t]hey had ab-
solutely no sense of guilt."[17]

The group solidarity of the Italian Americans resulted in their maintaining a
"studied aloofness" toward the prison authorities and a comparatively limited interest in members of other groups in the inmate population. They would engage
with other prisoners if they found "a common ground," Hiss told the journalist
Brock Brower in 1960. But the common ground "ha[d] to be a real interest, nothing
egregious." Although MacCormick had predicted that Hiss would find the organized crime figures the most congenial of his fellow inmates, Hiss had been warned,
"[t]he first day I was there," to approach all of his incarcerated contemporaries cautiously. "[N]ever speak at breakfast," he was told. "Everyone's got his own problems, and the guy next to you may be in a rage." Hiss was well aware of the
"ever-present possibility of involuntary involvement in some fracas brought about
by prison tensions." He was also conscious of his own notoriety.[18]

So on the morning after he was released from quarantine, assigned to a dormitory in the general population, and marched to breakfast with his fellow inmates "in
sullen silence," Hiss waited an interval until asking "if anyone at my part of the table
knew Mike M.," the brother-in-law of "Danny F.," Hiss's acquaintance at the West
Street detention center. Hiss then recalled what happened next:

> A black-haired, dark-eyed man almost directly across from me said quietly
> that he was Mike M. and asked the reason for my query. I told him of my
> coming to know Danny F. at West Street and of his telling me to seek out
> Mike M. Danny's name proved a password. Mike's guarded manner
> changed instantly. He smiled in a warm, friendly way. His prompt accept-
> ance of me brought with it a relaxation of manner and mood at our end of
> the table. Mike plainly had standing among my new companions. His ready
> acceptance of me helped me to fit in quickly and easily with the others in
> my dormitory. Our relationship became a close one. We were constant
> companions.[19]

Hiss had been planning to approach Mike M. ever since his encounter with Danny
F., having learned from MacCormick that the racket guys were likely to carry the

greatest amount of influence among his fellow inmates. But he had not known that Mike was "the unquestioned, though tacit, leader of the Italian American contingent and thus one of the two or three most important men in the prison population." Mike had been convicted of racketeering, and had turned down a plea bargain that would have kept him out of jail in exchange for testimony against more highly placed organized crime figures. Hiss discovered that members of organized crime families were "routinely locked up on contempt of court charges" for failing to disclose information to federal investigators. Mike's combination of offenses resulted in his receiving a comparatively lengthy sentence, and his "relative seniority among those of his fellows" serving comparable sentences was, given the hierarchical relationships among participants in organized crime, a source of his leadership. But Mike also possessed, Hiss observed, "calm good judgment and common sense," so that "[p]roblems of personal conflict were brought to him."[20]

Mike "was always the center of a small group" to which Hiss regularly attached himself during his time in Lewisburg. The group, primarily consisting of racket guys, discussed "prison gossip and the doings of the group's friends in the outside world, but also politics, religion, and history." At times "[o]ur conversations were interrupted by a supplicant seeking Mike's solution of a dispute." The dispute would sometimes be aired in the presence of the group, but on other occasions "Mike would leave us and walk around the cinder track as the case was presented to him." "My Italian American friends," Hiss noted, "treated serious matters seriously. Problems that came before Mike were explained in sober fashion and considered with gravity and decorum. Formality and courtesy were valued."[21]

In discussing his time in Mike's circle in Lewisburg Hiss singled out several incidents that demonstrated the group's code of conduct and served to explain why the organized crime figures accepted Hiss. Danny F.'s introduction to Mike might have broken down some barriers. That alone, however, would not have explained the access that Hiss enjoyed to Mike and his friends. That came from the fact that Hiss was a lawyer, and thus a potential source of advice to men who fully expected to encounter law enforcement authorities in their future careers. "Every day," Tony Hiss reported, when Alger arrived at the exercise yard, "there was a line of 40 to 50 people with legal papers they wanted him to go over." Alger "couldn't bring himself to say no" to the requests, and the public setting in which they took place meant that the Lewisburg authorities were aware that Hiss was dispensing advice. Mike warned Hiss to be more circumspect lest he "wind up in Atlanta." But at the same time Mike called upon Hiss to give discreet legal advice to his organized crime colleagues.[22]

One example involved the "famous underworld figure" (as Hiss called him), Frank Costello, who served a short sentence in Lewisburg for contempt of the United States Senate. Hiss wrote about meeting Costello in his memoirs. After being subpoenaed by a Senate committee investigating organized crime, Hiss recalled, Costello declined to answer "six or seven questions," then, on the advice of his lawyer, answered all but one of the remaining inquiries. Although his "right to refuse to answer the remaining question" was upheld in court, Costello was convicted of contempt and sent to Lewisburg. Shortly after he arrived, Hiss "received word" from Mike "that 'Mr. Frank' would like to meet me and have a private talk. It was arranged that we should meet in the yard and have such a talk during the recreation period. Two of my new friends accompanied me. Costello was attended by two others. The two parties came together, there were formal introductions, and Costello and I then walked around the track by ourselves."[23]

The "decorum" of the Hiss-Costello meeting, reminiscent of meetings between leaders of organized crime families, tacitly confirmed Hiss's acceptance in the circle of inmates centering around Mike M. The purpose of the meeting was for Costello to seek legal advice from Hiss about his contempt conviction. He brought along an appellate brief, written by Robert Benjamin, who had also represented Hiss, challenging the conviction. After Hiss gave the opinion that Costello's voluntarily answering some of the Senate committee's questions had "purged him of contempt" as to those questions, and that he had a constitutional right to decline to answer the other questions, Costello, Hiss reported, "expressed . . . sympathy" about Hiss's own "miscarriage of justice." Costello added that "his favorite political figure" was Eleanor Roosevelt.[24]

Another example of the affinity between Hiss and Mike's circle of regular guys was Mike's delegation to Alger the task of teaching one of the younger organized crime figures to read and write. As Alger told it to Tony Hiss, one day in the exercise yard "Leo M.," (whom Tony referred to as "Pasquale" or "Pat"), approached Mike and asked him to read a letter from his wife, and to help him write her a reply. Mike, Tony reported, "couldn't take too much of this, and he got [Alger] to take on the job" of teaching Leo to read. Hiss agreed, but was only able to secure "Dick and Jane" books from the prison's Education Department. Eventually, by devoting about two hours a day for months to Leo M.'s tutelage, Hiss was able to help his pupil read and write at a seventh-grade level. Leo had been completely illiterate when Hiss started working with him. He had dropped out of school at the age of seven, when truant officers, searching for him at his home after he had left school without permission, beat his mother, who could not speak English, and was uncooperative in their efforts to find him. He had become a boxer, and then a strong-arm man in organized crime.[25]

Mike M. played handball with Hiss, and was his regular companion during intervals of leisure time when Hiss was not tutoring Leo. On one occasion Mike served as a reality check for Hiss after Chester Lane, who had introduced a "forgery by typewriter" argument in Hiss's unsuccessful appeal from his perjury conviction, reported that typewriter experts hired in connection with that defense had produced a machine which seemed to be "an exact copy" of the Woodstock typewriter produced at the perjury trials. Hiss was so buoyed by the information, he recalled, that he leapt to the conclusion that the duplicate typewriter "would spring him immediately, . . . and asked [Mike] what errands he could run for him on the outside." Mike suggested that the information was unlikely to gain him a new trial, and when his lawyers made the motion "old Judge Goddard turned [it] down . . . like a shot."

The most important consequence of Mike's friendship with Hiss came in the summer of 1953, when Hiss was in his third year at Lewisburg. Hiss described the incident in his memoirs:

> On one occasion . . . I was warned by my Italian American friends that I should, for a day or two, be circumspect and remain in their protective circle. I was told that two undisciplined young Italian Americans had just joined the population and had been assigned to the early morning task of cleaning the kitchen. The guard on duty, who was particularly disliked by the prisoners because of his hostile manner, had said to the newcomers that something should be done about Hiss. He had pursued the subject by saying that the Rosenbergs were dead, so why should Hiss continue on? The two young men had taken this as a hint that they should do me harm.[26]

Julius and Ethel Rosenberg had been executed for conspiracy to commit espionage in June 1953, bringing the issue of Soviet agents penetrating the workings of the United States government once again to the fore. The guard was suggesting that Hiss, as a fellow "traitor," should meet the same fate. "Fortunately for me," Hiss recalled, the recent arrivals "consulted Mike M. and his associates, who assured them that I was 'one of them.'" In Tony Hiss's version, Mike said, "This guard can't help you, can't make your life any easier here. Forget it. I know Hiss, he's not so bad." The guard, whom Hiss speculated was emotionally unstable, subsequently killed himself.

Mike, Tony concluded, had saved his father's life.[27]

The regular guys called Hiss "Alberto," believing that "Alger wasn't a real name." In addition to keeping Hiss alive at Lewisburg, the regular guys represented the closest thing Hiss had to a circle of companions. But the outstanding characteristic of Hiss's social interactions during his time in prison was, as one regular guy put it in a 1964 interview, his independence. "In there we all run in what you call 'packs,'" the regular guy said, but "Hiss never joined one. . . . Hiss went about his own way." From the time he entered Lewisburg part of Hiss's strategy of maintaining a sense of self was to scrupulously avoid too close an emotional involvement with any of his inmate contemporaries, while at the same time seeking to convey an unfailingly positive attitude toward them, and to his obligations as a prisoner. This included not only performing acts of kindnesses toward inmates such as Leo, but responding stoically to the petty abuses occasionally enacted upon him by prison authorities and fellow prisoners. "Hiss always had something good to say about everybody," an organized crime figure noted. He added that "Hiss was denied a lot of privileges," but "never complained."[28]

In addition to the camaraderie and psychological resilience he found in the racket guys, Hiss discovered that other inmates, or prison authorities, possessed qualities or interests he found stimulating. The ex-soldier Klaus and he compiled a "basic list of symphonies, concertos, choral works, chamber music, and instrumental pieces" for the Education Department to use in requesting copies of recordings from radio stations. Murph swapped his handball expertise for the sympathetic companionship Hiss provided. The prison librarian and members of the Education Department helped Hiss circumvent a Bureau of Prisons ruling that no prisoners at Lewisburg could receive books from the outside. The ruling was made after a columnist revealed that the Lewisburg prison, had allowed Hiss to receive books from Kenneth McCormick of Doubleday Publishing Company. McCormick had a right of first refusal on any book Hiss might produce after leaving prison. Lewisburg's librarian, who had a limited budget, had encouraged this arrangement when Hiss promised to leave the books with him after being from prison. The Bureau of Prisons ruling threatened to nullify this arrangement.[29]

Hiss and the librarian fought back. An inmate in the Lewisburg population had recently "turned to God," Hiss recalled, "and was engaged in serious religious study in prison, including a correspondence course" that featured "a steady stream of books." Hiss and others "prevailed upon the deprived student to complain to his congressman about the godless ruling" denying him and other prisoners any access to outside reading matter. After the congressman protested to the Bureau of Prisons, Lewisburg was permitted to make an exception for books of religious content. The librarian liberally interpreted this exception, and eventually "works of science, history, . . . biography, . . . art, philosophy, geography, travel, and even politics were included."[30]

Hiss also had some companions with whom he discussed ideas. One was "Lester W.," a "slight young rabbinical student" from Austria who worked with him as a clerk in the storeroom. Lester, who had been arrested for smuggling diamonds into the United States, had been planning to use the income from smuggling to "marry and go to Israel." He was "devout, studious, well read, and retiring," and he and Hiss "spent many hours together" engaging in "long discussions of religion, the Bible, history, philosophy, German literature, and world politics." Another, "Clovis," was a "Jewish intellectual" who had refused to serve in the Korean war because he was a conscientious objector. Hiss discussed art and literature with him, and introduced him to the *New Statesman* magazine, which, along with the *New Yorker*, he was allowed to receive at Lewisburg. In 1964 Clovis, using the name "A. Bergdoll," gave his impressions of Hiss:

> I can't say I was one of Mr. Hiss's best friends at Lewisburg, though he is one of the few people there who helped make my stay a relatively pleasant one, kept my mind operating by discussions of most art and literature. . . .
> Mr. Hiss at Lewisburg quickly got the respect of most of the staff and in the end I would say very, very nearly 100 percent of the inmates. . . .
>
> Mr. Hiss showed great adaptability. At one time were both in a large dormitory. . . . The noisiness and lack of privacy made it very difficult. . . . Mr. Hiss however took it all in stride, and seemed quite happy, though the noise, etc., could not have been entirely what he liked.[31]

Although Hiss was able to carve out some opportunities for stimulation and companionship at Lewisburg, he never deviated from the position, which he expressed to John Chabot Smith in the 1970s, that "jail is a terrible place." "Hostility," he said in his memoirs, "is inherent in prison procedures," and his surroundings at Lewisburg were "grim" and "oppressive." Privacy was nonexistent, but at the same time the setting fostered an "isolation that seemed designed to make each man feel alone and helpless." And all the while there was a constant underlying tension, the result of "the close confinement of men trapped in emotional ordeals." Hiss observed that in the weekly movie the "Italian Americans strove to sit as far as possible to one side or the other of the auditorium." This was because the theater was a dark, crowded place, where "the possibility of a riot" was always present, and "[t]he Italian Americans had an extraordinary sensitivity to even faint signs of potential danger." After being in Lewisburg for a while Hiss himself could sense the "sudden quietness from one area" that "might signal the tense moments when a quarrel has deteriorated into violence."[32]

In this atmosphere Hiss not only sought occasional companionship and diversion, but attempted to maintain the posture of stoical calm Clovis had commented on. This was particularly important to him because he knew that he was a notorious prisoner, the kind that was not likely to get any public favors from authorities and might be resented by inmates. He perceived, correctly, that his notoriety would make him a visible inmate, and he was determined not to be seen as someone who agitated for special treatment or complained when he appeared to be mistreated. With MacCormick's advice in mind, he did not request interesting jobs or special favors, and when he seemed to be being disadvantaged because of his notoriety he accepted the treatment without complaint.

MacCormick had asked Hiss what jobs he might like to perform during his stay at Lewisburg. Hiss's first choice had been to work as an orderly in the prison hospital, which appealed to the sense of power and satisfaction he found in altruistic activities. MacCormick strongly cautioned him against volunteering for hospital duties. He would have access to drugs in a hospital, and would thus be pressured by inmates to smuggle them drugs, placing him in a vulnerable position whatever he did. His next choice was to participate in the Education Department, for which he was eminently qualified, given his academic background and achievements. That position would not materialize, MacCormick predicted, because the authorities would be concerned about perceptions that Hiss might be teaching Communist ideology, or Soviet propaganda, to his fellow inmates. In sum, MacCormick concluded, Hiss was not likely to be placed in any comparatively desirable job, including ones, such as positions in the prison library, that were coveted because the duties were thought to be light. MacCormick correctly guessed that Hiss would be made an inmate clerk in the storeroom, assisting the official in charge of non-edible supplies. That job required regular physical labor and constant supervision, because both guards and prisoners had access to the items on shelves. The storeroom was also, Clovis recalled, a "very lonely, depressing place."[33]

But Hiss, as he put it, made the best of his assignment. He "heaved stuff around all day," including, occasionally, food. "[O]nce or twice he got a chance to snag a couple of steaks" out of a batch designed for the prison staff. Mike thought this behavior too risky, but another of the regular guys, Angelo, secured "a little electric plate from one of his friends in the radio shop," and he and Hiss "broiled the steaks while Angie stood at the window waving a towel to get the smell out of the room." Alger stated that he "enjoyed storeroom work," because "moving things around was something real to do, as well as good exercise." He had good relations with the prison officer in charge of supervising the storeroom, who "let him read books when there was nothing else to do." Hiss did not receive any discretionary time off his sentence for meritorious conduct, nor were any of his applications for parole granted, although the storeroom guard periodically recommended that he receive those dispensations. When, in the middle of his sentence, he was offered a transfer from the storeroom to the kitchen, he turned it down, perhaps believing that access to food would subject him to pressures comparable to those caused by access to drugs in the prison hospital. Years later Tony Hiss was given access to the file on his father during his time at Lewisburg. It revealed that Hiss had consistently received the maximum number of rating points for job performance, based on criteria such as "dependability," "interest," "attitude," "comprehension of job," and "cooperation." During the last month of his incarceration his supervisor described his performance as "very outstanding."[34]

Making the best of his surroundings not only involved squeezing out the small pleasures that were associated with a dull and lonely job. It also required that Hiss be perceived by his fellow inmates as "just a knockabout guy." Hiss was able to achieve this status, in part, because he convinced other inmates that despite his notoriety he was able to endure the routine deprivations and injustices of prison without complaint. And he received more than his share of deprivations and injustices while at Lewisburg.

In the 44 months he spent in Lewisburg Penitentiary Hiss only received one set of privileges, a transfer from a general dormitory to the "honor block" of cells. This was a benefit, but it was routinely dispensed to prisoners with no history of violent crimes and meritorious records. None of the discretionary privileges accorded to Lewisburg inmates, such as reductions from incarcerated time for good behavior, early release on parole, or even the opportunity to work outdoors, in less supervised conditions, on the prison farm, was given to Hiss. Given his consistently good record of performance and cooperation, his failure to receive any discretionary privileges was clearly a product of his visible status. If the Lewisburg authorities had not been aware, before Hiss's incarceration, that any evidence of their according him favorable treatment ran the risk of generating a public outcry, the public reception to the column protesting his being permitted to receive books from the outside would have convinced them.

After first being allowed to participate in debates with nearby colleges, which the Education Department at Lewisburg encouraged as part of prisoner rehabilitation, Hiss was barred from that activity because the authorities felt they might be thought of as encouraging his success as a debater. As this decision suggested, Hiss not only received few privileges while at Lewisburg, he was sometimes not allowed to engage in activities approved for the general prison population. In addition, the authorities ignored attempts on the part of other inmates to express their animosity toward him. One of Hiss's friends summarized some of the deprivations Hiss endured:

> Hiss was denied a lot of privileges in Lewisburg. He couldn't debate because he would win all his debates with Bucknell University and in time the officials stopped him from that.
>
> He didn't receive any . . . "meritorious good days" because the officials were afraid of public opinion.
>
> This man wore old clothes while he was there, never got new clothes, wore old shoes. And, although you're entitled to two pairs of new shoes a year, he never received those. [The inmates] that worked in our clothing issue used to cut his trousers one leg higher than the other when he'd send his clothes to the laundry . . . and the officials that worked in the clothing issue knew this was going on.[35]

In detailing this list of deprivations, Hiss's friend added that "Hiss never complained" about his treatment. He "would never go to the officials to complain." The harassment, the friend suggested, was eventually "straightened out by cons like myself and others who liked Hiss." It had originated with "[a] few fellows, the so-called flag-raisers, [who] called him a Commie. . . . These were the only ones [who] would try to harass Hiss and in time they quit this."[36]

As the cutting of Hiss's trousers suggested, despite his generally good relations with other prisoners his image as a "Commie" persisted during his time at Lewisburg. That image was generally dangerous to Hiss in a world in which violence was never far from the surface and in which relations between the United States and the Soviet Union were openly antagonistic, but it was also dangerous in a more concrete fashion. During the years of Hiss's incarceration at Lewisburg the facility was the principal place of residence for the growing number of persons convicted of subversive advocacy, or subversive activities, under congressional statutes that began to be zealously enforced in the late 1940s and 1950s. One of the persons housed at Lewisburg was Ethel Rosenberg's brother, David Greenglass, who had received a reduced sentence for testifying against his sister and her husband Julius. Another was Gus Hall, the longtime secretary of the Communist Party of the United States. "All the top Commies in the country that were in jail at that time came through Lewisburg," one inmate reported. The constant influx of "Commie" prisoners provided recurrent reminders, to the general prison population, that another alleged Communist, Alger Hiss, was in their midst.[37]

Hiss had resolved, on entering Lewisburg, not to discuss controversial issues with his fellow inmates and not to comment extensively on his own case. He was careful to avoid extensive contacts with Smith Act prisoners or others identified with Communism. Although he "met a couple of Communist leaders who had been convicted just about the same time he was," Alger told Tony, he did not "talk to them much," and "he never talked politics with them." This, in Tony's view, "convinced . . . a number of the prisoners . . . of Al's innocence." Mike M. reported to Tony that "Alberto [as he called Alger] has never once said anything to me on this subject, except that he was innocent." Mike added that Hiss was "not the kind of man who if he believes something would pretend he didn't." He based this conclusion on his experience in "running the numbers," where "[y]ou have to know people." "Alger Hiss is no Communist," Mike concluded. Another inmate made the same assessment, saying that "I don't think Hiss was a Communist" because "while I was in jail with him I had time to observe and study this man." He described Hiss as "a very liberal man" who "sees only what is good in people."[38]

By enduring petty abuses without complaint, being circumspect in his contacts, adhering to the prisoner-of-war code of the racket guys, avoiding discussions of his own case, consistently performing his duties, occasionally filching from the authorities for the benefit of his fellow inmates, giving advice and instruction to those who asked for it, and remaining seemingly imperturbable in the crowded, noisy, invasive atmosphere of prison life, Hiss had successfully created another reputation for himself: that of a "good con." In 1978 Murray Kempton, a believer in Hiss's guilt, wrote that "I shall never dismiss Alger Hiss as no better than a traitor so long as I know that he never finked at Lewisburg." Kempton was referring to comments made to him by "one or two ex-convicts who were there with [Hiss]." "Their reverence," Kempton reported, "was authentic beyond question." Hiss, as an inmate, "was kind; he was helpful; he was indeed a comrade you could ask to hide your contraband and know he'd never either use it himself or hand it over to the guard." Kempton found a "curious moral purity" in Hiss's stance, as if by declining to "fink" on his fellow prisoners he was protesting against the authority of the system that had unjustly incarcerated him.[39]

It is possible that Hiss hoped that his willingness to occasionally participate in inmate-generated subterfuge would be taken by his peers as evidence of his innocence. But it seems more likely that it was part of his strategy of remaining as

inconspicuous as possible in an atmosphere in which his image as a Communist traitor might trigger hostility at any time. As he prepared to leave Lewisburg in the fall
of 1954, he had already experienced one such response, the threats to him Mike M.
and his associates had headed off. Then, two weeks before his scheduled release on
November 27, another prisoner, William Remington, was killed by "a violent moun-
taineer from Kentucky." Remington's death once again raised the issue of Hiss's special vulnerability to his fellow inmates.[40]

Remington, like Hiss, was serving a sentence for perjury in connection with alleged spying for the Soviets. In 1945 Elizabeth Bentley had named him, along with
Hiss, as a Communist and Soviet agent in the series of interviews she gave to the FBI
after defecting from the Soviets. Bentley alleged that Remington had been a conduit
of information for the Soviets when employed by the War Production Board, for
whom he worked until 1944, when he entered the Navy and ceased espionage activities. The FBI recorded Bentley's information and began an investigation of Remington, but he remained in government service, and in 1946 was about to join the
White House as a special assistant when the FBI's information came to light, and his
appointment did not materialize. In 1947, he applied for a job with the Atomic Energy Commission, and the FBI, in the course of interviewing him, confronted him
with Bentley's charges.

In the course of the interview Remington admitted having met with Elizabeth
Bentley and two other persons who were known Communist Party members and
Soviet agents, but denied having passed on any classified information. He denied
ever having been a member of the Communist Party of the United States, and volunteered to make further contacts with the Soviet agents as an FBI informant. As a
result of his statement about his Communist Party membership, he was summoned
before a grand jury, and repeated the denial. He was subsequently indicted for perjury, and the prosecution produced incriminating testimony from his former wife
about his Communist Party membership. The scope and importance of Remington's
espionage activities paled in comparison to those of Hiss, but he was one of the few
persons on Elizabeth Bentley's list who sought to refute her charges rather than flee
the country or invoke the privilege of self-incrimination. As a result Remington
ended up in Lewisburg.[41]

Remington's death came about when he discovered the Kentucky prisoner attempting to steal cigarettes from his bathrobe pockets as he napped in his cell. By
awakening, and catching the thief in the act, Remington provoked him to retaliate,
and the Kentucky prisoner hit him several times on the head with a rock that he had
concealed in a sock. Remington suffered severe head injuries, and died despite receiving blood transfusions. Although the attack on Remington apparently had no po-

litical significance, when news of it reached the Justice Department the Lewisburg authorities were instructed to take special care to protect Hiss for the remainder of his time there.[42]

Hiss was summoned to the Lewisburg warden's office, and told that he would be taken from his cell in the honor block and placed in a locked cell in the quarantine wing until his release. He vigorously protested this action, arguing that his fellow inmates would take it as evidence that he was asking for special protection from them, a violation of the inmate code. Hiss asked that the head of the prison guards be solicited as to whether he thought Hiss in any particular danger. "I said [to the warden,]" Hiss recalled, "that if I were segregated, I would not cooperate with the move, would have to be carried, and in every way would make it plain to the other prisoners that the charge was not of my doing."

A compromise was reached in which a guard who was inoffensive to the prison population was assigned to "keep me in sight whenever I left my quarters." Hiss insisted that the guard "not come closer than 20 paces" to him, so that he did not interfere with Hiss's conversations during leisure activities. By the time of the Remington incident Hiss had become aware that the best way to ensure his safety in Lewisburg was to symbolically align himself with the inmates rather than the authorities. He knew, from the earlier incident, that protection was much more likely to originate from the former than the latter source. Moreover, the gesture of publicly refusing to be isolated from his fellow prisoners was consistent with adherence to the stoical code of the prisoner of war.[43]

The Lewisburg authorities' inclination to link the attack on Remington to the prospect of one on Hiss was a testament to the fact that during Hiss's time in prison the public had retained its general view of him as a notorious figure, whose arrest lent credibility to McCarthy's charges. Although Stalin died during Hiss's incarceration, relations between the Soviet Union and the United States, now complicated by the fact that both nations possessed nuclear weapons, had not improved. Bomb shelters were built throughout America, and the Soviets tightened their grip on the East European members of the "Communist bloc." Hiss's placement at Lewisburg prompted members of the public to write numerous "vitriolic" letters about him to prison officials during his stay there. One official reported that "[t]here was a public uproar" when Hiss's sentence was automatically reduced from 60 to 44 months under the applicable "good behavior" statute, and Lewisburg authorities received several threats to Hiss's well-being as his release became imminent. The officials' insistence that Hiss be shadowed by a guard after Remington's murder may have irritated Hiss, but it was not irrational, given Hiss's provocative image in the early 1950s.[44]

On November 27, 1954, Chester Lane, now Hiss's chief litigator, drove to Lewisburg in a red convertible, with Priscilla and Tony, to pick Alger up. The group drove uneventfully from central Pennsylvania to New York City, but Tony later remembered that the police helicopter hovered above Lane's car for part of the way. Tony also recalled that Priscilla "kept pounding the back of the front seat and shouting, 'Keep calm, Chester! Keep calm!' " No threats materialized, and when Hiss settled himself in New York, he could take some comfort in having successfully coped with 44 months in an environment that contained the usual privations of prison and added dangers for him. He had kept the fiction of his innocence intact, but, from all accounts, had not overplayed his hand, saying little about his case. He had shrewdly observed the groups within the prison population and managed to form associations with the best-adjusted and most powerful group. He had carefully refrained from making critical comments about other inmates, so that some who observed him closely believed that he was a tolerant person with a capacity to see good in everyone. A conversation Hiss reported to Tony suggests that stance of tolerance might not have been wholly spontaneous. One day in the exercise yard, Tony noted, "another guy asked [Hiss] what he thought of the people in there." Alger's initial response was that "he thought they were interesting."[45]

That response was very likely genuine: Hiss was a person of great intellectual curiosity whose subsequent comments on his Lewisburg experience indicated that he was highly attentive to the social backgrounds and attitudes of individuals and groups in the prison population. But Hiss's companion was seemingly puzzled by the response. "Interesting," he said to Alger. "What the hell does that mean?" Hiss then said, "I mean I like them." His companion responded, "Oh, why didn't you say so? That's different." After recording the conversation, Tony added, "One way and another, [Alger] learned a lot. The first things to learn were manners." "Manners," in this case, were the art of not suggesting that an educated, cultured person such as Hiss might be looking at his companions as he might study animals in a zoo. His "interest," the response suggested, was a form of affection.[46]

Hiss's stance toward his fellow prisoners at Lewisburg demonstrated his remarkable powers of self-control. He had entered a situation radically incompatible with his personal fastidiousness, his highly developed intellectual and cultural tastes, and the many years in which he had functioned as a privileged and accomplished figure. He nonetheless managed to convey an impression that the striking discontinuity between his past life and his present situation had not adversely affected him. This was all the more intriguing because Hiss hated prison. In none of his accounts of his Lewisburg experience did he portray it as helping inmates to live better lives. He de-

Hiss's "mug shots" on leaving the Lewisburg penitentiary in November, 1954.

clined to participate in efforts at prison reform after being released. In 1974, when the Nixon White House was in disarray and the prospect of jail time threatened to extend to Nixon himself, Hiss had a conversation about Nixon's prospective incarceration with his brother Donald. "Don't ever send anybody to jail, it's a terrible place," Donald recalled Alger saying.[47]

As part of his effort to develop a prisoner-of-war mentality, Hiss resolved to maintain contacts with some of his fellow inmates after he and they had been released. This prompted a conversation, which he reported in his memoirs, about the interpretation of the standard parole condition that a former inmate not "associate with criminal elements" during the parole period. Hiss told the Lewisburg authorities that he "could not in good conscience" agree to the condition, and that if it were to be strictly enforced, "there was no sense in my leaving the penitentiary, for I would not attempt to live up to the restriction." After some delay, he was informed that the requirement, whose strict enforcement could hardly have been anticipated, would "not be so construed in my case."[48]

The bonding with fellow inmates reflected in this exchange was apparently reciprocated by those who had spent time with Hiss in Lewisburg. In addition to the inmate Murph's effort to meet Hiss when the prison bus containing released inmates arrived in New York, a story surfaced that when Hiss was released from Lewisburg the prisoners left behind saluted him with cheers and applause. The story first appeared in print in 1960, when Brock Brower, in the course of stating that "Hiss's success in prison derived from human qualities that it would be hard to fake," asserted that "there were rousing cheers from the bleak prison windows" when Hiss "went out of the gates on November 27, 1954." Meyer Zeligs repeated the story in 1967, and in *Laughing Last* Tony Hiss said that when Alger "walked out the main gate other inmates jammed the windows and cheered and applauded." In his memoirs, however, Hiss only said that "[a]s I walked through the prison courtyard and the gates, I was surprised and touched to hear farewells called to me by many friends crowded behind the barred windows." The last account seems most plausible. But whether or not Hiss's fellow inmates actually applauded him when he left Lewisburg, the story demonstrates that Hiss was able to separate his antipathy for the experience of prison from his responses to some of the inmates he met there.[49]

The various accounts Hiss and some of his contemporaries gave of his time at Lewisburg offer comparatively little information about his inward reactions to his prison experience. Two sources, however, provide some sense of those reactions. One is a set of comments Hiss made to the psychiatrist Meyer Zeligs in the 1960s about the "continuing and intensive self-examination" that he "start[ed] in on" while at Lewisburg. The other is a series of letters, published in 1999 by Tony Hiss, which Alger wrote to Priscilla and Tony from prison. Both sources need to be used with care. Hiss's comments to Zeligs have the distinctively cautious and impersonal tone Hiss adopted to anyone except intimates, and his letters to family members were mindful of censoring authorities and designed to appeal to an adolescent male in a sometimes precarious emotional state. But both contain some clues to Hiss's inner thoughts and feelings as he sought to cope with the prospect of nearly four years in a federal penitentiary.[50]

Zeligs, in the course of researching a book on the psychological relationship between Hiss and Whittaker Chambers, prodded Hiss to become "more knowledgeable about psychic forces." Eventually Hiss made an attempt to characterize some of the thinking he had done at Lewisburg in psychological terms, even though he was disinclined to "inflate the significance of my effort by suggesting an analogy to real psychoanalysis." He had, he told Zeligs, devoted time "at night after lights out at 10 P.M., and the not-infrequent periods when I was left alone in the storeroom . . . with no books" to "prolonged and undistracted concentration." During those periods, he recalled, "[I] examine[d] my major goals, tolerance for types of strain, ethical standards, capacity for affective relations, self-control, willingness to assume responsibility, sense of affirmation, ability to live in and savor the immediate, historical outlook, ... spontaneity, forthrightness, consideration for others."[51] This process enabled him to identify the dominant "attitudes" he held. He then sought to discover the sources of those attitudes, reflecting on "early family relations and atmosphere and training; church, school, neighborhood, summer farm life, the Scouts, camp, college, and professional influences." He considered "the impact of my own marriage and being a parent." He then attempted to associate his "emotional responses" with the attitudes. Those responses included "anger, affection, pride, pleasure, serenity, euphoric states, [and] boredom." He tried to identify the sources of those responses, and to chart his reactions to "pain, to intensive work, [and] to long hours of work night after night."

His goal, in undertaking this self-examination, was to "know better what my capacities were for the immediate future [in Lewisburg] and for later on." By "concentrated attention" to his defining attitudes and responses, he was seeking to "reexamin[e] and extend my personal philosophy." He told Zeligs that the self-examination "was not done *in vacuo*," but included observations of "my daily reactions to my fellow prisoners and the guards and officials," as well as "considerable reading and thinking" about "ethics," "social customs," "history," and "psychology."[52]

The introspective exercise Hiss described to Zeligs appears initially to be part of a strategy for coping with the prospect of several years of prison. Tolerance for types of strain, self-control, willingness to assume responsibility, ability to live in and savor the immediate, spontaneity, forthrightness, and consideration for others were attitudes conducive to making the task of living in a prison population easier. Anger, affection, pride, pleasure, and boredom were emotions commonly triggered by the deprivations of prison and efforts to cope with them. The more Hiss was able to channel his attitudes to generate positive emotional responses, the better time he was likely to have in Lewisburg. The more he understood the sources of those attitudes, the more likely he might be to accomplish that channeling. In one respect, then, the "continuing and intensive self-examination" that Hiss undertook at Lewisburg was part of his coping strategy. It was designed to help him "make the best" of his time in prison.

In some of his letters to Priscilla, Alger provided more detail on the process of applying his self-examination to the experiences of prison life. In one he addressed "the theme of tests of essential personal *values,*" characterizing values as "quite different from the optimum *circumstances* which allow them full expression." Prison, he felt, "can be an excellent test of one's basic values . . . [f]or those who so regard it." He contrasted two states of being: "peace of mind" or "serenity," which came from "a complex blending of experience with understanding" that produced "inner growth without self-absorption," and "bitterness," which came from the "inability of inner values to accommodate [and] permit continued spiritual *growth* from . . . external events." Prison was an experience filled with "[e]vents that wound," potentially "disarrang[ing]" one's values. But "the adult personality," the "large of soul" could surmount "[c]ircumstances [that] may block the normal sharing and giving of the personality."[53]

The key to serenity and fulfillment, as Hiss put it in another letter to Priscilla, was "respect for man's potentialities and the attempt always and everywhere to further their growth." He resolved to treat prison as an experience in which he would be constantly learning and growing, and he found that his charm and resonance enabled him to serve as a confidant for other inmates and even officers. He was exposed to "letters, family photos, reminiscences, future plans, personal problems," sometimes in the form of "aimless and rather pathetic chatter," which induced "boredom." But in his conversations he also experienced the "natural dignity and psychic candor" of some of his acquaintances, which freed them from "self-abasement, over-assertiveness, [or] self-consciousness." In his conversations with racket guys and other prisoners Hiss not only learned about the codes and customs of a prisoner-of-war ethos, but also of "the affirmative outreach and aspiration of spirit which is the natural accompaniment and source of wholesome human growth and maturation." He asked Priscilla to help supply additional words of "affirmation, outreach, and aspiration" so that he could better describe "the emotionally healthy man."[54]

The last comment suggests that Hiss's efforts to reexamine his attitudes and emotional responses while in prison were not simply designed to help him cope with incarceration. They were also, as he had put it to Zeligs, part of a "plan for later on." The self-analysis Hiss undertook at Lewisburg can be seen as connected to his superordinate goal of convincing others of his innocence and thereby vindicating his reputation. Here one gets a glimpse of Hiss's abiding, even fanatical dedication to that goal. He knew that he was not innocent, and that any vindication would be the successful selling of a lie. He also knew that to achieve vindication he would need to exhibit many of the qualities, and assume many of the intellectual and emotional attitudes, that he felt would help him cope with the deprivations of a prison envi-

ronment. He would need to be flexible and at the same time dogged in the face of periodic strain. He would need a considerable measure of self-control. He would need
to cultivate a resonance and empathy with others who might be inclined to support
him. He would need an ability to project a "sense of affirmation," and of serenity,
as part of the process of convincing others that he was innocent. He would need to
suppress anger, and channel it into persistent, dedicated campaigning against his
enemies. He would need to be mindful of history and the phenomenon of change
over time, and he would need an awareness of "social customs" and of human psychology.[55]

One can see how some of the successes Hiss achieved at Lewisburg might have
energized his pursuit of the goal of convincing others that he had been an innocent
victim. He had entered a prison atmosphere conducive to humiliation and fraught
with personal danger, and emerged as an inmate whom most of his peers accepted
and liked. He had avoided being labeled a pariah or a malcontent, and had done so
without any modification of his claim of innocence. He had demonstrated to himself that he could endure, and even prosper, in an inmate population whose members, on the whole, had very little in common with him and many reasons to distrust
or despise him. When he left Lewisburg, he may have felt that the first major test of
his self-conscious response to adversity had gone rather well. Prison might be a terrible place, but he had reason to believe that he had, within limits, fashioned it to his
advantage.

Meanwhile, as Hiss remained incarcerated from the spring of 1951 to the fall of
1954, the outside world moved around him, and bits of information from it pene-
trated Lewisburg. In addition to the *New Yorker* and the *New Statesman*, Hiss also had
access to newspapers, so that he was not entirely bereft of news from outside. He
was, however, severely restricted in his correspondence. On entering Lewisburg he
was asked to make a list of seven persons with whom he would be permitted to
communicate. He was allowed to write a total of three letters a week to those persons. He could only receive a total of seven letters a week. He designated Priscilla,
Tony, Timothy Hobson, Minnie Hiss (who was 83 when he entered Lewisburg),
Donald Hiss, his sister Anna Hiss, and his lawyer Helen Buttenweiser. He told Minnie that she could only write him once a week, and she did for the duration of his
sentence, writing on Sundays. Priscilla sent him at least four pieces of mail each
week, many of them envelopes containing postcards with reproductions of paintings that Alger admired.[56]

The restrictions on Hiss's correspondence meant that most of his letters from Lewisburg went to Priscilla and Tony. The letters to Tony were not only circumscribed by the fact that prison authorities would be reading them, but by the emotional reaction Tony had to his father's imprisonment. Tony later characterized his condition during those years as "lost, totally out of my depth, struck dumb, frozen solid, a real boy transformed into a block of wood." In the fall of 1952, when Tony was 11, Priscilla took a job, and Tony became a latchkey child, coming home to an empty apartment after attending the Dalton School. By early 1953, after Tony had suffered a series of accidents and begun to talk of urges to stand in front of subway trains, he was taken to a psychiatrist twice a week after school, and on other days, Priscilla began to leave work early. Aware of Tony's predicament, Alger took special pains to write letters that his son might appreciate, which may have contributed to their resolutely upbeat tone. But it is likely that the "supportive, cheerful, chatty" quality Tony remembered in the letters was not simply a device to reassure him and Priscilla. By adopting that stance in his letters Hiss was also reinforcing his determination to make the best of his immediate present and to set forth a positive vision of his future.[57]

As Hiss entered his second year at Lewisburg, working in the storeroom and lodging in a second-floor dormitory, Whittaker Chambers's autobiography, *Witness*, began to be serialized in the *Saturday Evening Post*. The book was to become a best seller, in part because the serialized excerpts exposed readers to Chambers's dramatic writing style. *Witness*, which appeared as Senator Joseph McCarthy's charges that Communists had infiltrated the federal government were gaining national attention, and as the Soviet Union's successful development of nuclear weapons had been made public, was a gripping drama of Cold War espionage. Hiss found himself in the uncomfortable position of lingering in prison while his chief accuser made money by accusing him all over again. Nonetheless he began reading Chambers's excerpts as soon as they appeared, writing Priscilla, on February 7, 1952, that she "must read what [the *Post*] has added to the Great Books." He added that "[a]ny enlightened layman will realize at once that [*Witness*] is the product of a seriously disturbed psyche." In evaluating *Witness* he drew a contrast between the "liberating affirmation" he was seeking to achieve in prison and the "self-imprisoned despair" that "doomed" Chambers.[58]

This sort of letter, with references to outside events and his enemies, was rare among Hiss's prison correspondence. Much more common were letters taking up three more mundane themes. One set of letters, called "Nature Notes" or "Window Watching," consisted of sketches of and reflections upon the natural surroundings of Lewisburg. Another was a series of fictional stories for Tony, modeled on the

Uncle Rebus stories, featuring a "sweet, simple, mischievous, and comically vain-glorious" figure called the Sugar Lump Boy. The third was a running commentary on Alger's effort to teach Leo M., whom he referred to as the "B.R." and "M.R." ("Beginning" and "Middle Reader"), to read and write.

All three sets of letters were designed to entertain and amuse Tony, thereby distracting him from the loss of his father's companionship and lifting his spirits. They had another purpose as well. In those "cheerful and chatty" letters Alger was seeking to demonstrate to Priscilla, and to convince himself, that he was strong and resolute enough to make the best of his personal ordeal, and to help others along the way. The letters were designed to provide evidence that he was performing acts of "liberating affirmation" in circumstances that might have seemed more conducive to bitterness or despair.

The "Window Watching" letters were vivid descriptions of uneventful features in the landscape outside Hiss's prison window. They were also designed, however, as testaments to the benefits of cultivating a capacity to "observe" one's surroundings in a meaningful way. In an August 1952 letter Hiss defined what he called that "[r]ewarding" version of "observation." It consisted of learning to recognize "the constant and ubiquitous marvels of life," as distinguished from what was conventionally termed "something worth looking at." His point was that most humans simply took their natural environment for granted, only reacting to unusual phenomena. The cultivated observer, however, appreciated the distinctive elements in a landscape, and how those elements subtly changed on a daily basis. He also understood that trees and fields and the sky were remarkable phenomena in themselves, sustaining human life and surviving over eons of time.

Hiss tried to capture this dimension of observing natural phenomena in the prose of his "Window Watching" sketches. Central Pennsylvania, he wrote in October 1951, was a "land of rolling fields and second-growth woods," where autumn was "long and leisurely and full of ripe fruition, with none of the New England sense of summer's death and of urgency to batten down the hatches of life." A "long and stunning" sunset on November 1951 ended with "numerous large purple clouds dominating the south and west." On March 1, 1953, he mentioned "a baby blizzard" followed by "a brilliant dazzling hour in cold sunlight." The moon, as it set in the morning sky one late September morning in 1953, appeared "quick-silver, with the sheen of a fish's belly flashing under water and the craters like global maps." A "real central Penn. autumn evening sky" featured "a long-lasting radiance that arches widely till it merges with a powder-blue after-sunset" color. "The luminosity is extraordinary and seems to have the pulsating quality . . . of Northern lights."[59]

In descriptions such as those Hiss employed words associated with sensual or physical stimulation (ripe, stunning, brilliant, dazzling, flashing, radiant, luminous, pulsating) to describe natural surroundings. The choice of words suggested that the observer of a fall landscape, a sunset, a moon in the morning sky, a sunset, or a twilight sky was being uplifted by affirming something elemental in nature and human responses to it. Sometimes Hiss sought to underscore the elemental dimensions of his observations by connecting them directly to experiences of his readers. After describing the luminosity of an October twilight sky, in a letter written after Priscilla and Tony had visited him at Lewisburg, he added, "I hope thy little group has a clear and 'typical' sky to light it homeward." On another occasion, after describing the "positive ecstasy" of birds chirping "over the damp meadows," he felt that "[t]he paper [of his letter] must have absorbed some of it." "Perhaps if thee and T sit very still," he told Priscilla, "you can hear a faint repetition."[60]

The point of the "Window Watching" letters was obvious enough. A man in a prison cell, in the midst of a largely grim and oppressive environment, looks at sunsets and skies and landscapes through a barred window. By noticing the beauty of the outdoors, the man was coming to appreciate the ways in which common qualities of the natural world were always available to bring beauty and pleasure to humans. The man, as Hiss put it, was "learning and growing." He was making the best of a bad situation, and letting his loved ones know that he was doing so.

Hiss's window watching was thus a way of reaffirming goals he had set for himself on entering prison. Each time he wrote an evocative description of his natural surroundings to Priscilla and Tony, he demonstrated to himself that he had learned how to extract something uplifting and useful from mundane features of his environment. Window watching was a kind of reward for the iron discipline Hiss was imposing on himself while trapped in Lewisburg.

The "Sugar Lump Boy" Hiss created for Tony also served multiple purposes. Those stories featured a "Tony" character, a mentor to the Sugar Lump Boy. The Sugar Lump Boy habitually needed guidance, made mistakes, or got discouraged, but despite his foibles, the Tony of the stories was invariably good-natured, patient, and helpful. When the Sugar Lump Boy wanted to pass a swimming test before learning to swim, Tony taught him to dog-paddle, and then float, and then kick his feet, and eventually he swam across the width of a pool. When the Sugar Lump Boy, having watched Tony practice basketball, brought out a Ping-Pong ball and a basket made from paper clips, Tony "laughed and told the S. L. B. his ideas were very good," but they could use "baskets and a ball from [a] mechanical basketball game."

When the Sugar Lump Boy "missed 6 shots in a row," and declared, "I *hate* basket-ball," Tony "very calmly . . . asked the S. L. B. to come and sit by him and watch the others for a while." Then he told the Sugar Lump Boy, "Don't worry if you miss. I used to miss a lot when I started, too." Sometimes, despite Tony's help, the Sugar Lump Boy didn't learn as quickly as Tony. One day he came home from the grocery store with fresh baked bread that he had squashed to fit inside a toy cart. Tony "ex-plain[ed] that it would have been easier to ask the grocer to cut the bread in half." Subsequently the Sugar Lump Boy came home "with half a grapefruit, cut-side down, in the rather dirty wagon." Looking "very proud," he told Tony, "I wasn't going to make the same mistake twice!"[61]

After rereading the "Sugar Lump Boy" letters as an adult, Tony Hiss concluded that they were efforts to "show . . . me how to do something, or encourage . . . me to try again when I was feeling defeated." They were also efforts on the part of Alger to encourage himself to make the best of his time in prison. Faced with the prospect that his absence, as Tony entered puberty, might further erode Tony's self-esteem, Alger had invented stories about a figure who "was in worse shape and needed [Tony's] help right away." Creating the "Sugar Lump Boy" stories helped Alger deal with any guilt associated with his required withdrawal from his family at a critical time in Tony's maturation process. Alger could feel that he was making use of his imaginative and communicative talents to reach out to his son despite their separation. That feeling helped sustain him as well as Tony.[62]

The "Window Watching" and "Sugar Lump Boy" letters, although covering different topics, were thus parallel exercises. Hiss was simultaneously seeking to shore up the emotional reserves of his family, especially Tony, and to execute strate-gies for preserving his own self-respect in an environment where humiliation and degradation were familiar conditions. That exercise took its most direct form in the largest group of Lewisburg letters that Alger wrote on any particular topic, those in which he described to Priscilla and Tony the process by which he taught Leo M., a member of the racket guys, to read and write. In his memoirs Hiss described Leo M. as natively intelligent but "[c]ompletely illiterate," someone whom the prison's Ed-ucation Department was "not equipped to teach . . . basic reading and writing skills." Hiss took on that task, and after regular sessions that extended over several months, succeeded. He called Leo, in his letters to Priscilla and Tony, the "Beginning Reader," or "B.R.", and eventually the "Middle Reader."[63]

The importance Hiss attached to his education project with Leo M. can be seen in the fact that he devoted 87 of the 445 letters he wrote Priscilla and Tony from Lewisburg to descriptions of his work with the B.R. or M.R. The letters began in

the fall of 1951 and continued through March 1954, when Leo was released on parole. In the earliest of the letters Alger, then living in a dormitory, told Tony that
"one of the young New Yorkers in my dorm never learned to read or write," and
was "very sensibly using some of his spare time to do so." Hiss advised him to get
his wife to send him some "new readers [from] the school in their neighborhood,"
and expressed "hope that he'll let me help whenever he gets stuck." But five months
later, in March 1952, he continued to characterize Leo as a "non-reader." A "modest birthday gathering" for Leo had been held in Alger's cell in the honors block,
to which Alger had been assigned the previous December. Leo, who received permission to come to the honors block for the party, told Alger that "[h]is studying
[had] been zero for the past four months." Because the winter weather had kept the
prisoners indoors, and Leo and Alger had been in separate quarters, Alger had
"had no chance to help him." Leo had gone through "a period of negativism"
about reading and writing in the interval. But he told Alger at the party, "I *must*
learn to read. This way I am blind," and Alger hoped to "be able to nudge him along
a bit."[64]

By May 1952, Leo had been transferred to the honors block, rejoining Alger and
Mike M., whom Alger typically called the "t.o." ("tall one") in letters to Priscilla and
Tony. This development, and the return of mild weather, enabled Alger to "help the
Beginning Reader with his letter from home . . . each day." From that time on he
spent "[t]he noon hour, regularly, and the pre-supper and pre-yard time, often,
[with] reading lessons." Leo's prison job had nighttime hours, so after going over "2
new pages at noon" every day with Hiss, he reviewed the pages in the afternoon
while Hiss worked in the storeroom. Although learning to read and write was "hard
and discouraging," Alger wrote Tony, Leo's "enthusiasm and perseverance is wonderful."[65]

For the next several months Alger provided an account of Leo's quest. In June
1952 Leo "wrote the last 4 or 5 lines of his letters to his wife." By December he
could "spell and write over 350 words," which had "led to a new interest in words and
in spelling by some of my other friends." They would "'casually' slip into a conversation about some $5.00 word like 'fastidious' and wait expectantly for a rise from
someone." They "started a vocabulary list," and had "impromptu spelling bees."
When some remained "blocked by writing," which "[made] them very self-conscious
and their good, quick brains just freeze," Alger and Mike M. would "ask . . . quietly
what [they] wanted to say." One, "the Barber" (given that name because that had
been his profession before coming to Lewisburg), "gulped, sighed, and quite naturally and sensibly told." Hiss and Mike "then said, 'That's fine, go ahead and write

it just that way.'" "'The Barber' looked at us in great surprise, saw we meant it, relaxed and finished in 10 minutes."[66]

By January 1953, Alger reported that "[t]he B.R. is now getting interested in long words," such as "'possibilities.'" He asked "the tall one [t.o.] challenge him to spell it—then very proudly [spelled] it correctly." Tony had been dutifully impressed, and when Alger reported this to Leo, the Beginning Reader was a "little disappointed" that Alger hadn't also mentioned his mastery of "audacity," which "he quite rightly regards as still trickier." By the end of January Leo was "justifiably proud of having written for the first time a letter to his wife entirely without help." "He said," Alger wrote to Tony, "he had a kind of feeling he had never had before and that the words came to him as if he had always known them."

Meanwhile Leo had begun to read a book on American history, *Heroes, Heroines, and Holidays,* in the Education Department's library. The book was one the Beginning Reader could easily grasp. "He read over several pages with me right before supper," Alger reported. "Since then he hasn't been able to leave it alone—he finds it so amazing that he . . . can now read something he is interested in for what it tells him, not just to practice reading." "That book's like a toy," he told Alger, "with his face shining."[67]

By March 1953, Leo had written a letter to his brother without help. By September he was reading *Robinson Crusoe* in what Alger judged to be "about at 5th grade vocabulary." He was also scanning newspapers and magazines. By November Hiss was able to introduce Leo to John Beaty's *The Mountain Book,* designed for older children, which contained "much sound geologic information interestingly presented and illustrated." Leo's "progress is so marked," Alger told Tony, "that he must hereafter be known as the Middle Reader!" After Thanksgiving Alger reported that "the real holiday event . . . was the terrific achievement of [Leo] in reading 25 pages of *The Mountain Book,* which in Alger's view was "up to 7th grade standards." Leo's "enthusiasm, progress (actually from day to day), and his pleasure in accomplishment" were "pretty to see."[68]

January 1954 produced the culminating event in Leo's journey out of illiteracy. He "wrote a letter for a friend who is unable to write." Alger saw the episode as "an important symbol to [Leo] of how much he has accomplished." The event came at "a good psychological moment" as well, Alger thought, because Leo's time in prison was coming to a close, and he was being transferred to the prison farm, reserved for inmates of good behavior who were soon to be released. "[I]t is good for him," Alger wrote Priscilla and Tony, "to realize that he no longer needs help, *but on the contrary can give it.*" By March Leo had "made parole on a reconsideration of his case," and after reporting the news to Hiss, "skipped and danced happily down the road to the farm, turning from time to time to wave at the storeroom window where I stood applauding the celebration." Leo left Lewisburg on March 25, 1954, in Hiss's view "a very happy and self-possessed young man."[69]

On one occasion Whittaker Chambers spoke of Hiss's "great gentleness and sweetness of character," and on another of his "deep considerateness and gracious patience." That impression of Hiss was echoed by many others who encountered him over the years. Some were struck by Hiss's notable talent for making strangers feel welcome and at ease in his presence, as if he appreciated their company and cared about them. Others noted his capacity for random acts of kindness, sometimes to persons he encountered on the street or barely knew. Commentators on Hiss's career, in the course of summoning up reasons for their belief in his innocence, often pointed to examples of his sweetness or selflessness.[70]

Hiss's tutelage of Leo seemed to be another illustration of those qualities. He and Leo had been thrown together in prison, Hiss learning of Leo's illiteracy only because of his connection with Mike. Leo was so devoid of reading and writing skills that the prison educators could not help him, and tutoring him was going to require so laborious an effort that not even Mike could summon up the energy to attempt it. But Hiss took on the task, even after recognizing that he must give up his leisure time to accomplish it. The result was that he devoted hours treasured by inmates to patiently attending the efforts of an illiterate to decipher written English in its most elementary versions. Alger Hiss, whose life before Lewisburg had been marked by a thirst for highly sophisticated forms of written and artistic expression, consequently spent months sitting alongside an inmate while he traced his finger across the pages of books designed for first-graders.

Hiss's tutelage of Leo was clearly a generous endeavor. He not only endured Leo's efforts, he committed to a practice of regular advisory sessions, even though he did not occupy the same position of responsibility to the other racket guys that persons such as Mike held. Moreover, Leo could hardly have failed to notice that Hiss was taking great pleasure in his progress. That fact shines through the B.R. and M.R. letters. Not only did Alger report more regularly on Leo's quest than on any other topic, he eventually announced to Priscilla and Tony that Leo's learning to read and write had changed him from a depressed person who thought himself "blind" to a "self-possessed," happy individual who can come to realize that he not only could read and write, but could help other illiterates learn to do so.

The qualities that led Alger Hiss to use his precious leisure time at Lewisburg to help Leo need to be considered, in any assessment of his personality, along with the qualities that led him to take advantage of the need of several persons to trust in his veracity and believe in his innocence. It is possible to fashion an explanation for Hiss's acts of kindness and generosity, coupled with his acts of clinical detachment and conscious betrayal, that views both sets of acts as part of an overriding personal and social agenda; Hiss's quest to integrate his self-absorption with his altruistic public goals.

Hiss recognized that he was an instinctive and a habitual altruist. He liked helping people in need, even if the help imposed burdens on him. Caring about, and helping others, reinforced his sense of his own powers. "I like people when they are in trouble," Hiss said to his son Tony in the 1970s. "[T]hen they have to like you, and you can feel powerful by helping them." The transforming moment for Leo in his journey out of illiteracy, Hiss thought, came when he realized that he could read and write well enough to help an illiterate write a letter. The transforming moment for Hiss in his journey along with Leo had likewise come when he was able to report that his pupil had realized that he no longer needed help, but on the contrary could give it. Hiss italicized the last words to show their importance to him. Those who could help others no longer needed help themselves. Altruism, for Hiss, was a means of demonstrating his own independence and control of his destiny.[71]

Control over his own life, including the secret dimensions of that life, was a state that Alger Hiss deeply cherished. He took pleasure in his ability to carve out a favored slice of life, and, when his life became less favored, to carve out a thinner slice within that. The slice had included helping others as long as he could remember, from the time when he implicitly realized that he needed to help his mother by being, in addition to a talented son, a dutiful and appropriately directed one. He had helped his brother Bosley during his last illness, his brother Donald when he became seriously ill, Priscilla Fansler when she faced the loss of a potential husband and an unborn child. In his mind he had even helped Justice Holmes expand the pleasures of reading.

In helping Leo to read, in being a friend to Mike and the other racket guys, in assuming the role of a diligent, uncomplaining prison worker, in seeking to improve the educational resources of Lewisburg prisoners but never crossing the line between well-behaved inmate and agitator, in doling out legal advice in the exercise yard, in never ratting on inmates who abused him, Hiss was demonstrating to himself that he could shape a potentially dangerous, brutalizing experience into a slice of life where his powers of self-control were actually strengthened. He emerged from

Lewisburg chastened about the experience of prison—he never placed any faith in incarceration as a rehabilitative exercise—but more confident than ever about his capacity to create a life for himself that might eventually approximate the life he had contemplated before his perjury trials. Prison had threatened to break Alger Hiss, perhaps even eradicate him as it had eradicated William Remington, but Hiss had emerged more sure than ever that his essential self was intact, and his search for self-fulfillment still on course.

That search's social dimension also survived Lewisburg. By carefully distancing himself from his notorious past—neither admitting complicity nor seeking to portray himself as a victim—Hiss began to convince his inmate acquaintances that he was innocent. But that had not been his principal goal. His principal goal had been to ensure that the social agendas to which he had dedicated himself—agendas precipitated by his loyalty to the ideals and aspirations of Soviet Communism—remained intact, undisturbed by his prison experience. He did not choose to enlist any of his prison acquaintances in the campaign for vindication he had promised to undertake after being convicted of perjury. Only his lawyers, his family, and intimate friends on the outside remained engaged in that campaign while he was in Lewisburg. Those persons were to learn, if they had not already done so, that Alger Hiss's campaign to "prove" his innocence would be an integral part of his social agenda when he was released from prison. For Hiss, convincing the public that he had been an innocent victim of a malevolent political culture, not a Soviet agent, was intimately connected to the overriding goal of helping the ideals of Soviet Communism spread throughout the world. He was prepared to betray the trust of loyal friends, and family members, to pursue that goal. He had demonstrated to himself, in prison, his great capacities for self-discipline under stress. He had structured his prison relationships with that goal in mind. Even the obvious delight he took in teaching Leo to read had been a way of disciplining himself and opening up possibilities to the common man.

But Hiss's social agenda was primarily a secret agenda. He chose to conceal it from most of his acquaintances, burying it beneath a narrative in which he portrayed himself as the unreconstructed survivor of a breed of New Dealers who were dedicated to alleviating the lot of the economically disadvantaged, fighting Fascism, and achieving international peace. In that cover role, he was occasionally passionate but usually lighthearted and good-humored. As a secret Soviet Communist, he was a highly disciplined, extremely dedicated true believer: someone resembling a fanatic. When he left prison, and circulated in the ordinary world, he allowed his "deep considerateness and gracious patience" to infuse many of his personal relationships, so that to some admirers he appeared a person who radiated inner tran-

quility and a kind of saintliness, very far, despite his notoriety and reduced circumstances, from being a bitter or broken man. By helping others, Hiss helped himself
make the best of his lot. But all the while he was devoting energy to the welfare of
others, he was keeping some things for himself. His secret life, with its unarticulated
but deeply held social goals, remained intact.

An advertisement for *Friendship and Fratricide* by Meyer A. Zeligs, 1967.
The description of Zeligs's book appears on the left, and a close-up photo
of Whittaker Chambers on the right.

CHAPTER FOUR

The Campaign for Vindication

On November 28, 1954, after Alger Hiss was released from Lewisburg, he and Priscilla began to take stock of their lives.[1] The prospects were not particularly rosy. Hiss had lost his license to practice law, and anticipated that "informal blackballing" would affect his efforts to find a job. He quickly found that assumption confirmed. "Friendly prep schools and college administrators," he recalled in his memoirs, "were politely negative," being "aware of the likely attitude of trustees and contributors." He explored opportunities in the publishing industry, and in other "business concerns." Nothing materialized. For the time being, the Hisses's financial situation was not dire, because while in prison Alger had secured advances from American and British publishers for the book he planned to write. They amounted to $10,000, which, together with Priscilla's salary from her work at the Doubleday bookstore, enabled the Hiss family to live "simply but certainly not in penury."[2]

Hiss's decision to write a book meant that he intended to remain in the public eye. But he was initially unclear about the scope or content of the book. He first thought of writing "a philosophical discussion on civil liberties, the limits of court procedures in times of public hysteria." He did not plan "to argue the case, or to write another *Witness.*" But "literary friends" suggested that he write on his own case rather than attempt "a generalized commentary." One of his lawyers, Robert Benjamin, urged him to "keep [the book] accurate," even if "that would make it dull." Benjamin told Meyer Zeligs that he thought Hiss was in an awkward position. His prospective audience, Benjamin felt, "would have been satisfied only by a confession of guilt or of covering up for someone else who was guilty." Benjamin didn't see "how one who has been convicted of perjury could have proclaimed his innocence with flourishes and expected the public to believe him." Then there were "the extraordinary emotional qualities" of Whittaker Chambers's *Witness,* Benjamin noted, and Alger Hiss was not known for his emotional prose.[3]

Hiss eventually did write on his own case, taking two years to produce a draft manuscript. But he was determined to give a first priority to some public statement proclaiming his innocence. This decision did not sit well with Priscilla. "[D]omestic troubles began within half a year of my return" from Lewisburg, Alger wrote in *Recollections of a Life.* Priscilla "had been deeply wounded by the trauma of the trials," and had "met with various slights and acts of hostility, or thought she did." When Hiss was released, "Priscilla wanted us to flee the scenes of her torment. She suggested we change our names and try to get posts as teachers at some remote experimental school oblivious to public opinion."[4]

Hiss's view was "directly to the contrary." His "objectives" and "personal needs," he believed, required that "public prejudice should be confronted and faced down." He intended to "write about the travesty of the HUAC hearings and the trials" as a step "toward my ultimate vindication." Priscilla found that decision "profoundly distasteful." She thought that Alger's efforts to retrace the story of his trials would be "sure to keep . . . her worst times of nightmare . . . alive." She "distanced herself" from the book, and although he dedicated it to her, took "no pleasure" in its appearance. Her resistance to the book became a symbol of the "fixed gulf" between them as their "disagreement as to our future goals became irreconcilable."[5]

The estrangement of the Hisses would eventually free up Alger to change the focus of his campaign for vindication. He had initially claimed that his personal life was uninteresting, and that he greatly valued his privacy. When his book appeared in 1957, it was a legal brief for his innocence, almost devoid of comments about the Hisses's private life. Although Hiss was initially more comfortable with such an approach, it also had the advantage of forestalling further scrutiny into the effect of the Hiss case on Priscilla and the Hiss family.

Alger knew that Priscilla had reacted emotionally to his indictment. Her reaction, he later suggested, bordered on hysteria. In conversations with his son Tony in the 1970s, Alger described life with Priscilla during the period of his trials:

> Prossy [went] into a type of collapse. I tried to impart courage to her. I'd always known that she frightened easily. . . . [T]here was this constant . . .

anxiety that . . . was impossible to calm. If you eliminated one damned thing, talking rationally and reasonably, there was always another. God, it was burdensome to go over her anxieties at length. Every day seemed a new wound to her. One blow after another. I felt I wasn't getting across. And, by God, the last thing I wanted after a long day with the lawyers was a long anxious talk session with Prossy. . . . Prossy got into a near paranoid state. She believed the walls of our apartment were bugged.[6]

During this period, Hiss recalled, he felt that "it was essential before anything else that [Priscilla] be supported." He attributed this feeling to that fact that "[l]oyalty is a very big thing in my life," an "old southern tradition." He saw Priscilla as "dependent on me, and I had to support her." When Alger was released from prison, he attempted to change the dynamics of their relationship. "I suggested that we not be so closely entwined, that we each have independent activities." In his campaign for vindication, he noted, "I had to speak more frankly." Priscilla "would not accept suggested changes," stating that "any change was disloyal to the noble, splendid, beautiful ideals we'd shared."[7] The campaign, for her, became a symbol of Alger's refusal to let go of a period in their lives that she associated with feelings of anxiety and disgrace. She wanted for the Hisses to disappear, to the point of changing their names; he wanted to keep public attention on the Hiss case.

Eventually the irreconcilable attitudes of the Hisses toward Alger's campaign for vindication would result in their separating. The decision to separate came in the fall of 1958, but they resolved to continue living together until Tony, a senior at the Putney School at the time, returned for the Christmas holidays. Alger then spent "the next several years in rented rooms and friend's apartments," Priscilla remaining in their Greenwich Village residence.[8]

Throughout the 1960s, Alger recalled, he and Priscilla "made several attempts at reconciliation, but the differences that had developed were too great, and the wounds we had dealt each other were too deep." The "differences" may have been accentuated by the fact that Alger and Priscilla no longer had the bond of participating in espionage together. Although Alger may have been interested in a kind of vicarious reliving of his covert career as he proceeded on his campaign for vindication, he could hardly resume his career as a Soviet agent, even had he wanted to. He was, in the jargon of the spy trade, "blown," and Priscilla was as well. To an important extent, the shared activities in Alger and Priscilla's marriage, from the early 1930s to the mid-1940s, had consisted of children and espionage. By 1959 Timothy Hobson was living his own life, Tony was about to go to college, and Priscilla and Alger were out of spying forever. And by the 1970s Alger's "loyalty" to Priscilla had apparently diminished, and the abiding sense of personal and family privacy he had referred to after returning from Lewisburg had lessened as well. He began conveying to sympathetic biographers some quite personal information about Priscilla and the Hiss family.[9]

In interviews with Tony and John Chabot Smith in the 1970s, which were undertaken with books about his life in mind, Alger revealed that the "major operation" Meyer Zeligs described Priscilla as having in the fall of 1929 had been an abortion.[10] He also told Alden Whitman, his initial choice as authorized biographer, that the name of the man who had fathered the child was William Brown Meloney. Hiss also mentioned that his elder son, Timothy Hobson, had been discharged from the navy after a homosexual episode, and was not called as a witness during Hiss's perjury trials so that that family secret would not be revealed. On the basis of that information John Chabot Smith offered an explanation for why Priscilla had been such an ineffective witness at the trials (she was afraid she would be asked about the abortion) and why Hiss had not allowed Timothy to testify when his evidence—that he had been in the Hiss home on an occasion when Whittaker Chambers had claimed to have received stolen papers from Alger, and had not seen Chambers—would have been helpful to the Hiss defense.[11]

Priscilla's attitude toward Alger after their separation seems to have been ambivalent. Tony said that after he graduated from college in 1963 and "moved back to Prossy's apartment" in New York while working for the *New Yorker,* she "alternated between cursing Al for leaving and making plans for what she'd do after he came back." She refused to divorce Alger, who had become involved with another woman as early as 1960. When Alger was asked to give some lectures at the New School for Social Research of the City University of New York in the 1960s, Priscilla attended all of them. "[S]omewhere in her psyche," Alger speculated, "with all the trauma the case represented, the rope she clung to was: loyal wife."[12]

Priscilla's comment about Alger's proposal that the Hisses lead more independent lives after his return from Lewisburg is suggestive. He recalled her as stating that any change would have been a betrayal of the "noble, splendid, beautiful ideals" they had shared. By that she might simply have meant ideals of solidarity and mutual support in a marriage. But she might also have meant the ideals of dedication to the better world that she believed the Soviet Union to represent. By pursuing his campaign for vindication, she might have felt, Alger was only increasing the risk of his definitive exposure. It was clear, however, that Alger was prepared to take that risk. And with his estrangement from Priscilla, responsibility for shielding her from public scrutiny no longer needed to be one of his priorities.

Hiss's decision to make a book publicly defending himself his first project after Lewisburg previewed the grand theme of the remainder of his life. When he was released from Lewisburg he had already decided that that theme would be a campaign to vindicate his reputation by convincing the public of his innocence. Each of the looking-glass wars that remained for Hiss would be connected to his campaign for vindication. He would die, 42 years after being released from prison, still proclaiming his innocence.

Whittaker Chambers, on noting that Hiss planned to mount a campaign to establish his innocence after being released from Lewisburg, thought he understood why. All Hiss needed to do, Chambers suggested, was to persist in his campaign until one elderly resident of Hartford, Connecticut, said to her companion, "I don't see how Alger Hiss could brazen it out in that way unless he were innocent." At that point, Chambers said in his vivid fashion, "that is victory" for the Communists. Alger Hiss, Chambers thought, would have succeeded in hoodwinking the American public with the Big Lie. That was what one should expect from Communist agents.[13]

But no other Soviet agents who were Hiss's contemporaries, once exposed, responded by launching a massive, lifelong campaign for vindication. Julius and Ethel Rosenberg, even more notorious figures at the time of their 1951 conviction for passing atomic secrets to the Soviets, insisted on their innocence, but they were facing the death penalty, and their execution precludes any speculation as to how they might have reacted over time. The same might be said of William Remington, who claimed that he had been wrongfully convicted of perjury in 1951: Remington's death at Lewisburg forestalled any campaign he might have launched. Morton Sobell, who was associated with Rosenberg's network and was convicted of atomic espionage in 1951, has continued to maintain his innocence, but not in the vociferous fashion of Hiss. The same can be said of Judith Coplon, convicted in 1950 for giving Justice Department counterintelligence files to a Soviet undercover agent. Coplon's conviction was subsequently reversed because of illegal searches and seizures on the part of the government. She has never admitted working for the Soviets, but her habitual stance has been to avoid public exposure altogether.

Several other less well-known persons, convicted of spying for the Soviets between 1955 and 2001, have denied participating in espionage, but have not chosen to publicly proclaim their innocence and seek vindication. In addition, a number of Americans accused of espionage have cut deals with the authorities, publicly recanting their sins in the process, or taken advantage of the privilege against self-incrimination and quietly dropped from public view.[14] Protestations of innocence and deal-cutting are not unusual among persons accused and convicted of crimes, and may be particularly evident where espionage is involved. Nonetheless Hiss remains unique in two respects. One was the length, energy, and public nature of his exoneration campaign. The other was its remarkable success. Of all his contemporary Soviet agents, only Hiss was exposed, convicted, imprisoned, and then nearly vindicated. And his near vindication came without his producing a shred of credible new evidence that tended to exonerate him.

Thus the first project on which Hiss embarked after prison, and the first major consequence of his effort, his estrangement from Priscilla, were symptomatic of his life to come. By entering into a campaign for vindication Hiss signaled to his closest friends and supporters that there would be no getting beyond his central mission in life. One could either enlist in Hiss's campaign or distance oneself from it. One could either choose to believe that Hiss was an innocent scapegoat or refuse to participate in the fashioning of a narrative of innocence. There was no other alternative. To believe in Alger Hiss, one had to believe in his campaign for vindication.

One of the earliest opportunities afforded to Hiss to publicize his campaign came in the spring of 1956, when he was invited to Princeton University to speak on the "Meaning of Geneva," a disarmament conference between the United States and the Soviet Union held in the summer of 1955. The invitation came from an undergraduate debating organization, the Whig-Clio Society, which, in an effort to boost sagging attendance, had sent out invitations to a number of visible public figures, including Vice President Richard Nixon, Senator Joseph McCarthy, and labor leader John L. Lewis, in March 1956. Hiss had remained on parole for 16 months after being released from Lewisburg, and had been prohibited from making any public appearances during his parole period. That period expired at the end of March 1956, enabling him to accept the Princeton invitation.[15]

When the Whig-Clio Society announced that it had invited Hiss to speak on April 26, an outcry began among Princeton alumni. Prior to the invitation's being made public, Princeton administrators had attempted to dissuade the society from issuing the invitation, one arguing that Hiss, a convicted perjurer, was "using Princeton's prestige to launch his rehabilitation effort." But once the invitation was made, the Princeton administration defended it. Its principal argument was that although the Whig-Clio Society had been "rash, stupid, and silly" in inviting Hiss, student organizations should have the autonomy to make their own decisions. The Princeton student newspaper supported the administration, stating in an April editorial that it was better for Princeton to host controversial speakers than to buckle to "outside pressure groups," including alumni. Alumni who opposed Hiss's invitation stressed that he was a "convicted traitor," and argued that his presence sullied the idyllic place that Princeton represented.[16]

After he learned of the reaction to his invitation, Hiss contacted the president of the Whig-Clio Society and asked if they wanted to reconsider inviting him. When the president responded that the invitation was still open, Hiss said that he was planning to come. Meanwhile the Princeton Board of Trustees, at a regularly scheduled April 20 meeting, unanimously disapproved of the invitation to Hiss, but voted, 26 to 4, to "leave upon the students' shoulders the responsibility for their action." By then the invitation had become the subject of debate in Congress and had received ample coverage in the press. Over 500 representatives of the press asked for credentials to cover Hiss's speech, and the Princeton administration was faced with a potential circus. Accordingly, Princeton took a number of steps to minimize fallout from Hiss's appearance. His talk was limited to 20 minutes, with a 10-minute question period. Only 200 students, and 50 members of the press, were permitted to attend. No photographs were permitted, and the usual post-speech reception was canceled.[17]

Before the speech, Hiss had dinner at the home of Princeton history professor Elmer Beller, a friend. He and Beller were accompanied to the speech by a police escort, Hiss recalling that "as I walked with two faculty friends to the building where I was to speak, we were forced to pass between lines of irate American Legion veterans and alumni." Paper-mache pumpkins and signs with pictures of typewriters had appeared on the Princeton campus the morning of the speech, and the message "Traitor Hiss" was painted on the steps of Whig Hall, where the speech took place. Seven hundred persons, many of them representatives of the media, thronged outside Whig Hall as Hiss spoke. But the speech itself was an anticlimax. Hiss himself called it "moderate, rather dull I was told," and a Princeton administrator described as "duller than *The New York Times* editorial." "The story ended when Hiss walked in the front door," a reporter on the scene commented.[18]

Although Hiss had seen the Princeton invitation as his "initial opportunity to break out of Coventry," it had only confirmed his pariah status in the 1950s. Although Princeton alumni and administrators vigorously debated the invitation to Hiss, no one advanced the position that Hiss's incarceration had been a miscarriage of justice. Both sides agreed that he was a "convicted traitor": the issue in the debate was whether students, when they showed themselves capable of making bad judgments, should be permitted to do so. Not even those in the Whig-Clio Society who had urged inviting Hiss indicated that he might have been innocent. To the extent they knew who Hiss was, they had wanted to invite him because he was controversial and would boost their attendance. Their assessment was correct on both counts.[19]

Thus as a potential step toward rehabilitation and eventual vindication, the Princeton speech was hardly a success. And other events in the 1950s brought home to Hiss how far away he was from those goals. The range of opinions among commentators on his case remained strikingly narrow. To illustrate, between 1950 and 1952 five essays appeared in literary journals on the Hiss case, precipitated by the jury verdict or the publication of Chambers's *Witness*. The essays were written by Leslie Fielder and Diana Trilling, who combined literary analysis with a liberal political perspective, and Arthur Koestler, Granville Hicks, and Sidney Hook, each of whom had been popular-front Communists in the 1930s and had subsequently become outspoken in their denunciations of Communism. All of the essayists declared their belief that Hiss had rightly been convicted of perjury and had engaged in espionage, and that Chambers should be honored for his efforts to oppose Communism, including his frank admission of his own Communist past. The essays can be seen as forecasting the widely shared perception of Americans, throughout the 1950s, that Alger Hiss was a convicted traitor.[20]

Two defining themes of American culture in the period between the later 1930s and the early 1960s had contributed to the widespread public acceptance of Hiss's convicted traitor status. The first was the recoil of American intellectuals from Soviet Communism, and the resultant collapse, in the community of persons who regarded themselves as political "progressives" or "liberals," of any sympathy for the popular-front collectivism of the 1930s. The Stalinist purges, which began in earnest in 1937 and precipitated Chambers's defection, were one signal of the dark side of the Soviet state; the Hitler-Stalin pact in 1939 another. The official entry of the United States into World War II in 1941 escalated the stakes for supporters of collectivist policies, which were practiced by the Nazis as well as the Soviets. By the close of World War II the *Partisan Review*, a symbol in the 1930s of popular-front politics and avant-garde culture, had become an organ for anti-Communism and the integration of liberal politics with mainstream artistic ventures. In this altered intellectual and cultural climate, there was precious little space for former enthusiasts of the Soviet ideal. Their only hope for respectability was to follow Chambers's path, that of open renunciation of their former pro-Soviet sympathies and vigorous engagement with anti-Communism. By the 1950s, anti-Communist ideology dominated not only American foreign politics but domestic politics as well.[21]

The other theme was to combine with anti-Communism to make Senator Joseph

McCarthy into a cultural icon for a brief stretch in the 1950s. It was the emergence of a powerful wave of anti-intellectualism.[22] As postwar America integrated returning service personnel into the population, large numbers of persons began moving out of cities to suburbs, and institutions of higher education proliferated, the cultural influence of elites and intellectuals began to wane. McCarthy's appeal was not only to rabid anti-Communists but to those who identified with his antiestablishment stance in the Senate: he was a junior senator, with few connections, when he first announced the number of Communists who had infiltrated the federal government. The 1952 and 1956 presidential elections, pitting a plain-spoken, sometimes inarticulate general against the cultured, witty, and gentlemanly Adlai Stevenson, represented a version of culture wars, and Eisenhower won decisively.

In this atmosphere Hiss was a charged figure, although perhaps somewhat inaccurately perceived. He had appeared at his trials as the very model of a cultured, liberal, establishment intellectual, with ties to Johns Hopkins, Harvard Law School, Holmes, and the State Department. But although he was regularly described as "patrician" (and continued to be portrayed as such in subsequent literature on the Hiss case), his immediate family had had only a few years of wealth, which ended when he was an infant: his elite educational training had been the result of scholarships or the contributions of his uncle George. Although Hiss and Chambers, an unprepossessing former "Bohemian," seemed to be contrasting social types, their economic and educational backgrounds, up to the time they entered college, had been quite similar. But none of this mattered in the face of the inflammatory dimensions of Hiss's career that emerged at his perjury trials. He was, on the surface, a spoon-fed representative of the eastern upper class who had turned leftward, joined the Soviets, and infiltrated the federal government. He was an example of the potential consequences of the otherworldiness of the elite intelligentsia.

These public perceptions of Hiss had some practical consequences as well. After submitting his manuscript to Knopf in the fall of 1956, Hiss began to look for a job. He took a typing and shorthand course in order to make himself a more marketable private secretary, but found he could not master touch typing, nor acclimate his earlier "speedwriting" technique to the course's shorthand system. He approached each job interview with a "boundless self-confidence," but after several months, nothing had materialized.[23]

A portrait of Hiss in this period of his life was supplied by Hiram Haydn, an editor at Random House publishers, who was asked to give Hiss an interview in 1954, shortly after Hiss had been released from prison. Hiss, Haydn recalled, "was looking for any kind of freelance editorial work," and he was curious about Hiss. Haydn then described the interview:

For the first ten minutes of our meeting, I was much impressed. . . . He was quiet, dignified, and—most of all—bore himself with no trace or either defensiveness or aggressiveness.

More than an hour later, I was bewildered. Mask succeeded mask, role role, personality personality. There was a half hour during which our actual situation was reversed, as though *he* had granted *me* an interview. He asked me many questions about my work, suggested improved methods for running the editorial department, etc. All, no doubt, with an eye for how he might fit into the Random House structure. But the authority with which he spoke suggested he was *in charge*.

Suddenly something brought this phase to an end, and he became gaminlike, elusive, answering my questions with the manner of a shrewd, precocious boy who was playing games and admiring his skill at them.

Another shift, and he seemed abruptly defensive. There were fear and suspicion in his expression, and he answered me in guarded monosyllables. This attitude passed like a summer storm, and he reverted to his original personality. We concluded our talk pleasantly, no hint at his (unconscious) other impersonations remaining.[24]

Haydn had been one of the early recipients of a technique Hiss practiced on many other potentially sympathetic persons he encountered in the years after his release from prison. Perhaps because of the circumstances of his interview, which might have led to a job for Hiss, Haydn had a fuller exposure to Hiss, and was able to get a sense of Hiss's complex and layered personality. Several other persons who met Hiss derived only the impression that Haydn got during the first ten minutes of his interview: Hiss was a gracious, dignified figure, without any traces of bitterness or defensiveness. Many took this impression to be a kind of proof of Hiss's innocence. But Haydn had seen more. There was Hiss's formidable managerial side, which had brought him success as a government bureaucrat. There was his cultivated evasiveness, exhibited in a talent for not quite answering questions and creating false impressions without actually lying. There was his occasional defensiveness, which would surface when a wall in an elaborate cover story threatened to be breached, as when his interviewer expressed sympathy for a person Hiss, in his cover life, was not supposed to have known. All told, Haydn had discovered Hiss's talent for manipulating others. He had glimpsed it more readily because Hiss was not simply settled into a familiar role in his cover story. He genuinely wanted something from Haydn, so he was more inclined to reveal his talent for taking over a conversation.

In the end Hiss did not get a job offer, as was the case with all of his interviews in the first two years after he left prison. But finally, in the spring of 1957, his book, *In the Court of Public Opinion*, was published, and in connection with its publication Peter Kihss of *The New York Times* wrote a profile of him. In the profile Kihss mentioned that Hiss was looking for a job. One of the persons who read Kihss's profile was Andrew Smith, the president of a company called Feathercombs. Smith had designed a "backless comb made of looped piano wire" that was particularly effective in holding women's hair in place when swept up on the top or back of a head. He used a type of resilient piano wire from Sweden, and employed Japanese workers to bend it. He then added rhinestones, producing a light, strong, and decorative hair barrette. He had secured a patent for the comb.[25]

Smith wanted to hire someone to restructure Feathercombs's operations so that the company could expand and eventually issue stock. He was not interested in the details of the restructuring, and he felt he could secure Hiss's services for less than market value. In this he was correct. Hiss agreed to go to work for $100 a week, and Smith rejected that figure as unconscionably low, paying him $6,000 a year. By 1959 Hiss's salary had been raised to around $11,000. Feathercombs, however, was under siege. Although Hiss's efforts to reorganize the corporation had been effective (despite the fact, Smith recalled, that "[e]veryone eventually had a run-in with Alger because he was such a driving perfectionist"), Feathercombs' market position was being undermined.[26]

A "major manufacturer of women's hair accessories," Hiss recalled, "brought out a plastic comb similar to ours." The comb was not as effective at keeping hair in place, but it was sold at a cheaper price, and the manufacturer had "long-established relationships with stores in every sizable city." After being hired Hiss had retained Walter Beer, a partner of Chester Lane, as "general counsel to pass on contracts and other corporate problems," and Beer recommended a suit against the manufacturer for patent infringement. The suit appeared promising, but when Feathercombs failed to get an injunction prohibiting its competitor from selling combs while the patent suit was pending, its financial future became troublesome. The denial of the injunction meant that the manufacturer's lawyers could engage in delaying tactics while its combs remained in the market. Feathercombs was vulnerable to those delays because its competitor's combs had cut into Feathercombs' sales, and Feathercombs only made combs. Smith, however, believing that the patent suit would eventually succeed, turned down offers from the manufacturer and the Gillette Company to buy Feathercombs. By August 1959, the company was "living from hand to mouth," and Hiss proposed that he "should leave as soon as I could find another job."[27]

Five months later he had not found one. After leaving Priscilla, he had moved into what a journalist in 1960 described as "a third-floor walk up, a sad building with a tattered green awning over a vacant store front." His savings had been exhausted paying for his legal appeals. Congress had passed a statute, openly directed at him, which denied a pension to any employee of the federal government convicted of perjury in a case involving national security. His perjury conviction had also resulted in his losing his license to practice law in Massachusetts and New York. He lived off of unemployment benefits for most of the winter of 1959, and when he eventually found a job selling stationery in the spring of 1960, his starting salary was about $75 a week. Brock Brower, who wrote a profile of Hiss that appeared in the December 1960 issue of *Esquire,* described him as "more or less broke" and "in straitened circumstances."[28]

His book had neither been a literary nor a financial success. Reviews described it as "heavily legalistic," "dully written," having "a curiously flat quality," and "not very interesting." It relentlessly argued again the case that Hiss had lost on appeal, and was almost entirely devoid of emotional vitality. Brower found the book "steadily more wearisome," and noted that reviewers found that it "offer[ed] no new evidence that might change the public's mind." But Hiss told Brower that "[t]he book," which had been "written as a lawyer's brief," was "all I have to say about the case." He did not plan to write an autobiography, he said, nor "to write about my time in prison" because he felt there was "nothing that interesting about my life" and "I hold certain strong views about privacy."[29]

One might have thought from Brower's interview that Hiss was about to disappear into the inconspicuous, prosaic life of the average American. The last paragraph of Brower's article described Hiss as walking "across lower Fifth Avenue . . . going after that most mundane of American goals, . . . a customer." Hiss was seeking, Brower felt, a "retiring but useful life . . . much below the high drama of the Case." Although continuing to proclaim his innocence, he had not sought out publicity. But Brower had run across Hiss at a time in which he felt that most members of the public continued to think of him as a convicted traitor. Joseph McCarthy was dead, but the Soviet Union and the Cold War were still in the forefront of American consciousness.[30]

Brower quoted the sole public comment Whittaker Chambers made on Hiss after his conviction. Chambers, noting that Hiss had been granted a passport in 1959, had supported the decision, but added that "I cannot say . . . that Alger Hiss has paid any effective penalty" because "he has defiantly refused to . . . speak the truth" about his involvement with Soviet espionage. Most Americans would have agreed with Chambers. Knowing that, Hiss did not seek the public limelight. But his campaign for vindication remained as central to him as it had been when he left Lewisburg.[31]

Hiss had not fully represented his attitude to Brower in 1960. A few months before Brower interviewed him, despite his claims to Brower that he valued privacy, had no interest in writing an autobiography, and did not think his life was particularly interesting, Hiss had begun to engage in a series of intensive personal interviews with Meyer Zeligs, a psychiatrist who was preparing a book on the relationship between Hiss and Whittaker Chambers. Although Hiss began his discussions with Zeligs by "express[ing] the feeling that his private life had little bearing on the case," he eventually agreed to talk about "all aspects of his life, private and public, personal and political." Over a six-year period, Hiss gave Zeligs access to his defense files, which included "all correspondence, confidential memoranda, investigators' reports, [and] legal briefs." Hiss's relatives provided Zeligs with "an abundance of anecdotes dating from his childhood." Hiss talked to Zeligs about the suicides of his father and his elder sister, the resentment he felt toward his mother, the anguish he experienced when his brother Bosley died, his courtship and marriage to Priscilla, and Priscilla's and his subsequent estrangement and separation.[32]

Here was an apparently radical about-face from the posture toward his personal life and feelings Hiss had adopted in the Brower interview. Nonetheless Hiss had his own reasons for thinking that broad-ranging cooperation with Meyer Zeligs might help his campaign for vindication, and that his campaign might appeal to some new audiences. Among those reasons, four were probably of greatest importance to Hiss.

First, Hiss had exhausted the legal arguments for his innocence. After being stymied, at his trials, by the problem of the similarity of the typeface on Hiss family correspondence and that on the stolen government documents Chambers testified to having received from Hiss, the Hiss defense team had sought to surmount that problem, in their appeals, by producing new evidence that Chambers, or someone in league with him, could have built a typewriter whose typeface was nearly identical to that owned by the Hisses. They did not succeed in that effort. But if one believed that a forged typewriter could have been produced, this left the question of why Whittaker Chambers would have been motivated to frame Hiss. Lawyers for Hiss had already attempted to produce an answer to that question. Chambers, psychiatrists for the defense had testified at Hiss's second trial, was a deeply disturbed individual, a "sociopathic personality" with a tendency to engage in pathological lying. He also had an obsession, perhaps homoerotic in nature, with Hiss.

If one were inclined to find this view of Chambers credible, and one believed that Chambers or his cohorts had the capacity to build a typewriter with a matching typeface to that on the Hiss family machine, a demonstration of Hiss's innocence—or at least a demonstration of reasonable doubts about his guilt—turned on more concrete evidence about the nature of Chambers's pathology, and about his relationship with

Hiss. In short, the case for Hiss's innocence now rested on extralegal evidence. No one was more aware of this than Hiss himself. He had not only exhausted his legal appeals, but he had made an effort to summarize, in *In the Court of Public Opinion,* all the legal evidence on his behalf, and he recognized that the public had been indifferent to that appeal.

Cooperating with Zeligs appealed to Hiss because Zeligs was interested in the extralegal dimensions of the Hiss case, particularly in the psychological relationship between Hiss and Chambers. As such Zeligs was likely to engage in the sort of psychiatric speculation about Chambers's personality and his reaction to Hiss that the defense psychiatrists had attempted at Hiss's second trial. Hiss knew that Zeligs had an acquaintance with one of those psychiatrists, Dr. Carl Binger, who had pointed out in his testimony that one of the books Chambers had translated from German, Franz Werfel's *Class Reunion,* dealt with themes of obsession and betrayal that Binger felt were suggestive of themes in the Hiss case. Hiss was also aware that Zeligs was strongly attracted to Binger's "obsession and betrayal" hypothesis. "I felt I was definitely on the track of certain factors in [the] human equation that had not been examined in the literature on the [Hiss] case," Zeligs wrote in his preface to the book he eventually produced on Hiss's and Chambers's relationship.[33] By revealing personal information to Zeligs, Hiss believed that he could help Zeligs flesh-out a portrait of the Hiss-Chambers relationship that might incline readers to believe that Chambers had motives, however disturbed, to frame Hiss.

Hiss had an additional reason for cooperating with Zeligs. In two letters written to Hiss lawyers in 1960 and 1961, Zeligs revealed the likely approach he would take in his book and strongly intimated that he thought Hiss was innocent. In the first of those letters, written to Hiss's personal lawyer Helen Buttenweiser, Zeligs asked for copies of Binger's testimony at the second trial, as part of a "clinical . . . psychoanalytic investigation."[34] The fact that Zeligs was planning to make use of Binger's testimony provided a clue to his stance, which he was to make explicit in *Friendship and Fratricide.* "I . . . find it difficult to understand," he wrote, "how the reliability and credibility of Chambers could have been accepted or given serious consideration once his clinical picture had been portrayed" by Binger. Eventually Zeligs was to claim that Chambers's motives for framing Hiss centered on his associating Hiss with his elder brother Richard, for whom he had erotic feelings and who had committed suicide. Chambers, Zeligs believed, lead an "itinerant and vagabond existence," had a "sociopathic personality," was "amoral," and was an "unreliabl[e] . . . witness." And the "central issue" in the Hiss case "boiled down to" whether "Hiss or Chambers was lying."[35]

If there was any doubt about where Zeligs stood on the question of Hiss's innocence, it would have been dispelled by a subsequent letter Zeligs wrote to Claude Cross, Hiss's lead counsel at his second trial. "I can readily appreciate your strong sentiments about Hiss's innocence," Zeligs said in a March 13, 1961, letter to Cross. "[A]nd [I] must say that I share the same conviction." It appears that Chambers and his supporters may have likewise been aware of Zeligs's inclinations. Neither Chambers nor any of his family, friends, or attorneys cooperated with Zeligs in his project. Although Zeligs described his posture in the book as one of "careful analytic neutrality" toward his subjects, the fact was that he believed Chambers to be a disturbed liar and Hiss his victim. Hiss had every reason to alter his posture about his personal life and the Hiss case, given the opportunity that Zeligs's book presented.[36]

Zeligs's book was important to Hiss's campaign for vindication in one additional respect. It suggested that since the key to establishing Hiss's innocence was more likely to lie in human motivation rather than in legal evidence, it was crucial to emphasize features of Hiss's public persona that would resonate among American audiences. Hiss's conviction had actually rested on the strength of the prosecution's evidence rather than on the comparative credibility of the chief protagonists in the case. In his testimony Chambers admitted that he had been a Communist and a Soviet agent for several years, and that he had lied to the House Un-American Activities Committee about the nature of Hiss's activities. The Hiss defense strategy was centered on establishing his credentials and reputation for honesty and integrity, and on attacking Chambers's reputation. The testimony of the psychiatrist witnesses produced by the defense was designed to suggest that Chambers was a seriously disturbed personality. But none of these tactics was able to surmount the prosecution's evidence that Hiss had had a far closer relationship with Chambers than he had admitted to having, and that Chambers had access to documents that had been typed, as far as anyone could determine, on a Hiss family typewriter.

From the outset, then, the legal evidence gathered by the Hiss defense was weak, forcing it to rely on extralegal factors such as the credibility of the protagonists. Zeligs's book was projected as another exercise in undermining Chambers's credibility, suggesting reasons why he might have wanted to frame Hiss, and portraying Hiss as a sympathetic figure. As a work of scholarship, which it purported to be, *Friendship and Fratricide* was an almost comical failure. The book announced itself as an intensive psychological analysis of the Hiss-Chambers relationship, but Chambers declined to cooperate with Zeligs. Consequently Zeligs's extended speculations about Chambers's early life and personality were based on the testimony of psychiatrists employed by the Hiss defense and Zeligs's conjectures. In contrast, his speculations about Hiss were based on information mainly provided to him by Hiss and Hiss's lawyers and friends.

But *Friendship and Fratricide* was nonetheless an important event in Hiss's campaign for vindication. It succeeded in humanizing Hiss, and revealing some of the tragic events of his early life as no previous work on the Hiss case had done. And it collected some extralegal arguments that Hiss could use in his campaign. When a new audience for those arguments appeared on college and university campuses in the late 1960s, Hiss was poised to advance those arguments, and to offer a fresh portrait of himself.

Zeligs's said in his preface to *Friendship and Fratricide* that the idea for a book on the relationship between Hiss and Chambers had taken shape when he read the Earl Jowitt's 1953 book, *The Strange Case of Alger Hiss*, and Fred Cook's 1958 book, *The Unfinished Story of Alger Hiss*. Jowitt, who was in retirement when his book appeared, had been a distinguished English barrister, eventually becoming the Lord Chancellor of England. In the preface to *The Strange Case of Alger Hiss* he described how he first became interested in the Hiss case:

> Some time ago, when I was still Lord Chancellor, I had sent to me the full transcript of the second trial of Alger Hiss. . . . It had struck me, from the little I did know, as being a case of unusual interest. . . . But whilst I was still in office, I had no spare time to devote to a reading of the case. Now that I have more leisure, I have read the case and analysed the evidence.[37]

Jowitt's preface also revealed why he had a particular interest in the Hiss case. He referred to the "striking differences between a trial in the Courts of the United States and a trial in the English courts," which were made even more "far-reaching" for him by studying the transcript of Hiss's second trial. He also alluded to the "high reputation for integrity" that Hiss had "previously enjoyed on both sides of the Atlantic," which required that "the case against him should be established beyond any peradventure." Both those comments informed the critique of Hiss's conviction that Jowitt put forth in *The Strange Case of Alger Hiss*. Although he primarily focused on what he took to be the unacceptably liberal American rules about admitting and commenting on evidence at trial, he raised, along the way, the two themes that would form the heart of Hiss's extralegal defense. The first was that if Hiss had actually typed stolen government documents on a family typewriter and passed them on to Chambers, only an "utter fool" would have allowed that typewriter to remain in circulation once Chambers broke with the Soviets. Hiss's motivation, in short, seemed inexplicable if he were guilty, but explicable if he had been framed. The second was that some information Chambers revealed in *Witness*, coupled with psychiatric testimony at Hiss's second trial, made Chambers appear "quite out of the ordinary." Jowitt did not make precisely clear what information he meant, but he appeared to have thought that Chambers's suicide attempt, in which he planned to inhale gas fumes from rat poison while he slept, was bizarre, and that the possibility that Chambers may have wholly fabricated a trip he claimed to have taken with the Hisses reinforced the psychiatrists' suggestion that Chambers was a pathological liar.[38]

Jowitt also speculated that because of the anti-Communist paranoia in the United States at the time of the Hiss trials, agencies of the United States government had incentives to appear zealous in their pursuit of alleged Communists in the government, and Hiss might have been a scapegoat. He suggested that Chambers himself might have gained access to the Hiss family typewriter. Fred Cook was to elaborate on those themes in *The Unfinished Story of Alger Hiss*. Cook's book consisted of a popularization of the principal arguments raised by Hiss's lawyers in his unsuccessful motion for a new trial in 1952, to which he added speculations about Chambers's instability, his possible hatred of Hiss, and the "official collaborators" who may have helped Chambers "in the perfection of his story and the completion of his deed." He suggested that both the FBI and HUAC had political reasons for victimizing Hiss, and the FBI may well have had the resources to build a typewriter with a typeface that appeared to match that of the Hiss family. Hiss, Cook concluded, might have been "an American Dreyfus, framed at the highest level of justice for political advantage."[39]

A shorter version of *The Unfinished Story of Alger Hiss* had appeared in the *Nation*, a magazine that identified itself as solidly pro-Hiss in the 1950s. The *Nation* had been politically "progressive" since the 1920s, and under a series of editors and publishers had remained sympathetic to popular-front collectivism after many New Deal liberals had abandoned that stance. By the 1950s the *Nation* and another New York-based journal, the *New Leader*, had identified themselves with the two prongs into which New Deal liberalism split after the Soviet Union became identified as America's chief international antagonist.

Although the *New Leader* continued to support domestic programs associated with the liberal wings of the Democratic Party, it was virulently anti-Soviet and anti-Communist. In contrast, the *Nation* maintained that Fascism remained a larger global threat than Communism; that the Soviet Union's policies were nationalistic rather than ideological; that the Cold War was principally a product of American paranoia about the Soviets; that the Communist Party of the United States was lacking in influence and had no ambitions to undermine the American governmental system; and that Joseph McCarthy and the attacks on civil liberties that he helped foster were far more of a domestic threat than the Communists. The increasingly opposing views of the *New Leader* and the *Nation* came to a head in 1951, when Clement Greenberg, a former *Nation* staffer, wrote an article in the *New Leader* in which he accused the foreign editor of the *Nation*, Julio Alvarez del Vayo, of "consistently echo[ing] the interests of [the Stalin] regime" in his columns. The *Nation* sued the *New Leader* for libel. Although the suit was eventually dropped in 1955, the incident further polarized liberal opinion and identified the *Nation* as "soft" on Soviet Communism.[40]

The publishers and editors-in-chief of the *Nation* from the 1940s through the 1970s, who included Freida Kirchwey, George Kirstein, Carey McWilliams, and Victor Navasky, were all sympathetic to Hiss. Kirchwey was an advisor to Hiss during his perjury trials, and recommended Claude Cross as his lead counsel for the second trial. Kirstein's wife, Elinor Ferry, assisted Helen Buttenwieser's research on Hiss's 1952 motion for a new trial. McWilliams and Navasky, in their tenures as editor-in-chief of the *Nation*, would make it the chief outlet for articles sympathetic to Hiss in the 1960s and 1970s. Among the persons Zeligs acknowledged as providing him with assistance in the preparation of *Friendship and Fratricide* was Elinor Ferry, who gave him access to the notes and memorandum she prepared after interviewing some of Chambers's associates in connection with the 1952 motion for a new trial.[41]

Zeligs indicated that his "clinical curiosity about the lives of Hiss and Chambers" was "first stirred" after reading Jowitt, and that Cook's account "focused . . . my attention on the riddle of the [Hiss] case," which centered on the motivation of Hiss for allegedly being a Soviet agent, and that of Chambers for waiting ten years to accuse him. Thus Zeligs's book drew on the two strands of Hiss's extralegal defense: the pathological, possibly revengeful personality of Whittaker Chambers and the political incentives that agencies of the United States government, in the Cold War years, had for framing Hiss. He popularized the arguments that were to be central to Hiss's campaign for vindication from the 1960s on.[42]

From the appearance of *Friendship and Fratricide* through his death in 1996, Hiss's campaign for vindication sounded those themes. His campaign, increasingly, was about the character and personality of Whittaker Chambers, and those of his other prominent antagonists, notably Richard Nixon and J. Edgar Hoover, and about the "Cold War" political atmosphere in which he was tried. By the 1970s he would en-

Alger Hiss in 1967, when his campaign
for vindication was beginning to gain
momentum.

tirely reverse the emphasis of the defense
he had outlined to Brock Brower in 1960.
He had told Brower that he had said all he
had to say about his case in his "brief," *In
the Court of Public Opinion,* and that he
had no intention of talking about or writing about personal aspects of his life. By
the 1970s he had already cooperated with
one author who was writing about his
personal life and was in the process of cooperating with three more. And although
he would make one more legal attempt at
vindication, a *coram nobis* petition he filed
in 1978 to set aside the verdict in his second trial, he introduced no new exculpatory evidence in that petition.[43]

One of the major adjustments Hiss
needed to make, as he mounted his campaign for vindication over the years, was
to minimize the sorts of defenses with
which he was instinctively comfortable—defenses centering on the precise way in
which evidence was given, and introduced, in formal legal proceedings such as
committee hearings and trials—and to emphasize other kinds of defenses, those related to politics, political attitudes, and human sympathies and antipathies. Hiss
needed to learn that the acuity of his mind and his penchant for careful, precise language, which had stood him in good stead as a lawyer, were not much help to him
in mounting extralegal arguments for his innocence. They made him appear cold,
evasive, bland, and unsympathetic. He was better off, in his campaign, appearing as
a scapegoat, a victim, a dupe. He was better off characterizing his opponents as unscrupulous politicians or false friends. He was better off if the public thought that
he had been a quixotic champion of his wife, or the innocent casualty of Whittaker
Chambers's revenge, or Richard Nixon's ambition, than if it thought he was a highly
credentialed, self-possessed, shrewd New Deal lawyer.

It was helpful to Hiss that he did have a streak of blindness and naiveté, which caused him to engage in some acts that actually helped convince supporters that he was innocent. But, on the whole, he needed to shed the careful lawyer's skin he had worn at the HUAC hearings and at his trials, and take on another, artificial, campaign skin: that of the political victim. Hiss did a remarkably good job at that adjustment, given that he knew just how artificial the skin was.

Hiss also received the benefit of a new generation of persons who were more inclined to be sympathetic to his characterizations of himself as the victim of malevolent anti-Communist zealots, both in and out of government. As he had struggled to find a job and to secure a receptive audience for his campaign in the early sixties, the "New Left" movement in American politics was beginning to take shape. Three interconnected features distinguished the New Left from its "old" counterpart. One was a shift in the audiences to which radical criticism of the established political order was directed. The second was a broadening of the subject matter of radical ideologies, and the third was the merging of traditional political rhetoric with appeals that emphasized cultural and generational conflict and made use of the visual impact of television.[44]

The marginality of traditional radical politics in the years in which Hiss was accused of being a Communist, convicted of perjury, incarcerated at Lewisburg, and relegated to the status of a salesman for a stationery firm, was evident. Although the ubiquity of anti-Communism as a political principle was decisive in that development, there was another reason. The period between the close of the Second World War and the mid-1960s was a period of general economic prosperity, which extended not only to affluent groups in the population but to the traditional victims identified by popular-front ideology in the 1930s, industrial laborers and agricultural workers. To be sure, relative affluence did not extend to most members of the African American community, and labor conflicts continued. On the whole, however, a gap began to exist between the rhetorical invocations of worker exploitation that had dominated popular-front collectivism in the 1930s and the economic condition of those workers. In addition, the boom in American higher education in the 1950s and 1960s resulted in many more opportunities for the children of lower-income families to attend colleges and universities.

The New Left, as the movement came to be identified in the early 1960s, developed its identity in this cultural setting. The critiques of established policies and institutions launched by its leaders were designed to inspire college and university students rather than industrial or agricultural workers. The issues those leaders identified as worthy of attention and protest went beyond the labor context to include the civil rights of African Americans, the academic freedom of students, professors, and campus speakers, and the involvement of the United States in Vietnam. The political ideology that linked New Left responses to those issues was not a version of popular-front collectivism but a version of participatory democracy. That version presented radical politics through the filters of generational conflict, avant-garde culture, and mass demonstrations that could be seen on television.

The evolution of Students for a Democratic Society (SDS), the organization from which the much broader New Left movement originated, serves to illustrate the transformation of American radical politics in the 1950s and 1960s.[45] The founders of SDS were students at the University of Michigan, some of whom had family ties to radical labor politics, some of whom did not. The principal theoretician of SDS, Alan Haber, was the son of a University of Michigan economics professor who had been a labor organizer and a follower of the Progressive Wisconsin senator Robert LaFollette. Tom Hayden, who succeeded Haber as president of the Michigan SDS chapter when, in the summer of 1960, Haber became president of the entire SDS organization (a full-time job that required him to move to New York City), was from a family with no ties to political radicalism or labor. Hayden's youthful heroes were an independent fisherman whom he met while working near Lake Huron in the summers, Holden Caulfield of *Catcher in the Rye,* and Jack Kerouac, author of *On The Road.* Haber, three years older than Hayden, recruited Hayden for SDS at Michigan because Haber believed that Hayden's writing talent, charisma, and well-roundedness—Hayden was an athlete and gifted public speaker in addition to being on the staff of the Michigan student newspaper—could help SDS gain support within a broader community of students.[46]

Haber believed that SDS, while keeping ties with the progressive labor tradition, should tap into the avant-garde cultural currents he had encountered as an undergraduate at Michigan in the 1950s. Although Haber was 18 when he entered the University of Michigan in the fall of 1954, he had still not graduated by the spring of 1960, when Hayden was in his junior year. In a paper marking his succession to the SDS presidency, Haber wrote that a new student movement would emerge "out of a heritage of absurdity." "The term 'beat,'" Haber felt, captured one element of the movement's response to that heritage. It had "come to characterize all those who have deviated from the traditional college patterns. They are variously professional students, bohemians, political types, and nonstudents who still seem to be around." Haber was actually all of those "beat" types rolled up together. Between 1954 and 1960 he alternated between enrolling in classes at Michigan some semesters and dropping out of college at other times; he was "a part of this very avant-garde scene" in Ann Arbor; he was the most conspicuous political activist in the Michigan student body in the 1950s; and in 1955 he began "a protracted odyssey as an off-again, on-again student and free-lance gadfly."[47]

Haber also recognized that for financial and other reasons, SDS needed to maintain its connections with the "old left." SDS was the descendant of an organization known as the Student League of Industrial Democracy (SLID), which had been a branch and financial ward of the League of Industrial Democracy. The League dated back to 1905, when it was founded as the International Socialist Society. The League's original purpose was to "bring the message of socialism to American college students," but in the period between the 1920s and the 1950s both it and SLID, for a variety of reasons, ran into difficulties in getting that message out. By the time Haber went to Michigan, SLID was in a state of near-extinction, and the League of Industrial Democracy, which remained solvent because of support from trade unions and its tax-exempt status, "had become . . . a kind of dignified retirement home for aging social democrats." Nonetheless Haber recognized, when he decided to change the name and orientations of SLID to SDS in 1960 (in part because "SLID was . . . a laughable name . . . for an organization in decline"), that SDS could not survive without the League of Industrial Democracy's financial support.[48]

The League's continued patronage of SDS was not accomplished without some tension. Once Tom Hayden joined SDS, he became its principal public rhetorician, and between 1960 and 1965 Hayden's rhetoric more than once infuriated League members as being "soft on Communism." The League had struggled to make its anti-Communist stance plain in the 1930s and 1940s, and its members were sensitive to any suggestions that SDS was attracted to systems erected on Marxist premises. The League also tried to insist that SDS's principal focus be labor organization, although that issue was less volatile for its members. By 1965 SDS had tapped into the growing antiwar sentiment on college and university campuses, and its enrollment, and contributions from opponents of the war, had grown large enough to make the organization financially self-sufficient. In October 1965, on the pretext that its members wanted to engage directly in political activity and thus could not be identified with a tax-exempt organization, SDS severed relations with the League.[49]

Although Haber was deeply committed to a vision of SDS that would incorporate traditional political radicalism with the variety of impulses he saw in the community of 1950s beatniks, it was Hayden, who succeeded Haber as president of the national organization of SDS in 1962, who would put that vision into practice. Between 1960 and 1965 Hayden was the principal SDS liaison to student sit-in and picketing demonstrations, at Michigan and elsewhere, supporting the civil rights of

African Americans, championing the free speech rights of critics accused of taking
pro-Communist or pro-Socialist positions, and opposing the war effort in Vietnam.
He went to Georgia, Tennessee, and Mississippi to protest racial segregation, and in
a well-publicized incident in McComb, Mississippi, in the fall of 1961, he was dragged
from his car and beaten. He went to the University of California at Berkeley and observed demonstrations against HUAC and the administration's effort to censure
student protesters. He traveled to a number of campuses recruiting for SDS. He became so enthusiastic about the prospect of interracial economic development proj-
ects in impoverished neighborhoods that in 1964 he moved to Newark, New Jersey,
to encourage community organization. And in 1965, with the Communist historian
Herbert Aptheker and the pacifist historian Staughton Lynd, he visited Hanoi, North
Vietnam, at the invitation of the North Vietnamese and in defiance of a State Department travel ban.[50]

By his Hanoi trip Hayden, who had been replaced as the president of SDS earlier that year, had come to understand the value of media coverage of organized student demonstrations, and so had his colleagues in SDS. Although the membership
of SDS had been growing steadily in the first half of the 1960s, it was not until SDS
organized a March on Washington in the spring of 1965, opposing the escalation of
the Vietnamese war, that the group received coverage in national media. In April
1965 *The New York Times* ran a profile of the SDS, and in October CBS News, noting that SDS had organized "International Days of Protest" against United States
involvement in Vietnam, ran a two-day feature on the antiwar movement, centering on an interview with Paul Booth, who had authored a 1962 "Port Huron Statement" with Hayden describing SDS's commitment to interracial participatory
democracy. By the close of 1965, despite Hayden's inflammatory Hanoi visit, SDS
was poised to become the linchpin of the antiwar movement and the center of New
Left politics.[51]

The escalation of the war in Vietnam struck more deeply into the community of
college and university students in the 1960s than any of the other issues with which
SDS had come to be identified. Although deferments from military service were still
available to many male college and graduate students as late as 1967, Haber's pattern
of dropping in and out of college exposed one to the draft, and being drafted typically meant being sent to Vietnam. And in 1968 an executive order from President
Lyndon Johnson abolished student deferments for all males above the age of 18, including students that had not completed two years of graduate study. Although a
draft lottery allowed male students with high draft numbers to continue their education, the change meant that the Vietnamese conflict now directly affected the lives

of large members of college and university student bodies. SDS had found an issue that was guaranteed to capture the attention of its principal audience, and also to galvanize national politics and the media.[52]

From SDS's successful capture of prominence in the antiwar movement in 1965 to 1969, the organization, as if uncomfortable with the leadership of a mass movement, began to spin out of control. By 1968, as antiwar politics began to influence that year's presidential election, SDS had over 100,000 members, but by 1969 it had collapsed entirely. New Left culture and politics, in contrast, continued to thrive. Part of SDS's problems could be traced to its leadership. Hayden increasingly became convinced that politics, generational identity, and cultural activity were linked, and his slogan conveying that message, "a re-assertion of the personal," was interpreted by him and some of his age contemporaries as calling for increasingly confrontational and violent public acts. Other difficulties could not be traced directly to SDS, but contributed to a sense in America of the late 1960s that social disorder and radical politics were linked. Between 1967 and 1970 riots took place in cities, such as Newark, where Hayden had hoped to build economic initiative programs, Martin Luther King and Robert F. Kennedy were assassinated, student demonstrators disrupted the 1968 Democratic convention, student strikes shut down universities, and the National Guard fired at student demonstrators at Kent State University. In the midst of these developments Hayden was convicted of conspiracy to incite a riot at the Chicago convention and sentenced to five years in prison.[53]

At a broader level, however, the New Left's program of creating a version of participatory democracy that combined individual self-fulfillment, generational conflict, and symbolic political activity in a mass-media culture survived into the early 1970s. National political leaders endorsed civil rights, the war against poverty, and opposition to U.S. participation in Vietnam.[54] Paradoxically, at a time when the traditional focus of left politics on industrial labor issues was becoming increasingly marginal, the mainstream appeal of some New Left concerns revived the communal and participatory emphasis of the popular-front ideologies of the 1930s. It was as if a new generation of students could suddenly identify with the heady reformist spirit of young New Dealers.

Alger Hiss was to benefit from the political and cultural transformations in which the New Left movement took shape. Although he continued to deny unequivocally any connections with Communism or the Soviets, he readily admitted to having been a deeply committed New Dealer, interested in shaping federal government programs to help agricultural workers and industrial laborers in the Depression. He also readily admitted to being an advocate of international peace. His credentials in both categories were impressive, and some of them were unmistakably in a progressive political tradition, such as his legal work for farmers and industrial workers in the 1930s and his identification with the United Nations and international cooperation as an alternative to nuclear confrontation.

In the late 1960s Hiss began to receive invitations to speak at colleges and universities. Initially the invitations primarily came from English institutions, or American ones who were regarded as avant-garde. In 1967 the New School for Social Research in New York asked him to give four public lectures on the New Deal, and the following year he spoke on the same topic at The University of East Anglia and the University of London. Of the New School lectures, he recalled that "the questions I solicited after each lecture were lively and germane. I recall no heckling. . . . It had been 20 years since I had so enjoyed the feeling of being the right person in the right place at the right time."[55]

As his invitations to speak at colleges and universities increased, Hiss became a 1970s version of a consumer advocate. He began to make public appearances on college and university campuses at a time when other critics of established governmental institutions and policies, such as Rachel Carson on environmental issues and Ralph Nader on dangerous products, were directing their critiques at young audiences. The consumers, for Hiss, were not merely students attracted to the New Left movement. They were members of a new generation seeking information, and new perspectives, on his case and the Cold War atmosphere in which it had been tried. In being their advocate—in explaining to them how the bright vision of the New Deal had been corrupted by institutions such as HUAC and the FBI and by people such as Nixon and Hoover—Hiss was also, of course, being a spokesman for himself.

His new role as a college and university lecturer liberated Hiss. At a time in which his resources had been significantly deleted, it provided him with a source of income that, over the next decade, was consistent and not insignificant. He no longer bore the burden of being too closely associated with Communism; it was, after all, a rigid anti-Communist foreign policy that had drawn the United States into conflicts in Southeast Asia that were directly affecting the lives of Hiss's student audiences. Nor was he tarnished with the establishment connections that had been a liability at his trials. As a former inmate of a federal prison, and an obscure stationery salesman, he was one of society's outsiders. In the account of his case that he now emphasized, he had been a political victim of partisan zealots and sinister government officials, and he was telling the story of their misdeeds. That was a story, with its antiestablishment overtones, that his new audiences could warm up to. Without any substantial concrete evidence to bolster his campaign for vindication, by the early 1970s Hiss had redirected that campaign along profitable lines. He would partially reinvent himself in the process.

Hiss waving at his formal swearing-in ceremony,
the result of his successful 1975 petition to reinstate
his law license in Massachusetts.

CHAPTER FIVE

The Campaign Gains Momentum

I n 1962 Richard Nixon lost the gubernatorial election in California, and gave an
emotional speech in which he declared that the press would no longer have him
to "kick around." After Nixon's defeat ABC News ran a program, "The Political Obituary of Richard Nixon," in which they invited supporters and antagonists
of Nixon to comment on his future. Among the invitees was Alger Hiss. When
Nixon learned that Hiss was being asked to comment, he protested, as did thousands
of other viewers. Some ABC network affiliates refused to run the program. The reaction was one more piece of evidence that Hiss, eight years after being released
from Lewisburg, remained a convicted traitor in the minds of large numbers of the
public.[1]

Six years later, Nixon had been elected president of the United States and the
Vietnam War had emerged as the most divisive issue in American politics, driving
Lyndon Johnson from the White House and paving the way for Nixon's victory. Although Nixon was not identified with the administration that had run into such difficulties in Vietnam, he was to have his own problems in extricating U.S. forces from
southeast Asia. By 1972, when Nixon ran for reelection, the Democratic Party candidate was openly antiwar, and Vietnam had come to be seen as a reckoning point
in American foreign policy. In the minds of many critics, the political and military
effort in Vietnam had failed because it rested on outmoded assumptions identified
with the Cold War years. It was simplistic to assume that the United States had an

interest in preserving every anti-Communist regime, however inept or corrupt, throughout the globe.

By 1974 Nixon, and many of the leading participants in his administration, were in disgrace. A botched effort on the part of persons hired by the committee organizing Nixon's reelection bid to burglarize Democratic Party headquarters in the Watergate office complex in Washington had eventually been found to have originated in Nixon's White House. Nixon himself had been revealed to have made taped comments that suggested he knew about an attempt to cover up the Watergate break-in. When those tapes were made public, Nixon was forced to resign the presidency. Several high-level Nixon aides went to jail, and Nixon himself escaped only by virtue of a pardon from his vice president, Gerald Ford. In the process by which the Watergate conspiracy was made public, the Federal Bureau of Investigation was revealed to have participated in partisan investigations of persons identified as opponents of the Nixon White House. The very charges of partisanship, malevolence, and corruption that Hiss supporters had made against government agencies at the time of his perjury trials had materialized during Nixon's presidency.

Vietnam and Watergate were to change the cultural setting of the Hiss case, and with it the prospects for Hiss's campaign for vindication. With the defeat of his legal arguments, and the failure of *In the Court of Public Opinion* to resonate with most readers, Hiss had begun to explore, in the 1960s, the extralegal dimensions of his campaign. His extralegal arguments emphasized, as had his reputational defense at his trials, the comparative credibility of him and his accusers. He had not prevailed on credibility issues at the trials, but Vietnam and Watergate added new political and cultural dimensions to his arguments. In the late 1960s and 1970s Hiss crafted a new narrative of his innocence, blending theories propounded by Zeligs and his lawyers with overtures to audiences now more inclined to believe in the malevolence and partisanship of Hiss's accusers.

To conclude that Hiss was innocent, one had to believe in the theory that he had been framed. That theory attributed sinister motives to Whittaker Chambers, who had charged Hiss with committing espionage, Richard Nixon, who had led HUAC's pursuit of Hiss, and J. Edgar Hoover, whose FBI had collected most of the rest of the known evidence incriminating Hiss. If Hiss had not passed stolen government documents to Chambers, then Chambers, either on his own or in league with others, had somehow acquired or fabricated those documents. Of Hiss's antagonists, HUAC and the FBI had the strongest incentives to expose Hiss, and perhaps the best ability to produce documents with a fabricated typeface. It was possible, then, that Chambers, Nixon, and Hoover had been co-conspirators against Hiss. That scenario was no more implausible, in post-Watergate America, than the Nixon White House enlisting the FBI in persecutions of its political opponents.

The Watergate scandal thus had a dramatic effect on the comparative credibility of Hiss and his opponents. Although it did not furnish Hiss with any new evidence tending to exonerate him, it had the effect of reminding observers of the fact that two of Hiss's major accusers, Nixon and Hoover, had been prepared to use their offices for personal, partisan gains. Hiss's third accuser, Chambers, had died in 1961, and his legacy was now prominently associated with the virulent anti-Communism of the Cold War years.[2] Watergate helped give additional credence to the possibility that Hiss might have been a victim.

Meanwhile the debacle of Vietnam helped clarify the sort of victim that Hiss might have been. Opponents of the Vietnam war linked the United States' difficulties to a flawed foreign policy. They reasoned as follows. The war had demonstrated the bankruptcy, in a globe increasingly populated by postcolonial, "third-world" nations, of a foreign policy erected on the bipolar divisions of the Cold War. Not all Communist regimes, Vietnam showed, were the same. The success of the Vietcong rebels in South Vietnam had come from their being in closer touch with the citizenry of that region than the official South Vietnamese government. "Communism" in southeast Asia had indigenous versions that had little in common with the Soviet bloc. The mistake of those who supported increasing U.S. involvement in Vietnam had been in thinking that the political divisions in that nation mirrored those of the bipolar model of Cold War foreign policy.

The fallout from Vietnam caused some American intellectuals in the late 1960s and early 1970s to try to separate their current political culture from that of the period from the close of the Second World War through the Johnson years. They reasoned that if Vietnam had been the unfortunate culmination of an American obsession with anti-Communism, one of the first steps in internalizing the lessons of Vietnam was to demonstrate the contrast between the monolithic, bipolar foreign policy of previous decades and the more nuanced approaches required in the post-Vietnam world. That contrast could be underscored by studies that labeled the years between the end of World War II and America's awkward retreat from southeast Asia as a "Cold War" era.

Historians took up the challenge. A series of works that appeared in the late 1960s and early 1970s began to probe the dominance of anti-Communism in American foreign and domestic politics from the late 1940s through the early 1960s. The

works sought to explain the appeal of Senator Joseph McCarthy, and the great significance attributed to the alleged penetration of the federal government by Communists, by linking those phenomena to the triumph of Cold War thinking. Between
1969 and 1971, three publications appeared that identified the Hiss case as a central
episode of the Cold War era.[3]

One of those works, an article in the *American Scholar* by Allen Weinstein, then
in the history department at Smith College, called for a "thoroughly researched reassessment of the Hiss case." That case, Weinstein argued, had become a symbolic
point of entry into the Cold War period. Decisions about Hiss's guilt or innocence
had come to reflect judgments "concerning an entire range of public issues." The
Hiss case raised "the meaning and merit of the Cold War, the treatment of domestic Communists, the response by intellectuals to their own radical pasts, the true extent of Communist infiltration into government during the New Deal, and the
proper role of congressional committees in investigating subversion." Weinstein
proposed to reexamine the Hiss case as part of a larger study on "the Cold War and
American society." He began with the assumption that most students of the case perceived it as an exercise in comparative credibility. In deciding whether to believe Hiss
or Chambers, Americans brought their attitudes toward Communism, subversion in
government, and the appropriate role of investigative committees to bear on the
credibility question. He proposed abandoning the assumption that "*either* Alger
Hiss *or* Whittaker Chambers was a complete perjurer" and "confront[ing] the case
itself." This would allow the separation of the facts of the case from "the inconsis-
tencies of partisan accounts."[4]

Weinstein's strategy of "confronting the case itself" would eventually lead him
to abandon his study of the Hiss case as a symbol of the Cold War to directly reexamine the question of Hiss's guilt. In a 1971 article, he wrote that he was not convinced that Hiss was guilty, but doubted whether Hiss could be proven innocent
given the evidence about the case that had thus far been made public. He suggested
that a definitive understanding of the case would not be possible without the release
of "the executive files of HUAC," "the relevant FBI records," and "the grand jury
records." In 1972 he filed a Freedom of Information suit to obtain FBI and Justice
Department files on the case. Despite the fact that Weinstein's article had not taken
a strong position on the issue of Hiss's guilt, he identified the Hiss case with the
"Cold War era," and stressed that the question of guilt or innocence might be clarified by the release of hitherto confidential government records. A reader of the article might well have conjectured that Weinstein thought there was a possibility that
Hiss had been a victim of partisan politics. At least Alger Hiss and his supporters

made that inference, for when Weinstein asked for access to Hiss's defense files in 1973, that request was granted.[5]

Meanwhile Hiss was prospering on the lecture circuit. By the 1970s invitations had come from a wider spectrum of colleges and universities, including Brandeis, Columbia, Harvard, Johns Hopkins, Kenyon, New York University, Trinity, the University of Virginia, and Wesleyan. Princeton also invited him back. He expanded his topics, including the Yalta Conference, the United Nations, the Cold War, the McCarthy era, Justice Holmes, and the American press. He developed a "preferred practice" on his visits, spending "two to four days at a college or university," giving "several seminars" in addition to a public lecture. Although he did not include his case as a separate topic, "it usually came up as a matter of course, and I always answered questions about it from my audiences." He saw the visits as "learning experiences for me [and] the students," potential opportunities to gauge the attitudes of a new generation and enlist some of its members in his campaign. The very fact that institutions thought it appropriate for Alger Hiss to be lecturing to students on the Cold War and the McCarthy era suggested that a distancing from the era in which his trials had taken place had begun.[6]

In 1972 Hiss was given further evidence that he was no longer viewed as a pariah, at least in some circles. The American Civil Liberties Union successfully challenged the 1954 "Hiss Act," making any government employee convicted of perjury in a case involving national security ineligible for a pension, as applied to Hiss himself. The decision resulted in his receiving 11 years' worth of back payments on a pension. In the same year Harper and Row issued a paperback edition of *In the Court of Public Opinion*, believing that it might appeal to the college and university market. Both those developments were discussed in a profile of Hiss by Thomas Moore for the April 1972 issue of *Life*. Moore characterized Hiss as "back in the headlines," "mellow," and "full of surprisingly warm regard for the world." He quoted Hiss as saying that there had been a "swing of the pendulum back to a liberal-progressive trend in politics in the last decade," and that the decision on his pension had been "one small step in his eventual vindication." As Moore talked with Hiss, he noted, Hiss "[l]it up a pipe given him by actor Zero Mostel, who was once blasted for left-wing activities," and declared, "by the time I am 80, I expect to be respected and venerated."[7]

Hiss's willingness to be publicly associated with persons involved with "left-wing activities" represented a change from the posture he had adopted after being released from Lewisburg, in which he insisted that he had been, and remained, an enthusiastic New Dealer but an anti-Communist. In July 1972, the *Esquire* columnist

Robert Alan Aurthur described meeting Hiss at a New York party frequented by "tired old leftos." The political consciousness of most of the persons attending the party, Aurthur noted, had been "formed during the Depression," where they had come to see "Franklin Roosevelt [as] our savior [and] the New Deal the hope for a new world." They had been "stunned by the disastrous events of the past few years" and were now "rendered helpless." The atmosphere of the party made Hiss, for Aurthur, the "only . . . person of interest" at the event. This was because he was "optimistic" and "full of hope." "You listen [to him]," Aurthur wrote, "and, recognizing the brilliance as well as the courage and determination, you are almost ready to go along."[8]

After the party Aurthur resolved to do a profile on Hiss, and had lunch with him as preparation for it. He saw Hiss as "a man who'd been mangled in the awful crunch of a whole society shifting from left to right," and marveled at his upbeat attitude. Hiss explained that his optimism was a product of his "experiences at colleges around the country." It was "clearly rooted in the behavior of today's youth." "Young people and Hiss . . . seem[ed] . . . inseparable." Aurthur noted: Hiss was "deeply respectful, almost in awe, of the young activists." In his visits to campuses he assumed the posture "not just [of] a survivor," but "[of] a reminder" of a time when government service consisted of "positive action by dedicated men." Contemporary students saw him as a "link" to that period. In contrast, they were contemptuous of those who "work[ed] within the political establishment today," and Hiss shared their contempt. Asked whether he admired any "establishment" figure of the early 1970s, Hiss gave "a flat, emphatic, 'No!'" He believed that the mutual regard in which he and young 1970s radicals held one another was "all part of the vindication" that he would eventually gain.[9]

Buoyed by the favorable reception he was receiving from colleges and universities, and noting the recoil of many students from the mainstream politics of their seniors, Hiss began to take a more active role in publicizing the image of himself as a scapegoat of the Cold War. By the early 1970s at least two reassessments of his career were in progress, Weinstein's study of the Hiss case and an authorized biography by Alden Whitman, a former *The New York Times* staffer who had himself been tainted with alleged sympathy for left-wing activities in the 1950s. Whitman, who wrote obituaries for *The Times,* interviewed Hiss for a prospective obituary and received Hiss's assurance of his full cooperation with a biography. But Whitman was unable to secure access to Meyer Zeligs's files, and after developing health problems in the early 1970s, recommended that John Chabot Smith, who had covered the Hiss trials for the *New York Herald Tribune,* succeed him. Hiss was equally cooperative with Smith's project.[10]

While Weinstein and Smith were working on their books, Hiss decided to produce his own account of his life. He did so in the form of an extended conversation with his son, Tony Hiss. Alger Hiss had more than one motive for choosing to publish a memoir through Tony. In addition to the project's providing him with an opportunity to couple his continued claims of innocence with a more humanized self-portrait, it enabled him to have a series of conversations with Tony about the years in which Alger suddenly became a figure of notoriety, was put on trial, and went to prison. Those years had taken an emotional toil on Tony, whose life, in his early thirties, had finally showed signs of stabilizing. Revisiting the time of Tony's turmoil, and placing it in the context of a frame-up in which Alger was a victim, might have the effect of bringing father and son closer together. The timing for reconciliation was propitious. Tony had initially felt torn between his parents as they became estranged after their separation in 1959. In 1963, after graduating from Harvard and taking a job on the staff of the *New Yorker,* he had moved in with his mother. But by the early 1970s, after some years of professional and personal unrest, Tony had concluded that he needed to live on his own and to see his mother less frequently. When the time the conversations between Alger and Tony began, both of them had only minimal contacts with Priscilla.

The first installment of Alger and Tony's memoir project appeared in 1973 in the form of an article by Tony, "I Call On Alger," in *Rolling Stone* magazine. The choice of that journal was suggestive. *Rolling Stone* was directed at a youthful audience that aspired to be on the cutting edge of the creative arts and cultural issues; to the extent it had a political cast, it was that of the New Left. Tony, at the time, was working on the anonymous "Talk of the Town" column for the *New Yorker,* and had published two jointly authored nonfiction books, oriented toward young adults. Although "I Call On Alger" was primarily designed to publicize Hiss's narrative of innocence to a new generation of readers, it also was intended to introduce Tony to a set of readers who were probably unaware of his work.

"I Call On Alger" was presented as an interview, with Tony ostensibly acting as a spokesman for *Rolling Stone,* asking the sorts of questions its readers might be inclined to ask a once-notorious figure with whom they were just getting acquainted. But it was clear that Tony's questions, as well as Alger's answers, had been scripted by Alger Hiss. The conversation started as follows:

> [Tony]: Let's start with this. Do you have any advice for any of the Watergate people if it turns out that they have to go to jail?

[Alger]: Don't you have . . . any introductory material? Why are you interviewing me? Why does anybody want to hear what I have to say? Then you refer to the fact that I was involved in an appearance before a committee quite different from the Watergate committee, . . . and that those hearings developed into a case most people who read *Rolling Stones* . . .

[Tony]: *Rolling Stone.*

[Alger]: . . . who read *Rolling Stone* may never have heard of or have forgotten about. Some aspects of what happened then may be relevant to what's going on today. Some of the same things that have happened in the Ellsberg case, in the Berrigan case, in the Camden 28 case, and in the Gainesville trial that's on now. And that's why you're interviewing me about it.

[Tony]: Could be. But you're not just interested in pointing out historical parallels but in establishing that you got a bum rap.

[Alger]: No, but I thought I'd give some background. I was going to say that because of the big change in the political climate, the fact is that now people don't put up with what they used to put up with, and aren't as driven and led as they were then on the subject of hysteria. When the same kind of cases are brought now, they don't succeed.

[Tony]: Talk has been going around Washington recently that all the recent political trials, beginning with the Hiss case, were fixed.

[Alger]: Yeah, and there's a certain unpleasant similarity about all of them, that they're all contrived for political purposes. But the big difference, I think, is the difference in public opinion, so the juries now aren't led by the nose. At the time when my case came up, the Cold War was already well under way, there was a great deal of hysteria.[11]

Alger then went on to suggest that in the Ellsberg, Berrigan, and "Camden 28" cases juries had been less gullible, and had recognized the "contrivances" in the government's case. In contrast, "in the Forties and Fifties *all* the contrived cases were gotten away with by the prosecution." The difference, he felt, "has to do with the amount of education . . . throughout the country." There are "more college students" in the 1970s: "people can't learn something and then forget it. . . . The sophistication of most young people today is way . . . above what it was 25 years ago when my case first started."[12]

In these introductory exchanges of "I Call On Alger," Tony and Alger established the central argument that they wanted readers to take from the article. It consisted of six steps:

> Step One: Watergate was the latest example of a tendency on the part of government officials to use their power for partisan political ends.
>
> Step Two: Among the ways in which those officials used power was in "contrived" "political trials" designed to punish persons they considered opponents or dissidents. Recent examples of such trials were those of Daniel Ellsberg and Philip Berrigan, dissidents who had escaped conviction because juries had discerned the political dimensions of their prosecutions.
>
> Step Three: Alger Hiss's trial was the first twentieth-century example of a contrived political trial.
>
> Step Four: Hiss had been convicted, whereas Ellsberg and Berrigan had been acquitted, because juries in the 1940s and 1950s were unsophisticated about the political motives of government officials, unduly deferential to the government, and fearful of being labeled dissenters.
>
> Step Five: In contrast, current members of the American population, more of whom had college degrees, were more sophisticated, more independent in their thinking, and more likely to attribute partisan political motives to government officials.
>
> Step Six: As such, many current Americans, on being aware of the political nature of the Hiss case, would be inclined to suspect that Alger Hiss had gotten a bum rap.

Alger and Tony invited the readers of "I Call On Alger" to reason backwards from their experiences with Watergate, the partisanship of the FBI, and the political dimensions of prosecutions brought against persons who were unsympathetic to the war in Vietnam or otherwise critics of the "Establishment." If they did so, the Hisses suggested, they would see the prosecution of Hiss in the same vein. In subsequent responses to Tony's questions, Alger suggested how his trial resembled those of Ellsberg or Berrigan. The House Un-American Activities Committee, which had launched the investigation into Hiss's alleged sympathy for Communism, acted as a "prosecutor and judge all at once." Hiss had been singled out as a target for investigation, and eventually for prosecution, because two other more prominent New Deal officials suspected of having links to Communism, Harry Dexter White of the Treasury Department and Lawrence Duggan of the State Department, had died after HUAC began investigating them. Hiss was an ideal "target of the reactionaries" because he had been associated with the United Nations and had been a participant at the Yalta Conference. He was "a handy compendium of various prejudices and hates" held by the right wing in the Cold War era.[13]

Had jurors been more sophisticated at the time of Hiss's trials, his image as a scapegoat would have been more readily perceived, and the political reasons for indicting and prosecuting him would have been more clearly discerned. But there was still an opportunity to set the record straight. Richard Nixon, by revealing himself to be a deeply partisan and mendacious figure in the presidency, had cast doubt on his motives for pursuing Hiss. "Mr. Nixon is sort of a press agent for me," Alger told Tony. "I now have a chance to state my own position simply because of the fact that Nixon was one of my initial tormentors." In addition, "the whole atmosphere of Watergate is more conducive to truth telling than anything we've had since my trial." Hiss hoped that "[t]he people who know about the dirty tricks in my case" would "now come forward." "I Call On Alger" closed with an appeal by Hiss "to those who may know to come forward," because "I still am following every lead and working for the vindication I'm eventually going to get."[14]

In one respect "I Call On Alger" was a predictable effort on the part of Alger Hiss to take advantage of the fact that his unmasking had been associated with a man who had been forced out of the presidency for lying and corrupting government agencies. Hiss's claim that he had been the scapegoat of his political enemies seemed more credible once one recalled that Nixon had been one of Hiss's chief prosecutors. But in another respect "I Call On Alger," and the memoir of his father, *Laughing Last*, that Tony Hiss published in 1977 were more unexpected. They demonstrated that the principal bond between Alger and his son had been forged around Alger's campaign for vindication. By feeding his father the questions out of which the syllogism of "I Call On Alger" was constructed, and by committing himself to publicizing Alger's claims that he had been the victim of partisan political enemies, Tony, as he launched his career as writer, associated that career with his father's campaign for vindication. He not only helped Alger by recording the explanations and justifications of Alger's narrative of innocence. He identified himself among the persons who claimed to know Alger well and, for that reason, to know that Alger was innocent.

The enlistment of Tony in Alger's campaign for vindication was striking in two respects. First, Tony unqualifiedly concluded that his father was innocent, even though he had discovered almost no new evidence about the Hiss case, and the one piece of potentially exonerating information that he had learned came from a family member, his stepbrother Timothy Hobson. Tony's basis for believing in his father's claims of innocence was, essentially, that he trusted his father's account of events because he loved his father. Although *Laughing Last* contained considerably more detail about the Hiss case and the Hiss family than "I Call On Alger," Tony assumed the same role in both works. He was the conduit through which stories about the case were passed on, largely affectionate anecdotes about Alger and his family were told, and the importance of the bond between Alger and Tony was affirmed.

It is interesting that Tony Hiss, who had been bedeviled as a youth by having a notorious and absent father, would implicitly decide to defend him. But one can surely understand how, even though Tony had very few reasons other than those supplied by his father to think Alger was innocent, this might have come about. Tony and his father were reuniting after one period in which Alger had been in prison and had been genuinely concerned for the welfare of his troubled son, after another period in which Tony had demonstrated hostility toward his father by showing up late for appointments with Alger and being rude to Alger's associates. Now both were embarked on a mutual venture that was designed to help vindicate Alger and establish Tony as a writer. Finally, some of the material in *Laughing Last* suggested that Tony had come to associate his self-esteem, as a young adult, with distancing himself from his mother, as his father had done with his own mother. All of these reasons, plus the natural sympathy and affection a son might have for a beleaguered father who was seeking to become his friend and clear his reputation at the same time, may have inclined Tony to publicly identify himself with Alger's campaign for vindication.

There was, however, another feature of Tony's enlistment in Alger's campaign. If one assumes that Alger Hiss knew that his campaign for vindication amounted to an elaborate deception, why did he enlist his own son in the campaign? To do so meant not only to repeatedly lie to his son, but to encourage him to publicize the lies. It meant that even if Alger Hiss succeeded in convincing a large segment of the public that he had been a scapegoat rather than a Communist or a Soviet agent, he would know that he had duped his own son into helping him facilitate a cover-up. It might seem, on initial reflection, that if Hiss knew that his campaign for vindication was designed to conceal rather than reveal the truth, he would not have wanted to involve any of his family members with it. For if the campaign was successful, he would be left with the knowledge that he had manipulated and misled those closest to him, and if it failed, they would be exposed as among his victims. Instead, Alger Hiss was not content to let the story of his innocence be told by sympathetic biographers. He enlisted his son to tell the story with him. He did so knowing that the story amounted to a series of lies. At one point Tony Hiss quoted his father as saying:

> Loyalty is a very big thing in my life. I'd been brought up on stories of the
> Knights of the Round Table, and then loyalty is an old southern tradi-
> tion—something I couldn't ever get through to [Meyer] Zeligs when I was
> talking to him. . . . When I met Arabs in San Francisco [during the 1945
> U.N. Conference], I was quite frankly fascinated . . . because I saw in their
> traditions the same fierce loyalty to family and clan.[15]

If one takes this comment at face value, and adds to it the evidence of Alger's deeply
affectionate prison letters to Tony, one might be inclined to think that Alger reasoned
as follows when confronted with the option of enlisting Tony in his campaign. Here
is my son, who has lived much of his life as a child and adolescent with the stigma
of a convicted traitor for a father. Now, after being estranged from me for awhile,
he is pulling away from his mother, and he and I are making friends. He very badly
wants to believe in my innocence: his mother and I, and his uncle Donald, and all
our close friends, have always told him I was innocent. By keeping that illusion
alive for him, I help take away the stigma, and leave him, at least in his mind, a far
more inspiring family legacy. By doing that I am exhibiting a "fierce loyalty to family and clan."

Then there was another set of loyalties for Hiss to consider. There seems to be
no escaping the fact that once one assumes that Hiss was a dedicated Communist and
Soviet agent, his lifelong effort to convince others that he was not represented a decision to prefer the loyalty he had to the ideals of Soviet society and to the tradecraft
of Soviet intelligence over any personal sympathies that were inconsistent with
those loyalties. In enlisting Tony in his campaign for vindication, Alger knew that
he was going to have to sacrifice candor for all the loyalties that were prompting him
to seek Tony's involvement. In practical terms, the early 1970s seemed a particularly
propitious time for Alger Hiss to add Tony to the stable of publicists for his narrative of innocence. Tony was developing a new closeness with his father, and having his help in expanding the campaign was efficient. It also meant, however, that the
central premise from which Alger and Tony formed a bond in the 1970s—the premise that Tony need feel no shame in having Alger as a father because Alger had been
innocent—would differ significantly from the shared beliefs that had once linked
Alger to Priscilla Fansler Hiss and Donald Hiss.

Priscilla and Donald had known that Alger's claims that he was neither a Communist nor a Soviet agent were false because they had also participated in the Soviet
military intelligence cell of which Alger was the center. They had their own incentives to back Alger's story, since they had both publicly denied being Communists
or espionage agents at the perjury trials. Nonetheless their participation in Alger's

campaign for vindication was virtually nonexistent in Priscilla's case and muted in Donald's. Meyer Zeligs, John Chabot Smith, and Allen Weinstein all interviewed Priscilla in connection with their books on Hiss and the Hiss case. Priscilla cooperated most extensively with Zeligs, with whom she had contact between 1960 and 1963. After *Friendship and Fratricide* appeared, Priscilla was reportedly upset with Zeligs's portrait of her, and subsequently supplied one of Weinstein's researchers a copy of a criticial review of Zeligs's book by John Millet, a psychiatrist whom she had consulted. By the 1970s the estrangement between Alger and Priscilla was very deep, but the last public statement she issued about the Hiss case was an unequivocal statement of Alger's innocence.[16]

Donald was also interviewed by Zeligs, Smith, and Weinstein, but none of them made extensive use of him as a source. Although his quoted statements confirmed Alger's story, he had already done so at the trials, and if he was more forthcoming in interviews, Zeligs, Smith, and Weinstein did not choose to quote him. Donald's cautious posture about the Hiss case may have been connected to concerns that he could be exposed as well. As we have seen, Weinstein's research turned up some information that Donald had been less than candid with Hiss defense lawyers about his knowledge of the whereabouts of the Hiss family typewriter, and that he may have tried to mislead them about a previous association in the late 1930s with the Communist labor leader Harry Bridges. That information did not suggest by itself that Donald was a participant in espionage, but he may have felt that he would not be advantaged by too public an association with Alger's campaign.

Tony's association with Alger's claims of innocence was different. Alger knew, from the moment of Tony's enlistment, that he was feeding Tony a lie, and that he would need to do so as long as his campaign remained the abiding goal of his life. He may well have appreciated the potential psychological benefits to Tony from joining the campaign. But there were risks that the venture might turn out disastrously for Tony. If Alger, in the course of continuing to publicize the Hiss case, were to be definitely exposed as not only a dedicated Soviet agent but as a mendacious fraud, Tony would bear that burden, as well as the consequences of having his father lie to him. Alger's strategy, however, had always been to take risks, to minimize the negative consequences of his deceptions, and to act as if a few minor acts of duplicity paled alongside the momentousness of his ideological cause. Thus the joint project that Alger and Tony had begun with "I Call on Alger" grew into *Laughing Last*.

Alger Hiss's decision to enlist Tony in his campaign for vindication might initially seem quite different from his earlier efforts to preserve the fiction of his innocence and keep others away from his secret life. His defiant posture before

HUAC, his strident insistence that Chambers had committed forgery by typewriter, the iron discipline he exhibited in Lewisburg, and even his decision, after his release from prison, to launch his campaign for vindication in the face of Priscilla's opposition could be said to be examples of a relatively familiar strategy adopted by persons caught committing heinous acts. Once having staked out a claim of innocence, and having served a prison sentence, Hiss, and others in similar positions, may well have felt nothing would be gained from an admission of complicity. But, one might argue, it is one thing to persist in a lie, and quite another to encourage one's own child, unaware of the true circumstances of his father's life, in a campaign to publicize that lie. Although Alger Hiss may have rationalized his enlistment of Tony by imagining, as previously noted, that Tony would actually be better off believing his father was a victim than knowing he was a spy, the truth was that by engaging Tony to produce *Laughing Last*, Alger knew that he was taking advantage of his son's vulnerability, and that he had decided to give a higher priority to his own goals and needs than to that of his son's welfare.

One might not even find this decision surprising. Humans are capable of ruthless self-preference, and fathers are capable of lying and even betraying sons. Alger's decision to enlist Tony in a campaign of falsehoods becomes most interesting not because it reveals Alger Hiss to have behaved contemptibly but because it illustrates how important the idea of preserving and defending his secret life was to Alger's sense of self-fulfillment and self-worth. For Alger Hiss, being a committed Soviet spy, and enticing others away from that secret life, were essential to his belief in himself. As a master spy, and a master deceiver, he was living a meaningful, integrated life. As a convicted traitor, and an exposed fraud, he was a failure. As a failure in his efforts to live and preserve a secret life, he was thrown back on the pathos and turmoil of his ordinary life, with its painful memories. In order to avoid being placed in that position, Alger Hiss would betray anyone who threatened to expose him, and enlist anyone who might help him keep his secret life secret.

Laughing Last began with Tony's declaration that he would "tell . . . what no one else has told before—the private life of a man whose public life has been so melodramatic [and] whose private life has been the one piece of the puzzle that hasn't been available before." Tony added that "frankly it took me a while to persuade [Alger] this story is worth the telling." Although the last comment was of a piece with early statements by Alger that his private life had not been all that interesting, it was probably not accurate in two respects. The comment implied that Tony had been the one persuading Alger to do the book, whereas it is more likely that both had incentives to revisit Alger's life. Alger wanted to put out a certain version of his career and the Hiss case, emphasizing his innocence. Tony wanted to be a participant as his father rehearsed his reactions to significant people and events in his life. Tony also wanted to summon up his youthful memory of some of those events, and to juxtapose that memory against his reaction to the events as an adult in his mid-thirties.[17]

Three story lines circled through *Laughing Last*. The first line took up events and people in Alger Hiss's life that made a distinct impression on him. Some of those were connected to the Hiss case, but others, such as Hiss's year as legal secretary to Holmes, seemed of elemental significance to Alger, and reappeared in his 1988 memoir, *Recollections of a Life*. The second line consisted of Tony's observations on important events in his own life, some but not all of which were connected to his father. The final story line took up Tony's reactions to the issue of his father's innocence. The lines swirled around and intersected with one another as the narrative of *Laughing Last* progressed, resulting in the book's being, essentially, about Tony Hiss's coming of age as he confronted the fact that Alger Hiss was his father.

The voice of *Laughing Last*, for the most part, is Tony Hiss, which gave an occasionally quirky dimension to the information imparted about Alger's life. The book revealed that Alger was not fond of his mother, that he had had women as authority figures for most of his life as an adolescent, that he tended to acquiesce in his mother's domineering tendencies, and that he was popular and accomplished during his college years at Johns Hopkins. But this information was interspersed with other details that seemed to particularly interesting to Tony in his mid-thirties. For example, *Laughing Last* described Alger's squeamishness about sexual matters, his being a virgin on his wedding night, the possibility that one of his elder sisters, Anna, was a lesbian, and his older brother Bosley's sexual profligacy.[18]

In addition, Tony, perhaps to emphasize his writer's stance of detachment or to appeal to the irreverence of a younger audience, chose to portray some of the grimmer events of Alger's life in wry, almost flippant terms. One example was the suicide of Alger's father, Charles Alger Hiss, when Alger was two years old. Tony described that incident as follows:

> Minnie [Mary Lavinia Hughes, Alger's mother] persuaded [Charles Hiss] to find work for her only brother, Albert Hughes. . . . Al Hughes became treasurer of Daniel Miller & Company [Charles Hiss's drygoods firm in Baltimore] and . . . either misinvested or made off with ten thousand bucks. Charlie paid off the debt by selling his own shares in the firm and leaving the company. . . . Charlie had been making forty to fifty grand a year, big money in those days, and was now broke. So he went down to Carolina to see his

older brother George, . . . who was doing fine in the cotton business. . . . George offered Charlie half of a large cotton mill which he was about to purchase and urged him to move the family down to Charlotte. Charlie was ecstatic, and went back to [Baltimore] to break the good news. If Charlie had taken George's offer he would have become a millionaire, but Minnie said: "Leave Baltimore? Leave my horse and carriage? Never! Surely you can see that the simple life they lead down there would never suit your wife and children."

[On a] Sunday morning [in April 1907] Charlie called downstairs to Minnie and told her to summon the family physician. Then he cut his throat with a razor—"almost from ear to ear," the *Baltimore Sun* reported in its obit. . . . The headline on the obit was "CUT THROAT WITH RAZOR," but Al and his baby brother, Donald, were never told the truth about their dad's death and didn't find out until they overheard an old lady on the block gossiping about it. . . . Minnie never remarried, and she never left Baltimore.[19]

We have seen that there were two other tragedies in Alger Hiss's youth, the death of his brother Bosley from Bright's disease in 1926 and the suicide of his elder sister Mary Ann in 1929. As to the first, Tony wrote:

Bos was a young snob who liked being a police court reporter who went to fancy parties at night. He had girlfriends Al remembers as Scott Fitzgerald girls—Bos bedded down with them, remember—and he was always able to twist all the women in the family around his little finger. He drank a lot . . . and contracted Bright's disease, an alcohol-induced kidney ailment where you can't pee. Al thinks Bos could have gotten over it if he hadn't been nursed by Minnie, whose favorite he was. Instead, he went back to the [*Baltimore*] *Sun,* started drinking again, got sick again. . . . In the summer of 1926, the summer before Al went off to law school, Bos was dying. . . . Al had the job of driving him to the hospital, where the doctors punctured his abdomen to drain the water off. Bosley died that November.[20]

With Mary Ann's suicide, Tony was more laconic:

Minnie pushed Mary to marry money and helped her get hitched to Eliot Emerson, a rich, charming, well-connected Boston stockbroker . . . who bought stocks on margin and went blooey in the smash. . . . Mary liked him

better when he'd had money and so she ate some lye and committed suicide in 1929.

Mary Ann . . . had been threatening suicide for years. [She] finally went
through with it a month before Al graduated law school, during final
exams.[21]

Despite the somewhat callous style employed by Tony to describe events that
must have been devastating for the Hiss family, each of his descriptions contained
a quite similar message. Minnie Hiss, after inducing her husband Charles to hire her
brother, who was responsible for Charles's business losing so much money that
Charles was forced to leave the business in order to pay off the debt, then refused
to join Charles in Charlotte, North Carolina, where he had been given a chance to
regain financial stability, because she declined to leave Baltimore for what she perceived as too "simple" a community. Minnie, in the capacity of caretaker to her ail-
ing son Bosley, so irritated him that he returned to work, and to drinking,
endangering his health to the point that his condition became terminal. And Minnie
"pushed" her daughter Mary Ann "to marry money," "help[ing]" her to make a
marriage with Eliot Emerson, whom Mary found so unappealing, after Eliot lost his
money in the stock market, that she eventually became depressed and killed herself.
Minnie was the culprit, in a more or less direct fashion, in all of the Hiss family
tragedies.

The theme of Minnie Hiss's efforts to manage, and to dominate, her husband and
children was mirrored by another theme that surfaced as the narrative of *Laughing
Last* moved forward in time to cover the events of Alger Hiss's adult life and those
of Tony Hiss's adolescence and young adulthood. That theme was the dominating,
and emotionally demanding, personality of Priscilla Hiss, whose portrait resembled
that of Minnie. Tony had seen Minnie as a "tough old battleax"; he saw Priscilla as
a far more vulnerable, but equally difficult, figure.[22]

Alger married Priscilla, in the late fall of 1929, because she was the divorced
mother of a three-year-old child and had recently had a love affair with a married
man collapse when he, having gotten Priscilla pregnant, returned to his own newly
pregnant wife. After Priscilla had an abortion, and Alger visited her in the hospital,
"she tells him," Tony related, "he can stick around if he'll marry her right away."
When, after his year as Holmes's secretary, Alger took a job with a Boston law firm,
Priscilla came to "loathe Cambridge," where they lived, and "bitched about it."
This resulted in the Hisses moving to New York, where Priscilla's brother and sister-
in-law lived. Priscilla was responsible for Alger's developing a consciousness of the
plight of economically disadvantaged people in the early 1930s. That consciousness

played a part in his decision to leave private practice to join the Agricultural Adjustment Administration in 1933. During the years the Hisses lived in Washington, Priscilla "played the piano, took premed courses for a while, dropped them, worked in the Library of Congress, was a civil defense warden in World War II, and eventually became a schoolteacher." "People remembered her," Tony wrote, "as slim, pretty, with long hair, talkative, opinionated. Men rather liked her, women often found her a little scary."[23]

Priscilla's first appearances in the narrative of *Laughing Last* were thus reminiscent of Minnie's: the demanding woman to whom family members deferred but resented. But after Alger had been indicted by the grand jury in 1948, another side of Priscilla emerged. As the Hiss defense team prepared for trial, Priscilla "went into a panic." She remained in that state "almost continuously, and in fact nothing Al could do or say between [the indictment] and March 21, 1951, . . . when he went off to jail, could ever stop her from being overanxious and on occasion hysterical for more than an hour or two at a time." At that point in his narrative Tony devoted five pages to direct quotations from Alger about Priscilla. Alger characterized her as having gone "into a type of collapse," of "get[ting] in a dither," of having "this constant . . . anxiety that . . . was impossible to calm."[24]

After Alger returned from prison, his difficulties with Priscilla continued. When he realized that she was opposed to his campaign for vindication, he "suggested that we not be so closely entwined" because "I had to speak more frankly" in connection with the campaign. Priscilla resisted this. The trials, Alger felt, had "meant the abasement of Prossy," who "lost all status" with Alger's conviction. Looking back, Tony wondered whether "maybe [Alger] went to jail to get away from Prossy." When he asked his father that question, Alger responded that "[p]erhaps by the time I went in I could see certain advantages to a period of separation. . . . I was not altogether horrified."[25]

The final set of episodes in the portrait of Priscilla were taken from the time when Tony was in his twenties and thirties. Alger and Priscilla separated before Tony started Harvard in the fall of 1959, and visited him separately. Tony had a difficult time adjusting to the unstructured dimensions of college, "getting up after lunch" and initially failing courses in Greek and English. Eventually Tony found satisfaction in writing features for the Harvard *Crimson*, and wrote an honor's thesis in history and literature. Although when Priscilla visited him, she reported that he was in "terrible shape," Alger thought that she "exaggerated [Tony's] troubles—maybe even relished them." "When dad would come visit me at college," Tony recalled, "the future would often tend to look like a more reliable proposition than when mom was up for a visit." After college, Tony secured a job with the *New Yorker*, and "moved back to Prossy's apartment because she told me she wanted me there."[26]

This ushered in a period in which Tony, who was simultaneously confronting professional responsibilities and concerns about his sexual identity, increasingly found Priscilla's presence chafing. Priscilla "was in a bad way," "pac[ing] the floor and moan[ing] a lot," and "alternat[ing] between cursing Al and making plans for what she'd do after he came back." Tony "would see Al every week or two for lunch," but Tony "was usually half to three quarters of an hour late and picked fights with him and was rude to his friends." Then, a "couple of years after I started working at the *New Yorker* and went back to living with Prossy,"[27] Tony had an up-setting experience. After enticing a young woman to engage in sexual relations with him, he found himself unable to become aroused, and worried that he might be gay. He decided to "get a boyfriend," and "found one who hated me, which seemed only right."[28]

It was in this period that Tony decided to "move out on Prossy, realizing, finally, that it hadn't killed Al to do so." After he found "my own place on West 10th Street . . . my life started to change." As Tony entered his thirties,

> I started working at my job, instead of seeing how many weeks I could sleep through not picking up paychecks; I started meeting lots of people who en-joyed their lives; I met a nice girl and was able to fuck her; I got to be good friends with Al, even showing up on time when we had lunch; . . . I bought new clothes and wore aviator glasses instead of hornrims; I started going to a good barber; . . . I grew a mustache. . . . These things took a few years—something like five or six—. . . but they all happened. Last year I even got a driver's license—to me a miracle. So what changed my life? Well part of it was I finally started to get to know my dad, and he turned out to be Al rather than anybody else.[29]

The theme of a demanding woman, whose emotional dependence produced feelings of confinement among the males loyal to her, surfaced again in this excerpt. When Tony lived with Priscilla, he failed to find satisfaction in his job, had low self-esteem, and worried about his sexual proclivities. After deciding to live by himself, he began to take his job more seriously and entered into a heterosexual relationship. The decisions Tony associated with a positive change in his life were all masculine rituals: buying clothes, getting his haircut, and changing the style of his glasses so as to appear more attractive to his peers; getting his driver's license; forming a closer friendship with his father; having sexual relations with a woman. They all followed from his moving out of his mother's apartment.

Although the theme of the costs of being loyal to demanding women served to unify the various narratives of Alger and Tony's lives that swirled through *Laughing Last*, its relevance to the narrative of Alger's innocence was not prominently featured. At one point, however, Tony suggested that Priscilla may have been at the root of Alger's troubles in the Hiss case. "I have found it very interesting to discover, in talking to people associated with the case, how many people on all sides . . . thought that the real truth was that Al was innocent but was covering up for something Prossy had done." He added that "several of Al's own lawyers" and "one of the top FBI men investigating the case" were of that view.[30]

Here was a connection between the "demanding woman/loyal man" theme and the Hiss campaign for vindication. But Tony could hardly make a claim that Alger covered up for Priscilla central to *Laughing Last* unless he wanted to identify himself, and his father, as purveyors of his mother's complicity as a Soviet agent. So he advanced a modified version of the demanding woman/loyal man theme, in which Alger was not covering up any links between Priscilla and the Soviets, but was seeking to prevent other sorts of evidence, such as Priscilla's abortion or Timothy Hobson's homosexual encounter, from publicly surfacing to embarrass Priscilla. Because Alger took such pains to protect Priscilla, Tony claimed, he did not devote enough time to protecting himself.

That was the extent of *Laughing Last*'s claims about Alger Hiss's innocence. The book introduced no new evidence tending to exonerate Hiss, and did not focus on Whittaker Chambers. At one point Tony linked the increasingly public tenor of his father's campaign for vindication to Watergate, writing that "[t]hree years ago, when Al saw that Dick Nixon was well on his way to becoming an ex-President, he decided that instead of working on a book about the New Deal, he would take a shot at pressing for total vindication." But the examples Tony gave were related to the *coram nobis* petition Alger eventually filed in 1978 that sought to overturn his 1950 conviction. He did not suggest that vindication for Alger Hiss might be achieved if people understood his selfless, loyal nature.[31]

In discussing the possibility that his father had been so interested in protecting Priscilla from embarrassment that he had neglected his own defense, Tony referred to a theory advanced by John Chabot Smith in *Alger Hiss: The True Story*. According to Smith, Tony wrote, "Al *was* covering up, not for any Commie crimes by Prossy, but by suppressing that old abortion of hers and at the same time making sure

Tim's gay episode didn't get on the record. John's story is true enough—as far as it goes . . . Al was participating in a sort of cover-up for Prossy's feelings."[32] But the "cover-up" was of a more general kind, Tony suggested: Alger was "more concerned about being personally loyal to Prossy." It was this sense of loyalty and protectiveness that Priscilla's "hysterical" reaction to Alger's indictment engendered that distracted Alger from mounting a more effective defense of himself.

Tony never explained, however, how loyalty to Priscilla served to undermine Alger's defense. Nor did Smith himself, whose *Alger Hiss: The True Story* argued that Alger was severely disadvantaged because he refused to allow Timothy Hobson to be called as a witness, and that Alger's protectiveness toward Priscilla resulted in the defense lawyers "g[iving] up trying" to help Priscilla become a more effective witness. Timothy would have been helpful to the defense, Smith suggested, because he was at the Hisses's house in Washington on an occasion when Chambers claimed to have picked up stolen documents from Alger Hiss, and Timothy had not seen Chambers. The testimony of Priscilla "was going to be important," Smith claimed, "because she was the one accused of typing Chambers's so-called pumpkin papers. If she could prove she hadn't done it, her husband would almost certainly be acquitted."[33]

There is no particular reason to accept any of Smith's claims. To take just one of those claims, if Timothy Hobson had been called as a witness, the most he would have been able to state was that 11 years earlier, when he was 11 years of age, he had not seen Chambers at the Hisses's Washington house. The Hiss defense had no witness who could corroborate that testimony. Timothy's stepfather was the defendant in the case, and his mother was allegedly implicated in espionage. Although the alleged homosexual episode that caused Timothy to be discharged from the navy had no relevance to his credibility as a witness, the Hiss defense lawyers might have decided that a jury, had they known about the incident, might have attached some significance to it, and concluded that Timothy should not be called. So Smith, to put it mildly, was stretching matters to suggest that Alger had disadvantaged himself by protecting Timothy.

In a chapter entitled "Adding It Up," Smith claimed that Hiss had been framed by Whittaker Chambers, who had typed the copies of the stolen documents himself. Since that chapter presented the most accessible summary of Hiss's arguments for his innocence that had yet appeared, it is worth considering in some detail.

Smith's explanation for how Chambers was able to produce documents allegedly typed on a Hiss family typewriter, which he called "the only [one] that fits all the undisputed facts," ran as follows. Whittaker Chambers needed a typewriter in the translation work he was doing in the spring of 1938. He had "spent a few nights with the Hiss family . . . in the spring of 1935," and "must have noticed Priscilla's old Woodstock." Chambers then stayed in an "empty apartment" of the Hisses for three months, and that apartment was "still full of its owner's furniture," which might have included the Woodstock typewriter. This gave Chambers "three months to use the old machine itself, and perhaps type papers on it which he carried away when he left."[34]

Thus by the spring of 1938 Chambers might have "had in his possession either the old Woodstock typewriter he had seen in the Hisses's home, or another very like it." He could have found out the Hisses had given the typewriter to Pat and Mike Catlett, and "taken it from their 'den' one night and returned it three months later." He could have "brought samples of the Hiss machine's work" to "allies in the Communist underground," who could then have found a machine with a typeface very similar to that of the Hisses. After securing that machine from his allies, Chambers could have switched it for the Hiss family machine, so that when Priscilla gave it to the Catletts, she did not know it was a fake. Meanwhile Chambers could have typed documents on the Hiss family machine, now in his possession.[35]

Smith then turned to the question of motive. Here he found that "the obvious explanation" was that Chambers "was protecting his job [with *Time* magazine] by sticking to a story he had been telling the FBI for years," that Hiss was a Communist. Chambers needed to do that, not only for his credibility, but because otherwise Hiss would have been able to sue him successfully for libel. So Chambers, under the pretense of admitting that he had previously concealed the truth that Hiss was a Soviet agent "because he was a man of compassion and didn't want to hurt [Hiss]," manufactured evidence that Hiss was an agent in order to buttress his claim that Hiss was a Communist. Chambers's "position at *Time,* "Smith argued, "depended on his reputation as an expert on American Communism and Communists."[36]

But why did Chambers type the papers in the first place? Smith suggested that he did so as part of a campaign to "blackmail" someone in the Communist party in order to protect himself from reprisals after his break with the Soviets in 1938. "[I]f Chambers already had a typewriter that matched the Hiss machine" at that time, Smith asked, "what better target for his blackmail than Hiss?" Chambers apparently "assumed, in 1935, that Hiss was a Communist," even though Hiss was not. He had "abundant reasons to resent Hiss," who had not encouraged him after their initial contacts, and who was "a golden boy making a name for himself in public life." Of all the government employees whom Chambers accused of being Communists, Hiss was the only one he knew much about. "He really had no choice," Smith concluded. "[I]f his 'life preserver' was to blackmail anyone, it had to be Hiss."[37]

Thus Chambers had the means and the motive to frame Hiss, Smith claimed. He also, in Smith's view, had the opportunity. He had secured a job "as a report editor for the National Research Project." This gave him "plenty of opportunity to make his face known wherever he wanted to in the offices and hallways, of the Old State, War, and Navy Building." As such he could have learned the State Department's procedure for distributing and disposing of the large number of diplomatic telegrams its employees received on a daily basis. When a telegram arrived, copies of it were made and distributed to several State Department offices. After those copies had been read, they would be collected in wire baskets for a messenger to pick up. The messenger would take one copy of the telegram to the permanent records office for filing, and then arrange for the others to be destroyed. Chambers could have picked up batches of the telegrams that had been deposited in the baskets, made copies of ones he found might be of interest to potential Soviet spies, and burned the rest. In this fashion, Smith suggested, Chambers could have acquired the documents that he copied and secreted away after breaking with the Soviets.[38]

Although Smith's summary of the case for Hiss's innocence was inventive and easy to follow, it was implausible. His account of how Chambers could have typed copies of stolen government documents to frame Hiss made Chambers resemble a combination of magician and fool. Smith's scenario of the "forged" documents required Chambers to steal a typewriter, perhaps twice, slip in and out of the State Department with impunity, convince his friends in the Communist underground to make a typewriter matching that of the Hisses, and return that typewriter to the Catletts without their even realizing the original typewriter had been taken. All this extraordinary legerdemain, however, was designed to frame someone whom Chambers knew was *not* a Communist or a Soviet agent so that Chambers could gain leverage on the Soviet handlers of a network of underground Communists. In short, Chambers took extraordinary risks to frame a man despite the fact that framing him would not have helped Chambers in the least.

Other than that series of conjectures, *Alger Hiss: The True Story* was a straightforward account of Hiss's life and career, incorporating some of the claims made by Hiss and his lawyers with the suggestion, made less explicitly in *Laughing Last*, that Hiss was something of a naif, incapable of fully grasping that the idealism and internationalism of the New Deal had evolved into the virulent anti-Communism of the Cold War era. "Hiss's role in these events, which he blundered into without understanding," Smith suggested, "was to dramatize to the world something he didn't believe himself—the idea that Communism was an almost supernaturally corrupting influence."[39]

Laughing Last and *Alger Hiss: The True Story*, taken together, rested their defenses of Hiss primarily on two suppositions. They asked their readers to assume that the

Hiss leaving the ceremony holding the arm of John Reed, with John Groden partially hidden on Hiss's left. Reed and Groden were the lawyers that represented him in his reinstatement petition.

Hiss case had been an exercise in the comparative credibility of Alger Hiss and Whittaker Chambers. The more one learned about Hiss's personal qualities, the less he seemed capable of having lied repeatedly about his relationship with Chambers and his associations with Soviet intelligence. And the more one learned about Chambers, the less he seemed capable of telling the truth about any subject. Both books then asked their readers to believe that agencies of the United States government, in the paranoid climate of the Cold War years, were prepared to go to any lengths in order to "prove" propositions they wanted to believe. If the infiltration of Communists into the federal government was the paramount social and political issue of the Cold War period, and exposing government employees who were Communists the top priority for investigative committees and agencies, those agencies needed some targets. They were inclined to be as partisan and as corrupt as necessary in order to secure them. Cooperation between Whittaker Chambers, a psychopathic liar, Richard Nixon, an ambitious politician riding the wave of anti-Communism, and J. Edgar Hoover, who controlled an unscrupulous, partisan FBI, in order to make the naive idealist Alger Hiss a scapegoat had a kind of historical inevitability. "The Hiss case," Smith concluded, "contributed . . . to the popularity of fraud and deceit as instruments of politics and sometimes policy, because it was through the use of these instruments that the prosecution was successful."[40]

In retrospect, it may seem startling that readers of *Laughing Last* and *Alger Hiss: The True Story* would have been inclined to jump to Smith's conclusions, or to believe that the portrait of Alger Hiss by his son was a rounded and accurate one. But in a climate affected by the debacle of Vietnam, the exposure of Hoover's FBI as an overtly partisan agency, and the disgrace of Nixon, many more members of the American public were inclined to grant the starting assumptions of *Laughing Last* and *Alger Hiss: The True Story*, and to ignore the fact that neither book had presented any new evidence supporting Hiss's claims of innocence. By 1975, as the books were underway, Hiss had had his license to practice law in Massachusetts reinstated. The Massachusetts Supreme Judicial Court, in doing so, recognized that Hiss was continuing to insist that he had never been a Communist or a Soviet agent, and that his conviction for perjury was unjust. Tony Hiss reported that in the wake of his re-instatement, Alger was successfully "working on his [*coram nobis*] case and con-tributing to his legal fees by giving talks "on the college lecture circuit." Here was the audience, with its heightened consciousness of Vietnam and Watergate, that Alger and Tony believed would eventually tip the scales in favor of Alger's vindi-cation.[41]

Alger Hiss: The True Story was published in March 1976. While it was in prepara-tion, Allen Weinstein was also working on his reassessment of the Hiss case. In 1975 some additional FBI files had been released to Hiss and Weinstein pursuant to Freedom of Information Act suits, and on February 1, Weinstein published an arti-cle in *The New York Times* stating that a "preliminary look" at those files "fails to bear out the most commonly raised conspiracy claims" made by Hiss and his de-fenders. Weinstein stopped short of saying anything definitive about the Hiss case, suggesting that "[p]ersuasive answers . . . for the unresolved questions that remain" could only be obtained when "all the FBI data have been correlated with other newly available evidence." He did mention, however, Elizabeth Bentley's and Igor Guzenko's 1945 identifications of Hiss as someone having ties with the Soviets.[42]

Aware of the forthcoming publication of Smith's and Weinstein's books, the journalist Philip Nobile decided to write an article on "The State of the Art of Alger Hiss." The article eventually appeared in the April 1976 issue of *Harper's*, and con-tained "an unscientific poll by letter and phone" in which Nobile asked "approxi-mately 100 lawyers, journalists, and various intellectuals" a question. "[I]f you had to pronounce Alger Hiss guilty or innocent," Nobile asked, "what would your ver-dict be?"[43]

Nobile's poll was precipitated not only by the appearance of Smith's and Wein-stein's books, which he believed would result in "[t]he Alger Hiss affair . . . tending toward final judgment," but by his own investment in Hiss. In the course of outlin-ing the Hiss case, Nobile stated that "[d]espite the verdict and the Supreme Court's refusal to review, the reasonable doubt persisted with regard to Hiss's guilt." The "bizarre personality of Chambers, the perfervid interest of Richard Nixon, the prosecution's failure to link Hiss to the actual typing of the documents," and "the lack of any witness supporting Chambers's party association with Hiss," Nobile felt, "troubled many open minds." After lunching with Hiss "in Greenwich Village several months ago," Nobile wrote, "I could hardly imagine" Hiss's guilt. Hiss had told Nobile "the same old story of an unsound informer, forgery by typewriter, ruthless enemies of the New Deal, anti-Communist hysteria, and a poisoned jury." "Why would he be peddling this tired line of defense," and "risking boredom and fresh humiliation," Nobile asked, "if it weren't true?"[44]

Nobile, like many others, had been struck by the dissonance between Hiss's courteous, calm demeanor and the implications of his perpetuating a lie and enlisting others in it. "Even if one grants espionage in the service of a Thirties ally," Nobile reasoned, "what kind of monster would compromise his family and friends to save face?" Such "unmitigated evil" was the last impression Hiss conveyed at lunch. "Calm, rational, and strangely unembittered, he elicited sympathy and trust. Surely he could not be one of history's arch-deceivers."[45]

Nobile's poll revealed that, at least among a group of literate, primarily northeastern public figures and intellectuals, Hiss's image had evolved from that of convicted traitor to a genuinely ambiguous figure. Of the 104 persons Nobile contacted, 55 replied. Of those, "[t]he new Hiss jury split down the middle." Nobile's poll was not exactly a random cross-section of the American public. Most of the persons who responded had already made public statements on the Hiss case, and almost all the visible public figures in the poll did not comment or did not respond. But after receiving an approximately even sampling of votes to convict and to acquit Hiss—17 of those surveyed voted Hiss guilty, 15 innocent, 6 were undecided, and 17 declined to comment—Nobile was sufficiently reassured to "vote Hiss innocent," saying that "nothing else makes sense."[46]

Voting "guilty" were William Buckley, William Bundy, William Randolph Hearst, Jr., Laura Z. Hobson (the wife of Thayer Hobson, Priscilla Hiss's first husband), Sidney Hook, Eliot Janeway, Elizabeth Janeway, Stefan Kanfer, Russell Kirk, Clare Booth Luce, Dwight McDonald, Merle Miller, John Osborne, Norman Podhoretz, John S. Service, William Shannon, and Garry Wills. Most of those persons had been previously recorded as believing that Hiss had been properly convicted. Of them, Buckley, Hearst, Hook, Kanfer, Kirk, Luce, and Podhoretz were identified with the political right. Voting "innocent" were Robert Alan Aurthur, Alexander Cockburn, Thomas Emerson, Abe Fortas, Gus Hall, Lillian Hellman, Nat Hentoff, Bruce Mazlish, Carey McWilliams, Arthur Miller, Victor Navasky, Gerald Piel,

Marcus Raskin, Robert Sherrill, and Charles Alan Wright. That list was even more decisively on the political left, with Aurthur, Cockburn, Hellman, McWilliams, Navasky, and Sherrill having been prominent supporters of Hiss when few commentators were inclined to be, and Emerson, Hall (the general secretary of the American Communist Party), Hentoff, Mazlish, Miller, and Raskin being visible advocates of left-wing causes. Wright, a prominent law professor and litigator with no discernible political affiliations, may have been something of a surprise, since he had represented Richard Nixon.[47]

The list of people who were "undecided" might have been of greater interest to Nobile's readers. It consisted of James McGregor Burns, Norman Cousins, Anthony Lewis, Norman Mailer, David Riesman, and C. Vann Woodward. All of those persons were prominent political liberals, although none could have been described as an active lobbyist for liberal causes. Burns, Riesman, and Woodward were academics, and Cousins and Lewis were journalists of an academic bent. The presence of such persons in an "undecided" group suggested that they had not satisfied themselves that enough evidence existed to support conclusions about Hiss that they wanted to believe.[48]

Many of the persons who returned Nobile's survey, but declined to comment on the issue of Hiss's guilt, tended to be politicians or those holding visible positions in public life or the academic world. Their reluctance to take a position could have been taken, in some cases, as the caution of people aware of the political fallout associated with controversial views. The group consisted of Raoul Berger, Ben Bradlee, Kingman Brewster, McGeorge Bundy, Noam Chomsky, O. Edmund Chubb, Max Frankel, George V. Higgins, Leon Jaworski, Henry Cabot Lodge, Murray Marder, John J. McCloy, Elliot L. Richardson, Dean Rusk, William Styron, and Barbara Tuchman. Nobile could have hardly expected Bradlee and Frankel, prominent newspaper editors, or Jaworski, Lodge, Richardson, and Rusk, visible figures in the Nixon and Johnson administrations, or Brewster, president of Yale University, to comment. John J. McCloy's semi-mythical status as a pillar in northeastern establishment circles since the Second World War had not been achieved by remarks on charged public issues.[49]

Nobile probably had not expected many of the 17 persons who did not respond to his survey to comment. Some of them, such as the novelist Saul Bellow, the television newscasters David Brinkley and Walter Cronkite, and Edward M. Kennedy, Mike Mansfield, Eugene McCarthy, and George McGovern, seemed to have been contacted simply for their celebrity value. The same could have been said of John Dean, J. William Fulbright, Averell Harriman, and Bill Moyers. But Nobile might have been surprised that Owen Lattimore, who had himself been under investigation

for alleged sympathies to Communism, George Kennan, one of the original architects of a resolutely anti-Soviet foreign policy, and I. F. Stone, known to be outspoken in his defense of persons accused of holding left-wing views, declined to
respond. A particularly conspicuous member of the group of nonresponders was
Thomas Murphy, who had prosecuted Hiss in both trials. Murphy was a federal
judge, but he clearly held a view on Hiss's guilt, so that Nobile may well have expected a pointed "no comment." Another somewhat puzzling member of the nonresponders was John Kenneth Galbraith, who would subsequently repeat his view
that Hiss had been justly convicted.[50]

The 49 nonresponders came from a much more diverse group of persons than the
55 responses, resulting in Nobile's survey not even being a cross section of American journalists, intellectuals, and public figures. His respondents were, overwhelmingly, intellectuals based in New York, most of which had already taken
public positions on the Hiss case. Although Nobile's asking William Buckley or
Sidney Hook or Russell Kirk about Hiss's guilt was as calculated to elicit predictable
responses as his asking Gus Hall or Arthur Miller, his survey of intellectuals included
several (Aurthur, Cockburn, Emerson, Hellman, McWilliams, Navasky, and Sherrill) who were known to have been advocates of Hiss's innocence for many years.
And Nobile did not seem to approach the question of Hiss's guilt in an entirely neu-
tral fashion. He cited an interview with Abe Fortas, in which Fortas, aware of his status as a former Supreme Court justice, stopped short of directly saying he thought
Hiss was innocent. "I always had, and still retain, an extremely high opinion of
[Hiss]," he told Nobile, "as a man of character and integrity, and as a loyal and dedicated American citizen." On the basis of that comment, Nobile entered Fortas in the
group who voted Hiss innocent. In addition, he quoted Fortas's description of Hiss
to Dean Rusk, who had known Fortas as a Johnson administration intimate. Would
Rusk, who declined to comment on the issue of Hiss's innocence, "at least endorse
this description of Hiss?" Nobile asked. Rusk did not endorse it.[51]

Nobile concluded his survey with his own assessment of Hiss. He "would vote
Hiss innocent," he said, echoing Lillian Hellman's comment that "nothing else
makes sense." "My argument," Nobile noted, "turns on psychology. I cannot con-
ceive of a sane person perpetuating a quarter century of deceit, jeopardizing the welfare of family and the reputation of friends, in a doomed attempt to reverse what that
person well knows to be the truth." Nobile kept referring to his luncheon with Hiss
and his perception of Hiss's demeanor. "Hiss is not crazy," he felt. "Instead, he is
serene. He says he has never done anything in his life that he is ashamed of." Nobile felt that "[i]f this inner harmony is simply a routine repeated by a deranged
player since 1948, then Hiss has deluded me and a large audience of fools."[52]

With Nobile's survey, and his comments, Hiss's campaign seemed in full throttle. If one imagined the survey to be at least a marginally representative cross-section of elite northeastern public opinion in 1976, Hiss had come very far from the notoriety attributed to him 20 years earlier at Princeton. Now, Nobile suggested, "[r]easonable men differ on Alger Hiss, and they always will." To progress from being a convicted traitor to the ambiguous figure that emerged from Nobile's poll had been a considerable achievement.[53]

Hiss had not accomplished that transformation in his public image by discovering any new evidence that pointed toward his innocence. The most complete summary of his career that had appeared by 1976, Smith's *Alger Hiss: The True Story*, had not contributed anything in that regard. All Smith had done was to publicize the winning dimensions of Hiss's character, his loyalty, graciousness, and unembittered belief in his innocence, and to engage in a series of speculations—none of them supported by evidence—that Chambers might have framed Hiss. But the portrait of Hiss initiated by Meyer Zeligs, fleshed out by Smith, and eventually expanded upon by *Laughing Last* had begun to take root. Instead of Alger Hiss being a cold, evasive lawyer, he had come to be thought of as a warm, humane, selfless, somewhat naive idealist. He had believed in the ideals of chivalry in his marriage, New Deal reform, and international peace. Sinister personalities obsessed with anti-Communism, such as Whittaker Chambers and Richard Nixon, had made him into a scapegoat.

Nobile's "audience of fools" was growing. Hiss was profiting from Chambers's death, Hoover's eclipse, and Nixon's disgrace. He was making connections on college campuses. The Cold War was coming to be thought of as a not altogether pleasant memory. "A Good Life," the last chapter of *Laughing Last* read, "Is the Best Revenge."[54]

A close-up of Hiss, taken at the 1975
swearing-in ceremony.

CHAPTER SIX

The Intervention of Allen Weinstein

Allen Weinstein expected the interview he had scheduled with Alger Hiss in March 1976 to be awkward. He thought that it might be the last time he and Hiss met face to face, and it was. A good deal had changed since Weinstein first had a theory about the Hiss case in the early 1970s. A good deal more was to change after the interview.

In 1976 Weinstein was in his thirties, and had recently received tenure from Smith College. He had previously written a book, entitled *Prelude to Populism*, on the effort to make silver into a national currency in the years after the Civil War, coedited a reader on slavery for college courses, and coauthored a high school textbook, *Freedom and Crisis: An American History.* As his 1971 article on the Hiss case in the *American Scholar* had signaled, he had concluded that the case could be best understood as a product of the Cold War, and that there were some troublesome unanswered questions about Hiss's guilt.

Two years after his final meeting with Hiss, Weinstein talked in more detail about his state of mind when he wrote the *American Scholar* article. The article, he thought at the time, would be the first step in his uncovering "some kind of conspiracy" against Hiss. His argument in the article, that Hiss was probably not guilty beyond a reasonable doubt, had emphasized the discrepancy between Whittaker Chambers's claim that he had defected from the Soviets in 1937 and the fact that all the stolen documents Chambers produced, and attributed to Hiss, were dated in 1938. Weinstein had not been convinced by Chambers's explanation that he had initially confused the dates, and wondered why he had not originally accused Hiss of espionage. Although he suspected that Hiss knew Chambers better than he claimed, he did not believe "that there was sufficient evidence to support the notion" that Hiss had been a Communist or a Soviet agent.[1]

Weinstein's plan was to force the government to turn over FBI files on the Hiss case through a lawsuit under the Freedom of Information Act. Once he gained access to those files, he would then learn, he suspected, "that the Bureau knew a great deal more about the case than it was telling." Eventually he hoped to show that "most of what [the FBI] knew [was] in Alger Hiss's favor." He approached a book on the Hiss case "with the assumption that my . . . research would reinforce this analysis." In short, when Weinstein began his reassessment of the Hiss case, he was "living off accumulated evidence" from his 1971 article, and being driven by his working assumptions about Hiss, Chambers, and the FBI.[2]

It was in that frame of mind that Weinstein first approached Hiss and his supporters. He was not surprised when Hiss allowed him complete access to his defense files. "Given the fact that I published an article which had argued for his innocence, and given the fact that . . . my premise was that he seemed to be innocent," Weinstein later said, "why *not* cooperate fully with me? I expected to be finding evidence that would help clear him." Weinstein added that he doubted that Hiss "thought any truly incriminating material" remained in his files, or those of the FBI. He may also have expected that if Weinstein "found evidence that would not fit [his] assumptions, I would toss it off as unimportant or irrelevant."[3]

Weinstein thus began his reassessment of the Hiss case with the same advantages as Meyer Zeligs and John Chabot Smith: full access to Hiss himself and to the information gathered over several years by lawyers representing Hiss. When Hiss resolved to cooperate with Weinstein, he was obviously not aware of all the material in his defense files, and, in particular, he may not have known that both of the lawyers who directed his defense effort through the first perjury trial, Edward McLean of the New York firm of Debevoise, Plimpton, and McLean, and William Marbury of the Baltimore firm of Marbury, Miller, and Evans (now Piper and Marbury), had resolved to keep minute records of their participation in the Hiss case. Some of those records indicated some skepticism about their client's veracity.

By the time of the first perjury trial, McLean had concluded that "at the very least, Alger was shielding Priscilla Hiss." McLean's firm had participated in Hiss's 1948 libel suit against Chambers, and had been counsel of record at the two perjury trials. But in February 1950, as Hiss began to plan the appeal of his conviction, McLean withdrew his firm from the case.[4]

The basis for McLean's withdrawal was a combination of concern that Hiss was not being sufficiently forthcoming with him, and a dispute with Hiss over the strategy of the appeal. McLean's concern about Hiss's attitude was centered on the fact that he and the other lawyers working closely with Hiss had experienced a series of unpleasant surprises about Priscilla Hiss. They did not know that she had been a member of the Socialist Party, a fact she denied at the first trial, only to be confronted with a membership roll listing her name. They did not know that she had admitted to the grand jury that the Hisses had given George Crosley a car. They suspected that she knew both Whittaker and Esther Chambers far better than she acknowledged. And they believed that she was an accomplished typist, even though Alger claimed that she barely knew how to type. In short, McLean believed that Priscilla was far more closely linked with Communist underground activity and espionage than Alger would acknowledge.

The dispute about strategy centered on Hiss's insistence that McLean emphasize two arguments in his appeal that McLean felt were strikingly weak. One was the psychologically disturbed state of Chambers. That argument was primarily the contribution of Harold Rosenwald, and Hiss was strongly attracted to it. But it had been ineffective at both trials. In the first trial Hiss defense psychiatrists were not allowed to testify, and in the second trial they were subjected to merciless cross-examination, culminating in Thomas Murphy's exchange with Dr. Carl Binger, who had based his conclusion that Chambers had a "psychopathic personality" in part on Chambers's tendency to look repeatedly at the ceiling during his testimony. McLean thought the "psychopathic personality" argument dubious, especially before an appellate court, which would not be hearing the testimony of witnesses.

McLean was also not attracted to the argument that Chambers or an associate had committed "forgery by typewriter," by producing documents typed to match the face of a Hiss family machine. The forgery-by-typewriter argument had not been made at the perjury trials, Hiss initially raising it in post-conviction comments before his sentencing. In a meeting with Hiss after his conviction, McLean made it clear that his firm's participation in an appeal was contingent, as he put it in a letter to Hiss, on its having "an undivided responsibility and final authority to decide, in our best judgment, as to how the case should be briefed and argued." "[T]here have been a number of occasions in the past," McLean added, "on which you have preferred to follow other people's advice rather than ours." Hiss responded that he "did not wish [McLean's firm] to undertake the appeal on the basis which [it] proposed." He elected to choose a new group of lawyers, headed by Chester Lane, for the appeal. Lane's brief included an elaborate statement of the forgery-by-typewriter hypothesis.[5]

After withdrawing from the Hiss case, Edward McLean retained his records, which Weinstein consulted. Much of the incriminating material that Weinstein used to build a case against Hiss came from McLean's defense files. They included the December 7, 1948, letter from John F. Davis to McLean indicating that Alger and Donald Hiss knew that Priscilla had given a Hiss family typewriter to the Catletts. Weinstein found Davis's letter particularly significant because at the same time that Alger Hiss had a conversation with Davis about the whereabouts of the typewriter, Hiss had stated to the grand jury that Priscilla had given the machine to a Washington junk dealer, and he and Priscilla had no idea what had subsequently happened to it.

William Marbury also came to have reservations about the veracity of his client. By 1964, Marbury was willing to tell Meyer Zeligs that Hiss had not told him "the whole truth" about the case. Marbury suspected that Priscilla had been involved with Communists or Soviet intelligence, and that Alger was concealing that involvement. Marbury had written Hiss to the same effect in December 1963. Hiss had responded that Marbury "was wrong in his assumption of fact," but Marbury persisted in his view, and the longtime friendship between Marbury and Hiss came to an end. After interviewing Marbury, Weinstein gained access to a long memorandum Marbury had written after the Hiss trials began, summarizing his relationship with Hiss. The memorandum contained information about Alger and Priscilla Hiss that indicated that Marbury was highly skeptical of Priscilla's credibility and not always inclined to believe in Alger's. Weinstein was to refer to it repeatedly in his book on the Hiss case.[6]

Hiss's reaction to the skepticism of McLean and Marbury was characteristic. On February 2, 1950, he and McLean had a conversation that ended with McLean's firm withdrawing from Hiss's appeal. McLean summarized that conversation in a memorandum to Hiss, in which he wrote that "[y]ou said, in substance, that . . . you desired to select new counsel who you believed would be more sympathetic to your views as to how the case should be handled." When McLean declined to pursue strategies that Hiss proposed, Hiss responded that he would find someone who would. Throughout his trials, he had attempted to control every feature of his defense.

"By 1974," Weinstein recalled, he "had begun to have some very serious questions about the completeness of Hiss's account." A good deal of the material in the Hiss defense files consisted of efforts to test the authenticity of various details in Chambers's account of his relationship with Hiss and their mutual activities. Although Hiss had challenged many of the details, and denied having had the close relationship with Chambers that the latter claimed, Hiss's lawyers found, in several instances, that Chambers's account was more credible. Weinstein gave some examples. One witness told Hiss lawyers that three separate people, of whom Chambers was one, had told her that Chambers had first met Hiss in Washington in 1934 at the "Ware Group" of Communists in the federal government, even though Hiss had claimed to have met Chambers, as George Crosley, for the first time in 1935. The witness, Josephine Herbst, lied about this information when interviewed by the FBI, and was not called as a witness at the Hiss trials.[7]

A second example involved the Bokhara rug that Chambers, on behalf of his handler Boris Bykov, claimed to have given Hiss in early 1937. Although Hiss stated that he had had no contact with Chambers after 1936, he admitted having received a rug from Chambers, which he claimed was partial payment for rent on an apartment. Chambers had given him the rug, Hiss said, sometime in 1935. But when lawyers for Hiss interviewed Edward Touloukian, an employee of the Massachusetts Importing Company, which had sold the rug, and Chambers's friend Meyer Schapiro, whom Chambers had asked to buy the rug for Bykov, they confirmed that the rug, along with three other rugs, had been shipped to Schapiro, who sent them on to Washington, in December 1936. This was consistent with Chambers's account, not Hiss's. "At every important point," Weinstein concluded, "Chambers's testimony about his underground experiences and . . . about Hiss's complicity, checked out."[8]

None of the evidence that caused Weinstein to alter his assumptions about the Hiss case between 1971 and 1974 had come from the FBI files he sought in his Freedom of Information suit. The FBI files were not made available to Weinstein until the summer of 1975, and he did not make any public assessments of them until February 1976. Weinstein's evidence came, primarily, from two sources: the Hiss defense files and friends of Chambers. After material in the defense files caused Weinstein to find Chambers's account of the case increasingly credible, he sought interviews with persons loyal to Chambers. A particularly important contact was Meyer Schapiro, the Columbia art professor who had helped Chambers buy the rugs in 1936. Weinstein first interviewed Schapiro in October 1974. Schapiro told him, in that and subsequent interviews, that he had served as an intermediary between Chambers and Oxford University Press for the purpose of securing Chambers work as a translator in the early spring of 1938. He also indicated that Chambers had been in regular touch with him and Herbert Solow, a radical journalist who had become a fervent anti-Stalinist, from the fall of 1937 to the fall of 1938, the interval when Chambers resolved to defect from the Soviet underground apparatus and carried out that defection.[9]

Schapiro also told Weinstein that letters from Chambers to Solow might be available in a collection of papers deposited by Solow's widow, Sylvia Salmi Solow, at the Hoover Institution at Stanford. Weinstein contacted Sylvia Solow, secured access to the Solow papers, and found a notarized memorandum written by Solow in the fall of 1938, summarizing an account of Chambers's break with the Soviets given by Chambers to Solow at the time. The memorandum provided additional evidence that Chambers had secured for himself a life preserver of stolen government documents, which he planned to release as part of a process of exposing Soviet underground networks if the Soviets retaliated against him after his defection.

Here, for Weinstein, was the possible solution of the "central mystery" he had identified in his 1971 article: how Chambers, if he had broken with the Soviets in 1937, as he had originally told HUAC and the FBI, could have come into possession of documents in Hiss's handwriting, and allegedly typed on a Hiss family typewriter, that were dated between January and April 1938. In the trials Chambers had testified that he had originally been mistaken about the date of his defection, and had offered some evidence that he was still paying rent and utilities on a Baltimore apartment in March 1938. But he had not been able to supply any proof that he was working for the Soviets, or had access to Hiss, in the early months of 1938. Solow's memorandum, in which Chambers gave the date of his defection as April 1938 and indicated that he had secured life-preserver materials from fellow underground agents between December 1937 and March 1938, provided proof of the first claim.[10]

After finding Solow's memorandum and several letters from Chambers to Solow between the fall of 1938 and the spring of 1939, Weinstein secured Schapiro's help, and together they attempted to develop a chronology of Chambers's activities between December 1937 and early 1939. In that interval Chambers had written letters to Solow and Schapiro, two of the handful of people who knew about his defection. Many of the letters were undated, but Weinstein and Schapiro attempted to give them approximate dates. Weinstein also found, in the Solow papers, two unpublished articles on Soviet espionage in the United States written by Chambers in 1938, which Chambers believed he had destroyed. One of the articles contained "an almost verbatim transcription" of one of the four notes in Hiss's handwriting that were included in the documents Chambers produced at the trials. Chambers was apparently going to use the transcription of the note as part of an article exposing Soviet intelligence.[11]

The evidence Weinstein found from Schapiro and Solow was less than conclusive. Solow's memo had been written at a later date, and none of the letters Chambers wrote to Schapiro or Solow could definitively establish that Chambers was still working for the Soviets in the late winter and early spring of 1938. But the letters were at least supportive of the account of his defection Chambers gave at the trials, and there was no particular reason to think that in 1938 Chambers, Solow, and Schapiro were in the process of setting up Alger Hiss for a fall sometime in the future. By the time he shared Solow's evidence with Schapiro, Weinstein was convinced that Chambers was, on the whole, a credible witness. "In the end," he told Philip Nobile in 1978, "whether or not I wanted things to turn out this way, Chambers's version turned out to be truthful and Hiss's not."[12]

The last straw for Weinstein was when he read over 15,000 pages of FBI files on the Hiss case that were released between the fall of 1975 and January 1976. Weinstein had sued for the files in November 1972. In August 1973, Attorney General Eliot Richardson opened FBI records more than 15 years old to "qualified historical researchers." As late as 1975 Weinstein had received only a few hundred pages of files, heavily edited, but two court orders by federal district judges in the District of Columbia eventually resulted in 11,000 pages of Hiss files being released in October 1975, and about 3,000 more in January 1976. By February Weinstein was prepared to announce, in both *The New York Times* and the *New Republic*, that the files showed no evidence of an FBI conspiracy, or "malevolence," only that the FBI had occasionally been inept or incompetent. There were no files supporting the forgery-by-typewriter hypothesis, and there were some that supported Chambers's testimony, such as interviews the FBI conducted with William Edward Crane, an informant who had been one of the photographers associated with Chambers's underground network, who "fleshed out in fascinating detail" its workings. Weinstein stopped short of declaring that claims that the FBI or someone else had framed Hiss were unsubstantiated by the files, but he concluded that "a preliminary look . . . fails to bear out the most commonly raised conspiracy claims."[13]

Weinstein's meeting with Hiss came about a month after his articles on the FBI files had appeared. "I was very nervous," he recalled. "Hiss is an imposing figure. He has marvelous presence, if a bit stagy. He's gracious. After some small talk, I blurted out something like, 'When I began working on this book four years ago, I thought that I would be able to demonstrate your innocence, but unfortunately, I have to tell you, that I cannot; that my assumption was wrong.'" Although Weinstein had interviewed Hiss on six previous occasions, the atmosphere in those encounters had been markedly different. Now Weinstein was feeling the force of Hiss's formidable self-control when confronted with unpleasant information about him. He was also feeling the weight of the differences between the two men's age and professional status. Alger Hiss, at 72, was still in his prime, still the credentialed lawyer, diplomat, and public speaker, despite his notoriety in some circles. Allen Weinstein, 39 at the time, was a comparatively obscure academic, in the midst of his first encounter with a scholarly topic of potentially great contemporary interest.[14]

He had meant to say more, Weinstein noted, but then Hiss interrupted him. "I'm not surprised," Hiss said. Weinstein waited for him to elaborate, but Hiss said nothing more. Flustered, with his "hands trembling," Weinstein "muttered and sputtered" the following:

> I had a number of unresolved questions about Whittaker Chambers's testimony when I began. Even then I wasn't convinced that either of you had told the complete truth. I thought, however, that you had been far more truthful than Chambers. But after interviewing scores of people, looking at the FBI files, finding new evidence in private hands, and reading all of your defense files, every important question that had existed in my mind about Chambers's veracity has been resolved. At the same time, a number of questions about your veracity on key points arose, and . . . none of them have been answered satisfactorily.

While he was making these comments he "tried to get eye contact with Alger Hiss, but he refused." When Hiss "finally looked at" Weinstein, he said, "I've always known you were prejudiced against me."[15]

One might have thought, after this exchange, that the interview would have come to an end. But, Weinstein recalled, he wanted to ask Hiss "one major question," the state of Hiss's knowledge about the Hiss family typewriter in December 1948, when Hiss had told the grand jury that Priscilla had given the typewriter away and he had no idea of its whereabouts. Weinstein had seen John Davis's December 7, 1948, letter to Edward McLean which contradicted Hiss's assertions. Hiss agreed to respond to the question, but "became a bit irritated" when Weinstein asked about the typewriter. He "was very precise," Weinstein noted, "about the fact that he had not even an iota of *personal* knowledge [about the whereabouts of the typewriter] in December '48."[16]

Weinstein then pressed the point. He asked Hiss whether "he knew of any written evidence that . . . suggested he knew exactly where the typewriter was before December 15, the grand jury's last day." Weinstein was referring to the Davis letter, which stated that Hiss had known, on December 7, 1948, that the typewriter had been given to the Catletts. "Again," Weinstein remembered, Hiss "was very precise about his lack of any *personal* knowledge in December, whether from documents or any other source." At that point Weinstein decided to challenge Hiss openly. "What would you say," he said to Hiss, "if I told you that I had documentary evidence that you knew where the [Hiss family] typewriter was in December '48, at the time when you were telling the grand jury and the FBI many times that you did not know."

Weinstein thought that Hiss responded, "I would say now, as I said then, that I had no *independent* recollection." After "batting this around for ten minutes," Weinstein let the matter drop.[17]

The interview ended, and Weinstein walked with Hiss to an elevator. After Weinstein pushed the button to summon the elevator, he "realiz[ed] that this was probably the last time we would ever speak." Aware that he "had only a few seconds" to make a final comment, Weinstein said, "I don't think you'll believe me, but I want you to know how hard this has been for me and how terrible I feel that what emerges now may cause various of your friends, whom I have gotten to know as individuals, additional suffering." Hiss looked at Weinstein and replied, "You really believe that this is going to make me suffer?" The elevator arrived, and Weinstein "said goodbye and offered my hand." Hiss "stepped away and disappeared without saying goodbye or shaking hands."[18]

Hiss had not been candid when he said that he was not surprised that Weinstein had revised his initial impression of Hiss's innocence, and that he had "always known" that Weinstein was prejudiced against him. Had Hiss believed, from the onset of Weinstein's research into the case, that Weinstein believed him to be guilty and was "prejudiced" against his campaign to prove his innocence, he would never have cooperated with Weinstein to the extent that he did. Hiss's remarks about Weinstein's being prejudice illustrate the lightning speed with which he could react to the appearance of hostility. Weinstein, whom Hiss had thought enlisted in his vindication campaign, had suddenly declared that he no longer believed in Hiss's innocence, and Hiss immediately responded by claiming that he had always known that Weinstein had it in for him. By 1978 Hiss was describing Weinstein as "a small-time professor from a small college" who was "trying to get to the big time through me." "He can't hurt me," Hiss said defiantly.[19]

But when Weinstein's book *Perjury* appeared in the spring of 1978, the first reaction to it suggested that Weinstein had hurt Hiss's campaign for vindication a good deal. After abandoning his premise that Hiss was mainly telling the truth, and Chambers was not, Weinstein had made effective use of his research. He had turned up evidence that Hiss had not been candid with his own lawyers, and that some of those lawyers were aware of that fact and, accordingly, less than fully convinced of their client's innocence. He had also discovered why the Hiss defense had not challenged the prosecution's most crucial claim, that the typeface on the documents produced by Chambers matched that on correspondence typed on a Hiss family typewriter. The Hiss defense's own typewriter experts had agreed that the typefaces were identical, and they also believed that the typeface of one machine could not be duplicated by another.

By taking Chambers's account of events, however bizarre it may have appeared, as presumptively accurate, Weinstein had been able to gain access to additional evidence, supplied by friends of Chambers, that reinforced the account. By investigating FBI and State Department files, Weinstein established that a good deal of information incriminating Hiss had not been made public at his trials. By talking to some old associates of Hiss in leftist circles in the 1930s, Weinstein was able to give a relatively full description of the Ware Group that coincided with that given by Chambers in his testimony and in *Witness*. The narrative of the Hiss-Chambers relationship that emerged from Weinstein's research seemed solidly grounded, and generally tracked that that Chambers had himself put forth. The general effect of *Perjury* was to establish that Hiss had almost certainly lied about the degree and duration of his relationship with Chambers, and had very probably supplied at least some of the documents that Chambers produced from his life preserver. When Weinstein concluded that the jury in Hiss's second trial had properly convicted him on both counts of perjury, that conclusion carried impressive weight.

The first wave of reviewer reactions to *Perjury* was overwhelmingly favorable. George Will, in *Newsweek*, described the book as "stunningly meticulous, and a monument to the intellectual ideal of truth stalked to its hiding place." "The myth of Hiss's innocence," Will concluded, "suffers the death of a thousand cuts, delicate destruction by a scholar's scalpel." Christopher Lehmann-Haupt, whose political perspective was decidedly to the left of Will's, was also impressed, writing in *The New York Times* that "the immediate impact of *Perjury* is highly impressive, and, to say the least, extremely damaging to Alger Hiss." So was Irving Howe, who described *Perjury* in *The New York Times Book Review* as "lucidly written, impressively researched, closely argued," and "formidable." Some reviewers suggested that after *Perjury*, the Hiss case was closed. "So far as any one book can dispel a large historical mystery," Garry Wills wrote in *The New York Review of Books*, "this one does it, magnificently." Alfred Kazin suggested in *Esquire* that "it is impossible to imagine anything new in the case except an admission by Alger Hiss that he has been lying for 30 years."[20]

But, at the same time, reviewers expressed puzzlement at the implications of a definitive conclusion that Hiss had been guilty of perjury and espionage. If that were so, one was required to explain Hiss's motivation in mounting his campaign for vindication. "[T]he dogged and infectious air of innocence around Hiss," Wills thought, "will continue to give people pause." He wondered "how [Hiss] could have lied to his friends in the first place and maintained the lies with assurance—even with serenity—for over a quarter of a century." *Perjury* had focused on "the evidence for certain acts having occurred," not on Hiss's motivation for being a Soviet agent, and especially not on his motivation for widely and publicly proclaiming his innocence after having been released from prison. Another reviewer, T. S. Matthews, noted that *Perjury* had appeared in a climate in which "the tide has turned in Hiss's favor," and "most American liberals believe that he was deliberately framed." Matthews was inclined to believe that Weinstein's conclusions about Hiss were correct, and if they were, Hiss would have been better off, once convicted, in "let[ting] sleeping dogs lie." As a result Matthews found Hiss "simply—incredible," having no idea . . . [w]hat Hiss is."[21]

The most impressive dimension of *Perjury*, given the climate of opinion that Matthews identified, was Weinstein's implicit portrayal of his stance as that of the objective scholar, dedicated to seeking out truth, rather than the partisan who had prejudged Hiss for better or worse before investigating the evidence. Even though public perceptions of the Hiss case had been gradually swinging in Hiss's favor as the partisanship and corruption of government officials seemed more plausible, Weinstein, *Perjury* suggested, had resisted that trend. In 1971 he may have been inclined to believe that the FBI or some other government agency had participated in the framing of Hiss, but when he sifted through the evidence, he abandoned that hypothesis.

Unfortunately for Weinstein, he would find himself unable and to some extent unwilling to persist in this stance of scholarly detachment when confronted with partisan criticism of his findings about Hiss. Rather than ignoring criticism, and referring others to the text and notes of *Perjury* itself, Weinstein engaged in public debates with his critics in which he sometimes appeared to adopt a partisan stance. The result was that some of Hiss's more fervent supporters were able to shift the focus of attention on the Hiss case from the question of Hiss's guilt or innocence to the soundness or integrity of Weinstein's scholarship. Weinstein did not emerge from the debates unscathed.

Hiss had known since his March 1976 encounter with Weinstein that a book on the Hiss case, declaring him guilty of perjury and espionage, would soon be forthcoming. His strategy, between March 1976 and the appearance of *Perjury* in April 1978 was to refrain from any mention of Weinstein or his book. This was in sharp contrast to Weinstein's activity in that period. By March 1976 he had made a decision to preview some of his principal conclusions in *Perjury*, and to reveal some of the new evidence about the Hiss case he had discovered, even though the book had not been completed. As Weinstein increasingly thrust himself into the public eye between 1976 and early 1978, Hiss and his supporters largely kept silent. Then, a week after *Perjury* was published, the *Nation* magazine, that longtime defender of Hiss, pounced.

Around the time of his March 10, 1976, meeting with Hiss, Weinstein had received another opportunity to publicize his forthcoming book. It came in the form of an invitation from *The New York Review of Books* to review Smith's *Alger Hiss: The True Story*, which was being published on March 18. Weinstein, realizing that sooner or later he would need to confront Smith's conclusions accepted the invitation, although he later said that he would have preferred to produce "a systematic review of the evidence" in the Hiss case rather than to review Smith (as he was concerned that readers might see him as having a conflict of interest). The review was scheduled for the April issue of *The New York Review*, but when Weinstein produced a draft in mid-March the *Review* released its text to *The New York Times*.[22]

The result was the two front-page articles in *The Times* on the Hiss case, appearing on March 17 and 18, 1976. They alluded to the publication of John Chabot Smith's *Alger Hiss: The True Story* and gave a summary of Weinstein's views on the Hiss case and Hiss's initial reactions. Both articles were written by Peter Kihss, a former colleague of Smith's on the *New York Herald Tribune* in the 1950s. Kihss, who told *The Times* desk that he was not the best person to report on the Hiss case because of his prior connections with both Smith and Hiss, nonetheless was "sickened" by Weinstein's review. Despite Weinstein's "strong conclusion" about Hiss's guilt, "not all the stuff" Kihss observed in Weinstein's *New York Review* draft "had much to do with Hiss." Details revealed by Weinstein about "Chambers's spy network," Kihss felt, did not constitute proof that Hiss was associated with it. Kihss believed that *The New York Review* was "trying to smother Smith."[23]

The first of Kihss's articles contained encapsulations of several of the findings Weinstein was to emphasize in *Perjury*. Kihss mentioned the discrepancy between John Davis's December 28, 1948, letter to Edward McLean revealing that Hiss had telephoned Davis on December 7 and indicated he knew the whereabouts of the typewriter, and Hiss's several statements to the grand jury, between December 10 and December 15, claiming no knowledge about the disposition of the machine. He also mentioned Weinstein's claim that he had found evidence, in the Hiss defense files, that the defense's own experts had concluded that Priscilla Hiss had probably typed the copies of documents Chambers produced, and that interlinear corrections on some of those documents were in the handwriting of Priscilla and Alger Hiss. Weinstein noted that FBI files had revealed that three other persons allegedly identified with a Soviet underground network in the 1930s had corroborated details

Hiss addressing the Harvard Law School Forum, taken on May 3, 1977.

Chambers supplied about that network, and that State Department files had confirmed that one of the documents in Chambers's life-preserver collection was a
handwritten copy, in Alger Hiss's hand, of a State Department telegram known to
have found its way to Moscow in January 1938. Finally, Kihss reported Weinstein's
claim that he had solved the "central mystery" in the case by reconstructing Chambers's calendar in 1938 through letters Chambers wrote to Solow and Schapiro.[24]

Kihss's second article, in addition to reporting Hiss's impassioned defense of his
innocence at the press conference launching Smith's book, stated that Hiss could not

recall making any statement to John Davis about the whereabouts of the typewriter. Kihss had not been able to reach Weinstein for comment in the course of preparing his first article, but he quoted Weinstein, in his second, as saying that "he felt sorry" for Hiss and that "the whole fabric of evidence, . . . much to my surprise, [had] gone the other way in terms of the position I began with."[25]

When Weinstein's review of Smith in *The New York Review of Books* eventually appeared, its central findings were accompanied by some strong statements. Weinstein said that although much of the damaging evidence about Hiss came from his own defense files, Smith, who also had complete access to those files, had ignored the evidence. Weinstein stressed that the defense files revealed that Hiss's lawyers knew that Hiss family letters and the copies of the documents Chambers produced had been typed on the same machine, and that they also knew that several other witnesses had identified Hiss and Chambers as members of the Ware Group. Such examples, combined with "new evidence" he had unearthed, Weinstein said, demonstrated that "Hiss has been lying . . . for nearly thirty years."[26]

Weinstein doubtless knew that his attack on Smith, and his strong comments about Hiss, made in advance of *Perjury*'s publication, would draw some critical reaction, but he may not have anticipated how quickly it would come. Two correspondents' description of Weinstein as having been "consumed by exchanges with critics" in the spring of 1976 was something of an understatement. A week after his *New York Review* essay was published some of his conclusions about the Hiss case were called "flatly wrong" by Peter Irons, who had written a dissertation on the domestic political roots of the Cold War period and was a friend of Hiss's. I. F. Stone, in an April 1 column in *The New York Times*, referred to Weinstein's "attack on Alger Hiss in *The New York Review of Books*," and intimated that newly released FBI files suggested that the Hiss trials had "elements of a stage-managed fraud." Robert Sherrill, the *Nation*'s Washington correspondent, used the occasion of *The New York Times Book Review* essay on Smith's book to criticize Weinstein and to repeat the "frame-up" theories first aired by Fred Cook and popularized by Smith. Three scholars wrote lengthy critical responses to Weinstein's *New York Review* essay in the form of letters to the *Review*. Weinstein responded to his critics at even greater length.[27]

Meanwhile the date of publication for *Perjury* kept getting pushed back. When Weinstein published an essay on Nixon and Hiss in *Esquire* in November 1975, a sidebar announced that "Weinstein's book, *Alger and Whittaker: The Hiss-Chambers Case*, will be published next year."[28] That still appeared to be the schedule in early 1976, when the *New Republic*, in February, and *The New York Times*, that same month, stated that the book, now titled *Perjury: The Hiss-Chambers Case*, would ap-

pear "this year"[29] and "later this year."[30] But by March *The Times* was reporting that
Weinstein "hopes to complete [*Perjury*] about next December or January for publication."[31] In June, Kevin Tierney and Philip Nobile stated that Weinstein "intends
to finish the manuscript of . . . *Perjury* . . . on Cape Cod early this summer." Alfred
A. Knopf, they added, "will publish the book after Christmas."[32] But no book appeared in late 1976, or in 1977. Weinstein continued to interview persons connected
with the Hiss case throughout most of 1977, including Priscilla Hiss. The only 1977
interviewee whose comments he used in *Perjury* was Nadya Ulanovskaya, the wife
of a Soviet controller of an underground American network in the 1930s with which
Chambers was temporarily affiliated. Weinstein tracked Ulanovskaya down in Israel,
and she confirmed Chambers's account of some details in his early career as a Soviet agent. The last person whom Weinstein interviewed was Priscilla Hiss, whom
he reported visiting on August 23, 1977. That interview may have been intended as
a formal courtesy, since Weinstein had already written the final draft of his introduction to *Perjury* (he dated that on August 22), and because Priscilla had told him
earlier, in a 1975 interview, that "I don't want to remember [the case], and I can't
therefore be of any help to you."[33]

There was thus a considerable interval between the exchange that Weinstein's
New York Review essay had precipitated in 1976 and the appearance of *Perjury* in
March 1978. In that time period Alger Hiss gained access to the page proofs of
Perjury and read them, making occasional notes on his copy. Most of Hiss's notes
consisted of statements such as "not true" or "So?" in response to claims that
Weinstein made. One example was Weinstein's description of Hiss as having "lost
considerable self-control" and being "emotionally drained" at the August 17, 1948
HUAC hearing when he was first confronted with Chambers. Another was Weinstein's characterization of Hiss as "nervous and emotional" at the subsequent August
25 hearing. Hiss objected to both depictions. Hiss's comments, which he wrote on
the margins of his copy of the page proofs, apparently found their way to Weinstein
or his publisher, because one of them, written on page 181 of Hiss's copy of the
Perjury proofs, resulted in an alteration in the final version of Weinstein's book.
Hiss wrote that Weinstein had misquoted him in an interview, and the quotation to
which Hiss objected did not appear in the published version of *Perjury*.[34]

In the same interval another critic of Weinstein, Victor Navasky, had agreed to
become editor of the *Nation* in early 1978, and was in the process of completing research on a book on the investigation of Communists in the movie industry in the
Cold War years. Navasky, 28 years younger than Hiss and five years older than
Weinstein, was a graduate of Elisabeth Irwin High School in New York, an institution whose faculty, in the late 1940s and 1950s, included many persons who declined

to take New York's required loyalty oath or to testify about their political affiliations before investigative committees. "I grew up in a very liberal milieu," Navasky told *Publishers Weekly* in 1980. "I became aware, as I was going to [Elisabeth Irwin], that the parents of some of my classmates were out of a job because of their politics."[35]

After Swarthmore College, a stint in the Army, and Yale Law School, from which he graduated in 1959, Navasky entered the world of political journalism. He was the editor and publisher of *Monocle*, a political satire magazine, from 1961 to 1970, when he joined the staff of *The New York Times Magazine*. Between 1972 and 1976 he wrote a monthly column, "In Cold Print" in *The New York Times Book Review* and was affiliated in a teaching or scholarly capacity with New York University, Wesleyan University, and the Russell Sage Foundation. In the interval between the spring of 1976 and the appearance of *Perjury* in 1978, Navasky was primarily occupied with being a visiting professor of journalism at Princeton and writing his book, which would appear in 1980 under the title *Naming Names*.

Navasky had first met Alger Hiss at a social event in the New York area in the 1960s. He later said that he had been "awed" by Hiss, whom he saw as "a sad and noble man who was trying to vindicate himself." He had been listed as "voting innocent" on Hiss by Philip Nobile in 1976. His central purpose in the *Naming Names* book, he later told an interviewer, had been to show that those members of the motion picture industry "who resisted [HUAC] and refused to name names [of Communist sympathizers in Hollywood] were acting in the spirit of the Constitution and defending the First Amendment." In contrast, the HUAC investigations amounted to a "degradation ceremony."[36] As he was completing *Naming Names*, the *Nation* invited him to succeed Carey McWilliams as its editor.

After accepting that invitation, but before assuming the editorship, Navasky wrote the Knopf publishing house for an advance galley of *Perjury*. He was requesting the galley, he told representatives of Knopf, because the publication of *Perjury* "was going to be an important event in the political culture," and he wanted to use the galley proofs to prepare an early review. When the galleys arrived, they contained no endnotes. He did not receive the endnote galleys until much closer to the date of publication.[37]

Navasky had an idea that "much more of *Perjury* than one might deduce from the text or the [end]notes drew on Chambers himself." He believed that Weinstein had "lent Chambers a perhaps undeserved credibility" through "a narrative method" that presented "Chambers's version of events, sometimes in his own voice, sometimes in Weinstein's voice, and sometimes imputed to other characters in the drama." Since Weinstein regularly placed "one [end]note at the end of a paragraph which list[ed] a half-dozen sources," the reader could not easily determine the basis of Weinstein's claims. Navasky, however, suspected that "Chambers . . . was being used to corroborate Chambers—and in ways which were often invisible to the reader."[38]

Was Navasky's hypothesis accurate? Despite his comments to Nobile, Navasky was subsequently to claim that he had formed no judgment on Hiss's guilt or innocence. Moreover, Navasky's belief that Weinstein was excessively relying on Chambers as a source was another version of the longstanding Hiss defense argument that if one did not believe Chambers, there was no case against Hiss. But Navasky had exposed a weakness in *Perjury*. On some occasions Weinstein's method of documenting his claims about the Hiss case presented verification difficulties for readers,[39] and Navasky shrewdly took advantage of that fact. Although Navasky's interest in criticizing Weinstein's research techniques can fairly be described as a partisan effort to undermine the authority of Weinstein's central charges against Hiss—none of which Navasky was able to refute—Weinstein took the bait, vigorously defending his scholarship in the form of impassioned (and tedious) exchanges with Navasky.[40]

A week after *Perjury* was published, Navasky produced a nine-page essay in the *Nation*, "The Case Not Proved Against Alger Hiss." The essay signaled that the intervention of Allen Weinstein in Hiss's campaign for vindication was not going to be taken in some circles as derailing that campaign. The essay began with a polemical conclusion. "After reading and rereading *Perjury*", Navasky wrote,

> Whatever his original motives and aspirations, Professor Weinstein is now an embattled partisan, hopelessly mired in the perspective of one side, his narrative obfuscatory, his interpretations improbable, his omissions strategic, his vocabulary manipulative, his standards double, his corroborations circular and suspect, his reporting astonishingly erratic. . . . His conversion from scholar to partisan, along with a rhetoric and methodology that confuse his beliefs with his data, make it impossible for the nonspecialist to render an honest verdict in the case.[41]

Navasky's conclusion was based on two deficiencies he found in *Perjury*. One, previously mentioned, was Weinstein's tendency to rely excessively on Whittaker Chambers's version of events and to give the misleading impression that other sources corroborated Chambers. Navasky's principal example was the date that Chambers broke from the Soviets. Chambers had previously testified (Navasky claimed "on at least sixteen separate occasions") that his break had taken place in 1937. Later, in both Hiss's perjury trials and *Witness*, he fixed April 1938 as the date. Navasky argued that Weinstein had not produced any hard evidence corroborating the April date, because the evidence he cited in support of Chambers came from sources that only Weinstein had seen (Solow's memorandum and Chambers's letters to Solow and Schapiro), and were imprecise. He also noted that rather than treating Chambers's revised account of his departure date as contradicting his earlier accounts, Weinstein's narrative contained sentences such as "[w]hen Chambers defected in 1938" and "[a]fter defecting in 1938."[42]

The other deficiency was Weinstein's use of interviews with persons from Chambers's past to corroborate connections among Chambers, Hiss, and undercover Communist networks. Navasky recruited members of the *Nation*'s staff to contact seven persons Weinstein had interviewed. Six responded. Each "claimed he was misquoted or misunderstood." In five of those cases Weinstein had used the source to corroborate information supplied by Chambers in court testimony or in *Witness*. The sixth case was Donald Hiss, whom Chambers had identified as knowing about the whereabouts of the Hiss family typewriter in December 1948. Donald Hiss denied that in a September 29, 1975, interview with Weinstein he had even discussed the typewriter.[43]

On its face, the polemical impact of Navasky's essay was impressive. Weinstein was made out to appear sloppy in his research and suspect in his interpretive stance. But in the context of Alger Hiss's campaign for vindication, the essay was less than it may have seemed. Although Chambers had clearly changed his story about the date he broke with the Soviets, Weinstein, who had examined all of Chambers's testimony regarding the date of his break, could reasonably have found Chambers's later account more credible, especially since it was supported by information Weinstein had gleaned from the Solow papers and Schapiro.

Some of the claims by Weinstein interviewees that they had been misquoted appeared to be self-serving. Two examples were Maxim Lieber and Sam Krieger. Lieber, a literary agent who was a Communist in the 1930s and knew Chambers well, was cited by Weinstein as confirming some details Chambers gave about his underground network, with which Weinstein said Lieber had been associated. Lieber, after telling Weinstein that "most of [the details about the network reported by Chambers were] true," then told Navasky that Weinstein "made all these things up from whole cloth." But Lieber also told Michael Kernan of the *Washington Post* that "Weinstein came to see me under false colors, representing himself as very friendly to Hiss. I never would have said a word to him if I'd known he was friendly to Chambers."[44]

As for Krieger, who was an organizer for the Communist Party of the United States in the 1920s, he confirmed recruiting Chambers to the party, but denied, among other things, that Chambers had been admitted to the party at the first meeting he attended, or that he had subsequently brought two friends from Columbia to meetings in the hope of recruiting them. Weinstein's most extensive use of Krieger, however, was to corroborate Chambers's claim that Krieger had been responsible for "bringing him into the Communist party," as Krieger put it to Weinstein. Details about when Chambers actually joined the party, or whether he brought friends with him to its meetings, seemed comparatively trivial. In addition, Krieger seemed to have the same change of heart about Weinstein as Lieber. In 1975, after Weinstein's article on Nixon and Hiss had appeared, Krieger wrote Weinstein that he had been "distressed" by the article because it "wasn't decisive enough in branding [Hiss's] conviction a frame-up." "I do hope," Krieger continued, "that the two days we spent in tape recording will help to prove that Alger was framed and a victim of Mc-Carthyism. Otherwise, I was given a bum steer and my time and trouble was for nothing."[45]

Navasky attempted to draw quite damaging inferences about *Perjury* from his claims about the carelessness of Weinstein's scholarship, suggesting that "*Perjury* settles nothing about the Hiss case," and "[w]hatever new data Weinstein may have gathered are fatally tainted by his unprofessionalism, his apparent intolerance for ambiguity, especially when it gets in the way of his thesis." But Navasky did not produce any evidence that refuted Weinstein's claims that Hiss had known Chambers well, had been a Soviet agent, and had lied about it. None of the alleged errors Weinstein had committed in quoting interviewees were central to his arguments about Hiss's guilt. At most they suggested that Weinstein, after first concluding that both Chambers's and Hiss's accounts of events were suspect, had then come to believe that Chambers was, in the main, telling the truth, and that Hiss was lying.[46]

Nonetheless Weinstein could not resist responding to Navasky's essay. Navasky's review, which was published in the April 8, 1978, issue of the *Nation*, had been available on April 1. By April 6 Weinstein had told *The New York Times* and the *Washington Post* that he intended "to write a thorough article about Navasky's criticism," and that he was inviting "Navasky, Hiss, or anybody else" to examine the original manuscript of *Perjury* and his tapes and notes. He added that he would "meet Navasky anytime" to debate his findings, and that Navasky could "bring along all the experts he wants, including Hiss."[47]

Weinstein, obviously less acquainted with the world of partisan journalism, played to some extent into Navasky's hands. This became apparent when Navasky, after his review of *Perjury* appeared, was able to transform a request on the part of the *Nation* to inspect Weinstein's files into a minor media event. A letter to *Encounter* magazine in March 1979 gave a summary of the confrontation between Navasky and Weinstein:

When Weinstein's book came out, Victor Navasky, editor of the *Nation*, wrote to six people whom Weinstein had interviewed, . . . asking them whether Weinstein had reported accurately in his book what they had said when he interviewed them. All six reported in great anger that he had twisted and distorted their remarks. . . .

[Sidney] Hook, [in a review of *Perjury*], says triumphantly that Weinstein is vindicated because he has them all on tape, but Professor Hook appears not to know that Weinstein—in a fashion reminiscent of Nixon at Watergate—will not let anyone hear the tapes.

The appointment was set up for Navasky and two witnesses to hear them. . . . When Navasky and his witnesses showed up, however, Mrs. Weinstein met them at the door and said that Navasky had broken his agreement—in what way, was not specified—and that Weinstein would not let him hear the tapes. The inference is inescapable that the tapes do not back Weinstein up.[48]

The summary was not quite accurate. Navasky had made a request that he and two other *Nation* staffers be allowed to inspect some of Weinstein's files, including his tapes of the interviews whose accuracy he had challenged. Weinstein, after initially granting the request, had subsequently refused, and his refusal had come at the last minute. The summary did not reveal, however, that Weinstein had told Navasky why he was refusing him access. Weinstein had only agreed that Navasky could view files related to the matters that Navasky, in his essay, had accused Weinstein of reporting inaccurately. Shortly before the planned meeting between Weinstein and the *Nation* staffers, Navasky had asked Weinstein for access to many more files than previously specified. Weinstein believed that the request violated the conditions he had previously established for access to his files, and thus canceled the meeting, telling Navasky that he would be depositing all of his files in the Harry S. Truman library by the end of 1978.

Nonetheless Weinstein suffered in the exchange. He had previously said that anyone who disagreed with his findings, including Alger Hiss, could investigate his *Perjury* files. His response to Navasky's request was not consistent with that invitation. Once having publicly taken the posture of a truth-seeking scholar who invites the world to inspect his files, Weinstein ran the risk of undermining that posture by subsequently attaching conditions to Navasky's access. The episode made Weinstein look disingenuous and evasive. Navasky, far more experienced in a certain breed of journalistic infighting, may have cared far less about "scholarly truth" than about controlling the damage Weinstein threatened to do to Hiss, or about gaining publicity for the *Nation*. He may have set out to make Weinstein, rather than Hiss, the object of public discussion after *Perjury*. Weinstein gave him the opportunity to do just that.

Alger Hiss played no public role in the events just described. There is not much evidence that he played a behind-the-scenes role either. Between 1976 and 1978 a good deal of his energy in the campaign for vindication was directed toward the lawsuit that he filed in July 1978 seeking to vacate his 1950 conviction on the ground of prosecutorial misconduct. Other than describing Weinstein as childish in 1976 and a small-time professor in 1978, he had avoided any personal references to him. Tony Hiss had noted in 1977, however, that as part of his father's efforts to "take a shot at pressing for total vindication," he had "teamed up" with "Bill Reuben, the encyclopedia of the Hiss case who walks like a man," and who had "compiled an 800-page unfinished dossier on Chambers." Reuben was on the staff of the *Nation*, and had participated in the source-checking on which Navasky had relied in his critique of *Perjury*.[49]

One additional embarrassment for Weinstein came in the spring of 1979. Alexander Cockburn, a journalist who had told Philip Nobile in 1976 that he believed Hiss to be innocent, gleefully reported the details of a settlement in a libel suit filed by Samuel Krieger against Weinstein, Knopf, and the *New Republic*. Cockburn also drew the conclusion, from the lawsuit's settlement, that Navasky had hoped would be drawn by large members of the public when he published his 1978 critique of *Perjury*. "Weinstein's scholarship and research procedures," Cockburn wrote in the *Village Voice*, "have been plainly damaged by the whole [Krieger] affair." Cockburn suggested that the settlement of Krieger's lawsuit, in which he accused Weinstein of falsely stating that he was a fugitive from an arrest for murder, was a "vindicat[ion] for Krieger." Cockburn was correct about Weinstein's inability to defend the claims on which the suit had been based.[50]

Samuel Krieger had recruited Whittaker Chambers into the Communist Party in the 1920s. In his role as Party recruiter, he used the alias "Clarence Miller." Weinstein taped two interviews with Krieger in 1974, and listed Krieger's Clarence Miller alias in the index of *Perjury*, although he did not refer to Clarence Miller in the text. Unfortunately for Weinstein, there were two American Communists using the alias Clarence Miller in the 1920s. The other Clarence Miller had escaped from jail in North Carolina in 1929 and became a fugitive in the Soviet Union. Weinstein learned about the escape of Clarence Miller from reading the memoirs of another fugitive Communist, which included a photograph of Clarence Miller in the Soviet Union in the 1930s. On the basis of that information, and a personal recollection that turned out to be inaccurate, Weinstein wrote the following footnote about Krieger in *Perjury:* "Krieger became an important Communist organizer during the Gastonia textile strike of 1929. After being jailed by local authorities, Krieger and several other union leaders fled to the Soviet Union, where he lived for a time during the 1930s. In 1977 he was living in retirement in California." He added, in support of the footnote, "Interviews with Sam Krieger, August 14–15, 174. See also Fred Beals, *Proletarian Journey,* passim, for the Gastonia strike and Soviet Union phases of Krieger's life."[51]

Weinstein had the wrong Clarence Miller, and thus his statements about Krieger's being jailed and fleeing were erroneous. Worse, Krieger was able to show that the other Clarence Miller had fled after being arrested for murder. Thus an informed reader of the footnote could have drawn the inference that Samuel Krieger, as Clarence Miller, was still wanted on a North Carolina murder charge. Under libel law, persons falsely accused of committing serious crimes can recover damages without having to show any tangible economic losses. In addition, Weinstein had repeated the statements about Krieger in a 1978 essay in the *New Republic* responding to Navasky's critique of *Perjury.* Krieger, who was able to produce a letter from the FBI clearing him of any suspicion of being the Gastonia Clarence Miller, sued Weinstein and his two publishers for $3 million.[52]

Alger Hiss was subsequently to mention Samuel Krieger's lawsuit in his memoirs. In commenting on *Perjury,* Hiss wrote that "readers noted and published its scholarly shortcomings and many errors, of which I was the principal, but not the only victim." Another person, Hiss went on to say, "was misidentified as a fugitive Communist organizer, sued Weinstein for libel, and received damages and a public apology." Hiss's statement was essentially correct, and at the same time artful. Krieger settled the case for an award of $17,500, an erratum statement by Weinstein and Knopf in subsequent editions of *Perjury,* and public apologies by Weinstein and the *New Republic.* But the statement implied that both Hiss and Krieger had been misidentified as Communist organizers. Krieger had admitted to being a Communist organizer; he had been misidentified as a *fugitive.*[53]

Cockburn concluded his account of the Krieger lawsuit by noting that Weinstein had still not followed through on his "repeated offer to place all his files [for *Perjury*] on record." After "many promises over the last three years," Cockburn noted, Weinstein "has . . . let no one have so much as a glimpse of them." His inference was plain. Cockburn was intimating that Weinstein was shielding his files from scrutiny by scholars because their investigation would reveal that in many other places in *Per-*

jury he had engaged in the same process of leaping to unjustified conclusions from ambiguous or nonexistent evidence.[54]

This was a potentially damaging supposition about Weinstein, and he had contributed to his own difficulties. He had begun his response to Navasky's attack by issuing statements that suggested he would give anyone unlimited access to his *Perjury* files. He had then backtracked from that statement when Navasky and his *Nation* colleagues asked for fairly broad access, indicating that the request amounted to a "fishing expedition" conducted by persons with ulterior motives. He had, nonetheless, promised to deposit all his files in the Truman library by the end of 1978. Cockburn was accurate in stating that three years after Weinstein's original offer to make his files public, he had not given anyone access to them.

That situation continued into the 1990s. In the second edition of *Perjury,* which was published in 1997, Weinstein included a revised version of the "Note on Documentation" that he had included in the first edition. The original note, after discussing the decisions Weinstein had made about endnotes, bibliography, and footnotes in the text (he identified his goal as "providing adequate documentation without becoming too cumbersome for the interested reader"), had contained the sentence, "Those interested in closer scrutiny can consult the entire archive used in preparing the book, approximately 50,000 to 60,000 pages of material, at the Library of Congress and the Harry S. Truman Library, where it will be deposited." That passage was struck from the 1997 edition.[55]

In its place, Weinstein wrote the following:

> When *Perjury*'s original edition was published in 1978, my intention was to deposit the 60,000 pages of material used in preparing the book at the Harry S. Truman Library. A lawsuit apparently encouraged by supporters of Alger Hiss against the author, his publisher, and the *New Republic* magazine—subsequently settled without trial—made it advisable to maintain the files accumulated through personal research. The author has deposited the FBI files used in his research at the Truman Library. Also, various scholars, including Sam Tanenhaus, recent biographer of Whittaker Chambers, have made extensive use of my personal research files with permission.[56]

Sam Tanenhaus's *Whittaker Chambers,* which appeared in 1997, confirms that at least one scholar did have extensive access to Weinstein's *Perjury* files. Although by the time that Tanenhaus had begun his research not only the FBI files but those used by

Meyer Zeligs for *Friendship and Fratricide* and those of Herbert Solow were generally available, Tanenhaus made several references to materials in the Allen Weinstein
Papers, which Weinstein had deposited with the Center for Democracy, a Washington, D.C., institution of which he was the president and chief executive officer.
Among the files Tanenhaus cited as coming from Weinstein's collection were letters
from Chambers to Meyer Schapiro in the 1920s, a 1975 interview Weinstein had
with Maxim Lieber, Weinstein's 1975 interview with Robert Stripling, the chief investigator for HUAC in 1948, and some of the undated letters Chambers had written to Schapiro in 1938 and 1939, which Weinstein had used to establish the
chronology of Chambers's break with the Soviets. Tanenhaus also had access to
Herbert Solow's November 1938 notarized memorandum, the major source for
Chambers's defection, but he saw that in the Solow papers in the Hoover Institute.[57]

The account of the Hiss case in Tanenhaus's *Whittaker Chambers* was supportive
of Weinstein's findings in *Perjury*. Weinstein may have given Tanenhaus access to his
Perjury files because he anticipated that Tanenhaus would confirm his conclusions,
or he may simply have believed that Tanenhaus was a reliable scholar. Tanenhaus's
portrait of Chambers was generally favorable, and among Tanenhaus's supporters
were persons, such as William Buckley, Ralph de Toledano, and Meyer Schapiro,
who were close friends and advocates of Chambers. So it is hard to say whether
Weinstein's cooperation with Tanenhaus signaled his renewed inclination to cooperate with scholars interested in the Hiss case, whatever their perspective. It is clear,
however, that after Navasky's attack and the Krieger lawsuit Weinstein revised his
position about making his *Perjury* files generally available.[58]

As the partisan battles about *Perjury* raged on in the late 1970s, Alger Hiss prepared
to file his *coram nobis* petition. *Coram nobis* is a shorthand version of the Latin phrase
quae coram nobis resident (which things remain before us), which captures the legal
principle that courts are always available to correct highly prejudicial errors previously made in them. A petition for *coram nobis* review must be made in the same court
in which the original errors were made, in Hiss's case federal district court in the
Southern District of New York. Because a *coram nobis* petition, if successful, results
in the complete and final eradication (the "vacation") of an earlier judgment by a
court, the standard for judicial granting of the petition is very demanding. Hiss
needed to show by clear and convincing evidence that errors at his 1950 perjury trial
had been sufficiently prejudicial that he had been denied a fair trial. Because he had
faced criminal charges, he only had to show that the evidence of his innocence

raised a reasonable doubt about his guilt. But given the relatively scanty evidence he produced at his second trial, this was a heavy burden.

The basis of Hiss's petition was that new evidence, released to him under the Freedom of Information Act in the 1970s, had revealed prosecutorial misconduct in his second trial for perjury. Specifically, he put forth documents in previously classified FBI files allegedly demonstrating that the prosecution had had improper contacts with one of the Hiss defense investigators; that it had wrongfully suppressed three statements by Whittaker Chambers to the FBI that contradicted other statements Chambers made during the second perjury trial; that it had also wrongfully suppressed evidence that the FBI knew that the Woodstock typewriter produced by the Hiss defense could not have been the typewriter originally bought by Priscilla Hiss's father; that it had improperly coached two witnesses who had given perjured testimony that the government knew to be false; and that Thomas Murphy had made an improper argument to the jury in his summation in the second trial.[59]

Hiss and his lawyers had not been very successful in obtaining their new evidence speedily, or in having their *coram nobis* petition reviewed expeditiously by Judge Richard Owen, to whom it had been assigned. In his memoirs Hiss claimed that although successful Freedom of Information Act litigants who had been given access to previously classified government documents were supposed to have those documents released to them in ten days, he did not receive all the documents he requested for four years, so that it was 1978 before his lawyers were ready to file the petition. Then Owen did not schedule arguments on the petition for another two years, and waited another two years before rendering a decision on July 15, 1982. He rejected all of the grounds for Hiss's petition, some of them summarily. He concluded that Hiss's 1950 perjury trial had been "a fair one by any standard," and that the jury verdict "was amply supported by the evidence—the most damaging aspects of which were admitted by Hiss." None of the new evidence Hiss presented in support of his petition, Owen concluded, "places that verdict under any cloud."[60]

Of all the findings Owen made in his decision, the one that most infuriated Hiss was Owen's statement that the evidence about the "second typewriter" allegedly discovered by the FBI was irrelevant because no proof that a second typewriter existed was offered at Hiss's perjury trials. Hiss found it "almost unbelievable" that Owen would "ignore my demonstration from FBI documents that it was malfeasance by the government that had deprived me of that very proof."[61] What is remarkable about this statement is that Hiss had made no such demonstration in his *coram nobis* petition. He had only demonstrated that FBI agents were concerned that the serial number on the typewriter produced by the Hiss defense might not be consistent with Woodstock typewriters manufactured in the year that Priscilla's father had purchased one. He had not shown that the FBI *knew* that there were two typewriters involved, or that the prosecution deliberately concealed that information. And it was a very long way from suggesting that the typewriter produced by the Hiss defense might not have been the Hiss family typewriter to concluding that therefore someone other than a Hiss family member had typed the Hiss standards and Baltimore documents.

William Reuben wrote a critique of Owen's decision, which the *Nation Institute* published in 1983, in which he asserted that the opinion contained "over one hundred errors of fact, ranging from significant to trivial." That same year, on February 16, a three-judge panel of the United States Court of Appeals for the Second Circuit summarily affirmed Owen's opinion. Hiss subsequently stated that the members of that panel, William H. Timbers, Ellsworth A. Van Graafeiland, and Thomas J. Meskill, were "so inflamed by their prejudices that they brush[ed] aside the government's concealment of exculpatory evidence." Hiss had received that panel of judges, he said, "[b]y the wheel of chance," and "[m]y lawyer and I knew them to be among the recently appointed conservative 'stiffening' of the appellate court." He would "have preferred any other panel." He then petitioned once again to the Supreme Court of the United States, who denied his petition on October 11, 1983. At the age of 79, Alger Hiss, twenty-three years after being convicted for perjury, had finally exhausted his legal remedies.[62]

Weinstein's intervention could well have been fatal to Hiss's campaign for vindication, but it was not. The events set in motion by Navasky's review, and culminating in the Krieger lawsuit, had the effect of redirecting some of the impact of Weinstein's intervention in the Hiss case. The initially favorable reviews of *Perjury* were potentially very damaging to Hiss's narrative of innocence. A new, massive, apparently authoritative, and seemingly objective study of the Hiss case had reinforced the second jury's decision that Hiss had been guilty of perjury and, by implication, of espionage. Weinstein had skillfully cataloged the evidence supporting Chambers's account of events, and had supplied a good deal more evidence incriminating Hiss. The first edition of *Perjury* provided information from FBI and State Department files that demonstrated that Hiss had been under suspicion of being a Communist and possibly a Soviet agent since the early 1940s, and additional information indicating that the suspicion had intensified in 1945. A full-scale security review of Hiss was underway in 1945 and 1946, and by early 1946 the State Department had resolved to promote Hiss no further and to monitor his activities. By the fall of that year Hiss had been encouraged to leave the department. *Perjury* also presented evidence, from Hiss's own defense files, that at least two of his principal lawyers believed that he had not been fully candid with them, and that Hiss knew far more about Whittaker Chambers and the whereabouts of the Hiss family typewriter than he had acknowledged.

The impact of Weinstein's intervention, at first, seemed devastating to Hiss's campaign for vindication. One reviewer said that the mystery of the Hiss-Chambers case had definitively been cleared up. But as soon as the first wave of favorable reviews appeared, Navasky launched his polemical attack and Weinstein allowed himself to be drawn into petty exchanges with his critics. Questions were raised about the credibility and authenticity of Weinstein's research. Weinstein had to issue a public apology for making false statements about Samuel Krieger. Weinstein never fully regained the momentum he had achieved with the first appearance of *Perjury*. After the book's initial appearance, he was challenging the whole world to examine his files and daring critics to refute him, but after the second edition of *Perjury* appeared (with even more evidence incriminating Hiss), Weinstein had become wary of exposing his research base.

There was a certain amount of irony in Weinstein's retreat from his initial challenge to critics. He himself had been directly, or indirectly, responsible for bringing into public view almost all of the new information that, when it surfaced from archival sources in the 1990s, further established Alger Hiss's role as a Soviet agent from at least 1934 through 1945. But his 1978 intervention in the Hiss case had not marked the end of Alger Hiss's looking-glass wars. Because of the controversy surrounding Weinstein's research, Hiss was able to continue his campaign for vindication without most observers concluding it had already been derailed. Hiss was, in fact, to have one more shining moment in that campaign.

General Dmitri A. Volkogonov, in August 1995, four months before his death. In 1992 Volkogonov announced that a search of former Soviet archives had exonerated Hiss of all charges of being a Communist and a Soviet agent. Volkogonov subsequently admitted that his search had been confined to two days in one archive.

CHAPTER SEVEN

The Russian Connection

I n the 1990s Alger Hiss's longstanding connection with Soviet intelligence would come full circle. It was the Soviets who had enticed him into undercover work in the 1930s, who had encouraged him to move into the State Department, where he might have greater access to diplomatic and military information useful to them, and who continued to work with him long after Whittaker Chambers defected from them. Now, in the last years of Hiss's life, it would be former Soviets who would attempt to clear him from any complicity as an undercover agent. Their attempt was taken in many quarters as conferring on Hiss the vindication he had so long sought. And, in a final twist, that vindication would turn out to be fleeting, and it would be the Soviets and their American undercover agents, this time as voices from the 1930s and 1940s, who would eliminate any ambiguity from the Hiss case.

J ohn Lowenthal was to serve as the catalyst for Hiss's renewed connection with the Soviets. Lowenthal had become Hiss's most visible supporter and closest advisor as Hiss entered his old age. His 1980 film, *The Trials of Alger Hiss,* was a summary of the Hiss campaign's narrative of innocence as it had taken shape in the years between the publication of *Perjury* and the appearance of *Recollections of A Life.* The film, which alternated black-and-white footage of the HUAC hearings and perjury trials with subsequent interviews, was billed as "cast[ing] an objective eye upon both sides of this hotly debated case," and as "offer[ing] no conclusion, but rather present[ing]" the available information so that the viewer may judge." It contained newsreel footage and interviews with persons associated with both sides of the case, including Richard Nixon, Robert Stripling, Isaac Don Levine, Sam Krieger, and Hiss himself. Despite its surface impression as a documentary, however, it amounted to a restatement of the central messages of Hiss's campaign.[1]

The film opened, and closed, with selections from a lecture Hiss delivered to a group of students in 1977. Hiss appeared relaxed, good humored, and confident in his claims that he was an innocent scapegoat, framed by others for partisan reasons, and his audience was depicted as convinced by his claims. In the last scene of the film, a student asks Hiss what, now that he has been cleared, he plans to do. Is he going to reenter government service, or perhaps run for office? The statement was remarkable given that it appeared after Weinstein's *New York Review* essay, which at minimum had signaled that one close student of the Hiss case was convinced of his guilt. But Hiss seemed surprised by the student's comment only because it assumed that a 73-year-old man would be inclined to reenter public service. "I'm doing well just walking across this platform," he joked. The message was that, after sifting through the evidence, a new generation of Americans had concluded that Hiss was innocent.

Much of the film had prepared the viewer to reach that conclusion. Selections from interviews with Hiss were interspersed throughout the film, giving him an opportunity to counter potentially damaging evidence. He restated the two-typewriters and forgery-by-typewriter arguments. In an interview, filmed in the late 1970s, with one of the jurors in Hiss's second trial, the juror learned for the first time that some FBI documents released to Hiss under the Freedom of Information Act had suggested that the FBI had doubts about whether the typewriter produced by the Hiss defense in court was the Woodstock that had been originally bought by Thomas Fansler. The juror stressed how significant the Woodstock had been for her and her fellow jurors, and suggested that had she known the machine brought into court might have been different from that allegedly used by Priscilla Hiss to type copies of stolen documents, Hiss might not have been found guilty.

Another juror's recollections were also used by Lowenthal to undermine the verdict against Hiss. The juror was from Hiss's first trial, where the jury had been unable to reach a unanimous verdict, voting eight to four for conviction. When Lowenthal revealed to the juror that Whittaker Chambers had given a 1949 statement to the FBI admitting some homosexual encounters (the statement was not made public until 1976), the juror responded that had the jury at the first trial known of Chambers's admission, "there would have been no case" against Hiss. The impression created was that the first jury would have found Chambers an unreliable witness because of his sexual proclivities. Elsewhere, however, the same juror suggested that he had voted to convict Hiss, and believed in his guilt. Those comments revived the strategic dilemma the Hiss defense faced with respect to rumors about Chambers's homosexuality. Hiss's lawyers had no proof of it at the time of the trials, and were concerned that stirring up rumors might look like an effort to distract the jury with irrelevant speculations.

Hiss's demeanor in the film was consistent with his willingness to associate himself more openly with leftist views in the late 1970s. In reminiscing about the years in which he first joined the federal government, he described himself as in the "radical" wing of New Dealers, and as finding nothing objectionable about Communism in the early 1930s. He vigorously attacked Joseph McCarthy, J. Edgar Hoover, and Richard Nixon, and made regular connections between his trial and McCarthyism. Lowenthal juxtaposed Hiss's comments against ones made by another interviewee, Congressman Edward Hebert, who admitted that as a member of HUAC in the 1940s and 1950s he was inclined to find anyone with potential left-wing leanings a liar and a dupe of the Communists. This was in keeping with the general tone and message of *The Trials of Alger Hiss*. Hiss had been the scapegoat of red-baiting zealots and disgraced government officials, but he was now convincing a new generation of his innocence.

Lowenthal's film was not the only effort to dramatize Hiss and the Hiss case that appeared in the 1980s. In 1983 the "American Playhouse" series, produced by the Public Broadcasting System and filmed in Boston, offered "Concealed Enemies," four one-hour programs on the Hiss case. In contrast to *The Trials of Alger Hiss*, "Concealed Enemies" contained no newsreel footage and no interviews with Hiss or other participants in the Hiss case: actors portrayed all the central characters. Although the producers and writers of "Concealed Enemies" had clearly read Smith's *Alger Hiss: The True Story, Laughing Last*, and possibly *Perjury*, the production listed no references or cooperating scholars.[2]

Although the general purpose of "Concealed Enemies" was to present the Hiss case as a fascinating set of unresolved ambiguities, it left some distinct impressions along the way. One impression was that Hiss, in the course of his confrontations with Chambers at the HUAC hearings and at the trials, had made some foolish mistakes. In the last episode of the production, Richard Hamilton, playing a "club acquaintance" of John Foster Dulles, made a comment to Dulles (played by Henderson Forsythe) after Hiss had been convicted. Hamilton summarized the mistakes Hiss had made: agreeing to appear before HUAC to defend Chambers's initial charges; failing to invoke his privilege against self-incrimination after becoming aware of the extent of the charges; suing Chambers for libel; agreeing to appear before the grand jury; trusting that he would be vindicated in the courts; trusting that he could win the case on "character" alone. He concluded his remarks by noting that Dulles, supposedly a friend and confidant of Hiss's, had ended up "testifying for the prosecution." Dulles then stalked out of the club where the exchange had taken place.[3]

An additional impression left by "Concealed Enemies" was that the architects of the production had either been convinced by some of the arguments made on Hiss's behalf in *Alger Hiss: The True Story* and *Laughing Last*, or thought they made for good drama. The suggestion that Hiss might have been covering up for Priscilla was introduced in several ways. Priscilla, played by Maria Tacci, became extremely upset after Hiss's indictment, showing great anxiety that either Timothy Hobson's homosexual episodes or her abortion might come to light. In a scene in which Timothy visited the Hisses during the trials (in the company of a young male friend), he offered to contradict Chambers's testimony that he had been in the Hiss's house on a particular occasion. Alger, played by Edward Heerman, refused the offer. In another scene Alger confided to a psychiatrist that he was worried about Priscilla's becoming hysterical over her fears about disclosure of the abortion. He claimed that he had refused to take "truth serum" because he might "lose control" and mention the abortion, and asked the psychiatrist to tell his lawyers that his refusal "had nothing to do with the case."

A third impression was that some of Hiss's opponents had political motives, and were not above manipulating evidence. One scene showed an FBI agent placing a typewriter, along with several others, in a storage area. A subsequent scene depicted a conversation between two FBI agents and J. Edgar Hoover (played by Raymond Serra) in late 1948, when the FBI and Hiss defense lawyers were looking for the Hiss family typewriter. In that conversation the agents raised the possibility that everyone looking for the typewriter had the wrong serial number, because Thomas Fansler could not have purchased a typewriter with that serial number the year he had bought it. Hoover responded by instructing the agents to keep that information within the FBI. Taken together, the scenes portrayed a somewhat garbled version of Smith's two-typewriters argument.

Several scenes showed Whittaker Chambers (played by John Harkin) and Richard Nixon (played by Peter Riegert) having private conversations, implying that Nixon, the first member of HUAC to conclude that Chambers's account of events was more credible than that of Hiss, constantly kept Chambers informed of developments in the case, and that the two men plotted strategy during the trials. There is no evidence that Nixon and Chambers met alone during the trials, or that they met frequently after the 1948 HUAC hearings. In one conversation, after Hiss's conviction, Chambers was portrayed as criticizing Joseph McCarthy to Nixon. Chambers

was not enamoured of McCarthy, and was a strong supporter of Nixon's political career. But he was not an intimate friend of Nixon's, and he maintained a careful public neutrality toward McCarthy.[4]

Julian Wadleigh (played by Frank Warden) had a fairly large role in the production. He was presented as a spokesman for the view that if Hiss had been a Communist, as Wadleigh had, and if he had passed government documents to the Soviets,
as Wadleigh had, those offenses, given the international climate of the 1930s, were
trivial. In one scene a lawyer for Hiss attempted to enlist Wadleigh to testify for the
Hiss defense. Wadleigh's wife Edythe (played by Jean de Baer) strenuously resisted,
and denounced the atmosphere in which Hiss was being tried. "I feel so isolated,"
she said. "It was either the Communists or the Fascists in those days. My husband
felt he was helping his country. Doesn't anybody understand?" In another scene
Wadleigh declared that the Hiss trial was "about politics, not truth."

At the conclusion of "Concealed Enemies," Joseph McCarthy was shown making a speech denouncing Communists in the federal government, and Alger Hiss was
shown sitting in his cell in Lewisburg, smoking, writing, and thinking. A voiceover
stated that Chambers had died in 1961, that Alger and Priscilla Hiss had separated
in 1959 and continued to live apart, and that Alger was vigorously maintaining his
innocence. Although several characters in the production, ranging from Wadleigh
through Nixon and Hoover to Dulles, were identified as believing that Hiss had
been a Communist and a Soviet agent, the general message of "Concealed Enemies" was more muted. It tended to portray Hiss as an idealistic, somewhat naive
person whose class blinders and personal loyalties caused him to underestimate his
enemies and sacrifice his own welfare to protect others. That view of Hiss was far
closer to that of Smith's *Alger Hiss: The True Story* than to Weinstein's *Perjury*.

Hiss's ebullient participation in Lowenthal's film, and the comments made at the
close of "Concealed Enemies," indicated that he was still vigorously campaigning
for vindication in the early 1980s. But by 1986, when David Remnick interviewed
Hiss for a feature story in the *Washington Post* magazine, he found Hiss, though still
serenely proclaiming his innocence, affected by time and changing currents in American politics. Macular degeneration had forced him to abandon his public lectures,
and he was living quietly in a small red clapboard house in East Hampton, on eastern Long Island. Priscilla had died in 1984, and although Alger had asked her for a
divorce repeatedly since the early 1960s, she had never agreed to discuss the matter.[5]

In 1960 Hiss had met a woman named Isabel Johnson, whom Tony Hiss described
in 1977 as "a tall, good-looking blonde." Isabel and Hiss began living together

shortly thereafter, and in 1985, with Priscilla dead, they were free to marry. When Remnick visited in 1986, he likewise portrayed Isabel as tall and beautiful, "a kind of siren of the left" who had "once been involved with author Howard Fast and was briefly married to screenwriter Howard Cole, one of the Hollywood 10" whom Navasky had written admiringly about in *Naming Names*. Isabel "would say a quick hello" to Remnick during his visit, but she "would not be interviewed or photographed," either working in the garden, "go[ing] off shopping in town," or remaining in the house's single bedroom. The East Hampton house was "simple and sparse," with "a few books on birding and the Hiss case" displayed along with "a poster print of a typewriter" in the living room. Someone had put up "a row of ceramic, lettered blocks on the windowsill" that spelled out " 'Liberal Sage.' "[6]

The Supreme Court's denial of Hiss's petition for certiorari[7] from the dismissal of his *coram nobis* petition had taken place in October 1983. He told Remnick that he had a "modest income" from the years he had sold stationery, a trust fund set up by friends that yielded about $5,000 a year, Social Security, and the occasional practice of law. ("I have one client, a small foundation. But I have to have all the documents read to me.") At the time of his interview with Remnick, he was spending most of his time dictating his memoirs, which would appear in 1988. He described them to Remnick, who found them "strangely cheery and selective," and realized that "Alger Hiss, the man, is becoming a half-remembered face, a ghost."[8]

Remnick's first impression of Hiss, in fact, had been that he was old. His legs wobbled as he left his red clapboard house to take a walk with Remnick. He was unable to see more than shapes and colors. His breath was wheezy and short, and he had to stop about every 50 yards. He was still thin, with a "razory jaw and knobby arms." His vocal cords had "bowed with age, giving his voice a quavering, underwater sound." His failing eyesight had forced him to give up driving a car and working for the Novick stationery firm.[9]

But Hiss, despite his infirmities, was hardly feeble, Remnick concluded. He retained the "formal courtesy" that previous acquaintances had remarked upon, putting companions at ease and disarming them. He continued to maintain his innocence with "a terrible evenness, pulling out old anecdotes and character sketches with the ease of an aging vaudevillian." He took jibes at Whittaker Chambers and Richard Nixon, but said that he was not bitter about the former, "because I honestly think he was not responsible for his actions," nor about the latter, because "[h]e didn't seem worth it." He insisted that his vindication was "inevitable." Remnick thought he saw "only the slightest fissures" in the "shell" Hiss presented to others.[10]

Hiss patiently took Remnick through the familiar passages in his narrative of innocence. He said that when called to testify before HUAC in 1948, he had already resolved to leave public life and return to the Boston law firm where he had his first job. He could have refused to appear at the HUAC hearings, or declined to answer questions, but he believed his testimony would clear up the allegations against him. He had thought the committee would treat him fairly, and later, that he would be given a fair chance in court. But the FBI, together with the anti-Communist zealots of the McCarthy era, were determined to have a scapegoat Communist in government in order to discredit the New Deal. Harry Dexter White and Lawrence Duggan were their first choices, but they died before they could become objects of public scrutiny. Hiss, like "the Rosenbergs," was "the right size" scapegoat.[11]

The typewriter on which stolen State Department documents had been copied was a fake, "forged" by the FBI. The Pumpkin Papers documents were also plants, "trumped up" by Chambers and his allies. He had been chosen as a victim more or less at random, being someone in the wrong place at the wrong time. "It was purely accidental. . . . I got hit." He admitted to having been a dedicated New Dealer, who "regarded the Soviets as potential allies" against Hitler, and who was even convinced that the Soviets were "driven" to sign the Hitler-Stalin pact "by the appeasement policies of Britain." He remained committed to an international policy designed to "avoid confrontation." He had never been a Soviet agent. He had simply been among a group of New Dealers with dreams of a peaceful, cooperative international community. "I insist on making this lunch dutch," he told Remnick. "That was the way with us New Dealers. We paid our own way."[12]

The narrative was still intact, as smoothly recounted as ever. But the times had changed since Hiss had been invited to write a *Times* op-ed column outlining "six parallels" between his treatment by HUAC and the Nixon administration's behavior during the Watergate crisis. Now, he told Remnick, "the enmity has risen against me once more." Chambers was a hero to the Reagan White House. The president could quote passages from *Witness,* and credited Chambers with helping him move from his 1930s liberalism to the distinctive brand of anti-Communist conservatism that would define his political career. Within the inner circles of the Reagan administration, one staffer told Remnick, Hiss was "thought of like Quisling or Benedict Arnold and the other great traitors of history." In addition to Chambers's posthumous 1984 Presidential Medal of Freedom, Reagan joined the staff of the *National Review,* in their 30th anniversary celebration in 1985, in tribute to Chambers.[13]

As for Hiss, he continued to move in left-wing circles in the 1980s. Remnick prepared for his session with Hiss by interviewing William Reuben, who had "devoted much of his adult life to vindicating Alger Hiss [and] clearing the Rosenbergs," and Victor Navasky, still editor of the *Nation.* Reuben described himself as "to the left of Alger and just about everyone else" among Hiss's supporters, and indicated that if he had heard that on his deathbed Hiss had confessed to being a Communist and Soviet agent, he "wouldn't believe it." He expressed frustration that Hiss had not been "angrier," "more passionate" about his innocence. "He doesn't have a Marxist or Socialist view" of the Hiss case "like I do," Reuben suggested. Hiss was "distracted by all the parties" in the Hamptons. Navasky characterized the parties as being composed of "what I'd call 'the old Left set'" and "the sort of cultural bohemian set."[14]

When Remnick asked Hiss about his politics, Hiss made no effort to conceal his sympathies. He "rip[ped] the president at length, especially for his policies in Nicaragua." He spoke of becoming "radicalized" by the Depression, and remembered Franklin Roosevelt's greeting to New Deal staffers: "Good morning, fellow socialists." Asked whether he admired Stalin, Hiss said, "Oh yes. In spite of knowing the extent of his crimes, he was very impressive. . . . He was decisive, softspoken, very clearheaded." Hiss remembered being able to read, while in prison, books that would have "made Joe McCarthy scream," such as the memoirs of Lenin's widow and "a radical interpretation of American slavery." That reading "kept me in touch with progressive, humane aspects of my life," he recalled. Reminded that Irving Howe, whom Remnick described as a "democratic socialist," had indicated that he had come to be convinced of Hiss's guilt, Hiss responded, "Howe? I don't consider him on the left."[15]

Remnick began his profile of Hiss with a quotation from a 1949 journal entry of Delmore Schwartz. "Alger Hiss," Schwartz wrote, "charmed everyone because he was so corrupt that he could tell anyone a lie and he could brazen out any lie." Remnick did not identify Schwartz, or elaborate on the view of Hiss expressed in the quote.[16] But he let the possibility that Hiss might have been lying about his associations hang in the air. Periodically he returned to the theme. He referred to John Lowenthal's once saying, "Anyone who has known Alger must entertain it: Might he be lying to me, his good friend?" He described Hiss as having "[o]ne of the most suspect memories in history." And he asked Hiss whether the world would ever "learn anything more about you. . . . Do you have a secret to tell?" "I have none," responded Hiss. "No secrets."[17]

But Remnick ultimately concluded that Hiss's life "will end in ambiguity." That "has been the triumph of Hiss's dotage," Remnick felt. "His persistence gives him the possibility of martyrdom." He quoted Victor Navasky's interpretation of the Hiss case. "Everybody comes to it," Navasky said, "with values and preconceptions. It's not surprising that in a case . . . where many of the principals are dead, where the charges of espionage introduce a whole world of lying, deception and code . . . you are left with ambiguity." He also quoted Allen Weinstein. "For Hiss, generations come and go," Weinstein suggested, "and since his accusers were Hoover, Chambers, and Nixon, he can always revive his own myth."[18]

Although Remnick believed that Hiss was "probably not" a martyr, he thought that "ambiguity [had] been a savior" to Hiss, making him "more important than he ever could have been either as a loyal servant to Franklin Roosevelt or to the Communist Party." "Even the most ardent partisans on either side," Remnick concluded, "sense the ambiguity." Weinstein himself, Remnick said, told him that after all his work on the Hiss case "he reserves the doubt every historian must have."[19]

Remnick's profile suggested that by the 1980s Hiss's image had not reverted to that of a convicted traitor. But from Remnick's perspective in 1986, the high-water mark in Hiss's campaign for vindication appeared to be the years between 1973 and 1975, when he was a welcome guest on campuses, publicizing a reissued edition of *In the Court of Public Opinion*, receiving an occasional favorable column, and profiting from Richard Nixon's disgrace. After Weinstein's *Perjury* appeared, Hiss's campaign had never achieved the same momentum. Remnick reported that Hiss's face "tighten[ed] into a walnut" when Weinstein's book was mentioned, and that he referred to it as a "mendacious piece of work." He also noted that "the reviewers, including many on the left, sided with Weinstein." Still, the question of Hiss's guilt had not been definitively answered for Remnick.[20]

Nothing in Hiss's memoir, *Recollections of a Life*, clarified matters for those who found the Hiss case intractably ambiguous. Most of the book was a collection of pleasurable reminiscences, including much of what Hiss had found stimulating and enjoyable in his life and leaving out most of its darker themes. Only in the last 20 pages of the book did Hiss attempt to leave readers with a vivid impression of the injustice that his conviction represented. In a chapter entitled "An Unholy Trinity" he lambasted his principal antagonists in the Hiss case, Nixon, Hoover, and Chambers, and in his final chapter, "Which Things Remain Before Us," he gave an emotional account of the denial of his 1978 *coram nobis* petition.[21]

As late as his 1986 interview with Remnick, Hiss had been measured in his comments about Nixon and Chambers, suggesting that they weren't worth becoming excited about and that Chambers, at any rate, couldn't help being unstable. But in *Recollections of a Life* Hiss decided not to hold back the depths of his antagonism. "I have had forty years to reflect on the origins of my case," he wrote, "as it was fabricated by an unholy trinity bound together by the theology of anti-communism." The members of that trinity were Nixon, "the power-hungry politician," Hoover, "the ultimate bureaucrat," and Chambers, "the perfect pawn." Although he had not previously "expressed my feelings publicly about these three men," he now, with "all judicial procedures . . . exhausted," felt "no such constraint."[22]

A comparable tone marked Hiss's account of his unsuccessful *coram nobis* petition, with which he concluded his memoirs. Hiss's description of that petition suggested, in fact, that after so many years of fashioning a story of how he had been framed for partisan purposes, he had actually come to believe it.

Hiss began his chapter on the *coram nobis* petition by stating that it was based on documents he had obtained from FBI files in his Freedom of Information Act suit. He claimed that the documents revealed that the government withheld "evidence so damaging to the prosecution's case . . . that the outcome would undoubtedly have been different" had it been revealed. He also asserted that the FBI documents "show government tampering with witnesses and infiltration of my legal staff." Specifically, he charged that a private investigator hired by the Hiss defense, Horace Schmahl, had given the prosecution details of the defense's trial preparation; that the government had withheld statements made by Chambers to the FBI that contradicted his testimony at the trials; that the prosecution had "manipulated . . . two of its important witnesses . . . to testify falsely"; and that the FBI had known that the typewriter produced in court could not have been the Woodstock owned by the Hisses. He buttressed the last argument with the claim that by the 1940s the FBI had the technology to alter the typeface on a typewriter, so that it could have produced documents matching those on the Hisses's Woodstock.[23]

Hiss then described the way the judges who passed on his *coram nobis* petition reacted to that evidence. "From the start," he suggested, "my case has been peculiarly 'political' in the sense that most people who judge it do so based on their political sentiments, fears, and desires rather than an appreciation of the facts." That had been the case with the *coram nobis* judges. Judge Richard Owen, the district judge who initially entertained the petition, was "a former assistant United States attorney whom President Nixon had appointed to the bench." Owen, who concluded that the two-typewriters argument was irrelevant to Hiss's conviction, since it had not been made at his perjury trials, "had decided against me even before he read the petition."[24]

When Hiss appealed Owen's decision to the United States Court of Appeals for the Second Circuit, he there encountered more partisan judges, Meskill, Timbers, and Van Graafeiland. They treated his counsel, Victor Rabinowitz, "with vociferous rudeness and hostility." They repeatedly noted that the two-typewriters argument had not been raised at the perjury trials, but then went on to "raise the pretext that Priscilla's father might have owned two Woodstocks." Hiss was "more shocked by this outburst of unreasoning hostility that I had been by the verdict thirty-three years earlier." He believed that when "appellate judges . . . are so inflamed by their prejudices that they brush aside the government's concealment of exculpatory evidence, evidence that, had it been timely disclosed, would have resulted in a different verdict, . . . the pillars of justice . . . are undermined." Hiss called the Court of Appeals' denial of his petition "the most depressing experience of my life."[25]

That passage reveals how deeply Alger Hiss had invested in the forgery-by-typewriter and two-typewriters arguments. He appeared to have been convinced that the FBI had deliberately withheld evidence that it was in possession of a second typewriter, and had that evidence come out at trial, he would have been acquitted. But both Owen and the Second Circuit had been on solid ground in finding the forgery-by-typewriter and two-typewriters arguments irrelevant to Hiss's initial conviction and by no means weighty enough to suggest that the conviction should be vacated. This raises the question why Hiss reacted so strongly to the Second Circuit judges's apparent indifference to his petition and hostility to his lawyer. To call their denial of his petition "the most depressing experience of his life," in light of all the other painful experiences he had encountered, was a striking response.

If one looks at the two-typewriters and forgery-by-typewriter arguments as essential components of the narrative of innocence that Hiss had been constructing for over three decades, however, the depth of Hiss's reaction becomes more comprehensible. The two arguments had been designed to fit within the general strategy of Hiss's campaign for vindication. They were arguments that emphasized the partisan, conspiratorial motives of his adversaries. They were intended to highlight Hiss's status as a scapegoat and a victim, beset by anti-Communist and anti-New Deal zealots. They also complimented the image of government agencies, when staffed by persons such as Richard Nixon and J. Edgar Hoover, as corrupt and vindictive. Finally, they reinforced the portrait of Whittaker Chambers as a pawn or a disturbed psychopath.

All of these features of the arguments lent an ideological, emotional weight to Hiss's campaign for vindication. Having very few solid legal defenses, he had been forced from the outset to emphasize the instability and unreliability of Chambers and the machinations of the prosecution. Nearly 40 years after his conviction, he had still not been able to adequately explain how Chambers could have gotten copies of stolen government documents except from Alger Hiss himself. Nor had he been able to provide convincing evidence of why Chambers, ten years after losing contact with him, would have suddenly decided to frame him. The arguments sought to take the Hiss case from the world of courtroom evidence to the hazier, more fantastic world of spying. One was supposed to believe that persons such as Chambers and Hoover were so thoroughly creatures of that latter world that they would think nothing of manufacturing documents on a typewriter to frame a former New Dealer just to execute some personal and partisan revenge. Hiss needed the arguments to maintain the fabric of his narrative of innocence intact, and when his *coram nobis* petition was contemptuously dismissed, his reaction was an emotional one.

From a sample of reviews of *Recollections of a Life,*[26] Hiss had impressed some readers with his evocative reminiscences, and reminded them of his dogged, but apparently serene, maintenance of his innocence. But *Recollections* had not changed the posture of the Hiss case appreciably from the late 1970s. Reviewers continued to be invested in the case for partisan reasons, although more calls for surmounting passions appeared. A group of reviewers retained a belief that Hiss must have been framed by some combination of Cold War antagonists.[27] Several reviewers, on both sides of the Hiss case, concluded that Hiss probably knew Chambers better than he acknowledged, and that he may well have been a Communist.[28] Although some continued to wax indignant about Hiss's espionage activities and were infuriated by his continual protestations of innocence,[29] others suggested that if he had spied, he had done so for understandable ideological reasons and the espionage he produced was relatively harmless.[30] A few continued to believe that the real importance of the Hiss case lay in the anti-Communist hysteria that nurtured it.[31]

On the whole, Hiss benefited from this state of affairs. If his campaign had not resulted in vindication, it had at least produced the state of ambiguity that Remnick identified. By denouncing his antagonists as an "unholy trinity," and repeating, over the years, that he was an ideal scapegoat for anti-New Dealers, that the atmosphere of the Cold War had made it impossible for his trial not to be "political," and that subsequent events had revealed the degree to which U.S. government agencies could become partisan and corrupt, Hiss had managed to shift his status from "convicted traitor" to that of an ambiguous figure who was either America's Dreyfus or a mendacious spy. As more commentators suggested that it was time to confine the Hiss case, and its protagonists, to the less partisan realm of historical curiosities, it appeared that Alger Hiss might end his days being thought of as an enigma. Given that on his release from prison in 1954 authorities had reason to believe that someone in the general public might attempt to kill him, that was something of a triumph. And then in 1992 came an apparent opportunity for unqualified vindication.

In December 1991, the Soviet Union collapsed, and the individual republics contained within it faced the prospect of becoming autonomous governmental units.

The largest and most prominent of those republics, Russia, seized the property of the former Soviet government, including the archives of the Communist Party. Boris Yeltsin, the new president of Russia, announced his intention to open up exchanges with the West, including visits by Western scholars who were interested in the history of the Soviet Union. In the new atmosphere created by these developments, John Lowenthal and Alger Hiss conceived a plan.

The Trials of Alger Hiss demonstrated that John Lowenthal, by the 1970s, had succeeded to the role once played by Helen Buttenweiser, that of the chief legal coordinator of Hiss's campaign for vindication. In contrast to Buttenweiser, who in the 1960s had admitted some frustration in efforts to turn up evidence helpful to Hiss, Lowenthal had aggressively sought to keep up the momentum of the campaign, releasing *The Trials of Alger Hiss* two years after *Perjury* had appeared. Although by the 1986 interview with David Remnick Hiss's eyesight had deteriorated to the point where he could no longer give public lectures and travel long distances, the campaign continued to drive both him and Lowenthal. With the opening up of Russia to Westerners in the early 1990s, Lowenthal concluded that Hiss had another opportunity to find evidence that might exonerate him.[32]

In August 1992, Hiss wrote a letter to several Russian officials, seeking information about himself in former Soviet archives. In the letter he stated that he was 88 years old and wanted to die peacefully, and he asked for evidence that would confirm that he was "never a paid, contracted agent for the Soviet Union." He also said that Lowenthal, representing him, would be visiting Moscow in September, and that he would seek appointments with the recipients of the letter. When Lowenthal arrived, one official, General Dmitri A. Volkogonov, met with him. For many years Volkogonov had served the Soviets as an official historian, producing an edition of the *History of the Great Patriotic War* and a biography of Stalin. When the Soviet Union disintegrated, Volkogonov emerged as a deputy in the new Russian Parliament and a military advisor to Boris Yeltsin.

After meeting with Lowenthal, Volkogonov promised to search Soviet archives for information about Hiss. He secured materials from KGB archives provided to him by Yevgeny Primakov, then the head of Russia's Foreign Intelligence Agency. Lowenthal returned to Moscow in October, and Volkogonov presented him with a one-page letter on Russian Federation stationery. The letter stated that after examining "a great amount of materials," Volkogonov had found "[n]ot a single document . . . that substantiates the allegation that Mr. A. Hiss collaborated with the intelligence sources of the Soviet Union." Hiss, Volkogonov concluded, "had never and nowhere been recruited as an agent of the intelligence services of the U.S.S.R.," and "was never a spy for the Soviet Union." "The fact that [Hiss] was convicted in the '50s," he added, "was a result of either false information or judicial error. . . . You can tell Alger Hiss that the heavy weight should be lifted from his heart."[33]

Lowenthal asked Volkogonov if he would supplement the letter with some video-taped comments, and Volkogonov agreed. In those comments he said that he had also found no evidence that Whittaker Chambers had been a Soviet spy. "I only found," Volkogonov said, "that [Chambers] was a member of the . . . American Communist Party." Lowenthal then returned to the United States with the documents containing Volkogonov's comments. On October 29, 1992, Lowenthal released Volkogonov's letter to the press, and he and Hiss held a news conference.[34]

The New York Times and *Washington Post* followed up Lowenthal's announcement with stories whose headlines reported that Volkogonov had "called Hiss innocent" and offered a "latest twist in the Hiss case." Both papers called Hiss to comment. He told *The Times*, "It's what I've been fighting for 44 years . . . I think this is a final verdict on the thing. I can't imagine a more authoritative source than the files of the old Soviet Union." He added that "[r]ationally, I realized time was running out, and that the correction of Chambers's charges might not come about in my lifetime." But "inside," he noted, "I was sure somehow I would be vindicated." To the *Post*, he said that he was "overjoyed, pleased as punch," and that "[t]he whole jury process [in his perjury trials] was tampered with by the propaganda of the time." "J. Edgar Hoover," he claimed, "acted with malice trying to please various people who were engineering the Cold War." The *Post* ran a picture of Hiss and Isabel Johnson embracing at the news conference.[35]

Hiss supporters were quick to claim that Volkogonov's statement exonerated Hiss. Lowenthal, whom *The Times* described as "a historian and filmmaker," and *The Post* as "a filmmaker, law professor, and longtime student of the Hiss case," told *The Times* that Volkogonov was a "professional historian who has spent decades in the archives," and who "would not lightly render an official opinion without being sure of his research." In a subsequent statement, commenting on Volkogonov's claims about Chambers, Lowenthal said that "[t]here are other scholars who have long suspected that Chambers was a total fantasist," and that Volkogonov's announcements "pull[ed] the rug out from under" Chambers's charges against Hiss.[36]

The *Nation*, whom *The Times* reported as having "back[ed] Lowenthal's studies of the Hiss case," promptly endorsed Volkogonov. Victor Navasky, reached by *The Post*, called Volkogonov's memorandum to Lowenthal "a very powerful statement," and "a major development in the case." Volkogonov was "in charge of all military intelligence," Navasky claimed, "and they did an exhaustive search." He noted that next week a *Nation* editorial would say, "We await with glorious anticipation the con-

Hiss and Isabel Johnson, whom he married in 1984 after Priscilla's death, taken on October 29, 1992. The occasion was Hiss's press conference announcing that Volkogonov and the Soviets had confirmed that he had never been a Communist or a Soviet spy. That announcement probably formed the basis of *ABC World News Tonight*'s erroneous statement, made the evening of Hiss's death on November 15, 1996, that Russian President Boris Yeltsin had said that KGB files supported Hiss's claims of innocence.

sternation that General Volkogonov's apparent vindication of Hiss . . . will cause in the neoconservative and far right communities."[37]

Some media seemed instantly convinced that Hiss had been vindicated. ABC, CBS, and NBC television reported Volkogonov's memorandum to Lowenthal the evening it was released, with CBS adding the next morning that Hiss had been "apparently exonerated" by Volkogonov. *USA Today* reported that "Russian files" indicated that "Hiss never spied." One CNN commentator asked why, in light of Volkogonov's comments, "Hiss's own government has not exonerated him," and Raymond Bonner, a guest on National Public Radio's *Weekend Edition*, called the Volkogonov memorandum a "vindication" of Hiss that revealed the excesses of anti-Communism.[38] By November 9 *Newsweek* was prepared to announce that "Russian documents seem . . . to clear [Hiss]," and that Volkogonov, "a highly re-spected general, historian, and politician," had "no reason to lie." It described the event as "bittersweet vindication for a man whose life has spanned most of this cen-tury," and quoted Hiss as saying, "This is a day of real rejoicing for me." And the *New Yorker*'s November 16 issue contained an essay by Tony Hiss, entitled "My Fa-ther's Honor," in which Tony declared that "my father's story" had been "suddenly given a very public happy ending, and I'm still finding what has happened almost too good to be true." "[N]ow people everywhere know," Tony said, "what my family and my father's devoted friends and well-wishers have always known—that Alger Hiss was not a Communist, not a spy, not a traitor. . . . Now my father can rest easy."[39]

From the outset, however, Volkogonov's announcement had been greeted with skepticism by Soviet specialists and some partisans. William F. Buckley told *The Times* that "[o]ne declaration by a General cannot undo the typewriter and all the evidence that overwhelmed the Hiss defense," and added, to the *Post*, "There is no way that a Soviet general has the power to vaporize judicial findings. The notion that Hiss has been exonerated is a huge laugh." The comments of some Soviet scholars suggested that they were equally unimpressed with Volkogonov's claims. *The Times* contacted Richard Pipes at Harvard, and he suggested that "there are a lot of things [Volkogonov] might not have seen. . . . There are archives within archives." For Volkogonov to "say that that there was no evidence in any of the archives," Pipes thought, was "not very responsible." Alexander Dallin of Stanford and Robert Tucker of Princeton were of a similar view, cautioning that "given the labyrinthine nature of the Soviet bureaucracy and the sensitivity of military and foreign intelli-gence operations," Volkogonov might have "unknowingly overstated his findings." "It was beyond the powers of even the most highly placed Russian official," they suggested, "to reach into every nook and cranny of Soviet intelligence."[40]

Allen Weinstein was also contacted by *The Times* and the *Post* for his reaction. Be-tween the appearance of the first edition of *Perjury* and 1992 he had left Smith Col-lege to become the head of a Washington-based organization, the Center for Democracy. After the Soviet Union collapsed, Weinstein and the publisher Random House, who had issued a paperback edition of *Perjury* in 1979, became interested in a project to secure Weinstein and other Western and Russian scholars access to KGB files. An agreement between Random House and a group of retired KGB agents was negotiated in 1992, with the sanction of the Russian Intelligence Service under Yevgeny Primakov. The agreement called for Weinstein, in collaboration with a Russian journalist who had previously worked for the KGB, Alexander Vassiliev, to write a history of Soviet intelligence operations in the United States in the 1930s and 1940s. Weinstein was thus once again engaged in the pursuit of archival material about Alger Hiss.[41]

Although Volkogonov's statement directly contradicted Weinstein's conclusions in *Perjury,* his initial response to it was cautious. He told *The Times* that Volkogonov's memorandum "reopened the [Hiss] case," requiring "every serious scholar . . . to take a fresh look." Perhaps with his forthcoming research in Russian archives in mind, he added that "[w]e have to see all the documents on Soviet espionage." He was somewhat more critical to the *Post.* "We know that Volkogonov looked at KGB files," he said, "but Chambers, by everybody's account, worked for military intelligence. Has Volkogonov looked at military intelligence files? Does . . . Yevgeny Primakov endorse this statement?" (Primakov had not).[42]

The *Post* invited Weinstein to elaborate on his comments in a November 4, 1992, op-ed column. Weinstein suggested that Volkogonov's "research" on Hiss might have been cursory. He noted that Volkogonov had apparently only consulted KGB files, and that Chambers had testified that both he and Hiss worked for the GRU, Soviet military intelligence. He also mentioned that in the period Volkogonov allegedly consulted the KGB files on Hiss, he told the *Moscow Times* that he was "devoting the majority of his time to research in the presidential archives" for information about Americans who had been reported as missing in action in Vietnam, and who may have been brought to the Soviet Union. Finally, he found it significant that Yevgeny Primakov had "made no comment on the matter" of Hiss and the KGB files, and stated that when he had visited Moscow in September 1992, and met with Primakov in connection with launching the arrangement between Random House and former KGB officials, Primakov had not mentioned Volkogonov's request to see KGB files.

But most of Weinstein's column amounted to a plea for support for his research into Russian archives. He stated that he and Primakov had had "an extensive discussion of possible subjects for joint Russian-U.S. scholarly research, including my request for release of KGB files of historical interest related to Soviet espionage in the United States during the 1930s and 1940s." He indicated that he planned to return to Moscow later in November "to raise with both Volkogonov and Primakov the concern for scholars . . . for early and complete release of [the KGB] records" he had discussed with Primakov. He declared that "the months ahead constitute a moment of truth in efforts by President Yeltsin and other Russian democrats to consolidate their fragile post-Communist open society," and called on "Western supporters" to "maximize efforts to provide our friends with immediate . . . government aid, private investment, technical help, and political support." "One unique aspect of Boris Yeltsin's leadership," he concluded, has been his commitment to ensuring that the Russian future includes a complete and honest record of the Soviet past."[43]

Weinstein's comments had raised the question of how Volkogonov, in the space of a comparatively short time, had been able to do a sufficiently exhaustive search of Soviet archives to make the categorical exoneration of Hiss that he provided to Lowenthal. "We do not even know," Weinstein said in his column, "whether the general has read a single book or article . . . on the [Hiss] case, despite having pronounced its closure so confidently." And as Weinstein prepared to return to Moscow, Volkogonov himself retreated from his position. In a letter published in the Moscow *Nezavisimaya Gazeta (Independent Gazette)* on November 24, 1992, Volkogonov revealed that he had only looked for "two days" in KGB archives, that "what I saw gives no basis to claim a full clarification" of Hiss's status, and that his more categorical comments had been an accommodation to Hiss and John Lowenthal. Hiss had "wanted to die peacefully," Volkogonov recalled, and Lowenthal had "pushed me hard to say things of which I was not fully convinced." He said that his motives for writing the memorandum, and assembling the videotape, for Lowenthal had been "primarily humanitarian."[44]

Volkogonov's retraction made it clear that his research on Hiss had established nothing that specialists on the Hiss case did not already know. Hiss was not a KGB agent, so it would have been unusual for any communications regarding him to have shown up in KGB archives. (As a matter of fact, there were a few such communications, but Volkogonov apparently did not see them.) Hiss had never been a "paid, contracted" agent for the Soviet Union: he had been a volunteer, working for ideological reasons. Volkogonov had only looked at KGB files for two days, a very short time to canvass records that, in Hiss's case, would have needed to extend from 1934 to 1946. In short, Volkogonov had not exonerated Hiss at all of being an agent for the Soviets, and he could have cleared him of being a "paid, contracted" agent without looking at any records.

Volkogonov's retraction did not gain anything like the attention among American media that his initial memorandum had garnered. No American newspaper reported the contents of Volkogonov's letter to the *Independent Gazette* until December 17, although the Federal Broadcast Information Service, based in Washington, broadcast the contents of the letter on December 3. As late as December 13, *The New*

York Times ran an article stating that Volkogonov had exonerated Hiss and indicating that Chambers had never been a Soviet agent. None of the television networks that had reported Volkogonov's "exoneration" of Hiss ran coverage of his letter to the *Gazette*.[45]

On December 17, 1992, however, Serge Schmemann, a Moscow correspondent for *The New York Times*, interviewed Volkogonov. "I was not properly understood," Volkogonov was quoted as saying about his initial communications with Lowenthal. "The Ministry of Defense also has an intelligence service, which is totally different, and many documents have been destroyed. I only looked through what the KGB had." Volkogonov told Schmemann that he was "a bit taken aback" by the reaction to his first comments on Hiss. "This was only my personal opinion," Volkogonov added. He repeated that he had written the memorandum primarily for humanitarian reasons, that Hiss had "wanted to prove that he was not a paid, contracted spy," and that Lowenthal had pressured him to exaggerate his claims. "But I did spend two days swallowing dust," Volkogonov said of his investigation of KGB archives.[46]

The Times contacted Hiss for a comment on Volkogonov's retraction. "If the general and his associates haven't examined all the files," Hiss said, "I hope they will examine others, and they will show the same thing." The *Washington Times*, reporting on Schmemann's interview with Volkogonov on December 18, ran the same photograph of Alger Hiss and Isabel Johnson embracing at the October news conference announcing Volkogonov's "exoneration."[47]

On January 11, 1993, George Will offered a summary of the Volkogonov episode in *Newsweek*, and found a moral in the tale. Will noted the number of American media outlets who had rushed to publicize Volkogonov's comments in October, and contrasted them with the absence of coverage of his November letter and his December interview with Schmemann. Will characterized the arguments advanced by "[t]he remnant of Hiss true believers" for his innocence as "ever more rococo." Although "only the childish or the paranoid," Will thought, could believe that Hiss had been framed, "slipshod journalism" of the kind associated with the Volkogonov episode, when combined with the general ignorance of the public about "the arcana of [the Hiss] case," made "most Americans . . . at the mercy of Hiss's continuing mendacity." Episodes like "the spurious 'exoneration' by Volkogonov" could "linger . . . in the air like the Cheshire cat's grin." They were "Hiss's reward for his cold persistence in exploiting American amnesia."[48]

At the time of the Volkogonov episode it was clear to most Americans that the Soviet Union was no longer a monolith, and that the Russian Republic would be experimenting with Western political and economic models. But not much else was clear. Was Boris Yeltsin, persistently rumored to be in ill health, the equivalent of a

Soviet premier, or a figure with much less power and influence? Did the collapse of the Soviet Union mean that Russians would now wholly repudiate their immediate past? To what extent would the records of the Soviet state be opened up? To what extent could Americans trust former Soviets in the post-Soviet world? In some respects the ease with which some American media accepted Volkogonov's "exoneration" of Hiss represented a longing to trust the Soviets. Once again Hiss had shrewdly assessed the changing political climate in which he continued to conduct his campaign.

The Volkogonov episode was significant in another respect. It was one more example of the distinctive combination of artfulness and recklessness that characterized Hiss's campaign for vindication. Like the two-typewriters argument, it had originated in a practical piece of strategy and mushroomed into a categorical affirmation of Hiss's innocence. Hiss's original request to the Soviet archivists had been to support him in a claim that he knew was easy to support. He assumed that even with the collapse of the Soviet Union, Russian officials had no incentive to publicize the Soviets' successful recruitment of a prominent American in the 1930s and 1940s. He also assumed that they could easily respond affirmatively to a request for proof that he had not been paid for his services. So Hiss's initial request was close to a no-lose proposition. But then, when Lowenthal persuaded Volkogonov to issue a much more sweeping exoneration of Hiss, Hiss decided to publicize it. In doing so he knew that Volkogonov's statement was based on so thin, and so suspect, an evidentiary basis that it would invite others to scrutinize its credibility, and possibly derail Hiss's campaign. But Hiss took the risk anyway.

Of all the risky dimensions of Hiss's and Lowenthal's decision to publicize the exaggerated version of Volkogonov's "exoneration," the most striking was Hiss's claim, when that version was first released, that he couldn't imagine "a more authoritative source" for the truth about the Hiss case "than the files of the old Soviet Union." Notwithstanding the longing Americans may have had to trust the Russians in 1992, it is intriguing that Hiss would have believed that the American public, having experienced a 50-year history in which the "old Soviet Union" had been associated with the systematic distortion and suppression of truth—would suddenly decide that a former KGB official's search of KGB records contained unvarnished truth about the Soviet Union's intelligence activities. And yet we have seen that at least some visible American media decided just that.[49]

The Russian connection to Hiss was to continue beyond the Volkogonov episode, and beyond Hiss's death in 1996. It was, ultimately, to bring the Hiss case into its sharpest relief. Through a series of reactions, in both Russia and the United States, to the temporary opening of Soviet era archives in the early 1990s, a good deal of new evidence about Hiss came to light. All of that evidence confirmed the account of Hiss's life as an agent for Soviet military intelligence that Chambers had supplied, as well as evidence about Hiss previously furnished by Hede Massing, Elizabeth Bentley, and Igor Guzenko. But the extraordinary aspect of the evidence was not that it reinforced those sources. It was that it brought into the narrative of Alger Hiss's life some anonymous, or obscure, participants in Soviet and American intelligence in the 1930s and 1940s who had known a great deal about Alger Hiss, and who had recorded that knowledge for their limited circles. As Hiss was approaching death, in the mid-1990s, the comments of those persons about him were about to enter the public domain.

Random House had not been the only American publisher making arrangements with Russian groups after the collapse of the Soviet Union. In 1992 Yale University Press secured access for two American specialists on domestic Communism, Harvey Klehr and John Earl Haynes, and a Russian scholar, Fridrikh Igorevich Firsov, to a newly opened Russian archive, known as the Russian Center for the Preservation and Study of Documents of Recent History. RTsKhIDNI (pronounced *"ritz-kidney"*), the Center's acronym in Russian, housed files of the Comintern (the umbrella organization that directed policy for Communist parties outside of Russia) and the Communist Party of the United States. Three American foundations, the John M. Olin Foundation, the Open Society Fund, and the Smith-Richardson Foundation, supported the project, as did a Russian foundation, the Foundation for Cultural Initiative. Russian translators were hired to work with the documents, and Klehr and Haynes each made two visits to Moscow in 1992 and 1994.[50]

The first work to emerge from the RTsKhIDNI project was Klehr, Haynes, and Firsov's *The Secret World of American Communism,* published by Yale Press in 1995. The book was a collection of 92 documents from the RTsKhIDNI archives, primarily from the 1930s and 1940s, with commentary by the authors. The documents consisted of communications between members of the American Communist Party and officials in Moscow. The documents conclusively demonstrated that the actions and policies of the Communist Party of the United States were directed by Comintern representatives in the Soviet Union, and that the American Communist Party was used as a device to recruit American undercover agents for Soviet intelligence. Although Hiss's name did not appear in any of the documents, they confirmed a number of details in Chambers's account of the joint espionage in which he and Hiss allegedly participated. They confirmed, for example, that Joszef Peter, known as "J. Peters," was installed as the controller of the American Communist Party's secret

apparatus in 1932, and funneled American Communists whom he thought had potential as undercover agents to the Soviets through 1938, when he was replaced.
Whittaker Chambers had identified Peters as the liaison between the Ware Group
and Moscow in the early 1930s, and the person who had recruited him and Hiss to
espionage.[51]

The documents also confirmed that several persons whom Chambers, and Elizabeth Bentley, had identified as being Soviet agents in United States government agencies in the 1930s were known as such by Moscow. Many of the documents in question
were communications initiated by Pavel Fitin, the head of the foreign intelligence office of the NKVD from 1940 to 1946. Fitin's duties included coordinating with the
Comintern about the identity and tasks of American-based Soviet agents. He regularly dispatched telegrams and other communications to Comintern officials asking
for information about the agents, typically giving their actual names. Fitin's communications, and the replies to them by Comintern representatives, confirmed the status of several American agents whom Chambers, and Elizabeth Bentley, had identified
as officials of the United States government who were working for the Soviets.[52]

Although the opening of the RTsKhIDNI archives produced additional evidence
buttressing the credibility of Chambers's version of events, its greater significance
came in its ramifications for expanded access by scholars to secret intelligence files
in the United States as well as in Russia. While working in the RTsKhIDNI files,
Klehr and Haynes found communications from Fitin about three American, British,
and French agents for the Soviets, Judith Coplon, Klaus Fuchs, and Pierre Cot. All
of them had been subsequently identified as spies by American and British intelligence, and anecdotal evidence suggested that they had been exposed because en-
crypted telegrams from Soviet agents had been decoded. That evidence, provided
in the 1986 memoir of Robert Lamphere, a retired FBI agent, and the 1987 memoir
of Peter Wright, a retired officer with British counterintelligence, pointed to a brief
period during the Second World War when American intelligence had broken the
codes of Soviet transmissions from Washington and New York to Moscow. The
code-breaking project, known by insiders by the name Venona, had apparently been
engineered by the United States' National Security Agency.[53]

As they were completing *The Secret World of American Communism*, Klehr and
Haynes attempted to learn more about the Venona project. They interviewed an official of the National Security Agency, who confirmed the existence of Venona, indicated that it had produced a good deal of helpful information during the Second
World War, and stated that all of the information was classified. There matters
stood until *The Secret World of American Communism* was published in 1995. Shortly
after its publication Klehr and Haynes were contacted by Senator Daniel Patrick

Moynihan, who had been named the chair of a Commission on Protecting and Re-
ducing Governmental Secrecy created by the Clinton administration. Moynihan
asked Klehr and Haynes to testify before a meeting of that commission in May 1995.

At the meeting Klehr and Haynes described the cooperation they had been given
by Russian officials in their investigation of the RTsKhIDNI archives, and stated that
they found it ironic that messages in the 1940s from Soviet officials to their
American-based contacts were available in Russian archives, but their decoded versions, if they existed, remained in a closed archive in the United States. Given the
National Security Agency's previous response to their questions about the Venona
archives, Klehr and Haynes remained pessimistic that they would be opened. But in
July 1995, at a ceremony in Langley, Virginia, attended by representatives of the
CIA, the FBI, and the National Security Agency (NSA), a batch of Venona messages
was released. It consisted of deciphered Soviet telegrams and cables between 1942,
when the Soviets, responding to the pressure of wartime traffic, began to use a less
secure coding system, and 1946, when a Soviet agent with NSA, William Weisband,
informed Moscow that the codes had been broken. NSA continued to decipher messages until the 1970s, but the only successfully decoded messages were within the
1942 to 1946 period.[54]

Some of the decoded Venona messages, however, amounted to major break-
throughs in the history of Soviet intelligence in America. In a 1999 book, *Venona:
Decoding Soviet Espionage in America*, Haynes and Klehr summarized the findings
of the Venona project:

> What [the Venona decryptions of Soviet telegrams and cables revealed,]
> however, stunned American officials. Messages thought to be between So-
> viet diplomats at the Soviet consulate in New York and the People's Com-
> missariat of Foreign Affairs in Moscow turned out to be cables between
> professional intelligence field officers and Gen. Pavel Fitin, head of the
> foreign intelligence directorate of the [NKVD] in Moscow. . . .
>
> By 1948 the accumulating evidence from other decoded Venona cables
> showed that the Soviets had recruited spies in virtually every major Amer-
> ican government agency of military or diplomatic importance. . . . The de-
> ciphered cables . . . identify 349 citizens, immigrants, and permanent
> residents of the United States who had a covert relationship with Soviet in-
> telligence agencies.[55]

Among those identified by the Venona decryptions as having a covert relationship
with the Soviets was Alger Hiss.

The first decrypted Venona cable alluding to Hiss was one in September 1943, from "Mol'er," (identified by the NSA as Pavel P. Mikhailov, the Soviet Vice Consul in New York who doubled as the controller of military intelligence for the NKVD) to the "director" in Moscow, Pavel Fitin. It was only partially decoded, and appeared to be a response to one of Fitin's periodic requests for information about American-based agents. Fitin's requests were particularly useful to United States intelligence agencies, and also to subsequent scholars, because they often asked for the real names of the agents along with their code names. In this case Mikhailov supplied Fitin with the code names ("Matvej, Frank, Gustav," etc.) of several agents, and their actual names ("Milton Schwartz, Arthur Moosen, George Gorchoff," etc.). He also added: "The Neighbor has reported that [undecipherable] from the State Department by the name of Hiss."[56] Schwartz, Moosen, and Gorchoff were all New York-based GRU agents, controlled by Mikhailov. Under Soviet intelligence procedure at the time, Mikhailov would not have known the code names, or identities, of Washington-based GRU agents unless someone in Soviet intelligence circles told him. The NKVD had the authority to demand information from the GRU in the 1930s and 1940s, so Mikhailov's reference to the "Neighbors," a generic code word used by the GRU and the NKVD to refer to one another, probably meant that someone from the NKVD had told him that the GRU had a Washington-based agent named Hiss who worked at the State Department. Apparently neither Mikhailov nor his source knew Hiss's code name.[57]

That evidence was cryptic, but the second Venona cable identifying Hiss was far more extensive. It was sent to "Moscow" (probably for Fitin's attention) by Anatoli Gromov, the controller of Washington-based NKVD agents, on March 30, 1945.[58] Gromov's cable referred to a "chat" an official called "A" had recently had with an agent called "Ales." "A" was identified by Venona cryptographers as "Albert," one of the code names of Iskhak Akhmerov, a longtime NKVD controller in the Washington area.[59] It is not clear why Akhmerov sought out Ales and passed on the details of his chat to Gromov, or why Gromov communicated those details to Fitin. It would have been unusual, but not unprecedented, for a NKVD controller to talk to a GRU agent, and Gromov, who was a very experienced controller of Soviet agents in high places,[60] may have taken an interest in Ales.[61] The discussion between Akhmerov and Ales, as summarized in Gromov's cable, revealed that:

1. Ales has been working with the Neighbors continuously since 1935 . . .
2. For some years past he has been the leader of a small group of the Neighbors' probationers, for the most part consisting of his relations. . . .

3. The group and Ales himself work on obtaining military information only. Materials on the Bank [the State Department] allegedly interest the Neighbors very little and he does not produce them regularly.
4. All the last few years Ales has been working with Pol, who also meets other members of the group occasionally.
5. Recently Ales and the whole group were awarded Soviet decorations. . . .
6. After the Yalta Conference, when he had gone on to Moscow, a Soviet personage in a very responsible position (Ales gave to understand that it was Comrade [Andrey] Vishinski [the Deputy Foreign Minister]) allegedly got in touch with Ales and at the behest of the Military Neighbors passed on to him their gratitude.

On August 8, 1969, an analyst at the National Security Agency added a footnote after the first mention of Ales: "Probably Alger Hiss." The analyst was being cautious. Nearly all of the details Gromov supplied about Ales in the cable fit Hiss. Chambers had testified that Hiss first began to work with Joszef Peter, through the Ware Group, in 1935. He also stated that Peter had moved Hiss out of the Ware Group to his own parallel apparatus, and, because of Hiss's contacts with the Nye Committee, linked that apparatus to Soviet military intelligence. Although most of Hiss's work in the State Department was not involved with military affairs, on at least one occasion, in 1945, he had requested classified reports on atomic energy and Far Eastern military policies that were outside the parameters of his office. Another decoded cable would confirm that he and the other members of his group were awarded Soviet decorations, probably in early 1945. And Hiss, after attending the Yalta Conference as an assistant to Secretary of State Edward Stettinius, had stopped off briefly in Moscow with Stettinius and two other officials, H. Freeman Matthews and Wilder Foote (none of whom was ever suspected of being a Soviet agent).

In addition, in the Cyrillic alphabet, used by Russians, Ales looks like a contraction of "Alger Hiss," and a former KGB official, Oleg Gordievsky, stated that Hiss's code name was Ales in a history of the KGB he published after defecting to Great Britain in 1985.[62] The only puzzling feature of Gromov's cable was his statement that "[a]ll the last few years Ales has been working with [Pol], who also meets other members of the group occasionally." The NSA analysts could not identify the code name "Pol" or "Paul."[63] However, Nathan Gregory Silvermaster, who was the organizer of a loose group of Washington-based NKVD agents in the 1930s and 1940s, had the code name Pal.[64] But Hiss did not work for the NKVD, so if Pol referred to Silvermaster, it is not clear what Gromov meant in saying that Hiss "worked with" him. Perhaps there was a Pol who has yet been identified, or perhaps Gromov only meant to say that Hiss and Silvermaster, whose group was quite large, were both working in the Washington area.[65]

A final piece of evidence supporting the hypothesis that the Ales of Gromov's cable was Hiss came from another communication involving Pavel Fitin, discovered by Allen Weinstein in KGB files in Moscow. As Haynes and Klehr were proceeding with their investigation of RTsKhIDNI archives and Venona documents, Weinstein and Alexander Vassiliev were examining the files opened to them by Russian authorities in 1992. When the Venona transcripts were released in 1995, Weinstein became aware of the decoded cables mentioning Hiss and "Ales," and incorporated them in the second edition of *Perjury*, which was published in 1997. Meanwhile he and Vassiliev found, in KGB files, an April 25, 1945, memorandum sent by Fitin to his supervisor, Vsevolod Merkulov, the Soviet Commissar for State Security. In the memorandum Fitin asked for a decoration of the Order of Red Star for an American-based Soviet agent whose code name was "Ruble." He described Ruble's contributions":

> Our agent Ruble, drawn to working for the Soviet Union in May, 1937, has been passing . . . initially through the military "neighbors" and then through our station, valuable information on political and economic is-sues. . . . According to data from Vadim, the group of agents of the mili-tary "neighbors" whose member Ruble had been earlier, was recently decorated with USSR orders. About this fact, Ruble learned it from his friend Ales who is the leader of the mentioned group. Taking into account Ruble's devoted work for the USSR for 8 years and the fact that as a result of transfer to our station, [he] was not decorated together with other mem-bers of Ales's group, [we] consider it expedient to recommend him for the decoration with the Order of the Red Star. Ask your consent.[66]

Venona transcripts revealed that the Ruble in the memorandum was Harold Glasser, a Soviet agent in the Treasury Department, and in *The Haunted Wood*, Weinstein and Vassiliev identified "Vadim" as a code name for Anatoli Gromov. Ales was Hiss. The memorandum stated that Glasser had recently been working for "our station" (Fitin was affiliated with the NKVD), but that he had previously worked for Ales's group, affiliated with the GRU. According to Gromov, Hiss had told Glasser that his group of agents had recently received Orders of the Red Star for their serv-ice. This was consistent with what Gromov had reported to Fitin on March 30, 1945.[67]

The April 25 Fitin memorandum was on a routine covert intelligence matter. American-based Soviet agents were not typically paid for their services in the 1930s and 1940s: they participated in espionage because of ideological commitments, which included opposition to Fascism as well as support for Soviet Communism. But their Soviet handlers believed that periodic appreciation of their services was necessary. The Bokhara rugs given to Hiss and three other agents in late 1936 was an example of that appreciation. Military decorations, and, in Hiss's case, the personal thanks of a highly ranked Soviet official were other examples. Thus there was nothing earth-shaking in Fitin's memorandum. But it confirmed some details about Glasser and Hiss previously supplied by Elizabeth Bentley and Whittaker Chambers. Bentley had told the FBI, in 1945, that Glasser had asked her to help get him transferred from the agent group with which he was working to her group, affiliated with the NKVD. Bentley tried to facilitate Glasser's transfer, but was unsuccessful in getting him routed to her group. Subsequently she found out that a person "named Hiss . . . in the State Department" had "turned Glasser . . . over to some Russian."[68]

Meanwhile Chambers, in *Witness,* had said that in 1937 Glasser, an assistant to Soviet sympathizer Harry Dexter White at the Treasury Department, had been told by Joszef Peter to encourage White to cooperate more fully with the Soviets. Peter asked Chambers to make contact with Glasser in order to increase White's output of intelligence, but Glasser convinced Chambers that White was producing all he could.[69]

Thus three independent sources, Gromov, Bentley, and Chambers, had learned the same information about Glasser and Hiss. Moreover, they had learned it from different sources. Gromov's information had come from conversations with Glasser and Hiss; Bentley's from a conversation with another Soviet agent, Charles Kramer;[70] and Chambers's from Joszef Peter. All of the sources identified Alger Hiss as an agent for Soviet military intelligence in 1945, and all indicated that he had been an agent at least since 1937. And all of the sources were themselves involved in undercover Soviet intelligence. When one adds to these facts the routine nature of the details provided about Glasser and Hiss, the idea that all of the sources would have been fabricating information about Alger Hiss as an undercover agent in the 1930s and 1940s becomes wildly implausible.

The RTsKhIDNI files and the Venona transcripts enabled Weinstein and Vassiliev to approach the NKVD files opened to them in a more informed manner. They knew code names for many of the American-based agents and Soviet handlers of intelligence networks in the 1930s and 1940s, and they knew more about the relationships between the Communist Party of the United States, the Comintern, and the NKVD and GRU. With that background, they were able to find, in the same archival base that Volkogonov had apparently examined, documents in which members of the Soviet intelligence community identified Hiss, by his real name, as a Soviet agent in the 1930s.

The first set of documents was related to a story about Hiss that had been told by a former Soviet agent, Hedda Gumperz (known in the United States as Hede Massing) at Hiss's second perjury trial. Massing, who had defected from the Soviets in 1937, had told the same story to the FBI in 1948. The story was about a conversation between Massing and Alger Hiss that took place at a Washington dinner party in 1935. In the conversation, Massing recalled, Hiss had said that he and Massing, as recruiters for Soviet networks, were in competition for the services of Noel Field, then an employee of the State Department. Hiss teased Massing that she was trying to get Field away from him, but that he would prevail. When Massing testified at his 1950 perjury trial, Hiss admitted to knowing Field, but denied knowing Massing and produced a witness who claimed that Massing had told him she couldn't remember ever having met Hiss.[71]

The dinner party, Massing claimed, had taken place sometime in the winter of 1935. In the spring of 1936 she learned from Field, who was about to leave for Europe, that Hiss had renewed contact with him. This prompted her to write a lengthy memorandum to her superiors in Moscow. In the memorandum, located by Weinstein and Vassiliev in the NKVD archives, Massing said,

> Alger Hiss turned to [Field, whom she referred to by his code name "Ernst"] the day before his departure to Europe. Alger told him that he was a Communist and that he knew "that [Field] also had connections but he was afraid they were not solid enough. . . ." Alger asked [Field] several other questions. . . . He also asked [Field] to help him get to the State Department. Apparently [Field] satisfied this request.
>
> When I pointed out to [Field] his terrible discipline . . . he did not seem to understand it. He thought that just because "Alger was the first to open his cards, there was no reason for [Field] to keep a secret." Besides, Alger announced that he was doing it for "us."[72]

Massing also told the story to Boris Bazarov, her NKVD controller in the Washington area. Bazarov was sufficiently agitated by the story that he cabled Moscow as well, pointing out that "[Field] and Hiss have been openly identified [as agents]," and that "[Massing, called by her code name "Redhead"] and Hiss several months ago identified themselves to each other." Bazarov proposed that the NKVD not attempt to cultivate any more prospective American agents for a time, indicating that "the persistent Hiss" would likely "continue his initiative in this direction" for the GRU. Moscow was furious at the development, cabling Bazarov on May 3, 1936, that they did not understand why Massing had met with Hiss (whom they referred to as "Lawyer," the NKVD's code name for Hiss at the time) at all. Two weeks later Itzhak Akhmerov, who had replaced Bazarov as controller of the NKVD's Washington agents, cabled Moscow back, attempting to palliate his superiors. He noted that Massing had only met Hiss once, and that after his network had learned of Hiss's GRU connections, none of them had met with Hiss. Akhmerov also reported that "by an accidental coincidence," Massing had run into a "brother organization worker . . . whom we know as 'Peter.'" Peter had told Massing, "You in Washington came across my guy [Hiss]. You better not lay your hands on him."[73]

This set of documents not only confirmed the story that Massing had told at Hiss's second trial, but also Whittaker Chambers's account of what he and Alger Hiss were doing in 1936. Chambers had said that Joszef Peter, after first using Hiss as a Ware Group agent reporting to him through Chambers, had decided to place Hiss in one of the old-line governmental agencies and have him report directly to Soviet military intelligence. In the spring of 1936, the documents revealed, Peter, who considered Hiss "my guy," had been informed that Massing had run into him in Washington, and had warned Massing not to recruit him. Moreover, because Massing and Hiss were in separate networks, Massing did not know his code name, so she openly identified him in her cable to Moscow. Nor did Bazarov, who worked for the NKVD, know Hiss's code name. The result was that two documents in NKVD archives singled out Alger Hiss as a GRU agent in 1935 and 1936.

The second set of documents established that Hiss was continuing to serve as a GRU agent in 1938. It was again prompted by the fortuitous interaction of Hiss with another Soviet agent. In this instance the agent was Michael Straight, the son of one of the owners of the *New Republic*, who had studied at Cambridge University in the 1930s and been converted to Communism by Anthony Blunt and Guy Burgess, two of the notorious Soviet agents with Cambridge affiliations. Straight joined the State Department in January 1938, and shortly thereafter reported to Akhmerov, his Soviet handler, that Hiss was "a very progressive man . . . who occupied a responsible position" and might be a potential recruit. Akhmerov cabled Moscow for advice. "I can't tell ['Nigel,' Straight's code name] to stop seeing Hiss," Akhmerov noted, because "[i]f I tell him that he might guess that Hiss belongs to our family." Akhmerov added that "he was not sure who Hiss is connected to." That cable, sent in June 1938, also suggested that Akhmerov had either never known Hiss's code name or had forgotten it.[74]

A month later Akhmerov sent another cable. He had been "hunting for Hiss," apparently to find out with whom he was affiliated, and had run into Joszef Peter, whom he referred to as "Storm," one of Peter's code names. Peter had told him that "Hiss used to be a member of *bratskiy* organization who had been routed into the [State Department] and sent to the Neighbors later." In addition to being yet another document openly identifying Hiss as a Soviet agent, the cable was another confirmation of Chambers's version of events. Joszef Peter, Chambers had said, had first used Hiss's intelligence, funneled to Chambers, in his capacity as coordinator between the Communist Party of the United States and Soviet intelligence, and then, after Hiss had been routed into the State Department, had sent him to GRU. The term *"bratskiy* organization" in the cable referred to Peter's group of underground American Communist Party members who cooperated with the NKVD and the GRU.[75]

Finding documents in Soviet archives positively identifying Alger Hiss as a Soviet agent in the 1930s must have been a source of considerable satisfaction for Weinstein. His efforts to open up those archives after the fall of the Soviet Union had been directly or indirectly responsible for the RTsKhIDNI project, which had documented the Soviets' extensive use of the American Communist Party for intelligence purposes, the release of Venona documents, which had first revealed that Hiss had continued to work for the Soviets throughout World War II, and Weinstein's and Vassiliev's being granted access to KGB archives. Partisanship, the success in the 1970s of Hiss and his supporters in publicizing a conspiratorial, "political" explanation of his conviction, and Weinstein's own miscalculations and excesses had resulted in the first edition of *Perjury* being unable to strip the Hiss case of its ambiguity. When Tony Hiss had proclaimed his father's vindication after Volkogonov's initial comments, he had done so without even mentioning *Perjury.* Now Weinstein could issue a second edition of *Perjury* in which he made use of Venona transcripts and some of the NKVD files he had found. Now, finally, the Russian connection to Hiss had revealed itself, in its own words and documents.

Alger Hiss did not live to see the publication of most of the archival evidence whose release had been precipitated by the collapse of the Soviet Union. In 1997 Weinstein released the second edition of *Perjury,* and in 1999 he and Vassiliev published their analysis of KGB files, *The Haunted Wood.* That year John Earl Haynes and Harvey Klehr's history of Soviet espionage in America, based on the Venona transcripts, also appeared. But Hiss had died in November 1996. In a memoir of his father's years in prison, *The View from Alger's Window,* Tony Hiss noted that in the last year of his life Alger's body was "almost completely worn out," making him "a prisoner of his own physical frailties." But his mind remained unaffected, and he continued to discuss current events.[76] One of those was the release, in March 1996, of the Venona cable summarizing Gromov's chat with Ales. The cable, with its footnote identifying Ales as "probably Alger Hiss," was the subject of newspaper coverage. Hiss was contacted, and replied, through Tony, that he was not Ales, and had only visited the new Moscow subway system when he stopped off there after the Yalta conference. Most of the articles reporting the release of the Ales cable, however, found it incriminating. Eric Breindel, for example, writing in the *Wall Street Journal*, called the cable "the smoking gun in the Hiss case." "[F]olks who refuse to recognize this document's implications," Breindel suggested, "are likely to be the sort who would insist on Mr. Hiss's innocence even if he confessed."[77]

The day Hiss died, however, Peter Jennings of ABC News reported that, in effect, he had been vindicated by the Russians. "Hiss . . . protested his innocence until the very end," Jennings said on the November 15, 1996, edition of "ABC World News Tonight." "And last year, we reported that the Russian president Boris Yeltsin said that KGB files had supported Mr. Hiss's claim. [Hiss] was 92 when he died today."[78] Jennings's claims about Hiss were not supported in most of the obituaries that appeared in major newspapers. Bart Barnes, in the *Washington Post*, referred to the "Ales" cable, and stated that although Hiss "insisted until his death that he was innocent," he "never established his innocence."[79] Columnists, on the whole, were less cautious about pronouncing Hiss a Soviet agent. Robert Novack, after pointing out that Volkogonov had retracted his statement and that Jennings had somehow not caught up with that retraction, referred to a "deep-seated reluctance within the American liberal establishment to acknowledge that Hiss was a liar, spy, and traitor."[80] Evan Thomas, in *Newsweek*, concluded that Hiss "probably was . . . a Soviet spy," and that in protesting his innocence he "was just a very good spy, deceitful to the end."[81] George Will, writing in the *Washington Post*, was the least restrained of all. Will had been a longtime observer of the Hiss case, reviewing the first edition of *Perjury* favorably and summarizing the American media's failure to publicize Volkogonov's qualification of his initial "exoneration" of Hiss. Now he denounced Hiss and his supporters: "Alger Hiss spent 44 months in prison and then his remaining 42 years in the dungeon of his grotesque fidelity to the fiction of his innocence. The costs of his unconditional surrender to the totalitarian temptation was steep for his supporters. Clinging to their belief in martyrdom in order to preserve their belief in their 'progressive' virtue, they were drawn into an intellectual corruption that hastened the moral bankruptcy of the American left."

Will rehearsed the "definitive" confirmation of Hiss's complicity by Weinstein in *Perjury*, Volkogonov's "recant[ing]" of his early statement that he was "familiar with all pertinent archives" about Hiss, the confirmation of Chambers's "account of the Communist underground in the United States" by the RTsKhIDNI files, and the identification of Hiss as "Ales" by Oleg Gordievsky and the Venona files. "There is no hatred so corrupting as intellectual hatred," he concluded, "so Hiss's supporters always responded to evidence by redoubling their concoction of rococo reasons for believing him framed. . . . Never has so much ingenuity been invested in so low a cause." Hiss, "enveloped in his enigmatic fanaticism," and his supporters, "impervious to evidence," were "monstrosities."[82]

Two weeks after Will's column, Victor Navasky provided an example of how a longtime Hiss supporter was prepared to view his life. Navasky's editorial in the *Nation* began by stating that the Hiss case "was politically motivated from the beginning" and that "no document was ever produced to corroborate the charges" against Hiss. Navasky divided Hiss's life into three acts. In "Act One," the "Republican right tried to use Whittaker Chambers's allegations against Hiss to discredit the entire New Deal." In "Act Two," "the right was joined by Cold War liberals (and eventually neoconservatives) who tried to use the Hiss case to prove that the brutal excesses of the domestic cold war . . . were justified by the internal Red Menace." The Hiss case, in Navasky's view, was "carried on in a cold war climate that precluded the possibility of a fair trial." "Act Three" consisted of Hiss's campaign for vindication, his showing that three of the Pumpkin Papers microfilm rolls consisted of harmless documents available to the general public, and Volkogonov's "exoneration." Volkogonov, Navasky claimed, conducted an "exhaustive search," and his only qualification was to say that "he couldn't say for certain that the case was closed." He had made no "retraction," except in the minds of "[l]atter-day cold warriors."

Also in "Act Three" was the Ales cable from the Venona project. Navasky noted that the claim that Hiss was Ales had been made in "an anonymous footnote . . . twenty years later." He found it "ironic" that Hiss, whom his enemies labeled a "traitor," was a "model citizen: courteous, curious, incapable of bitterness and dedicated to establishing his innocence through official channels such as the courts and the Freedom of Information Act." Navasky closed the editorial by noting that *The New York Times,* in its obituary, had departed from its usual practice of listing the survivors in the obituary's final paragraph, and ended it with a quote from William F. Buckley, whom Navasky described as having "built a career, a magazine, and a movement on the assumption of Hiss's guilt."[83]

The Times obituary was the most extensive, the length that Alden Whitman had predicted in 1986. Janny Scott had replaced Whitman as the author, Whitman having retired from the paper in 1976 and died in 1990. The obituary was nearly 3,200

words, and began on the front page. It briefly covered Hiss's early career and government service, and went into some detail on his perjury trials and the HUAC accusations by Chambers that lead to them. It described Hiss's campaign for
vindication, his public lectures in the 1960s and 1970s, the reinstatement of his government pension, and his unsuccessful *coram nobis* petition. It discussed Hiss's cooperation with Allen Weinstein and the latter's conclusion that Chambers, not Hiss,
had been telling the truth. It also mentioned Volkogonov's temporary "exoneration," and his subsequent qualification. It noted the release of the Ales cable in early
1996 and Hiss's public denial that he was Ales, including his comment that he had
stopped over in Moscow after Yalta only to look at the new Moscow subway
system.[84]

Scott's obituary also alluded to a paper published in 1993 by Maria Schmidt, a historian doing research on the Communist "show trials" in the Stalin era, in which officials who had allegedly conspired with anti-Soviet elements publicly confessed
their errors and were then executed. In studying records of the Hungarian secret police in connection with one of those trials, Schmidt had come upon testimony by
Noel Field, whom Hiss had tried to recruit for his network in 1935 and 1936. Field
had left the United States with his wife hurriedly in 1949, in part to avoid being
called as a witness in the Hiss trials. He had been promised a job teaching in Czecho-
slovakia, but the promise was a sham: the Soviets had wanted him as a witness for
one of the show trials. He was imprisoned in Hungary, and in 1954, prior to being
released, gave an interview to Hungarian authorities implicating Hiss as a Communist agent. In 1957 Field released a letter in which he stated that he believed Hiss to
be innocent of the charges of being a Communist and a Soviet agent, but Schmidt
found evidence of earlier drafts of that letter in Hungarian records, suggesting that
Field's statement was not entirely voluntary. Weinstein was to include the Schmidt
paper as additional proof of Hiss's guilt in the second edition of *Perjury*, and
Schmidt's findings were noted in *The New York Times* and *Washington Post* in October 1993.[85]

The difficulty with Schmidt's findings, as an article in the *Nation* in November
1993 pointed out, was their context. Field had obviously given the statements about
Hiss under duress, and it is not clear why Hungarian authorities, at the height of the
Stalin era, would have wanted to encourage Field to implicate Hiss. In fact the Soviet bloc was taking pains, at the time, to deny that it was conducting intelligence operations in the West, so "encouraging" Field to expose Hiss as a condition of his
release would seem perverse, all the more so because the other evidence Schmidt
found suggested that Hungarian authorities were helping Field construct a defense
of Hiss's innocence.[86]

Scott concluded her obituary by noting that Hiss had outlived Whittaker Chambers, his wife Priscilla, and Richard Nixon, and mentioned that Isabel Johnson and Tony Hiss, as well as Timothy Hobson, had survived him. Her last paragraph quoted William F. Buckley as a representative of a group of people "who believe [Hiss] guilty," but had "long ago given up their hope that he would come clean." Buckley said that "[i]t's probably understandable" that Hiss "would feel that he had let too many people down" if he admitted his guilt.[87]

In May 2000, Thomas Powers reviewed six books on Soviet espionage in England and the United States in the 1920s, 1930s, and 1940s, including *The Haunted Wood* and Haynes's and Klehr's *Venona*. Powers took it for granted that Alger Hiss had been a Soviet agent. In referring to the Ales cable in the Venona collection, Powers noted that

> the "Ales" cable is not proof that Hiss was a spy, just useful supporting evidence. Whether Hiss is mentioned in other Venona cables still unread is of course unknown, and no GRU intelligence files about Hiss or any other spy have been released.

But, he added,

> [M]uch additional evidence about Hiss's involvement with the Soviets has turned up since the voluminous and explicit claims by Whittaker Chambers and Elizabeth Bentley in the 1940s, claims which no serious scholar of the subject any longer dismisses.[88]

Powers cited the correspondence between Hede Massing, Boris Bazarov, and their Moscow superiors in *The Haunted Wood*. He added Itzhak Akhmerov's May 1936 cable to Moscow about Hiss, Joszef Peter, and Massing. He concluded that "anyone who wants to know what Hiss and his friends were up to can find a rich, convincing and vivid report in *The Haunted Wood* and *Venona.*" The evidence from those sources proved, he believed, that "while the excesses of McCarthyism may be fairly described as a witch hunt, it was a witch hunt with witches, some in government."[89]

After reviewing other books, Powers turned back to Hiss. As a "young reporter for the United Press in New York City in the late 1960s," Powers "had occasion to call Alger Hiss on the phone."

There had been some development in his efforts to rehabilitate himself—a court had said yes or no, I no longer remember the details. But I remember something curt and irritated in his voice which nevertheless conveyed the pain suffered by an innocent man wrongly accused. He sounded like a man running out of patience with the world for taking so long to grasp the truth of his innocence.

Powers then, "[a] few years later," read Weinstein's *Perjury*.

The experience was something of a shock. The case was not even hard. What Whittaker Chambers had claimed was true, and it was convincingly and obviously true by the time Hiss went to jail for perjury. Hiss's denial, and his persistence in it for decades, and his support in it by so many otherwise smart people, was one of the great intellectual contortion acts of history. The evidence now . . . is simply overwhelming.[90]

Powers then turned to a question about Hiss that continued to haunt him.

What continues to astonish and bewilder me now is why Hiss lied for fifty years about his service in a cause so important to him that he was willing to betray his country for it. The faith itself is no problem to explain: hundreds of people shared it enough to do the same thing, and thousands more shared it who were never put to the test by a demand for secrets. But why did Hiss persist in the lie personally? Why did he allow his friends and family to go on carrying the awful burden of that lie?[91]

Alger Hiss had told David Remnick in 1986 that there would be no deathbed confession; he had "no secrets." In fact he had lived with a large secret for over 50 years at that time, and would live for ten more. He had apparently known, from the first time he realized Whittaker Chambers was about to reveal their shared past, that denial, artifice, and a contrived search for "vindication" would be his response to the case. He never deviated from that strategy, and he never admitted, even to his own son, that it was a strategy. Powers thought that keeping to this lifelong lie was "an awful burden," and found himself astonished and bewildered by Hiss. That has been the response of most people who have come to believe in Hiss's guilt. As Powers put it, why did Hiss "persist in the lie personally?"

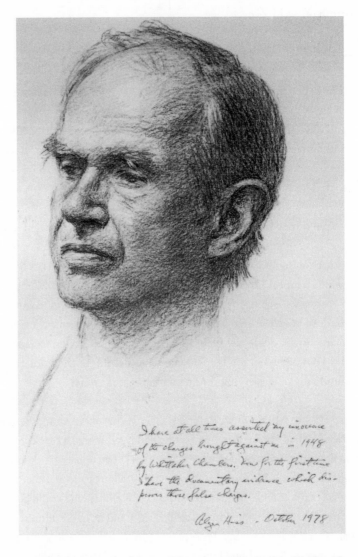

A 1978 photograph of a pencil drawing of Hiss by Joss Melik with
the inscription, "I have at all times asserted my innocence . . .
Now for the first time I have the documentary evidence which
disproves those false charges." Hiss's *coram nobis* petition to
vacate his 1950 perjury conviction was filed that year.

CHAPTER EIGHT

Alger Hiss's Looking-Glass Wars

hapter four included a comment Whittaker Chambers made when Hiss was released from prison, declared his innocence, and announced his campaign for vindication. Chambers predicted that all Hiss needed to do was to continue to maintain that he had been a victim and a scapegoat, and that sooner or later one respectable inhabitant of Hartford, Connecticut (or any other American city), would say to another respectable inhabitant, "[r]eally, I don't see how Alger Hiss would brazen it out that way unless he were innocent." At that point, Chambers said, the Communist Party would have achieved "victory."[1]

Chambers's comments were made when the Cold War was still raging, and they reflected his increasing pessimism that the American public would grasp the lessons of the Hiss case. Hiss was just one, Chambers thought, of a dedicated band of Communists and Communist sympathizers who were determined to replace the American system of government with something resembling that of the Soviet Union. Chambers believed that the American people, being innately decent and trustworthy, had not yet fathomed the depths of deceit and subversion to which Communists were willing to go to achieve their goals. He took Hiss's protestations of his innocence as consistent with the Communist strategy of the Big Lie.

As Vietnam signaled the waning of 1950s-style Cold War ideology in American foreign and domestic policy, and members of American elites began to recoil from the excesses of McCarthyism and the crudities of a bipolar conception of international affairs, Chambers's interpretation of Hiss's campaign for vindication came to be seen as Manichean, and Chambers himself as an unreflective species of anti-Communist, sharing the somewhat simplistic judgments and tastes of his Cold War-era contemporaries. And as Watergate followed on Vietnam, attitudes toward government powerholders became ever more cynical, and a discernibly different generation of college and university students surfaced, Chambers found himself associated with some undeniably patriotic, but nonetheless partisan and sinister figures of the Cold War generation, Richard Nixon and J. Edgar Hoover.

Out of these developments, and Hiss's dogged maintenance of his innocence, evolved the perceived ambiguity that began to envelop the Hiss case. Whereas in the 1950s Hiss had been seen unambiguously as a convicted traitor, and the investigations of alleged Communists in government as evidence that there *were* Communists seeking to infiltrate governmental agencies, by the mid-1970s investigative agencies had come to be seen as suspect in themselves, and anti-Communism as a cover for right-wing partisanship. As those who had lead the prosecution of Hiss fell from grace, the possibility that Hiss had been a victim or a scapegoat seemed more credible.

The early books on the Hiss case had wrestled with the question whether Hiss's conviction had really resolved the irreconcilable accounts of events and human motives presented by Hiss and Chambers. The books wrestled with such questions as whether Hiss or Chambers was lying, whether Hiss was a Communist or simply a dedicated New Dealer, whether Hiss was a Soviet spy or just an anti-Fascist internationalist, whether Chambers was an honest patriot or a malevolent intriguer, whether those who had helped Chambers expose Hiss were decent Americans who had come to grasp the evils of Communism, or partisan zealots, seeking to strike at the New Deal and the United Nations through Hiss. The first books on the case, such as Alistair Cooke's *A Generation on Trial,* sought only to raise those questions. Some subsequent books from the 1950s, such as Jowitt's *The Strange Case of Alger Hiss* and Cook's *Alger Hiss: The Unfinished Story,* tilted toward resolving them in favor of Hiss. Other books from the same time period, such as Victor Lasky and Ralph de Teledano's *Seeds of Treason* and Chambers's *Witness,* identified Hiss as just one among several "Communist traitors" in American government.

Despite Hiss's general status as a convicted traitor in the 1950s and early 1960s, doubts remained about the case. After 1967 all the subsequent twentieth-century books on the case took as their central premise not that Hiss was innocent, but that the American public could not make up its mind about Alger Hiss's guilt. Meyer Zeligs suggested that Whittaker Chambers had made Hiss into the subject of his distorted fantasies, and that Hiss had been too naive and too chivalric to see it. Smith's *Alger Hiss: The True Story* and Tony Hiss's *Laughing Last* picked up on those themes, arguing that it would have been much easier for Chambers or others to frame Hiss than most people understood, and that Hiss himself, far from being a fanatical Soviet spy, was an ingenuous, otherworldy, almost saintly figure.

Allen Weinstein, having started a project to get past the perceived ambiguity of the Hiss case by historicizing it, found himself drawn into the puzzle of Hiss's guilt, and devoted all his efforts to resolving it. But after all his dogged research and his skirmishes with partisan critics, Weinstein confessed that he still found Hiss an enigma. And Weinstein's conclusions, for all their power, did not dislodge the conventional framework in which the Hiss case continued to be viewed. In 1986 Remnick referred to the Hiss case's essential ambiguity. In 1992 American television networks were quick to publicize Volkogonov's "exoneration" of Hiss. And in 1999, after the Venona transcripts and NKVD archives had made it clear that Chambers had been accurate and Hiss had been lying, Tony Hiss published a book in which he said that he knew his father was innocent because his stepbrother, Timothy Hobson, had told him that Chambers had never visited the Hiss household on a day he had supposedly had a clandestine meeting with Alger Hiss. One of the comments on the dust jacket of Tony Hiss's *The View from Alger's Window* said that it was "likely to have a profound effect on the ongoing debate over Alger's character and culpability."[2]

It is time to replace this framework for looking at Alger Hiss with a different one. Instead of seeking to determine whether Hiss was a Communist and a Soviet agent, and whether he lied about that, and about his relationship in espionage with Whittaker Chambers, we need to ask some other questions. Given that Hiss *was* a dedicated Communist, from the early 1930s on, and an agent for Soviet military intelligence from at least 1934 through most of 1946—given that he lied about every essential issue raised at his two perjury trials—why did he go on publicly proclaiming his innocence for the remainder of his life? Why did he enlist his friends and family in that lie? Why did he mount a campaign for "vindication," and seek "exoneration," when he not only knew that those states of being would be false, but that *he could never prove them to be true?* And how, given mounting evidence of his guilt, was he able to persuade so many others of his innocence?

I have tried to explore those questions by reconceiving Alger Hiss's life as a series of looking-glass wars. By that phrase I mean to suggest that Hiss's life was a series of critical episodes in which a secret portion of his life—the portion concealed, as it were, behind the looking glass—was threatened with exposure. In each of those episodes Hiss sought to defend his secrets in a distinctive way. Understanding his distinctive response helps us understand why he chose to be a Communist and a Soviet undercover agent. And understanding the response also helps explain why he chose to fashion a lifelong narrative of innocence, in which he projected himself as a victim and a scapegoat, all the while knowing that his narrative was false. Finally, understanding Hiss's approach to his several looking-glass wars helps make sense of the two largest puzzles of his life. Why did he enlist his strongest supporters, and the most loyal members of his family, in perpetuating his false claims, and how was he able to transform his public image from that of convicted traitor to that of someone who might have been one of the casualties of Cold War excesses?

The first of Hiss's looking-glass wars confronted him with the awkward option of putting off his marriage to Priscilla Hiss, at a time when circumstances had combined to make her suddenly available to him, or violating one of the conditions of his employment with Justice Oliver Wendell Holmes. Once Priscilla, with whom he had been smitten for many years, signaled her willingness to marry him, Hiss knew which of the options he would choose. He then had to figure out how to break Holmes's no-marriage rule without enraging Holmes. His strategy was to plan a virtually secret marriage while pretending that he did not know about Holmes's rule. This was to be a common technique of Hiss's in his looking-glass wars. He not only denied having a secret life that many people would have found objectionable. He also sought to project the image of person who, by reason of his character and personality, *couldn't* have had such a life.

Hiss's next looking-glass war began in August 1948 when Whittaker Chambers reappeared from his past to accuse him of being a Communist. His response to Chambers's testimony was strikingly similar to his response in the marriage episode. He could have admitted knowing Chambers and being a Communist in the 1930s, adding, perhaps, that he had renounced Communism at some earlier period. He could have declined to appear before HUAC, or declined to comment on Chambers's allegations, citing the privilege against self-incrimination. Instead he appeared before HUAC without a lawyer and categorically denied being a Communist and even knowing Chambers. He offered a reputational defense.

As directed at Chambers's accusations, the strategy nearly worked. Hiss's demeanor reinforced the credibility of his denial. Alger Hiss was very good at convincing others of his sincerity. He could project a "terrible evenness," an absence of bitterness or outrage, even a sympathy for his accusers. He nearly convinced HUAC. Only Richard Nixon, who had his own attraction to secret machinations, found him too smooth by half.

Hiss's reputational defense against Chambers's accusations and his strategy in the marriage episode were of a piece. Both were based on his belief that he could keep others away from a secret part of his life by convincing them that he was not the sort of person who could conceivably have such secrets. The strategy worked well in the marriage episode. It only failed as a defense to Chambers's accusations because it forced Hiss to attack Chambers's credibility in order to reinforce the persona he was presenting. As it turned out, Chambers had far more damaging evidence than Hiss suspected.

The trials were extensions of the looking-glass war that began with Chambers's appearance before HUAC. Once again Hiss employed a reputational defense. He produced numerous persons who held high office as character witnesses: they testified to his impeccable character and integrity. He calmly, for the most part, denied knowing Chambers except as George Crosley, the mooching journalist. He denied ever being a Communist, and he denied passing any stolen papers to Chambers. Once again, his strategy nearly worked. Had the prosecution not secured copies of Hiss family correspondence that matched the typeface on the documents Chambers produced, Hiss might have been acquitted of the far more serious perjury count, lying about passing the documents to Chambers.

Hiss next responded to being sent to prison in a distinctive fashion. Recalling the life he had lead before being convicted of perjury can highlight how distinctive his response was. For 11 years he had simultaneously performed the roles of an employee of the United States government and a committed Communist and spy for the Soviets. He had spent the day at the Department of Agriculture discussing farm policies with government lawyers and bureaucrats, while spending some of his evenings meeting with his Ware Group comrades. He had served as counsel to the Nye Committee, processing reports about the munitions industry in World War I and preparing for hearings, while at the same time trying to determine whether he could procure some classified military information for the Soviets.

Beginning in 1936, he had become a State Department bureaucrat, working his way up the career ladder, making friends with Dean Acheson, Stanley Hornbeck, Francis Sayre, and Edward Stettinius. All the time that he was maintaining cordial relations with those persons, he was searching for ways to help Soviet military intelligence. When his favorite courier to Boris Bykov defected in 1938, he did not decide to shut down the cell he was running. Although he had limited access to confidential military information, he made the most of the strategic information he did pick up. Even after he knew that people in the State Department and the FBI considered him a security risk, he took the opportunity to meet secretly with the Soviets in Moscow in 1945, although he had traveled there with Stettinius himself.

In short, by the time Chambers first exposed him Hiss was already a master at compartmentalizing his working life, and at partitioning truth from lies. He was well prepared to continue that partitioning in his campaign for vindication. The discipline of years of being a spy would help him in prison, and it would help him in the campaign. Hiss knew, more than anyone else, how successful he had been in simultaneously frequenting overt and covert worlds.

Once Hiss left Lewisburg and began his campaign for vindication, there was one feature of his campaign that he hoped to turn to his advantage. This was the fact that the case was still, fundamentally, about the irreconcilable testimony of Hiss and Chambers. As such, public understandings of the case would be as grounded on perceptions of the principal actors as they would be on new evidence that surfaced. The importance of public perceptions had been vividly brought home to Hiss when, in the wake of the perjury trials, Chambers, an active Communist for 12 years, had emerged as a kind of Cold War hero, and Hiss had faced death threats. If he could convince the public that he was a person of character and integrity, and his accusers were less admirable persons, his claims that he was an innocent scapegoat were likely to appear more credible. So by persistently asserting that he *was* innocent, even after he had served his time in prison, Hiss might help convince others that he was *the kind of person that wouldn't go to such lengths unless he had been.*

This strategy also harmonized with Hiss's desire to prevent others from learning about his secret life as a Soviet agent. By keeping that life secret, Hiss was being loyal to the Soviet cause and to the ethos of the secret world. And by maintaining the fiction of his innocence, Hiss was exhibiting a kind of loyalty to those who themselves needed to believe him innocent, such as the persons who had supported him through the years when most saw him as a convicted traitor. Hiss stood to benefit in all respects from the strategy.

Weinstein's *Perjury* represented the closest anyone had yet come to penetrating Hiss's secret worlds. *Perjury* required Hiss and his supporters to fashion a more embroidered statement of his innocence. That statement came in the form of Hiss's 1978 *coram nobis* petition, which Hill and Wang published in 1979. The petition raised once more the forgery-by-typewriter and two-typewriters defenses, adding the suggestion, based on evidence in newly released FBI files, that the agency believed that the serial numbers on the Woodstock found by the Hiss defense indicated that it could not have been the typewriter originally purchased by Priscilla's father. The petition argued that the prosecution had misled the jury by concealing this information, letting it believe that the machine its members had sampled in court was the Hiss family Woodstock. That argument wonderfully suited both the forgery-by-typewriter and two-typewriters hypotheses, for it raised the possibility that the FBI had "planted" the second Woodstock where Hiss lawyers could find it after determining that its typeface closely resembled that of the Hiss family machine. When the arguments were summarily dismissed by Owen and the Court of Appeals, Hiss responded, in his memoirs, by asserting that the entire *coram nobis* process had been a partisan charade.

Hiss approached death realizing that his secret life was on the brink of full exposure. That is why his response to Volkogonov's exoneration can be seen as particularly revealing. He had asked Russian officials to provide him with an endorsement he knew they could furnish: a statement that he had never been a paid, contracted agent of the Soviet Union. He may have underestimated, however, the extent to which officials in Boris Yeltsin's Russia were prepared to cultivate good relations with the West. The result was that when John Lowenthal pressed Dmitri Volkogonov for a far more extensive declaration of Hiss's innocence than Hiss had himself requested, Volkogonov supplied it, even though he had not done the research his endorsement implied.

Volkogonov's exoneration was too tempting for Alger Hiss not to try to capitalize upon. It was the final proof, that Hiss *really was* the saintly figure who had been framed by Chambers, Nixon, and Hoover but had never let that catastrophe embitter him or dampen his zeal to establish his innocence. Claiming total vindication, on the basis of Volkogonov's comments, was an act of loyalty to Lowenthal, Tony Hiss, and all the other hard-core supporters. It was also a way to stoke the satisfactions Hiss received from keeping his secret life to himself. When he made the news of his exoneration public, Isabel embraced him and Tony wrote an essay on his "honor." Alger's joy may have been as much for the fact that he had been able to reward their loyalty as for his apparent success in once more defending his secret space.

Hiss's gesture ultimately led to the definitive exposure of his secret worlds. We are now in a position to see the recklessness in that gesture as a central ingredient of his character. His recklessness was connected to his idealism, to his fanatical devotion to his goals, and to his distinctive mix of ingenuousness and deceptiveness. When those characteristics are combined with Hiss's instinctive altruism, the high priority he placed on loyalty, his singlemindedness and self-control, and his strong faith in his own competence, the portrait of a person ideally suited for the life of a secret agent emerges.

When the Ware Group brought Hiss to Joszef Peter's attention, and Peter offered Hiss the opportunity to launch himself on a career path that would include spying for Soviet intelligence, that option was attractive to Hiss in several respects.

He believed in popular-front collectivism, and had a benign vision of Soviet Communism. His being chosen for secret work, and given his own "parallel apparatus," confirmed his sense of competence. The network in which he was placed would revolve around him.

Whittaker Chambers, when Hiss first met him, was another candidate for Hiss's altruism. Despite Chambers's interesting past and obvious intelligence, he was a lesser being in Peter's networks, and he was impoverished and apparently friendless. Hiss could find some pleasure in helping Chambers, offering him an apartment, loaning him a car, taking him on trips, lending him money. All of those acts were not only consistent with the ethic of Communist solidarity, they were ways in which Hiss could serve as a caretaker. And the fact that the Hisses and the Chamberses, as members of an underground Soviet network, were breaking rules in becoming close friends, was no barrier to someone as accustomed to secret spaces as Alger Hiss.

Hiss's acquiescence in the espionage procedures suggested by Boris Bykov, by which the Hisses kept stolen government documents in their residence, typed copies of them on a family typewriter, and circulated them in the Soviet underground, was very risky. It made it much more likely that the Hisses could be associated with stolen government papers, and it increased the possibility that someone in Hiss's network might eventually betray him. Yet there is no evidence that Hiss ever showed any reluctance to produce typed copies of stolen documents. He liked secrecy, he liked taking risks, and Bykov's procedure was a tribute to the amount of useful information he was able to extract from the State Department. The procedure also assumed that Hiss was competent enough to make it work. In the past, when faced with the prospect of taking risks to achieve goals he strongly desired, Hiss had not hesitated, and he had succeeded in attaining the goals.

Hiss also ignored the increased risks to him resulting from Chambers's defection from the Soviets in 1938. Not only did he rebuff Chambers after Chambers told him that he was defecting and implored him, as a friend, to do so as well, he sought to expand his espionage activities. After his responsibilities in the State Department increased, he attempted to use his greater authority to gain access to more classified military information, much of which bore little connection to the official duties he performed. When he became aware that the FBI was investigating him, he did not stop his attempts to obtain information that he believed might be useful to the GRU.

This risk-taking was accompanied by an assumption, on Hiss's part, that he could competently master any difficulties that might arise from his being a Soviet agent in the midst of the State Department. Hiss proceeded, in the 1940s, as if he could easily persuade others of his innocence if challenged. Even though he knew that he had come to the FBI's attention by 1942, and that by 1945 both the FBI and State Department security officials were deeply suspicious of him, and even though his friends, such as Dean Acheson, advised him to leave the Department in 1946, he continued to take the position that he was reluctant to leave before he could be definitively cleared of any suspicion. He was seeking that clearance in the same time frame in which he received the Order of the Red Star from the Soviets and was personally thanked by Andrei Vishinsky for his work as a Soviet agent.

By the perjury trials, then, Alger Hiss had developed a longstanding pattern of engaging in secret intelligence work that he found stimulating and rewarding, and that he plausibly denied. Denying that secret worlds existed in his life had become as natural to him as participating in those worlds. Denying his secret life, in fact, had become a way of demonstrating his loyalty to all of those who inhabited it, from Joszef Peter and Boris Bykov (whom Hiss never admitted to having known) to Priscilla and Donald Hiss. By not exposing those who participated in his secret world Hiss was acting as their caretaker. By doing such he was reinforcing his own sense of competence, boosting his self-esteem.

Maintaining his innocence and campaigning for his vindication, after his release from prison, was another gesture of loyalty and altruism. Loyalty to the ideals of Soviet Communism and to the secret work in which he had participated. Loyalty to those who had joined him in the campaign: Chester Lane and Helen Buttenweiser, who had helped him at the height of his legal troubles; John Lowenthal, who had assumed the role of his chief advisor and publicist; Meyer Zeligs and John Chabot Smith, sympathetic biographers; Timothy Hobson, who had come forward to declare his stepfather's innocence; and especially Tony Hiss, who had been nurtured on the illusion of that innocence and who had willingly helped his father keep his campaign in the public eye. Tony was also an object of altruism. Once so devastated by his father's humiliation and imprisonment that he contemplated suicide, Tony had recovered well enough to anticipate the prospect of a successful career as a writer. Alger could help promote Tony's career by freeing him from the burden of having a notorious figure as a father. If Alger was vindicated, his honor would be Tony's as well. Finally, Priscilla and Donald were also persons in need of Alger's caretaking. They had been spared exposure as agents, but they bore the burdens of being associated with him. If he were thought to be innocent, they would be as well.

And there was always the prospect that his campaign might someday succeed. By just remaining in the public eye, maintaining his persona of grace and gentleness, continuing to adopt his "terrible evenness" about the Hiss case and his enemies, he might someday convince a large segment of the public that his case was, after all, a "political" trial, a symbol of the excesses of the McCarthy era. Between the 1950s and the mid-1970s he had managed to cloak himself in ambiguity. And when he chose to publicize Volkogonov's sweeping "exoneration," many media outlets reported it as the final truth in the Hiss case. The gesture was risky, but then Hiss had always traded off the possibility of vindication against the risk of definitive exposure.

Alger Hiss can no longer be seen as a figure of ambiguity. This is so even though his psychological makeup was highly complex, and his motivation resists easy characterization. The ambiguity associated with Hiss was created by his regularly asserting things about himself and his life that were not true, and by others—for their own ideological reasons and because of Hiss's extraordinarily convincing persona—choosing to believe them. In thinking about the Alger Hiss that remains after that aura of ambiguity is lifted from him, the place to start is to summarize the qualities that have attracted Americans to him, and to begin to see him as a rare, but constant presence in our world: the consummate spy.

The persona that Hiss presented, as his campaign for vindication evolved, contained qualities that resonated for overlapping circles of late twentieth-century Americans. Hiss was a product of elite academic institutions in a time period in which education was becoming the most important index of social status in America. He was identified with Justice Oliver Wendell Holmes, the judge most familiar to twentieth-century Americans. He was associated with the birth of the United Nations, an aspirational symbol of international peace. He was one of numerous Americans who had been optimistic about the prospective path of the Soviet Union in the 1930s. If he had been in the left wing of the New Deal, seeking to experiment with collectivist solutions to the problems of farmers and industrial laborers in the Depression, many other Americans similarly felt that only thoroughgoing reforms could alleviate the economic crisis of the 1930s. If he had believed that the United States and the Soviet Union would cooperate to further world peace through the United Nations, so had most Americans at the close of World War II.

In short, many Americans found qualities in Hiss they could identify with or admire. And many found qualities in Hiss's antagonists that, retrospectively, they found distasteful. The anti-Communism of the Cold War era appeared to many as simple-minded and repressive. Richard Nixon demonstrated that becoming president of the United States did not divest a person of mean-spiritedness and a lack of principles. J. Edgar Hoover's carefully constructed image as a virtuous "G-man" came apart under closer scrutiny. When one totaled up Hiss's favorable associations and the notoriety of his enemies, his continued professions of innocence took on to some an air of nobility.

Many people thus wanted to believe that Alger Hiss was innocent, and Hiss helped them by embroidering his narrative of innocence over the years, tailoring it to the changing tastes of an elite segment of public opinion, from which almost all of the information and perceptions about Hiss originated. As he shaped and re-shaped his campaign for vindication, Hiss maintained his constant air of persistent, patient evenness. From Brock Brower in 1960, to Robert Alan Aurthur and Philip Nobile in the 1970s, to David Remnick in 1986, being in the company of Alger Hiss, and hearing him talk about his case, was a seductive experience. When one was outside the company of Hiss, and looked at the evidence, his guilt might have seemed more probable, but when one encountered him, and became exposed to his combination of graciousness and apparent serenity, ambiguity began to take over.

How was Hiss able to project, over so many years, an air of absolute confidence, even serenity, about his eventual vindication? How, especially, was he able to do so when he knew that his campaign was a confidence game, and that vindication would be a massive falsehood? Hiss's remarkable ability to sell himself and his campaign came from the vital role that his narrative of innocence played in his efforts to fashion, and to preserve, an integrated vision of his life. Integration—I am using that term in the psychological sense of completeness, self-fulfillment, and inner peace—was achieved, for Hiss, not by *being* innocent of covert espionage activity but by successfully *pretending* to be innocent.[3] Succeeding at this pretense of innocence—his version of vindication—would have meant that Hiss could see himself as an integrated personality who had lived a complete life.

Vindication meant that Hiss could take enhanced satisfaction in the work he had put in as a Soviet agent, now found not to have happened, and thus shoved, perhaps forever, behind the looking glass. It meant that he could take pride in acting as Soviet agents in the United States were instructed by their handlers to act. Never reveal your covert existence, they were told; if exposed, categorically deny any complicity; if convicted, strenuously maintain your innocence as long as you live.[4]

A long time KGB agent recalled that "[w]hen Hiss was accused at the end of the 1940s, his behavior followed instructions he may have learned in the 1930s: never admit anything." Apparently the Soviets particularly stressed this response for American-based agents because of their belief that American authorities, unlike their British counterparts, would never allow exposed agents to defect to the Soviet

Union. None of the celebrated British-based agents known as the "Cambridge Five," Guy Burgess, Anthony Blunt, John Cairncross, Donald MacLean, and Kim Philby, was ever brought to trial: Burgess, MacLean, and Philby died in Russia.

Never admitting his espionage meant that Hiss could help his supporters retain the illusion of trying to help a victim of history, and not think of themselves as fools. And it meant that he could see his life as he had described it in the last paragraph of *Recollections of a Life,* a description that now took on a striking concreteness:

> My goals still seem to me bright and attainable. In any event, I subscribe to the view that the way the journey is traveled counts for more than the goals reached. . . . I have pursued my goals in mine own ways.[5]

Had Hiss not maintained his innocence—had he adopted Priscilla's strategy of changing his name and quietly disappearing after being released from Lewisburg— he could never have achieved the feeling of having an integrated life. He would have been just one other undercover agent who had lied, betrayed his country, and gotten caught. By denying that he was a Communist, let alone a Soviet agent, Hiss was in effect asserting that he had not been exposed after all. To be sure, he had been accused by Chambers, convicted of perjury, and served time in prison, but all of that had been a miscarriage of justice. The accusations were false; the conviction erroneous; the prison time undeserved. With vindication, the grace with which he had responded to these tribulations would give him an aura of nobility. He could be an inspiration to his supporters, and a reminder of the excesses of the Cold War. And he could be a Soviet agent too. Those achievements, taken together, gave him a sense that his life had a completeness and a fundamental meaning. It became a beautifully integrated whole instead of the shambles it might otherwise have been.

One might compare the British atomic spy Klaus Fuchs, who said the following while confessing, in 1950, that he had given the Soviets information about the use of uranium and plutonium in the manufacture of nuclear weapons.

> I used my Marxist philosophy to establish in my mind two separate compartments. One compartment in which I allowed myself to make friendships, to have personal relations, to help people . . . I could be free and easy and happy with other people without fear of disclosing myself because I knew that the other compartment would step in if I approached the danger point. . . . It appeared to me . . . that I had become a "free man" because I had succeeded in the other compartment to establish myself completely independent of the surrounding forces of society.[6]

A biographer of Fuchs speculated that he had been "[d]ominated by the religious and ethical righteousness of his father" and "devastated by the suicides of his mother and sister," and had "retreated into the world of Communism and espionage, where he felt morally virtuous, politically active, and personally fulfilled."[7] Although Hiss associated dominance and suicide with a different set of parents, the parallels are striking.

I believe that Hiss should be understood as one sort of human actor in the sweep of history, not as another. If Hiss is to be seen primarily as an actor connected to a distinctive time in twentieth-century American life, when the domestic and international politics of the United States first reoriented themselves around the ideology of Cold War anti-Communism, and then distanced themselves from that ideology, he will be in danger, as are all historic personages identified with particular eras, of disappearing from view as that era comes to be perceived as remote. He should be thought of, instead, as one of the successful spies in American history, not only because of the quality and duration of his espionage for the Soviet Union, but because of his singular ability, in his successive looking-glass wars, to deceive so many persons about the secret dimensions of his life.

Hiss was a complex, troubled, ingratiating, formidable personality who was in many respects ideally suited to maintain a secret life. If there is such a person as a natural successful spy, who could conceal the existence of his covert activities as skillfully as he engaged in them, Alger Hiss seems to have been one. Thomas Powers's question, to which this chapter has partly been directed ("[W]hy did Hiss persist in the lie personally? Why did he allow his friends and family to go on carrying the awful burden of that lie?") answers itself if one thinks of Hiss as someone for whom spying for the Soviets, and lying about it for the rest of his life, was a way of demonstrating his multiple loyalties, channeling his altruism, and achieving self-fulfillment. Not many people seek psychic integration through spying and lying. Even fewer are so good at those tasks that they come close to achieving their version of it. Alger Hiss was one. There have been and there will be others.

AFTERWORD

Two weeks before he turned 93, John Davis and I had our last conversation about Alger Hiss. John died three weeks later. He had been in robust physical and mental health for so long that he seemed indestructible, but by the time of the conversation he was failing. He had not been able, or willing—he was capable of responding to unwelcome information by ignoring it—to pay close attention to the appearance, in 1999, of *Venona* and *The Haunted Wood*. At one point in the conversation he said something that made me think he was changing his mind about Hiss, but he also said other things that suggested he remained convinced that Hiss had been innocent.

After John's death some of his personal effects found their way to my household in circuitous ways. Recently, in the course of cleaning out an attic storage room, we found some papers that John had asked be given to us. Among those papers were carbon copies of the Reporters's transcripts of selected portions of HUAC hearings, ranging from August 5 through August 30, 1948, dealing with the accusations against Hiss and Hiss's responses. John, as Hiss's counsel, testified at a few points in the August 25 hearing, eventually being sworn in as a witness.[1]

John Davis's copies of the HUAC transcripts contained very few handwritten notes, none of which cast any light on the Hiss defense strategy. He had added paperclips to a fairly large number of pages in his copy of the August 16, 1948, hearing, in which Hiss was first confronted with Chambers in person, but there were not many other tracks of his presence, let alone any new information. But even though John's copies of the transcripts mainly duplicated materials I had already examined, they were a help to me. They seemed yet another link to John and the book's origins.

Many others besides John Davis have helped with this book. John Monahan, in the course of reading selected portions of drafts, gave me the benefit of his expertise in psychology, which supplemented my understanding of Hiss's motivation. Stephen Jones, Esq., of the Oklahoma bar, who has followed the Hiss case closely since the 1970s, favored me with several instructive communications on the case and my draft manuscript, as well as sending me a copy of the 1983 American Playhouse production on the Hiss case, "Concealed Enemies." Kenneth Abraham, Brian Balogh, Curtis Bradley, Barry Cushman, Ross Davies, Neil Duxbury, Daniel Ernst, Jack Goldsmith, Risa Goluboff, John Earl Haynes, Laura Kalman, Harvey Klehr, Alfred Konefsky, James Ryan, John Henry Schlegel, and Paul Stephan have read the entire manuscript in various drafts, and Professors Abraham, Cushman, and Stephan have also read drafts of law journal articles related to the book. John Jeffries, currently the dean of the University of Virginia School of Law, encouraged me to think about a book on Alger Hiss in the days in which our faculty offices were adjacent. Despite becoming dean, John read drafts of articles, and the entire book manuscript, as they appeared. This book would probably be better had I followed all the suggestions John (and my other readers) made to improve it, but I did follow many of those, and appreciate the help.

Portions of the book are based on endowed lectures I delivered at Ohio Northern University, Boston University School of Law, and Oklahoma City College of Law in 2001, 2002, and 2003. Two of the lectures were published as "Hiss and Holmes," 28, *Ohio Northern University Law Review*, 231 (2002) and "Alger Hiss's Campaign for Vindication," 83, *Boston University Law Review*, 1 (2003). My thanks to those institutions, and also to my colleagues at the University of Virginia School of Law, where I presented a draft of the Boston University article in a September 2002 faculty workshop. Thanks also to Elizabeth Lang, Rachel McKenzie, and the reference staff of the University of Virginia law school library for research assistance, to Kirsten Thorsen for her assistance with proofreading and the index, and to Dedi Felman and Peter Ginna of Oxford University Press for their help as the book progressed. The illustrations on pages 2, 34, 67, 116, 135, 142, 166, 172, 185, and 236 are courtesy of the Art & Visual Materials Special Collections Department, Harvard Law School Library. Those on pages 80 and 101 are courtesy of the U.S. Bureau of Prisons. Those on pages 200 and 215 are courtesy of AP/Wide World Photos, and that on page 15 courtesy of the Estate of John Knox. My thanks to Lesley Schoenfeld and Virginia Whitehill for their good auspices in procuring illustrations.

Two more persons deserve special mention. Marcus John Davis, John Davis's son, has been a very welcome addition to our extended family in the years since John's death, and I anticipate many more good visits with Marc. Susan Davis White has had a special interest in this book, which has not prevented her from getting sick of it, and Alger Hiss, at times. Although I asked her to read and edit as much of the final manuscript draft as she chose, the usual disclaimer that no one who helped with the book should be taken as endorsing its arguments applies pointedly to her. As always, however, she helps me write books by being there in countless ways. This book is for John Davis's daughter and my wife.

G. E. W.

Charlottesville

Summer, 2003

NOTES

Note on Citation Style

Readers familiar with the style and form of legal citations might appreciate some explanation of the method and style for documenting sources used in this book. As a general rule, endnotes in the text appear at the ends of paragraphs, and multiple sources are grouped together in the notes. When a source is cited more than once, a short title reference is used, with one exception. If the source being cited is the same source listed in a previous note with only one reference, "Id." is used. Endnotes occasionally appear within paragraphs, typically when a more extended quotation appears or when an endnote contains additional text.

When a quotation appears in a paragraph in which multiple sources are cited, a portion of the quotation is repeated in the notes to clarify its source.

When archival sources are used, scholarly works making use of those sources are often listed in combination with those sources if the text is directed at the scholarly works being cited.

Except for the "short title" form, citations to archival sources, books, scholarly and popular journals and magazines, and newspapers follow the legal style.

Preface

1. For more detail on John Davis's career, see the tributes to him by Oscar H. Davis, Milton V. Freeman, Daniel M. Friedman, William L. Reynolds, and myself in 47 Maryland L. Rev. 613–625 (1988).
2. G. Edward White, "The Alger Hiss Case: Justices Frankfurter and Reed as Character Witnesses," 4 Green Bag 2d 63–83 (2000).

Introduction

1. Further details of the events leading to Hiss's appearance at the March 18, 1976, press conference, with documentation, are provided in Chapter Six.
2. The first comment in the collection of essays on the Rosenberg case was made by Ellen Schreker in "Before the Rosenbergs: Espionage Scenarios in the Early Cold War," in Marjorie Garber and Rebecca L. Walkowitz, *Secret Agents*, 140 (1995). The second was made by Alice Jardine in "Flash Back, Flash Forward: The Fifties, The Nineties, and the Transformed Politics of Remote Control," in id., 110.

3. George McGovern, "Nixon and Historical Memory: Two Reviews," 34 Perspectives 1, 4 (1996).

CHAPTER ONE

1. Murray Kempton, "Alger Hiss—An Argument for a Good Con," *New York Post,* April 22, 1978, p. 11.
2. Murray Kempton, *Part of Our Time,* 17 (1955).
3. Details on Alger Hiss's early life are drawn from interviews with Hiss in Meyer A. Zeligs, *Friendship and Fratricide* (1967); John Chabot Smith, *Alger Hiss: The True Story* (1976); and Tony Hiss, *Laughing Last,* 8–31 (1977). See also Alger Hiss, "Autobiographical Notes," in Alger Hiss Defense Files, quoted in Allen Weinstein, *Perjury: The Hiss-Chambers Case* (1st ed., 1978, 2d ed., 1997); and Alger Hiss, *Recollections of a Life,* 1–9 (1988). The details vary slightly in these sources, but are essentially similar.
4. Kempton quote: *Part of Our Time,* 16–17. Hiss comments on his mother: *Recollections of a Life,* 3.
5. "Under all circumstances": Alger Hiss quoted in Zeligs, *Friendship and Fratricide,* 159. In that book Zeligs noted that he had conversations and correspondence with Alger Hiss "over a period of six years," beginning in May 1960. Id., xii, 488.
6. For background on Anna Hiss and Mary Ann Hiss, see *Friendship and Fratricide,* 159–161, 174–176; *Alger Hiss: The True Story,* 49, 64–65. Meyer Zeligs quoted Hiss's reaction to learning about Mary Ann's suicide in *Friendship and Fratricide,* 175, apparently based on an interview with Hiss. See id., 137–138.
7. For details of Bosley's illness, see *Friendship and Fratricide,* 167–169; *Alger Hiss: The True Story,* 63–65. The quote about Bosley's condition is from *Friendship and Fratricide,* 168.
8. "I'm not sure I accepted fully the nearness of his death": Alger Hiss, quoted in *Friendship and Fratricide,* 168. "A family arrangement": Alger Hiss to Meyer Zeligs, quoted in *Friendship and Fratricide,* 168.
9. Alger Hiss to Meyer Zeligs, quoted in *Friendship and Fratricide,* 169.
10. Bosley's ability to relate to people "a good in itself," but related to "impulsive self-expression": Alger Hiss to Meyer Zeligs, quoted in *Friendship and Fratricide,* 169. Johns Hopkins yearbook entry describing Hiss, quoted in id., 166.
11. Alger "still a virgin on his wedding night in 1929": *Laughing Last,* 9. Alger's description of Bosley as "undisciplined" and "casual in sexual matters": Alger Hiss to Meyer Zeligs, quoted in *Friendship and Fratricide,* 168. Alger's supplying "practical aid": Alger Hiss to Meyer Zeligs, quoted in id.
12. For the outlines of Donald Hiss's career, see Katie Louchheim, ed., *The Making of the New Deal: The Insiders Speak,* 321–322 (1983).
13. "Did my homework with pleasure and pride": Alger Hiss to Meyer Zeligs, quoted in *Friendship and Fratricide,* 155. High school yearbook characterization of Alger Hiss: quoted in id., 159. Quotes about Alger's nature from cousins: id., 154–155. Alger as "model of good manners," without "hostility": id.
14. Details of Hiss family finances: *Friendship and Fratricide,* 142–149. "[H]ard up" quote: Jesse Slingluff to Meyer Zeligs, quoted in id., 164.
15. Lee Pressman, quoted in *Part of Our Time,* 20.
16. Pressman's background: *Part of Our Time,* 20, described Pressman as "a young man up from Brooklyn by way of Cornell University."

17. For details of Priscilla Fansler's early life, see *Friendship and Fratricide*, 166, 180–182; *Laughing Last*, 40–50; *Alger Hiss: The True Story*, 66–69.

18. The taxicab incident is described in *Friendship and Fratricide*, 181, and in *Laughing Last*, 42. Alger Hiss was the source of the story.

19. In an interview with Meyer Zeligs, Thayer Hobson stated that he and Priscilla "never should have married." She was, Hobson thought, "an impractical idealist, interested primarily in art, literature, and music. . . . [O]il and water don't mix." Quoted in *Friendship and Fratricide*, 181.

    The identity of William Brown Meloney was revealed by Allen Weinstein in *Perjury*, 1st ed., 79. Weinstein indicated that he learned Meloney's identity from Alger Hiss himself, and that Alger had also told Alden Whitman, who was at one point planning an authorized biography of Hiss, and John Chabot Smith, who succeeded Whitman on that project. In a 1975 interview with Weinstein, Priscilla Hiss expressed outrage at Alger's revelation of her 1929 abortion and Meloney's identity. See *Perjury*, 1st ed., 599. In *Alger Hiss: The True Story*, 70–71, Smith reported that Alger and Priscilla differed as to when she first told him that her 1929 operation was an abortion.

20. For details of Alger Hiss's life in the years between 1925 and 1929, see *Friendship and Fratricide*, 172–73, 181–82; *Alger Hiss: The True Story*, 55–56, 61–62. Alger Hiss's comments about marriage are quoted in *Laughing Last*, 41.

21. Pressman's comment about Hiss's impression on Frankfurter is from *Part of Our Time*, 20. Frankfurter's comment to O'Brian is in a letter, Felix Frankfurter to John Lord O'Brian, April 1, 1930, Felix Frankfurter Papers, Library of Congress. Weinstein quotes the letter in *Perjury*, 2d ed., 71. For a discussion of the connection between Frankfurter's youth as a Jewish immigrant in the Lower East Side of New York City and his attraction to symbols of elite WASP culture, which began at Harvard Law School, see H. N. Hirsch, *The Enigma of Felix Frankfurter*, 21–24 (1981).

22. For details on Holmes's criteria for his secretaries, and Frankfurter's role in the process of selecting them, see G. Edward White, *Justice Oliver Wendell Holmes: Law and the Inner Self*, 313, 359 (1993).

23. Holmes wrote a January 21, 1929, letter to Frankfurter in which he said that "[t]he account you give of Mr. Hiss sounds most prepossessing and if he is willing to take the chances I shall hope to have him." The letter is quoted in Robert M. Mennel and Christine L. Compston, eds., *Holmes and Frankfurter: Their Correspondence, 1912–1934*, 234 (1996).

24. Alger's comments to Tony about women are quoted in *Laughing Last*, 51.

25. The story of Alger's 1929 visit to Priscilla in New York is told in *Laughing Last*, 42.

26. Details of Alger's and Donald's visit to Giverny in the summer of 1929 are in *Recollections of a Life*, 20–30.

27. Id., 29.

28. The quoted material is from *Recollections of a Life*, 34–35.

29. Hiss's comment is from *Recollections of a Life*, 35. For more detail on Holmes's work on the Court, see *Justice Oliver Wendell Holmes*, 311–315.

30. For more detail on Holmes's letter writing, see G. Edward White, "Holmes as Correspondent," 43 Vand. L. Rev. 1707 (1990).

31. For more detail on the work of Holmes's secretaries, see *Justice Oliver Wendell Holmes*, 468–471.

32. The quote from Brandeis is from an April 21, 1929, letter to Felix Frankfurter, quoted in Melvin Urofsky and David Levy, eds., *"Half Brother, Half Son": The Letters of Louis D.*

Brandeis to Felix Frankfurter, 370 (1991). For a discussion of the marriage of Wendell Holmes and Fanny Dixwell, see *Justice Oliver Wendell Holmes*, 103–108.

33. Holmes's comment about Hiss is from an October 29, 1930, letter to Nina (Mrs. John Chipman) Gray, in *Oliver Wendell Holmes Papers*, General Correspondence, Reel 27 (Microfilm Edition, 1985).

34. For more detail, see *Justice Oliver Wendell Holmes*, 107–108.

35. Hiss described his experiences reading aloud with Lila in *Recollections of a Life*, 5–9, and *Friendship and Fratricide*, 144. The "favorite diversion" quote is from *Recollections of a Life*, 8. The "period of leisure" quote is from id., 36.

36. The quoted passages are from *Recollections of a Life*, 36.

37. Quoted passages from id., 36–37.

38. *Recollections of a Life*, 40.

39. Secretary asked to keep "simple accounts": Holmes to Frankfurter, December 11, 1925, in *Holmes and Frankfurter*, 195. Sutherland access to "Black Book": Arthur E. Sutherland, Memoir of a Year with Justice Holmes, Arthur E. Sutherland Papers, Harvard Law School Library. Holmes's inability to grip a pen after August 1931: *Justice Oliver Wendell Holmes*, 458–459.

40. "Enchanted year" and "most profound influence on my life": *Recollections of a Life*, 32, 51.

41. Holmes referring to his secretaries as "sonny" or "idiot boy": *Laughing Last*, 54. Holmes describing the position as "my intelligent valet," and a place where a "young lawyer [would] waste his time": Holmes to Frankfurter, March 30, 1932, *Holmes and Frankfurter*, 271. The secretaryship as "not a place for a young lawyer who wants to rise": Holmes to Frankfurter, March 25, 1932, *Holmes and Frankfurter*, 270. "I very much wish to have a young man": Holmes to Frankfurter, March 30, 1932, id.

42. For a list of Holmes's secretaries from the 1905 through the 1934 Terms, see *Justice Oliver Wendell Holmes*, 489. All were WASPs except Thomas Corcoran, the secretary for the 1926 Term, an Irish Catholic, and possibly Robert Benjamin, secretary for the 1922 Term, who may have been Jewish. Holmes's comments that he did not want a married secretary "till you tell me that is the only possibility," and that he had "put the case of the married man to my wife": Holmes to Frankfurter, December 19, 1915, *Holmes and Frankfurter*, 40.

43. Holmes's statements that he would not have taken Barton Leach "had I known earlier that he was married," and that "I want a free man, and one who may be a contribution to society": Holmes to Frankfurter, January 6, 1925, *Holmes and Frankfurter*, 178. Holmes's comment that he was "a good deal annoyed" at Sutherland's marriage, Holmes to Frankfurter, July 25, 1927, id., 215. Holmes's "waiv[ing] my objections" to Sutherland, Holmes to Frankfurter, July 29, 1927, id.

44. The quoted comments in this paragraph are from a letter Hiss wrote to Felix Frankfurter, December 13, 1929, Felix Frankfurter Papers, Library of Congress.

45. Alger's and Priscilla's needing persuasion to have a minister perform the ceremony, and to invite any guests: William Marbury, "The Alger Hiss Case," memorandum in Alger Hiss Defense Files, quoted in Allen Weinstein, *Perjury*, 2d ed., 539. List of the wedding guests: *Friendship and Fratricide*, 182–183. Story about Alger's waving his hand when the minister said "speak now or forever hold your peace," Charles Ford Reese (one of Alger's friends who attended) to Meyer Zeligs, February 18 and March 14, 1963, quoted in id., 183.

46. Marbury's comment about Hiss's knowing that in marrying during the year with Holmes he was violating one of the terms of the secretaryship: "The Alger Hiss Case," quoted in *Perjury*, 2d ed., 539.

47. Alger Hiss to Felix Frankfurter, December 13, 1929, Felix Frankfurter Papers, Library of Congress.
48. Smith's account of Hiss's discovery of Holmes's rule "on the morning of my wedding": *Alger Hiss: The True Story*, 68. Smith, who interviewed Hiss regularly from April 1974 to July 1975, did not specify on which occasion Hiss told him the story.
49. The quoted passages are from Hiss to Frankfurter, December 13, 1929, Frankfurter Papers.
50. Donald Hiss's story about the subject of Alger's marriage being "taboo" in Holmes's company: Donald Hiss to Katie Louchheim, quoted in *The Making of the New Deal*, 36 (1983).
51. Comments on Priscilla as humorless and demanding: *Alger Hiss: The True Story*, 69–70; *Friendship and Fratricide*, 183; *Perjury*, 2d ed., 70 (quoting February 24, 1975, interview with William Marbury). Priscilla's dislike of Alger's Baltimore friends: *Alger Hiss: The True Story*, 69; their reciprocal dislike of her: *Perjury*, 2d ed., 70 (quoting Marbury interview). Minnie Hiss's perceptions of Priscilla and telegram: *Alger Hiss: The True Story*, 67–68 (Smith's source for that information was very likely Alger Hiss). Alger's feeling "independent" on marrying Priscilla: Alger Hiss to Meyer Zeligs, quoted in *Friendship and Fratricide*, 182.
52. Both quotes are from Whittaker Chambers, *Witness*, 363 (1952).
53. Information about Alger and Priscilla Hiss's life between 1929 and 1931: *Alger Hiss: The True Story*, 71–73; *Friendship and Fratricide*, 184–186.
   The name partner of the Cotton law firm was Joseph Cotton, who had combined law practice with public service. One of Holmes's legal secretaries, Thomas Corcoran, who had worked for Holmes in the 1926 Term, had joined the Cotton firm after his year with Holmes, and had then been appointed to the staff of the Reconstruction Finance Commission. Corcoran was to become one of Roosevelt's close advisors in the early years of the New Deal. The best source of the details of Corcoran's career remains Monica Lynne Niznik, "Thomas G. Corcoran," (unpublished Ph.D. dissertation, Notre Dame University, 1981).
54. Priscilla's joining Morningside Heights branch of Socialist Party, and working in soup kitchens: *Perjury*, 2d ed., 85, citing documents produced at Alger Hiss's perjury trials; *Alger Hiss: The True Story*, 72–73. "[G]rowing breadlines . . . hard-pressed farmers": *Recollections of a Life*, 60–61.
55. Alger's joining International Juridical Association: *Alger Hiss: The True Story*, 186. "[B]ecame responsible . . . greed": *Recollections of a Life*, 61.
56. Lee Pressman's affiliations with Communist Party: *Perjury*, 2d ed., 116–117, citing Pressman's August 28, 1950, testimony before the House Un-American Activities Committee, in "Hearings Regarding Communism in the United States Government, Part 2," 81st Cong., 2d Sess., pp. 2844–2901. Pressman's and Hiss's affiliation with International Juridical Association: id., 86, citing Alger Hiss, memorandum to Edward McLean, September 1948, Hiss Defense Files. Joseph Brodsky member of IJA: id., citing Jerome Hellerman, April 5, 1949, interview, Hiss Defense Files.
57. Hiss made a fuller statement of his growing political awareness in the early 1930s in a draft chapter in a book he planned to write on the New Deal, "Foundations of My Liberalism," in the Alger Hiss Papers, Harvard Law School Library. Despite its detail, the chapter should be used with care: it scrupulously avoids any mention of Hiss's connections with radical groups in the period, and takes pains to portray Hiss as a mainstream New Deal Democrat. Some of the material in the draft tracks themes raised in portions of Hiss's chapter, "The Making of a New Dealer," in *Recollections of a Life*, 52–63.

58. Hiss's move to Washington to join AAA: *Recollections of a Life*, 62–63; *Perjury*, 2d ed., 116–117. Frankfurter telegram urging Hiss to join AAA: *Recollections of a Life*, 52. Hiss's drafting contracts for Department of Agriculture: id., 63. Hiss joins Ware Group: *Perjury*, 2d ed., 119–120, citing November 27, 1950, FBI interview with Nathaniel Weyl, FBI Files.

59. The best account of the controversy involving cotton industry contracts is in Robert Jerome. Glennon, *The Iconoclast as Reformer: A Biography of Jerome Frank*, 98–101 (1985).

60. Charles Kramer a member of Ware Group: *Perjury*, 2d ed., 118–119, citing FBI interviews with Lee Pressman, August 30 and 31, 1950, FBI Files.

61. *Perjury*, 2d ed., 57, quotes Chambers as identifying Donald Hiss as a member of the Ware Group in a 1939 memorandum he gave to Adolf Berle, who was working on security matters for the Roosevelt administration at the time.

62. Death of Harold Ware and his replacement by Joszef Peter: *Perjury*, 2d ed., 118–119, citing FBI interviews with Pressman, August 30 and 31, 1950. Hiss's transfer from AAA to Nye Committee: id., 125–126, citing Gardner Jackson, Oral History, Columbia University, pp. 468–469. Peter's "dream" of penetrating "the old-line agencies": Whittaker Chambers to FBI, quoted in FBI Summary Report, May 11, 1949, #3220, FBI Files, p. 72. Chambers is quoted in *Perjury*, 2d ed., 114.

CHAPTER TWO

1. Joszef Peter ("J. Peters") as "head of underground section of the American Communist Party," and placement of Hiss and others in government agencies "to influence policy . . .": Whittaker Chambers, *Witness*, 335 (1952). Corroboration of Chambers's account of Alger Hiss's joining Harold Ware's group of Communists and Communist sympathizers, his meeting Chambers and Peter at Ware Group discussions, and Peter's subsequent recruitment of him as an agent for Soviet military intelligence is provided in various sources cited in this and subsequent chapters.

2. Hiss separated from Ware Group and placed in "parallel apparatus" reporting to Soviet military intelligence: *Witness*, 335–336.

3. Chambers's meeting with Ware and Peter: *Witness*, 336.

4. Chambers's first meeting with Hiss: *Witness*, 349–350.

5. Chambers's second meeting with Hiss: *Witness*, 351.

6. Chambers's description of Ware Group: *Witness*, 343–344.

7. Ware Group's turn to espionage: *Witness*, 369–70. Bill's lack of enthusiasm for documents obtained by Hiss when at Nye Committee: id., 375. Elizabeth Bentley identified Bill, an Estonian Red Army officer, as her first Soviet comptroller. Elizabeth Bentley, *Out of Bondage*, 243, 267 (1951). See also David J. Dallin, *Soviet Espionage*, 404, 444 (1955).

8. Information on Hiss's and Chambers's early careers can be found in Allen Weinstein, *Perjury: The Hiss-Chambers Case*, 79–97 (2d ed., 1997); Sam Tanenhaus, *Whittaker Chambers: A Biography*, 49–90 (1997). Unless otherwise stated, references to *Perjury* are to the second edition (the first edition appeared in 1978).

9. Chambers's description of his relationship with the Hisses: *Witness*, 359–360.

10. Chambers's move to Baltimore in preparation for being sent to England: *Witness*, 357.

11. Details of Chambers's life in Baltimore: *Witness*, 359, 373, 393.

12. Bykov's replacement of Bill in 1936: *Witness*, 405–06. Identification of Gross, Silverman, and Wadleigh as additional agents: id., 384–385.

13. Original procedure for photographing stolen documents under Bykov: *Witness*, 421–422.

14. Hiss's moving from Justice Department to State Department at cut in salary: Weinstein, *Perjury*, 188, quoting documents in Alger Hiss Defense Files, to which Weinstein was given access in the 1970s. Assistant secretary's office in State Department as "best possible place" for espionage agent to work: John S. Dickey, assistant to Assistant Secretary of State Francis Sayre, in "Memorandum of Interview [With] John S. Dickey," January 15, 1949, Hiss Defense Files, quoted in id., 189.

15. Chambers's descriptions of espionage procedure with Hiss: *Witness*, 425, 428–429.

16. Chambers including copies of stolen documents in life preserver: *Witness*, 38. In December 15, 1948, testimony to a New York grand jury investigating Communists in the United States government, Chambers said that he kept documents supplied by Hiss, rather than other agents, because only Hiss, among the agents that passed him stolen documents, generated enough material to require copying the documents before transmission. Whittaker Chambers, December 15, 1948, in Transcripts of Grand Jury Investigating Communists in the Government of the United States, 8 vols., 1948, Special Collections, Harvard Law School Library, Vol. 8, pp. 4434–4485. Hereafter cited as Grand Jury Transcripts.

17. Hiss's including handwritten summaries of documents in material he passed to Chambers: *Witness*, 429.

18. Hiss's "Stalin always plays for keeps" comment: *Witness*, 248. (Chambers did not specify exactly when the comment was made.) Details of Chambers's defection from Soviets: *Witness*, 35–44; *Perjury*, 275–279.

19. Details of Chambers's activity immediately after defecting in 1938: *Witness*, 56–69.

20. Details of Chambers's last conversation with Hiss in 1938: *Witness*, 72–74.

21. For details of Hiss's career in the State Department between 1936 and 1946, see John Chabot Smith, *Alger Hiss: The True Story*, 108–139 (1976); *Perjury*, 310–316.

22. For confirmation, in decoded Soviet cablegrams, that Donald and Priscilla continued to work for the Soviets through 1945, see Chapter Seven. Alger's refusal to allow Donald to procure State Department documents for the Soviets: *Witness*, 418–419.

    Allen Weinstein emphasized an incident in 1938 in which the Labor Department requested Donald Hiss's services (Donald Hiss was then in the State Department), to preside over a deportation hearing for Harry Bridges, the Australian-born head of a West Coast longshoreman's union associated with radical politics. Hiss had previously been in the Labor Department, and had worked on a deportation hearing on the West Coast in 1937, but subsequently denied that that hearing involved Bridges. He asked not to be transferred, and Assistant Secretary of State Francis Sayre acceded to the request. Weinstein found suspicious the facts that Bridges may have had links to the Communist Party of the United States, that Alger Hiss was Sayre's assistant at the time, and that Donald Hiss subsequently gave misleading testimony about the incident. He stated that "the selection of a presiding officer for [Bridges's] deportation would . . . have been of keen interest to [American Communist Party] officials." *Perjury*, 198. But even if Alger Hiss intervened to prevent Donald from being publicly associated with a proceeding involving Harry Bridges, and Donald was evasive about any other connections he might have had with Bridges, the incident hardly furnishes proof of Donald's Communist affiliations, let alone his involvement in espionage.

23. Christopher Andrew and Vasili Mitrokhin, *The Sword and the Shield: The Mitrokhin Archive and the Secret History of the KGB*, 133–134 (1999). That book was based heavily on a former KGB agent's successful smuggling a cache of secret KGB intelligence documents out of the Soviet Union.

24. For more on that meeting, and how it came to the attention of the National Security Agency of the United States, see Chapter Seven.

25. Maclean was posted to the British Embassy in Washington in May 1944, remaining there until 1949. For much of that time he was first secretary of the embassy, having access to nearly all of the British government's contacts with the United States and other governments. He also had access to high-level British policy documents. He passed a good deal of this information to the Soviets. There are documented meetings between Maclean and Hiss between December 1945 and November 1946. See Harvey Klehr and John Earl Haynes, *Venona: Soviet Espionage in America*, 52–55 (1999), citing National Security Agency decoded transcripts of Soviet communications; Verne W. Newton, *The Cambridge Spies*, 130–143 (1991), citing FBI files in the Diplomatic Section of the National Archives. For a summary of Hiss's repeated denials of having known Maclean, see id., 142–143.

26. For a discussion of Hiss's request, citing State Department files, see *Perjury*, 320–321.

27. Chambers's going to work for *Time* in 1939, and his purchase of Westminster farm: *Witness*, 86–88.

28. The September 1939, meeting between Chambers, Isaac Don Levine, and Berle is discussed in *Witness*, 463–466; *Whittaker Chambers*, 161–163; and *Perjury*, 291–293. Names of the persons, including Hiss, whom Chambers identified as Communist agents in the government, and whom Berle listed in the "Underground Espionage Agent" memorandum, are set forth in *Witness*, 466–469.

29. Berle's memorandum being laughed off by Roosevelt: *Witness*, 470, quoting Isaac Don Levine. For details of the Dies memorandum to Biddle, and the subsequent 1942 interview of Hiss by the FBI, see *Perjury*, 311–312, citing FBI and State Department files.

30. Chambers's 1941 meeting with Berle and 1942 interview with FBI: *Perjury*, 293–294, 302. For details of the FBI's 1942 interview with Chambers, and Hoover's decision not to follow up on the information Chambers supplied, see id., 302–303, citing FBI files.

31. Details of Bentley's work for the Soviets and her defection: *Venona*, 97–113, 121–123. For a recent treatment of Bentley, see Kathryn S. Olmsted, *Red Spy Queen* (2002).

32. Details of Guzenko's defection: Igor Guzenko, *Iron Curtain* (1948); Robert Bothwell and J. L. Granatstein, eds., *The Guzenko Transcripts* (1982).

33. Murphy's March 20, 1945, interview with Chambers: Transcript of Record, *United States v. Alger Hiss*, Vol. 6, p. 3323 (10 vols., Murrelle Printing Co., Sayre, Pa., 1950). FBI follow-ups and Hiss placed on "pending" list: *Perjury*, 308, citing FBI files.

34. Hiss interview with Ladd: *Perjury*, 318, citing FBI files; decisions to place Hiss on "pending list," deny him security clearance, and monitor his activities, id., 323–324, citing State Department and FBI files.

35. Subsequently *The New York Times* was to report that a Detroit lawyer, Larry R. Davidow, had warned Dulles that Hiss "had a 'provable' Communist record" in December 1946. Dulles allegedly replied to Davidow "that Mr. Hiss's loyalty to the United States was above suspicion." "Warning to Dulles on Hiss Described," *The New York Times*, December 18, 1948, p. 2.

36. Hiss's discussions with Carnegie Endowment: *Perjury*, 326–329, citing John Foster Dulles Papers, Princeton University. Acheson's statement about Hiss following his advice: Testimony of Dean Acheson, January 14, 1949, Senate Foreign Relations Committee, Vol. 11, 81st Cong., 1st. and 2d Sess. (1949–1950), pp. 11–12.

37. On HUAC's early years, see August Raymond Ogden, *The Dies Committee* (1945). For its activities in 1948, see Walter Goodman, *The Committee*, 235–271 (1968). For an unsympa-

thetic portrait of HUAC's investigation of Communists in the motion picture industry, see Victor Navasky, *Naming Names* (1980).

38. On the shaky status of the Committee in 1948, see *The Committee*, 260–266. On the Bentley hearings, see id., 244–249.

39. Details of Chambers's being subpoenaed by HUAC and his opening testimony: *Witness*, 529–531, 540; U.S. House of Representatives, *Official Report of Proceedings of August 3, 1948 Hearing Held Before Committee on Un-American Activities*, Ward and Paul, Reporters, Vol. 2, pp. 155–160. Hereafter cited as HUAC Hearing, August 3, 1948. Further citations to official reports of HUAC hearings in August 1948 will be listed by date. Individual hearings were bound separately and paged consecutively; some hearings required several bound volumes. Copies of the official reports are in the author's possession.

40. "I reported to the authorities what I knew . . . darker charges of espionage": HUAC Hearing, August 3, 1948, Vol. 2, pp. 158–159; *Witness*, 542–545.

41. Details of Hiss's response to Chambers's charges and Priscilla Hiss's reaction: *Perjury*, 7–8, quoting Hiss's August 3 telegram to HUAC chairman J. Parnell Thomas, and citing an interview with Alger Hiss, September 20, 1974, and letters from Edmund F. Soule (a neighbor of Priscilla Hiss's in Peacham) to Alden Whitman, April 24, 1974, and August 2, 1974.

42. For details of the meeting between Hiss, Acheson, Marbury, and Donald Hiss, see *Perjury*, 9. Hiss's opening statement before HUAC is HUAC Hearing, August 5, 1948, Vol. 4, p. 357. See also House Committee on Un-American Activities, *Hearings Regarding Communist Espionage in the U.S. Government* (July 31–September 9, 1948), Vol. 6, pp. 642–643. Hereafter cited as *Hearings*, with volume and page numbers.

43. On the Committee's deliberations after Hiss's August 5 testimony, see Robert E. Stripling, *The Red Plot Against America*, 115–116 (1977); Richard M. Nixon, *Six Crises*, 10–11 (1962).

44. In *Six Crises* Nixon said that the morning of Whittaker Chambers's August 3, 1948, testimony "was the first time I had ever heard of either Alger or Donald Hiss." *Six Crises*, 4. But Allen Weinstein, relying on a November 27, 1975, interview with Father John Cronin, indicated that Cronin had previously informed Nixon that Alger Hiss was suspected of being a Communist. *Perjury*, 7, citing the interview with Cronin.

    For the statement by Robert Stripling that Nixon "had his hat set" for Hiss, see id., 15, citing April 28, 1975, interview with Stripling.

45. HUAC Hearing, August 7, 1948, Vol. 1, pp. 48–49, 60. For Nixon's account of that hearing, see *Six Crises*, 16–18.

46. Hiss's August 16, 1948, testimony is HUAC Hearing, August 16, 1948, Vol. 2, pp. 49, 51–53. See also *Hearings*, Vol. 6, pp. 955–970. For Nixon's version, see *Six Crises*, 23–29.

47. HUAC Hearing, August 16, 1948, Vol. 2, pp. 63–64.

48. For Nixon's and Hiss's exchange about the possibility of Hiss's taking a lie detector test, see HUAC Hearing, August 16, 1948, Vol. 2, pp. 71–75. For Nixon's memory of his reactions to Hiss at the time, see *Six Crises*, 30.

49. For the law firm affiliations of many of Hiss's lawyers at the time they defended him, see successive editions of the *Martindale-Hubbell Law Directory*. For McLean, Vol. 2, p. 1855 (3 vols., 1950); Marbury, Vol. 2, p. 1200 (3 vols., 1950); Davis, Vol. 1, p. 202 (3 vols., 1949); Stryker, Vol. 2, p. 1785 (3 vols., 1949); Cross, Vol. 1, p. 1289 (3 vols., 1950); Lane, Vol. 2, p. 1819 (3 vols., 1950); Buttenweiser, Vol. 2, p. 2731 (3 vols., 1956); Rabinowitz, Vol. 4, p. 1722B (7 vols., 1978); Lowenthal, Vol. 4, pp. 557, 830 (7 vols., 1980). For Rosenwald's and Benjamin's affiliations in 1950, see *United States v. Hiss*, 88 F. Supp. 559 (S.D.N.Y. 1950) and *United States v. Hiss*, 185 F.2d. 822 (2d. Cir. 1950). Rosenwald was identified as a solo practitioner in the

District of Columbia during the second Hiss perjury trial, and as of counsel to Beer, Richards, Lane, and Haller, New York City, during the appeal.

Helen Buttenwieser's connections to the Hiss family were more substantial than any of Hiss's other lawyers. After Hiss went to prison in 1951, Priscilla and Tony lived with Helen Buttenwieser and her husband Benjamin "in their Upper East Side townhouse half a block from Central Park." Tony Hiss, *The View from Alger's Window*, 89 (1999).

Buttenwieser, a graduate of New York University Law School, began practicing law in 1936. Over the course of her career she became an investor in The *Nation* and a trustee of the New York Civil Liberties Union. Her obituary reported that as "a tireless defender of Alger Hiss," she "was the host for Sunday brunches at her home, where [Hiss] and his advisers and friends would gather." Susan Heller Anderson, "Helen Buttenwieser, 84, Lawyer and Civic Leader," *The New York Times*, November 23, 1989, p. D21. See Tony Hiss's affectionate tribute to Helen Buttenwieser in *The View from Alger's Window*, 89–102.

John Lowenthal's contributions to Hiss's defense were also very considerable, continuing to Lowenthal's death on September 9, 2003. Lowenthal was born in New York City in 1925, graduated from Columbia College, and was a student at Columbia School of Law when he volunteered to help the Hiss defense in 1949. With that action he began a course of service to Hiss that lasted well beyond Hiss's death. Lowenthal was a solo practitioner in New York City who also taught at the New School for Social Research and the law schools of the State University of New Jersey and the City University of New York. He was an accomplished cellist who performed at the Salzburg Music Festival a month before his death. For an obituary, see Stuart Lavietes, "John Lowenthal, 78, Professor Who Made Film on Hiss Trials," *The New York Times*, September 21, 2003, Sect. 1, p. 33. For more on Lowenthal's film, and his other contributions to the Hiss defense, see Chapter Seven.

50. Hiss's and Chambers's comments are in HUAC Hearing, August 17, 1948, Vol. 1, pp. 3, 4, 8–10, 27–29, 33. Nixon's reactions are from *Six Crises*, 31–36.

51. HUAC Hearing, August 17, 1948, Vol. 1, p. 33; *Six Crises*, 36.

52. HUAC Hearing, August 17, 1948, Vol. 1, pp. 33–34, 63–64; *Six Crises*, 36–37.

53. But Hiss had probably never known Chambers as "George Crosley." Chambers recalled that he had several aliases while a member of the Communist underground, including Carl (or Karl), David Breen, and Lloyd Cantwell. In *Witness* Chambers said that it was "possible" that he used George Crosley as an alias, but "I have no recollection of it, and I believe that I have recalled all the other names I used in the underground without effort." Id., 373. Hiss was never able to produce another witness who had known a George Crosley, and it is likely that he deliberately chose an alias Chambers had not used in order to prevent some other person's identifying the alias as a Communist or a Soviet agent.

54. For background on the efforts of HUAC investigators to find a record of Hiss's having transferred title to a car in 1935 and 1936, see *Six Crises*, 39–40.

The transcript of the August 25, 1948, hearing, HUAC Hearing, Vol. 10, pp. 909–1238, is a particularly good summary of the state of the Hiss case at the time. It includes (pp. 1012–1034) Nixon's questioning of Hiss about the transaction involving the 1929 Ford, and (pp. 1128–1138) the text of an August 24, 1948, letter Hiss wrote to HUAC chairman Parnell Thomas, protesting HUAC's treatment of him and giving a long list of distinguished persons who were prepared to testify to his competence and integrity.

55. For more details on the August 25, 1948, HUAC hearing, in which both Chambers and Hiss testified, see *Perjury*, 39–46. HUAC's "Interim Report" was included in *Hearings*, Vol. 13, pp. 1347–1357.

56. The "Meet the Press" program is discussed in *Perjury*, 51–52.

57. The complaint filed in the suit did not state whether Chambers's statements, which were described as "false and defamatory," were the basis of a slander or a libel action. The question of whether such statements, when made on radio broadcasts, constituted slander or libel was undecided at the time (they are now treated as allegedly libelous). Representing Hiss in the suit were Edward McLean, William Marbury, and Charles Evans of Marbury's Baltimore law firm. A copy of the complaint is in the author's possession. The deliberations among Hiss's lawyers about the defamation suit are discussed in *Perjury*, 141–144, citing Hiss Defense Files.

58. Chambers made this statement during a November 5, 1948, deposition. See *Perjury*, 150, citing "Baltimore Depositions," Hiss Defense Files, 317.

59. Chambers's colloquy with Richard Cleveland about his shielding Hiss is in *Witness*, 730. For Chambers's account of how (in response to a "routine" request from William Marbury that he produce any communications he might have had with Alger Hiss) he secured the life-preserver documents he had secreted in 1938 and gave them to Marbury, see id., 736–738, 749. See also Alexander Feinberg, "Friend Hid Stolen Films Ten Years, Chambers Says," *The New York Times*, December 8, 1948, pp. 1, 3, quoting Chambers's December 7 testimony before the grand jury in which he identified his nephew as having secreted documents for him in a location in Brooklyn. *The Times* article incorrectly gave the name of Chambers's nephew, Nathan Levine, as Irving Levin. Chambers listed Levine's name in *Witness*, 735.

60. See Jason Roberts, "New Evidence in the Alger Hiss Case," 1 *American Communist History* 143–162 (2002), which makes excellent use of the Grand Jury Transcripts and recently released HUAC Executive Session Transcripts in the National Archives to demonstrate just how precarious Chambers's situation was between November 17 and December 15, 1948.

61. For details on the state of affairs between mid-November and early December 1948, see *Perjury*, 153–163; Roberts, "New Evidence in the Alger Hiss Case," 147–157.

62. For details on the Pumpkin Papers episode, see *Perjury*, 161–169; for Chambers's version, see *Witness*, 751–755. Nixon's account of negotiations between HUAC and the Justice Department after Chambers produced his second batch of documents is in *Six Crises*, 56–59.

63. On December 12 *The New York Times* printed copies of 12 documents released to the public by HUAC. One of them was a handwritten memo identified as being in Alger Hiss's handwriting. John D. Morris, "12 'Spy' Papers Disclosed, One Held Written By Hiss, Inquiry Here To Get Films," *The New York Times*, December 12, 1948, p. 1. The quoted material is from *Six Crises*, 58–59.

64. For details of Chambers's attempt at suicide, see *Whittaker Chambers: A Biography*, 310, 313, 320–321; *Witness*, 773–776. Sam Tanenhaus, in *Whittaker Chambers: A Biography*, 577, places the date of the suicide attempt as December 10, but concedes that no source has yet pinpointed it.

65. Testimony of Raymond Feehan, December 14, 1948, Grand Jury Transcripts, Vol. 8, pp. 4247–4251. For more detail on the FBI's efforts, see *Perjury*, 262–264, citing FBI and Hiss Defense files.

66. Stripling statement to the grand jury: Testimony of Robert Stripling, December 9, 1948, Grand Jury Transcripts, quoted in Roberts, "New Evidence in the Alger Hiss Case," 158. Communications between Stripling and experts: Ordway Hilton to Robert Stripling, December 13, 1948; Hilton to Stripling, December 23, 1948; Hilton to Stripling, December 30, 1948; Elbridge Stein to Stripling, December 30, 1948, in HUAC Executive Session Transcripts, all quoted in Roberts, "New Evidence in the Alger Hiss Case," 158–159.

67. Hiss had previously denied publicly that he had turned over any papers to Chambers or anyone else. Alexander Feinberg, "Alger Hiss Denies Ever Turning Over Any State Papers," *The New York Times,* December 13, 1948, p. 1. Hiss's denials that he had seen Chambers after "the late spring of 1936" ("not later than June 1"), and that he had turned over any original State Department documents to Chambers ("A flat no.") are in Grand Jury Transcripts, Vol. 8, pp. 4486–4496. See also Russell Porter, "Hiss Offers Not Guilty Plea, Tentative Trial Date Jan. 24," *The New York Times,* December 17, 1948, p. 1. Details of the arraignment and Hiss's reaction: "Hiss Offers Not Guilty Plea": pp. 1, 5.

68. Hiss was shown a picture of Hedda Gumperz, or Hede Massing, the name she used in America, in his testimony before the grand jury on December 9, 1948. He first stated cautiously that Massing's "appearance was completely unfamiliar" to him, and, when pressed, said that he was "quite sure" he had "never seen her before." See Grand Jury Transcripts, Vol. 8, p. 3818.

69. Marbury's comment is in a letter to Edward McLean, February 4, 1949, in Hiss Defense Files. It is quoted in *Perjury,* 338.

70. For a summary of the Hiss defense strategy, see *Perjury,* 338–340.

71. Hiss's testimony to the FBI was recorded in a memorandum on December 4, 1948, FBI files. He said much the same thing to his own lawyers in a memorandum, "Hiss Typewriters," December 7, 1948, Hiss Defense Files. Both documents are cited in *Perjury,* 253.

72. The Hiss defense team knew by January 1949, that, in the opinion of their expert, the samples of documents McLean had discovered had a typeface that matched that of Chambers's Baltimore documents. At that time they did not know the whereabouts of the Woodstock typewriter, in part because of efforts on the part of the Catletts to avoid searching for it. See J. Howard Haring to Harold Rosenwald, January 26, 1949, and Edward McLean, "Catlett Family: Additional Information Obtained April 13–16, 1949," Hiss Defense Files. Both documents are cited in *Perjury,* 352, 354.

73. Davis summarized the contents of Alger Hiss's December 7 telephone call to him in a letter to McLean, December 28, 1948, Hiss Defense Files, quoted in *Perjury,* 257. For an account of Edward McLean's efforts to track down the typewriter, and Pat and Mike Catlett's resistance to that venture, see id., 346–351.

74. Evidence that FBI experts and Hiss defense experts agreed that the typefaces on Hiss standards and the Baltimore documents were a match can be found in several FBI memos between December 1948 and November 1949, and in "Memorandum re Haring's Opinion," December 13, 1948, Hiss Defense Files. Those documents are cited in *Perjury,* 228.

75. The relevant espionage statutes at the time of Hiss's indictment were 50 U.S.C., Sec. 32 (a) (1946), 18 U.S.C., Sec. 581 (a) (1946), and 18 U.S.C., Sec. 582 (1946). 50 U.S.C., Sec. 32 (a) made unlawfully disclosing information affecting national defense to a foreign government punishable by imprisonment for not more than 20 years, unless the offense occurred in time of war, in which case the punishment was death or not more than 30 years. 18 U.S.C. 581 (a) governed offenses committed during wartime. It had no statute of limitations. 18 U.S.C. 582 governed espionage committed other than in time of war. It had a three-year statute of limitations.

Hiss was indicted on December 15, 1948, and charged with offenses stemming from his allegedly passing stolen government documents in 1938. The United States was not at war in 1938, so 18 U.S.C. 582 governed. In order for Hiss to have been indicted for espionage, the government would have had to prove that he had disclosed information affecting national defense to the Soviet Union between 1941 and 1945, when the United States was at war with Germany and Japan. Hiss had in fact disclosed such information to the Soviets in that time period. But evidence that he had done so did not surface until the 1990s.

76. Chambers's account of the gift of the rugs is in *Witness*, 414–417. The quoted passages are on p. 414.

77. *Witness*, 39.

78. The most concise summary of testimony at the trials about the car, loan, and rug incidents is Transcript of Record, Vol. 4, pp. 1982–2046. Irving Younger, "Was Alger Hiss Guilty," 60 Commentary 23 (1975), based on an analysis of the transcripts of the two Hiss trials, concluded that, taken together, the disposition of the Ford, the rug gift, and the car loan significantly undermined Hiss's assertion that he knew Chambers only casually.

79. For Hornbeck's testimony, see Transcript of Record, Vol. 3, pp. 1348–1382. For Sayre's, see id., pp. 1472–1524.

80. "I am personally convinced that Mr. Chambers has framed me," Hiss told the grand jury on December 14, 1948. He speculated that Chambers had broken into the Hiss's house to gain access to the Fansler typewriter. Grand Jury Transcripts, Vol. 8, pp. 4382–4443.

81. For an account of the first trial, including statements from the jurors, see Mac Johnson, "Five Hiss Jurors Express Belief Kaufman was Biased for Defense," *New York Herald Tribune*, July 12, 1949, p. 1.

82. For additional details on the first trial, see *Perjury*, 369–418; *Alger Hiss: The True Story*, 291–399.

83. Details of Mike and Pat Catlett's testimony, and of the testimony of Priscilla Hiss, are in *The First Trial: United States v. America vs. Alger Hiss, Stenographer's Minutes*, 1683–1757 (Mike Catlett), 1761–1780 (Pat Catlett), and 2284–2287, 2316–2367, 2423–2437, 2443–2445 (a) (Priscilla Hiss) (1948) (Microfilm edition, Scholarly Resources, Inc.). See also *Perjury*, 394–397, 406–410.

84. Massing's testimony, although it received a good deal of press coverage, was largely irrelevant to the central issues at Hiss's trials, and the defense confronted her with a witness who claimed she had been much less certain about having met Hiss. See *Perjury*, 425–426. For a discussion of Binger's testimony, see id., 432–437.

85. For Murphy's comment about "immutable documents," see Transcript of Record, Vol. 1, p. 167. For Cross's effort to introduce Murphy's earlier statement that the "government has no case" if the jury did not believe Chambers, see id., p. 1816.

86. For Wadleigh's testimony, see Transcript of Record, Vol. 2, pp. 1107–1153, 1164–1256.

87. For Cross's summation, see Transcript of Record, Vol. 5, pp. 3091–3175; for Murphy's, see id., pp. 3213–3262.

88. For Judge Goddard's sentence, see Transcript of Record, Vol. 5, p. 3295; William Conklin, "Hiss Sentenced to Five Year Term," *The New York Times*, January 26, 1950, p 1.

89. Both Priscilla Hiss, in December 10, 1948, testimony to the New York grand jury, and Alger Hiss, in December 15, 1948, testimony, denied knowing the whereabouts of the Fansler typewriter. Priscilla said she gave the typewriter away "to a junk man or the Salvation Army." Alger said "I have no idea" where the typewriter is. Grand Jury Transcripts, Vol. 8, pp. 3877–3937 (Priscilla Hiss), 4486–4496 (Alger Hiss).

CHAPTER THREE

1. As noted in Chapter One, petitions for certiorari are regularly presented to the Supreme Court of the United States. Certiorari petitions ask the Court, at its discretion, to review a

case from a lower federal court (typically a United States Court of Appeals for a particular circuit). For a petition to be granted, four of the nine justices need to vote to hear the case. When a certiorari petition is granted, the case is then set on the Court's docket, typically for the following Term (the Court's Terms extended in the 1950s, as now, from the first week in October to some time in June). When the Court denies a certiorari petition, the decision of the lower federal appellate court is finalized. In Hiss's case this meant that his 1950 conviction on two counts of perjury had been upheld.

2. Title 18, Chapter 309, Section 4161, 62 Stat. 853 (effective September 1, 1948; repealed October 12, 1984), provided that prisoners convicted of offenses against the United States, and confined in penal institutions for terms other than life, should be entitled to deductions from the terms of their sentences when their "record of conduct show[ed] . . . [faithful observation of] all the rules." That provision was implemented by Title 18, Section 3624 (b), the Criminal Procedure, Postsentence Administration section of the United States Code, which provided that credit toward service of the sentence would be given for "satisfactory behavior," which was defined as "exemplary compliance with institutional disciplinary regulations." Hiss received no discretionary "good time," and was not deemed eligible for parole before the expiration of his sentence, so the reduction in his incarcerated time from 60 to 44 months was solely because he came within the statute. Lewisburg officials had the option of declining to certify his behavior as "satisfactory," and had he violated any prison rules he would have forfeited the statutory deduction. But Hiss did not violate any rules, and within two years of his stay was transferred to an honors block cell, reserved for prisoners whose conduct had been exemplary.

3. The term "knockabout guy" was used by Hiss in a 1960 interview with the journalist Brock Brower, quoted in Brower, "The Problems of Alger Hiss," *Esquire*, December 1960, 142.

4. On MacCormick, see Alger Hiss, *Recollections of a Life*, 162 (1988). On Viola Bernard as the contact, see Tony Hiss, *Laughing Last*, 146 (1977). The prosecution's suggestion that Hubert James, the jury foreman in the first trial, was biased in favor of the defense came in exchanges between the prosecution and Judge Kaufman in chambers, quoted in *The First Trial: United States of America vs. Alger Hiss, Stenographer's Minutes*, 303 (1948) (Microfilm edition, Scholarly Resources, Inc.). The reference to Claude Cross's statement about "Austin MacCormick's brother-in-law . . . keeping the jury hung," is an interview of Cross by Allen Weinstein, July 15, 1974, quoted in Weinstein, *Perjury: The Hiss-Chambers Case*, 373 (2d ed., 1997).

5. Alger Hiss to Priscilla Hiss and Tony Hiss, August 10, 1951, quoted in Tony Hiss, *The View from Alger's Window*, 127 (1999).

6. For descriptions of Lewisburg, see *The View from Alger's Window*, 7–8; *Recollections of a Life*, 170–171.

7. For Alger's memories of West Street, see *Recollections of a Life*, 163, 165; *Laughing Last*, 148–149.

8. The Danny F. / Mike M. story is told in *Recollections*, 164.

9. The statement that Lewisburg was racially segregated during Hiss's time there is from *Recollections of a Life*, 171, and *Laughing Last*, 151. The characterization of some inmates as "middle-class tax evaders" is from *Recollections of a Life*, 163, and *Laughing Last*, 152.

10. On hearing that Hiss was to be released in November 1954, Priscilla and Tony drove to Lewisburg to pick Alger up. Murph, who was not aware of this, arranged to meet the prison bus that regularly deposited released inmates in New York City. Murph became concerned when Hiss was not on the bus, and eventually called Hiss to reassure himself that Hiss had

been freed and was safe. MacCormick's prediction about the soldiers in Lewisburg: *Recollections of a Life*, 163. The Klaus and Murph anecdotes: id., 176–178.

11. "Hillbillies" as an important segment of the Lewisburg population, mainly as a result of car thefts: *Laughing Last*, 150; *Recollections of a Life*, 163. See *Laughing Last*, 159, for the lack of resources among the "hillbilly" prisoners. See *Recollections of a Life*, 181, for the jailbreak story.

12. MacCormick on racket guys: *Recollections of a Life*, 163. "[C]lairvoyant": id. Mike M. and Angelo as Hiss's "closest friends": *Laughing Last*, 153.

13. Italian American prisoners adopting a prisoner-of-war mentality while incarcerated: *Recollections of a Life*, 171–172.

14. "New boy in school": *Laughing Last*, 147. "[S]ense of selfhood": *Recollections of a Life*, 166.

15. Inmate comment on Hiss: "A. Rocco" to Meyer Zeligs, February 1964, quoted in Zeligs, *Friendship and Fratricide*, 394 (1967).

16. On the prison grapevine, and quarantine, see *Recollections of a Life*, 167–170. *Laughing Last*, 150.

17. "Not incommoded": *Recollections of a Life*, 168. "Sense of solidarity": id., 173. "Wonderful family relations" among the Italian American prisoners: quoted in Brock Brower, "The Problems of Alger Hiss," 142. Italian American prisoners as having "no sense of guilt": Hiss to C. Vann Woodward, May 2, 1959, quoted in *Perjury*, 2d ed., 581.

18. "Common ground": Hiss to Brock Brower, in Brower, "The Problems of Alger Hiss," 142. "Never speak at breakfast": *Laughing Last*, 148. "[I]nvoluntary involvement in some fracas": *Recollections of a Life*, 181.

19. Hiss's first meeting with Mike M.: *Recollections of a Life*, 173. Although one should recognize the possibility that Hiss overdramatized his memories of Lewisburg, there seems no reason to doubt their credibility. Hiss cannot be relied upon when discussing the Hiss case or events connected with his secret life as a Communist and Soviet agent. But when his memories were pleasant, and uncontroversial, he tried to be meticulously accurate in recounting them. His memories of Lewisburg were by no means pleasant, but in some respects Lewisburg was a triumphant experience for him. Moreover, several of the stories Hiss told about his time at Lewisburg were corroborated by other prisoners.

20. "One of three most important men," "relative seniority," and "common sense": *Recollections of a Life*, 174. Italian Americans "routinely locked up on contempt": *Laughing Last*, 154.

21. Hiss's comments on Mike: *Recollections of a Life*, 174.

22. Hiss as lawyer in prison yard: *Laughing Last*, 156.

23. Hiss-Costello meeting: *Recollections of a Life*, 175.

24. Hiss's comments about Costello: id.

25. Leo M. story: *Laughing Last*, 155–156; *Recollections of a Life*, 176.

26. Mike's advice to Hiss: *Laughing Last*, 154–155. Intervention of Mike on Hiss's behalf: *Recollections of a Life*, 181.

27. Alger Hiss's version of the story: *Recollections of a Life*, 181; Tony Hiss's version: *Laughing Last*, 154.

28. "Alger not a real name": Alger Hiss to Tony Hiss, in *Laughing Last*, 156. The other quoted passages in the paragraph are from A. Rocco to Meyer Zeligs, February 1964, *Friendship and Fratricide*, 394.

29. Klaus and Murph stories: *Recollections of a Life*, 176–178.

30. Hiss's story about the Bureau of Prisons' "exception" to its policy of no books for prisoners: *Recollections of a Life*, 179–180.

31. Lester W. story: *Recollections of a Life*, 168–169. Hiss calling conscientious objector Clovis: *Laughing Last*, 152; Clovis as A. Bergdoll, to Meyer Zeligs, February 1, 1964, in *Friendship and Fratricide*, 394.

32. "Jail is a terrible place": Hiss to John Chabot Smith, quoted in Smith, *Alger Hiss: The True Story*, 433 (1976). "Hostility" in prisons: *Recollections of a Life*, 166. Prisons as "grim" and "oppressive": id., 167. Italian American prisoners' sensitivity to violence: id., 172–173.

33. MacCormick predictions about jobs: *Recollections of a Life*, 162; *Laughing Last*, 146–147. Clovis comment about storeroom: A. Bergdoll to Meyer Zeligs, February 1, 1964, in *Friendship and Fratricide*, 394.

34. Sneaking steaks and broiling them with Angelo: *Laughing Last*, 147, 156–157. Storeroom guard's help: id., 147; *Recollections of a Life*, 183. Turning down kitchen transfer: "Clovis" ("A. Bergdoll") to Meyer Zeligs, February 1, 1964, in *Friendship and Fratricide*, 394. Comments in Hiss's prison file: *The View from Alger's Window*, 228–229.

35. A. Rocco to Meyer Zeligs, February 1964, in *Friendship and Fratricide*, 393–394.

36. Id.

37. The principal statute employed to prosecute persons accused of engaging in subversive activities or advocacy in the late 1940s and early 1950s was the "Smith Act," formally known as the Alien Registration Act, 54 Stat. 670 (1940). See generally Michael Belknap, *Cold War Political Justice* (1977). Lewisburg as home for most Smith Act prisoners: *Laughing Last*, 152, 162. "[T]op commies": A. Rocco to Zeligs in *Friendship and Fratricide*, 394.

38. Alger's conduct with Smith Act prisoners: *Laughing Last*, 162. Mike M.'s comments: id., 162. Other inmate's comments: A. Rocco to Meyer Zeligs in *Friendship and Fratricide*, 394.

39. Kempton quotes: Murray Kempton, "Alger Hiss—an argument for a good con," *New York Post Weekend* magazine, April 22, 1978, 11.

40. "[K]illed by a violent mountineer from Kentucky": *Alger Hiss: The True Story*, 431, citing an interview with Alger Hiss.

41. Information on William Remington: John Earl Haynes and Harvey Klehr, *Venona: Soviet Espionage in America*, 161–162 (1999); Gary May, *Un-American Activities: The Trials of William Remington* (1994).

42. Details of Remington's death: *Alger Hiss: The True Story*, 431, citing interview with Hiss.

43. Details of Hiss's interview with warden after Remington's death: *Recollections of a Life*, 182.

44. "[P]ublic uproar" regarding automatic reduction of Hiss's sentence: James Bennett, the director of the Federal Bureau of Prisons during the time Hiss was at Lewisburg, commented on Hiss in his memoir, *I Chose Prison* (1964). Tony Hiss quoted from Bennett's observations about public reaction to Hiss in *The View from Alger's Window*, 121.

45. Lane and the Hisses's drive from Lewisburg to New York on November 27, 1954: *Recollections of a Life*, 184–185; *The View from Alger's Window*, 121–122. Discussion between Hiss and other inmate: *Laughing Last*, 147–148.

46. *Laughing Last*, 147–148.

47. "It's a terrible place": *Alger Hiss: The True Story*, 432–433, citing interview with Donald Hiss.

48. Story about associating with criminal elements: *Recollections of a Life*, 183.

49. Versions of the story: "The Problems of Alger Hiss," 141; *Friendship and Fratricide*, 395, quoting "The Problems of Alger Hiss"; *Laughing Last*, 163; *Recollections of a Life*, 184. When the leader of the Socialist Party, Eugene Debs, was released from prison in 1922 after being pardoned by President Warren Harding, he was cheered by his fellow inmates, and responded by saluting them. Debs had been sentenced to serve ten years in the federal peni-

tentiary in Atlanta for advocating pacifism in a 1917 speech, and, while in prison, had received over a million votes in the 1920 presidential election. See Eugene V. Debs, *Walls and Bars*, 162–163 (1927). Thanks to Alfred S. Konefsky for calling my attention to the Debs episode.

50. For a description of the "self-analysis" Hiss undertook while at Lewisburg, see Hiss to Meyer Zeligs, quoted in Zeligs, *Friendship and Fratricide*, 400–401. "There was the occasion," Hiss said in connection with his self-analysis, "for a reconsideration of first principles, of values, of objectives." Quoted in id., 401.

51. Hiss letter quoted in *Friendship and Fratricide*, 400–401.

52. Id.

53. Alger Hiss to Priscilla Hiss, November 24, 1951, quoted in *The View from Alger's Window*, 143–144.

Alger wrote 445 letters to Priscilla and Tony Hiss from Lewisburg. Although Meyer Zeligs was given access to some letters, and quoted from a few in *Friendship and Fratricide* (398–400), Priscilla Hiss declined to make them public during her lifetime. After her death in 1984, Tony Hiss continued to live in her New York apartment, along with the letters, but did not inspect them. In 1997, about a year after Alger Hiss died, Tony received permission to visit Lewisburg, and on his return retrieved and organized the letters. *The View from Alger's Window* contains excerpts from many of the letters. See *The View from Alger's Window*, 25–30, for Tony Hiss's discussion of his use of the letters.

54. "Respect for man's potentialities": Alger Hiss to Priscilla Hiss, April 22, 1952, quoted in *The View from Alger's Window*, 196. "[L]etters, photos,": August 28, 1951, quoted in id., 129. "[A]imless and rather pathetic chatter": August 22, 1951, quoted in id., 125. "[N]atural dignity and psychic candor": April 13, 1952, quoted in id., 196. "[A]ffirmative outreach and inspiration . . . emotionally healthy man": May 20, 1952, quoted in id., 197.

55. "Plan for later on," "social customs": Hiss to Meyer Zeligs, quoted in *Friendship and Fratricide*, 401.

56. *New Statesman* and *New Yorker: Laughing Last*, 152. Newspapers: *The View from Alger's Window*, 75 *(Times)*, 181 *(New York Herald Tribune)*. Restrictions on correspondence: id., 31–32. Priscilla's responses: id., 72–74.

57. Tony as "lost, etc.": *The View from Alger's Window*, 88. Tony's anxiety after Priscilla takes job, including accidents, fears of standing in front of trains and consulting psychiatrist: id., 214–218. "Supportive, cheerful": id. 29.

58. Hiss on Chambers: Alger Hiss to Priscilla Hiss, February 7, 1952, *The View from Alger's Window*, 182.

59. "Rewarding observation": August 2, 1952, *The View from Alger's Window*, 159. "[R]olling fields . . . hatches of life": October 30, 1951, id., 159–160. "[L]ong and stunning" sunset: November 20, 1951, id., 160. "[B]aby blizzard . . . brilliant dazzling hour in cold sunlight": March 1, 1953, id., 160. Moon as "quick-silver . . . flashing": September 24, 1953, id., 162. "[C]entral Pa. autumn evening sky . . . pulsating": October 15, 1953, id., 162.

60. "To light you homeward": October 15, 1953, *The View from Alger's Window*, 162. "[P]ositive ecstasy . . . faint repetition": April 16, 1953, id., 161.

61. "Sugar Lump Boys stories: September 15, 1951, *The View from Alger's Window*, 108–109 (swimming); December 15, 1951, id., 109–110 (basketball); January 1954, id., 110 (bread and grapefruit).

62. Tony's later readings of the stories ("showing me how to do something . . . worse shape"): *The View from Alger's Window*, 107.

63. Description of Leo M. from memoirs and reference to prison Education Department: *Recollections of a Life*, 176. Nicknames of Beginning Reader (B.R.) and Middle Reader (M.R.) for Leo: *The View from Alger's Window*, 163.

64. Predominance of Hiss's Lewisburg letters (87 of 445) being about Leo M.'s reading: *The View from Alger's Window*, 163. Earliest letter, Alger Hiss to Tony Hiss, October 6, 1951, id., 167–168. March letter: March 15, 1952, id., 168.

65. May 10, 1952, *The View from Alger's Window*, 168–169.

66. June 1952 references: June 26, 1952, *The View from Alger's Window*, 169–170. December 1952 references: December 30, 1952, id., 171–172.

67. Mastery of "possibilities" in response to tall one's challenge: January 20, 1953, *The View from Alger's Window*, 172. Reference to Tony's being impressed and "kind of feeling": January 25, 1953, id. "[B]ook like a toy": January 29, 1953, id., 173–174.

68. Letter to brother without help: March 12, 1953, *The View from Alger's Window*, 174. Leo reading *Robinson Crusoe* and newspapers and magazines: September 15, 1953, id., 177. Leo reading *The Mountain Book:* November 15, 1953, id. Leo reading 25 pages of *The Mountain Book:* November 26, 1953, id., 178.

69. Leo writing a letter for an illiterate, and realizing that "he no longer needs help, *but on the contrary can give it":* January 21, 1954, *The View from Alger's Window*, 179. Leo making parole and skipping while Hiss applauded, March 4, 1954, id., 180. Hiss describing Leo as "self-possessed": March 25, 1954, id.

70. Chambers quotes: "great gentleness and sweetness of character": House Committee on Un-American Activities, *Hearings Regarding Communist Espionage in the U.S. Government* (July 31 through September 9, 1948), Vol. 6, 666; "deep considerateness and gracious patience": Whittaker Chambers, *Witness*, 363 (1952). Others impressed by Hiss's ability to put others at ease and convey an impression that he cared about them: Brock Brower, "The Problems of Alger Hiss," 141; Thomas Moore, "Parting Shots," *Life*, April 7, 1972, 78a; Robert Alan Aurthur, "Hanging Out," *Esquire*, July 1972, 26; Allen Weinstein, quoted in Philip Nobile, "Allen Weinstein: Who Is He and What Has He Got on Alger Hiss," *Politicks*, February 28, 1978, 5; David Remnick, "Alger Hiss: Unforgiven and Unforgiving," *Washington Post* magazine, October 12, 1986, pp. W29–30.

71. "I like people when they are in trouble," etc.: Alger Hiss to Tony Hiss, quoted in *Laughing Last*, 87.

CHAPTER FOUR

1. For the details of Hiss's release from prison, see *Recollections of a Life*, 184–185 (1988); *The View from Alger's Window*, 120–121 (1997).

2. The quoted passages are from *Recollections of a Life*, 185, 186.

3. The quoted passages are from Meyer A. Zeligs, *Friendship and Fratricide*, 402–403 (1966), based on interviews Meyer Zeligs had with Hiss, Kenneth McCormick of Doubleday Publishers (January 3, 1964), and Robert M. Benjamin (January 7, 1966).

4. *Recollections of a Life*, 187.

5. The quoted passages are from *Recollections of a Life*, 187.

6. Alger Hiss to Tony Hiss, quoted in *Laughing Last*, 139–140 (1977).

7. Alger Hiss to Tony Hiss, quoted in *Laughing Last*, 140.

8. *Recollections of a Life*, 190–191.

9. "[S]everal attempts at reconciliation": Id., 191.

10. For Zeligs's description of Priscilla's surgery, see *Friendship and Fratricide*, 182. For Smith's characterization of it as an abortion, see *Alger Hiss: The True Story*, 70 (1976); for Tony Hiss's, see *Laughing Last*, 42. Both Smith and Tony Hiss were told about the abortion by Alger Hiss. William Brown Meloney was first identified as Priscilla's lover by Allen Weinstein in *Perjury: The Hiss-Chambers Case*, 79, 599 (1st ed., 1978), citing September 11, 1974, interviews with Alger Hiss and Alden Whitman.

11. Revealed Meloney's name to Whitman: see *Perjury*, 1st ed., 79. Smith's hypothesis regarding Priscilla's ineffectiveness as a witness: see *Alger Hiss: The True Story*, 287–290.

12. Tony Hiss's comments regarding Priscilla's attitude towards Alger are from *Laughing Last*, 185–186. "[L]oyal wife": Alger Hiss, quoted in id., 186.

13. Whittaker Chambers to William F. Buckley, November 28, 1954, in William F. Buckley, ed., *Odyssey of a Friend*, 87–88 (1988). Chambers's full statement was as follows:

> Alger Hiss is one of the greatest assets that the Communist Party could possess. What is vindication for him? It is the moment when one of the most respectable old ladies [gentlemen] in Hartford [Conn] says to another of the most respectable old ladies [gentlemen], "Really, I don't see how Alger Hiss could brazen it out that way unless he really were innocent." Multiply Hartford by every other American community. For the C.P., that is victory.

14. The less well known persons who were convicted of espionage with the Soviets, but have continued to maintain their innocence, include William Fisher (convicted in the United States in 1955), Mark Zborowski (1958), Robert Soblen (1961), Marian Zacharski (1981), Kurt Strand (1998), Theresa Squillacote (1998), George Trofimoff (2001), and Clyde Conrad, an American, who was convicted in the Federal Republic of Germany in 1990.

Then there is the example of Morris and Lona Cohen, Americans who were convicted in Great Britain in 1961. For years the Cohens denied any involvement in espionage, even after they were deported to the Soviet Union in exchange for the Soviets's release of a British agent. Ultimately they admitted being Soviet spies, but only after the collapse of the Soviet Union.

I am indebted to John Earl Haynes for details about the persons listed in this note. For more information on the subsequent lives of other American Soviet agents who were exposed around the same time as Hiss, see John Earl Haynes and Harvey Klehr, *Venona: Soviet Espionage in America*, 116–207, 287–330 (1999).

15. The fullest account of the controversy surrounding Hiss's 1956 appearance at Princeton is John D. Fox, "The Hiss Hassle Revisited," *Princeton Alumni Weekly*, May 3, 1976, 8–15.

16. The quoted passages are from unnamed Princeton administrators, quoted in "The Hiss Hassle," 9, 11.

17. The Board of Trustees Resolution, April 30, 1956, is quoted in "The Hiss Hassle," 13.

18. Hiss's description of walking to the speech is from *Recollections of a Life*, 188. The Princeton administrator describing the speech was Edgar M. Gemmell, administrative secretary to the president of Princeton. Gemmell's comment and the unidentified reporter's comment are quoted in "The Hiss Hassle," 15.

19. "Initial opportunity to break out of Coventry": Alger Hiss to John M. Fox, quoted in "The Hiss Hassle," 9. Fox interviewed Hiss in preparation for his article.

20. The essays originally appeared as Arthur Koestler, "The Complex Issue of the Ex-Communists," *The New York Times* magazine, February 19, 1950, 10, 49–50; Diana Trilling, "A Memorandum on the Hiss Case," *Partisan Review*, May–June, 1950, 484–500; Leslie A. Fielder, "Hiss, Chambers, and the Age of Innocence," *Commentary*, August, 1951, 109–119;

Sidney Hook, "The Faiths of Whittaker Chambers," *The New York Times Book Review,* May 25, 1952, 1, 34–35; and Granville Hicks, "Whittaker Chambers's Testament," *New Leader,* May 26, 1952, 19–22. They have recently been collected in Patrick Swan, ed., *Alger Hiss, Whittaker Chambers, and the Schism in the American Soul* (2002). For evidence of the common views of Koestler, Trilling, Fielder, Hook, and Hicks toward Hiss and Chambers, see id., 8–9 (Fiedler), 30–31 (Trilling), 51–52 (Koestler), 61–62 (Hicks), and 70–71 (Hook).

21. On the decisive shift of American intellectuals on the left from the late 1930s to the mid-1940s, with the *Partisan Review* treated as an index, see James Burkhart Gilbert, *Writers and Partisans: A History of Literary Radicalism in America,* 221–282 (1968). For details on the triumph of anti-Communism among American "liberals" in the 1950s, see Mary Sperling McAuliffe, *Crisis on the Left: Cold War Politics and American Liberals, 1947–1954* (1978). For some documentation of how "[a] belief in Alger Hiss's guilt [became] a litmus test of the Cold War liberals new realism," see Kenneth O'Reilly, "Liberal Values, the Cold War, and American Intellectuals: The Trauma of the Alger Hiss Case, 1950–1978," in Athan G. Theoharis, ed., *Beyond the Hiss Case,* 309–319 (1982).

22. The best treatment of this theme is Ellen Schreker, *No Ivory Tower: McCarthyism and the Universities* (1986). For a response closer to the events, see Richard Hoftstadter, *Anti-Intellectualism in American Life* (1963).

23. *Recollections of a Life,* 189.

24. Hiram Haydn, *Words and Faces,* 290 (1974).

25. The details of Hiss's profile and Smith's response are from *Recollections of a Life,* 189. Hiss's description of Smith's comb is from *Recollections of a Life,* 190.

26. For details of Hiss's work at Feathercombs, see Zeligs, *Friendship and Fratricide,* 408–410; *Recollections of a Life,* 189–192; Brock Brower, "The Problems of Alger Hiss," *Esquire,* December 1960, 142–143, quoting an interview with Hiss. In *Recollections of a Life,* Hiss stated, at p. 189, that his salary when he left Feathercombs was $11,000. In "The Problems of Alger Hiss," he told Brower, at p. 143, that it was $12,000.

27. The quoted passages are from *Recollections of a Life,* 191–192.

28. "Third floor walk-up" and "straitened circumstances": "The Problems of Alger Hiss," 139, 145.

29. Review finding Hiss's book "not very interesting": *New Yorker,* May 25, 1957, 141. "[H]eavily legalistic" and "dully written": "Historical Notes: The Alger Hiss Story," *Time,* May 13, 1957, 27. Brock Brower's reactions to *In The Court of Public Opinion:* "The Problems of Alger Hiss," 142. Hiss's comments to Brower about valuing his privacy: id., 140.

30. Brower's last paragraph: id., 145.

31. Chambers had made the comment in "Foot in the Door," *National Review,* June 20, 1959. For the circumstances of the comment, see Sam Tanenhaus, *Whittaker Chambers: A Biography,* 507. Brower quoted the comment in "The Problems of Alger Hiss," 145.

32. Quoted passages are from Meyer Zeligs, *Friendship and Fratricide,* xii (1966).

33. Id., xi.

34. Meyer A. Zeligs to Helen Buttenweiser, May 19, 1960, quoted in *Perjury,* 2d ed., 527. Weinstein apparently saw this letter in the Hiss Defense Files. See id., 588.

35. *Friendship and Fratricide,* 385–386.

36. "I can readily appreciate your strong sentiments": Meyer A. Zeligs to Claude B. Cross, March 13, 1961, quoted in *Perjury,* 2d ed., 527. "[C]areful academic neutrality": *Friendship and Fratricide,* xiv.

37. The Earl of Jowitt, *The Strange Case of Alger Hiss*, 5 (1953).
38. "[S]triking differences" between United States and English trials: id., 6–7. "[U]tter fool": id., 200–201. Chambers "quite out of the ordinary": id., 35, 166.
39. Jowitt's suggestion that Chambers had access to the Hiss family typewriter: id., 106–110, 205. "American Dreyfus": Fred J. Cook, *The Unfinished Story of Alger Hiss*, 2, 171–174, 176 (1958).
40. For more details of the *Nation-New Leader* split, see *Crisis on the Left*, 109–115.
41. *Friendship and Fratricide*, 448.
42. The quoted passages are from *Friendship and Fratricide*, ix–x.
43. A *coram nobis* petition is filed by a person who seeks to vacate the prior judgment of a court against him. It must be filed in the same court that rendered the previous judgment. The basis of a *coram nobis* petition is that the previous judgment was based on errors of law "so egregious," as Hiss put it in his memoirs, "that they command the attention of the courts no matter how many years have gone by." *Recollections of a Life*, 212.
44. The most comprehensive treatment of the origins of New Left ideology in the 1950s and 1960s is James Miller, *"Democracy Is in the Streets": From Port Huron to the Siege of Chicago* (1987). See also, on specific issues that were particularly important to the New Left movement, Nigel Young, *An Infantile Disorder?: The Crisis and Decline of the New Left* (1977); Todd Gitlin, *The Whole World Is Watching* (1981); Nancy Zaroulis and Gerald Sullivan, *Who Spoke Up?: American Protest Against the War in Vietnam, 1963–1975* (1984); and James Forman, *The Making of Black Revolutionaries* (1985).
45. Unless otherwise indicated, the details of SDS's history from the late 1950s through 1969 are taken from *"Democracy Is in the Streets."* Quotations from SDS participants are from interviews and documents also cited in id.

    In focusing on SDS I do not mean to suggest that it was the only institution responsible for the emergence of what came to be called the New Left in the late 1960s and 1970s. Until 1965 SDS had only a marginal presence on college and university campuses, and when its membership soared between 1965 and 1968, largely because of early and prominent opposition to the war in Vietnam, the resultant stresses caused it to fragment and collapse. The importance of SDS, for my purposes, is that it played a pivotal role in increasing the resonance of a new brand of radical leftwing politics to college and university students in the late 1960s. That development helped make Alger Hiss become a sought-out lecturer to student bodies, who had shown little interest in him for ten years after his 1956 appearance at Princeton.
46. Details on the early lives of Haber and Hayden can be found in *"Democracy Is in the Streets,"* 23–27, 42–44, 50–54.
47. "Beat" characterization: [Robert] Al[an] Haber, "From Protest to Radicalism: An Appraisal of the Student Movement 1960," reprinted in Mitchell Cohen and Dennis Hale, *The New Student Left*, 41–49 (1967). Haber's dropping out and reentering the Michigan student body: *"Democracy Is in the Streets,"* 27, 40–41, 71; as part of the "avant-garde scene" in Ann Arbor: Haber to Miller, February 28, 1985, quoted in id., 28; as the leading political activist at Michigan in the 1950s: id, 27–28; his "protracted odyssey: id., 28.
48. For the details of the history of the League of Industrial Democracy, see *"Democracy Is in the Streets,"* 28–29. The characterizations of the League's mission as "bring[ing] the message of socialism to American college students," and its status in 1950s as "a kind of dignifed retirement home for aging social democrats" are from id., 28, 29. Haber's decision to

continue an affiliation between SDS and the League: *"Democracy Is in the Streets,"* 65–70. The name change from SLID to SDS: Haber to Miller, February 28, 1985, quoted in id., 38.

49. For more detail, see *"Democracy Is in the Streets,"* 133–140, 235.

50. On Hayden's peregrinations, see id., 45–49, 55–61, 260–273.

51. *The New York Times* coverage of SDS first appeared in Fred Powledge, "The Student Left: Spurring Reform," *The New York Times,* March 15, 1965, pp. 1, 26. CBS Television's initial coverage of SDS was on October 11 and 12, 1965. See *"Democracy Is in the Streets,"* 248–249. The "Port Huron" statement, written by Hayden and revised by members of SDS at a conference at Port Huron, Michigan between June 12 and June 16, 1962, is reproduced in id., 329–374.

52. For details of the Johnson administration's struggles with the selective service system and compulsory military service in the wake of its escalation of the war in Vietnam, see James Patterson, *Great Expectations,* 630–635 (1996).

53. The official collapse of SDS came in June 1969 when it was absorbed by the Progressive Labor Party, an organization modeled on "old-left" totalitarian government, specifically China under Mao Zedong. The Progressive Labor Party had been attempting a takeover of SDS since 1967. See *"Democracy Is in the Streets,"* 284–285, 311. Miller, at 238, refers to "Hayden's old call for a 're-assertion of the personal,'" but does not indicate when the "call" first appeared.

54. The influence of the 1960s antiwar movement on national politics culminated, and peaked, with George McGovern's capture of the 1972 Democratic presidential nomination and his decisive defeat by Nixon.

55. *Recollections of a Life,* 198.

Chapter Five

1. Nixon's comment, in a press conference held after his defeat in the gubernatorial election, was reported in "Transcript of Nixon's News Conference on His Defeat by Brown in Race for Governor of California," *The New York Times,* November 8, 1962, p. 18. For a discussion of the reaction to Hiss's participation in the program, see Allen Weinstein, *Perjury: The Hiss-Chambers Case,* 471 (2d ed., 1997).

2. After resigning from *Time* when it became clear that he would be the defendant in Hiss's 1948 libel suit, Chambers never returned to the *Time* staff. In 1954 he began a friendship with William Buckley, who consulted him before launching the *National Review,* and offered him a position with the magazine in September 1955 (Chambers declined on the grounds of ill health). Between 1955 and his death Chambers was a virtual recluse, and his only public comment on the Hiss case came in the form of a May 9, 1959, article in the *National Review,* in which he opposed efforts to prevent Hiss from traveling abroad by denying him a passport. After his death Chambers was seen as one of the inspirational figures for the *National Review*'s brand of anti-Communist conservativism. For an example of that view of Chambers, see William F. Buckley, ed., *Odyssey of a Friend* (1969), a collection of letters Chambers wrote to Buckley from 1954 to 1961. Details on Buckley's invitation to Chambers to join the *National Review*'s staff, and the origins of Chambers's position on Hiss's travel abroad, are in id., 103–107, 240–241.

3. Earl Latham, *The Communist Controversy in Washington* (1969); George Van Dusen, "The Continuing Hiss: Whittaker Chambers, Alger Hiss, and National Review Conservatism," 11 Cithara 67 (1971); Allen Weinstein, "The Alger Hiss Case Revisited," 41 *Am. Scholar* 121 (1971).

4. "The Alger Hiss Case Revisited," 122, 132.
5. The quoted passages are from "The Alger Hiss Case Revisited," 132.
6. The quoted passages are from Alger Hiss, *Recollections of a Life*, 199–200 (1988).
7. Thomas Moore, "Parting Shots," *Life*, April 7, 1972, 78A.
8. Robert Alan Aurthur, "Hanging Out," *Esquire*, July 1972, 26.
9. Id., 26.
10. For a discussion of how Smith succeeded Whitman as an authorized biographer of Hiss, see Kevin Tierney and Philip Nobile, "Reopening the Pumpkin," *More*, June 1976, 8.
11. Tony Hiss "I Call on Alger," *Rolling Stone*, September 13, 1973, 49–50.
12. Id., 50. The Ellsberg, Berrigan, and "Camden 28" cases each involved efforts on the part of government authorities, during the Nixon administrations, to prosecute persons for allegedly criminal acts related to opposition to the Vietnamese war. The Ellsberg case, which involved Daniel Ellsberg's leaking of classified Defense Department papers to *The New York Times* and *Washington Post*, resulted in a decision in which the Nixon administration received a slap on the wrist by the Supreme Court of the United States. See *New York Times Co. v. United States*, 403 U.S. 713 (1971).
13. Id.
14. Id., 53.
15. Quoted in Tony Hiss, *Laughing Last*, 140 (1977).
16. The review was John A. P. Millett, "The Power of the Accuser," 1, *Psychiatry and Social Science Review*, 4–8 (April 1967). The review contained a passage that Priscilla obviously liked, and that Allen Weinstein quoted in *Perjury*, 484. It read, in part:
    > Dr. Zeligs has so little to say about Priscilla Hiss, whose complete devotion and loyalty to her husband throughout the years of his imprisonment and whose unaided dedication to the education of their son, Tony, made possible for Hiss a return to a welcoming family. Her patient acceptance of the situation in which she found herself . . . exhibited a spiritual courage which was the best proof of the integrity which had been so cruelly questioned during the trials.
17. The quoted passages are from *Laughing Last*, 2.
18. Id., 8–9, 10, 13, 14, 18, 35, 39–40, 52–53.
19. Id., 6–7.
20. Id., 11.
21. Id., 10, 53.
22. "[T]ough old battleax": Id., 5.
23. "[H]e can stick around if he'll marry here right away": Id., 42. Priscilla disliking Cambridge: id., 64. The Hisses in Washington: Id., 73.
24. Id., 137, 139–140.
25. Id., 140, 141, 142.
26. Id., 141, 174, 175.
27. Id., 176.
28. "[W]ent back to living with Prossy": Id., 176. "I finally got into bed with a girl": Id., 176–177.
29. Id., 177.
30. Id., 135.
31. Id., 190.
32. Id., 135–136.
33. John Chabot Smith, *Alger Hiss: The True Story*, 286 (Timothy), 288 (Priscilla) (1976).

34. Id., 406–408.
35. Id., 408–409.
36. Id., 410–411.
37. Id., 412–414.
38. Id., 414–416.
39. Id., 440.
40. Id., 442.
41. The quoted passage is from *Laughing Last*, 191.
42. Allen Weinstein, "F.B.I.'s Hiss Files Show Bumbling, Not Malice," *The New York Times*, February 1, 1976, sect. 4, p. 9.
43. Philip Nobile, "The State of the Art of Alger Hiss," *Harper's*, July 1976, 67, 73.
44. Id., 68.
45. Id., 68–73.
46. Id., 73, 76.
47. Id., 67. Charles Alan Wright represented Richard Nixon in the summer of 1973 as "special legal consultant," arguing unsuccessfully before Judge John Sirica that the constitutional separation of powers protected Nixon from turning over White House tape recordings to a special prosecutor, Archibald Cox. See Wright's obituary in the *The New York Times*, July 9, 2000.
48. Id., 68.
49. Id., 68.
50. Id., 73.
51. Id., 74.
52. "Reasonable men may differ": Id., 76.
53. Id., 73.
54. *Laughing Last*, 179.

CHAPTER SIX

1. Allen Weinstein, quoted in Philip Nobile, "Allen Weinstein: Who Is He and What Has He Got on Alger Hiss?" *Politicks*, February 28, 1978, 4, 26.
2. Allen Weinstein, quoted in "Allen Weinstein," 26.
3. Id., 27.
4. Id.
5. See Allen Weinstein, *Perjury: The Hiss-Chambers Case*, 443 (2d ed., 1997), quoting Edward McLean to Alger Hiss, February 3, 1950, in Hiss Defense Files, and an interview with Robert von Mehren, December 11, 1974, for the details of McLean's firm withdrawal from the Hiss case.
6. "[T]he whole truth": William Marbury to Meyer Zeligs, May 6, 1964, quoted in Meyer A. Zeligs, *Friendship and Fratricide*, 405 (1967). "[W]rong in his assumption of fact": Alger Hiss to Meyer Zeligs, quoted in *Friendship and Fratricide*, 405–406. Zeligs stated that Hiss had written him that he received a letter from Marbury in December 1963, indicating that he suspected Alger of covering up for Priscilla. Id. The Marbury memorandum was entitled "The Hiss Case," and was prepared by Marbury in late 1948, about the time that Hiss was indicted for perjury. Marbury also sent a copy to Weinstein: see *Perjury*, 2d ed., 538.
7. Allen Weinstein, quoted in "Allen Weinstein," 26.
8. Id., 26, 27.

9. Id., 27.

10. Herbert Solow's notarized memorandum of Chambers's activities was actually four documents, the original memo, dated November 12, 1938, and three supplemental memos, dated between December 3 and December 17, 1938. Weinstein found all the memos in Herbert Solow's papers in the Hoover Institute at Stanford University.

11. Allen Weinstein, quoted in "Allen Weinstein," 27. Weinstein acknowledged the help of Meyer Schapiro in estimating the dates of the letters Chambers wrote in *Perjury: The Hiss-Chambers Case*, 625 (1st ed., 1978).

12. Allen Weinstein, quoted in "Allen Weinstein," 27.

13. "[Q]ualified historical researchers": Lesley Oelsner, "25 Years Later, the FBI Will Tell What it Knew," *The New York Times*, November 18, 1973, sect. 4, p. 3. Weinstein's receiving only a few hundred heavily edited pages by 1975: Lesley Oeslner, "Historian Gets a Few FBI Hiss Files," *The New York Times*, January 28, 1974, p. 53. Court orders releasing FBI files: "Records on Hiss Released by FBI," *The New York Times*, September 4, 1975, p. 38. Weinstein's announcement that the FBI files showed no evidence of a conspiracy: Allen Weinstein, "FBI's Hiss Files Show Bumbling, Not Malice," *The New York Times*, February 1, 1976, sect. 4, p. 9; Allen Weinstein, "On the Search for Smoking Guns: The Hiss and Rosenberg Files," *New Republic*, February 14, 1976, 16, 20.

14. Allen Weinstein, quoted in "Allen Weinstein," 4.

15. Id.

16. Id., 4–5.

17. Id., 5.

18. Id.

19. Alger Hiss, quoted in "Allen Weinstein," 4.

20. George F. Will, "The Myth of Alger Hiss," *Newsweek*, March 20, 1978, 96; Christopher Lehmann-Haupt, "Books of the Times," *The New York Times*, April 7, 1978, p. C25; Irving Howe, "Alger Hiss Retried," *The New York Times Book Review*, April 9, 1978, p. 1; Gary Wills, "The Honor of Alger Hiss," *The New York Review of Books*, April 20, 1978, 28, 30; Alfred Kazin, "Why Hiss Can't Confess," *Esquire*, March 28, 1978, 21.

21. "The Honor of Alger Hiss," 30; T. S. Matthews, "Books Considered," *New Republic*, April 8, 1978, 27, 29.

22. Keven Tierney and Philip Nobile, "Reopening The Pumpkin," *More*, June, 1976, 8, 9, quoting Allen Weinstein.

23. Peter Kihss, quoted in "Reopening The Pumpkin," 8.

24. Peter Kihss, "Professor Says Alger Hiss Lied About his Links With Chambers," *The New York Times*, March 18, 1976, pp. 1, 74.

25. Peter Kihss, "Hiss Says FBI Files Support Some of his Claims of Innocence," *The New York Times*, March 19, 1976, pp. 1, 10.

26. Allen Weinstein, "Was Alger Hiss Framed?" *The New York Review of Books*, April 1, 1976, 14, 16, 19.

27. "Consumed by exchanges with critics": "Reopening The Pumpkin," 9. Peter Irons's attack on Hiss took place at an April 8, 1976, panel discussion on the Hiss case at the annual meeting of the Organization of American Historians. See Alden Whitman, "Historian Challenged on Report That Hiss Lied About Chambers," *The New York Times*, April 9, 1976, p. 20. On Irons's friendship with Hiss, see Peter Irons, *The New Deal Lawyers*, xi (1982). Sherrill's critique of Weinstein was in "Innocent, a New Book Says—Guilty, Another Will

Say—and the Trial Goes On," *The New York Times Book Review,* April 25, 26, pp. 31–32. For Weinstein's exchanges with scholarly critics of his *New York Review* essay, see the exchange of letters in *The New York Review of Books,* May 27, 1976, pp. 32–48.

28. Weinstein, "Nixon v. Hiss," *Esquire,* November 1975, 73.

29. "On the Search For Smoking Guns," 16.

30. "FBI's Hiss Files Reveal Bumbling, Not Malice," 9.

31. "Claims of Innocence," 10.

32. "Reopening The Pumpkin," 9.

33. See *Perjury,* 1st ed., 123–124, 546, 645–646.

34. Alger Hiss's marked copy of the page proofs of the 1978 edition of *Perjury* is in the Alger Hiss Papers, Special Collections, Harvard Law School Library. Hiss's marginal comments about Weinstein's characterizations of his demeanor at the August 17, 1948, and August 25, 1948, hearings were on pages 32, 33, and 43 of his copy of the page proofs. His claim that Weinstein had misquoted was in the margin of page 181.

35. "I grew up in a very liberal milieu . . .": Victor Navasky to John F. Baker, quoted in *Publishers Weekly,* October 10, 1980. On Elisabeth Irwin High School, and Navasky's attendance there, see Ronald Radosh, *Commies,* 25–28 (2001).

36. Navasky's being awed by Hiss: David Remnick, "Alger Hiss: Unforgiven and Unforgiving," *Washington Post* magazine, October 12, 1986, 23, 31. "Degradation ceremony": Navasky to *Contemporary Authors Online,* June 6, 2000.

37. "Transformation of Historical Ambiguity," 219.

38. Id., 222–223.

39. I have consulted many of the archival sources Weinstein used, and, with some trivial exceptions, his citations to those sources are accurate. But some of his citations were to personal interviews or letters in private collections that cannot be easily verified.

For example, Weinstein made a claim in *Perjury* that, if accurate, was very damaging to Hiss. He wrote that Priscilla Hiss had once revealed that she was "sick of all the lies and cover-ups" connected with the Hiss case. The paragraph in which Weinstein quoted Priscilla's comment read as follows:

> [I]n 1968, shortly after publication of Zeligs's book left Mrs. Hiss embittered over the author's treatment of her, Priscilla was visiting family members in Chicago . . . when, according to a guest of the family, someone made a "tactless remark" about the case over dinner one night at her sister's house. Priscilla exploded and, according to another guest: 'Pros announced that she was sick of all the lies and cover-ups—or whatever it was that she said. Jane didn't remember the words but immediately remembered the painful tension between Pros and her sister-in-law, each being fairly polite and covering up intense dislike and animosity. Jane remembers that the party blew up and Prossy was the cause.'

Perjury, 1st ed., 546. At the end of the quotation Weinstein placed an endnote, which read as follows: "Abbott Millspaugh to the author, November 18, 1973; Roberta Fansler to Alden Whitman, December 7, 1974, courtesy of Mr. Whitman." Id., 632. A close reading of the quoted paragraph, along with the endnote, would reveal that the source for the "lies and cover-ups" quote was Abbott Millspaugh, relying on his memory of a conversation his wife Jane had overheard five years earlier. In essence, a man had written Allen Weinstein in 1973 that in 1968 his wife had remembered tension between Priscilla Hiss and her sister-in-law at a dinner party, that Priscilla had said *something like* "she was sick of all the lies and cover-ups," and that the party subsequently "blew up" because of Priscilla's attitude. There was no other source for the statement. Roberta Fansler's December 7, 1974, letter to Alden Whitman, which Weinstein also cited in the endnote, only stated that a "tactless remark" about the Hiss case had been made at a dinner party at the house of Priscilla Hiss's sister.

The "lies and cover-ups" statement thus had far weaker corroboration than Weinstein's paragraph implied. The endnote, on its face, makes it difficult for a reader to identify who the corroborating source for the statement was. Finally, both the sources Weinstein cited were in his personal files, to which he has restricted access.

40. Readers interested in the details of those exchanges can consult G. Edward White, "Alger Hiss's Campaign for Vindication," 83, Boston U. L. Rev. 1–146 (2003).

41. Victor Navasky, "The Case Not Proved against Alger Hiss," *Nation*, April 8, 1978, 393, 394.

42. Id.

43. Id., 394–397.

44. See *Perjury*, 1st ed., 128–129, indicating that Maxim Lieber confirmed details of Chambers's life as a member of the Communist Party and citing interviews with Lieber. "[M]ade all these things up from whole cloth": Navasky, "The Case Not Proved," 397, quoting Lieber. Weinstein's reporting Lieber as having confirmed most of the details of *Witness* is in *Perjury*, 1st ed., 129, citing May 10 and May 13, 1975, interviews with Lieber. "[F]alse colors": Michael Kernan, "A Literary Skirmish Over Hiss," *Washington Post*, April 6, 1978, p. B1.

45. Krieger's denials: "The Case Not Proved," 396, quoting Krieger. Weinstein's use of Krieger: See *Perjury*, 1st ed., 100. "I do hope . . . will help to prove that Alger was framed": Weinstein quoted these comments from a letter Krieger had written him in "Perjury, Take Three," *New Republic*, March 29, 1978, 16, 19.

46. The quoted passages are from "The Case Not Proved," 401.

47. Weinstein's intention to "write a thorough article about Navasky's criticism": "Author Defends Hiss Book against Attack in Article," *The New York Times*, April 6, 1978, p. A17 (quoting Weinstein). Weinstein's invitation to examine his tapes and notes: "A Literary Skirmish Over Hiss," p. B3 (quoting Weinstein).

48. "Arguments (New and Old) About the Hiss Case," *Encounter*, March, 1979, 82 (letter from Margaret Stern).

49. Hiss's teaming up with William Reuben: *Laughing Last*, 190.

50. The quoted passages are from Alexander Cockburn, "Krieger Victorious Over Hiss Author" *Village Voice*, May 28, 1979, pp. 31, 77.

51. *Perjury*, 1st ed., 100. Weinstein erroneously gave the last name of Fred Beal, the author of *Proletarian Journey*, as Beals.

52. At about the same time that the Krieger suit was being settled, Victor Navasky made a decision that resulted in the *Nation*'s corporate owner, National Enterprises, joining Weinstein, Alfred A. Knopf, and the *New Republic* as defendants in lawsuits. In March 1979 Navasky received, from an undisclosed source, an advance copy of former President Gerald Ford's memoirs, about to be published by Harper and Row. Believing that Ford's memoirs, which dealt with his controversial pardon of Richard Nixon for any possible criminal offenses related to the Watergate burglary, were "hot news," Navasky excerpted and paraphrased portions of the memoirs, centering on Ford's account of his decision to pardon Nixon, in an April 3, 1979, article in the *Nation* entitled "The Ford Memoirs: Behind the Nixon Pardon." Harper and Row and the *Reader's Digest*, which had copyright agreements with Ford that gave them exclusive rights to the publication of his memoirs, sued the *Nation*'s corporate owner, National Enterprises, for copyright infringement, claiming that Navasky's belief that the Ford memoir was "hot news" did not constitute "fair use" under the existing fed-

eral copyright statute. They proved that *Time*, which had agreed to pay them $12,500 for the right to run an excerpt from Ford's memoirs, had declined to do so after Navasky's *Nation* article appeared.

National Enterprises lost at the district court level, won a reversal before the U.S. Court of Appeals for the Second Circuit, and eventually lost before the Supreme Court. Navasky's "fair use" defense, that some of the details of Ford's pardon were "hot news" and thus "fair use" of copyrighted material, did not succeed, ultimately, because the "hot news" he identified—that in the course of considering the pardon Ford had had a conversation with Alexander Haig that might have constituted obstruction of justice—had already been revealed in a 1974 Congressional hearing. See Harper and Row Publishers et al. v. Nation Enterprises et al., 557 F. Supp. 1067 (1983) (the district court decision), 723 F.2d. 195 (1983) (the Court of Appeals for the Second Circuit's reversal of the district court), 471 U.S. 539 (1985) (the Supreme Court of the United States' reversal of the Court of Appeals, and reinstatement of the district court's judgment against Nation Enterprises).

53. Details of settlements are rarely made public, but a large gap between the amount demanded by a plaintiff in a libel action, especially when punitive damages are an option, and the actual settlement, especially when it includes a public apology, is a common feature of libel litigation.

54. "Krieger Victorious," 77.

55. *Perjury*, 1st ed., 591.

56. *Perjury*, 2d ed., 532.

57. Sam Tanenhaus, *Whittaker Chambers: A Biography*, 520, 534, 545, 553, 554, 555, 566 (1997). For evidence that Tanenhaus had seen the Solow memorandum, see id., 522, 542 note 40.

58. Id., 607.

59. Hiss's *coram nobis* petition was reported as *In re Hiss*, 542 F. Supp. 973 (S.D.N.Y. 1982). For Hiss's comment that the normal ten-day requirement for governmental responses to requests for information under the Freedom of Information Act had in his case "stretched to four years," see *Recollections*, 216. For Judge Owen's finding that the original jury verdict in Hiss's second perjury trial was amply supported by the evidence, see *In re Hiss*, 542 F. Supp. at 799.

60. For Hiss's comment on the delay in getting the government to respond to his request for information under the Freedom of Information Act, see *Recollections*, 224. For Owen's statement see 542 F. Supp. at 999.

61. *Recollections*, 224.

62. Reuben's critique was William A. Reuben, *Footnote on a Historic Case: In re Alger Hiss* (1983). For Hiss's invocation of Reuben's pamphlet, and his reactions to the judges who decided his petition, see *Recollections*, 224–225.

CHAPTER SEVEN

1. John Lowenthal, *The Trials of Alger Hiss*, ISBN 1-55974-239-9 (1980), dust jacket.

2. "Concealed Enemies" was produced by Peter B. Cook and directed by Jeff Blockiner (with Lindsay Law and David Elstein as executive producers). The actors playing the principal characters in the Hiss-Chambers case were Edward Heerman as Alger Hiss, Maria Tacci as Priscilla Hiss, John Harkin as Whittaker Chambers, Peter Riegert as Richard Nixon, Raymond Serra as J. Edgar Hoover, Richard Dysart as Lloyd Striker, and Frederick Cooper as Thomas Murphy. Of Hiss's lawyers, Harold Rosenwald, played by Michael Tucker, re-

ceived far more attention than William Marbury or Edward McLean, probably because "Concealed Enemies" chose to emphasize the Hiss defense's unsuccessful effort to use psychiatric testimony about Chambers at the second trial, a strategy that originated with Rosenwald.

3. The last comment about Dulles was technically accurate, but Dulles had not appeared voluntarily for the prosecution. At the first trial Murphy had subpoenaed him as a rebuttal witness, hoping to show that in the course of discussing the Carnegie presidency with Dulles, Hiss had misled Dulles about the FBI investigation of him as a security risk. Lloyd Stryker strongly objected to Dulles's testimony on the ground that it did not contradict anything Hiss had said in court, and thus he had been inappropriately been called as rebuttal witness. For more detail, see *The First Trial: United States of America vs. Alger Hiss, Stenographer's Minutes,* pp. 2551–2667 (1948) (Microfilm edition, Scholarly Resources, Inc.).

4. See Sam Tanenhaus, *Whittaker Chambers: A Biography,* 477–478, 487, 497 (1997).

5. Remnick's impression of Hiss: David Remnick, "Alger Hiss: Unforgiven and Unforgiving," *Washington Post* magazine, October 12, 1986, p. 23.

6. Tony Hiss, *Laughing Last,* 185 (1977); "Unforgiven and Unforgiving," pp. 28, 32, 33.

7. The Supreme Court has discretion to grant or to deny certiorari petitions, and denies most of the ones submitted to it. To grant a petition, the votes of four out of nine justices are required. Once granted, a case is set for argument before the Court.

8. "Unforgiven and Unforgiving," 29, 33, 34.

9. Id., 23, 24, 25, 29.

10. Id., 24, 28, 29.

11. Id., 21, 30.

12. Id., 29, 31, 34.

13. Id., 25, 26, 31.

14. Id., 27, 28, 31.

15. Id., 27, 31, 32, 34.

16. Id., 23. Delmore Schwartz was a writer and editor who was born in 1913. In 1949 he was an associate editor of the *Partisan Review* and a visiting lecturer at Princeton. He suffered from mental illness, and his work, mainly of poetry, received mixed reviews. He had published an article in the *Marxist Quarterly,* a journal with a Trotskyite orientation, in 1937, but his identification with the *Partisan Review* in the late 1940s would have signaled that he held an anti-Communist perspective. It is unclear how he had become acquainted with Hiss. Remnick had probably seen the journal entry in *Portrait of Delmore: Journals and Notes of Delmore Schwartz, 1939–1959,* which was published in 1986. On Schwartz, see Richard McDougall, *Delmore Schwartz* (1974). On the *Partisan Review* in the 1940s, see James Burkhart Gilbert, *Writers and Partisans,* 253–282 (1968).

17. Id., 29, 33, 35.

18. Id., 27, 35.

19. Id., 27, 29, 35.

20. The quoted passages are from id., 27.

21. Alger Hiss, *Recollections of Life* (1988).

22. Hiss's attitude toward Nixon and Chambers in the Remnick interview: "Unforgiven and Unforgiving," 29. Hiss's attitude towards Nixon and Chambers in *Recollections of a Life,* 202.

23. *Recollections of a Life,* 217–220.

24. Id., 216, 217, 224, 225.

25. Id., 225.

26. The principal reviews of *Recollections of a Life* were Jim Christy, "The Man Behind the Symbol," *Toronto Star*, July 23, 1988, p. M6; Michael Kazin, "Alger Hiss's Unreflective Look Back," *Washington Post*, May 10, 1988, p. E1; Christopher Lehmann-Haupt, "Alger Hiss Recalls Emotional Side of His Two Trials," *The New York Times*, May 12, 1988, p. C33; Patricia MacMillan, "Alger Hiss's Wry Look Back," *Chicago Tribune*, July 7, 1988, p. C3; Connor Cruise O'Brien, "Truth-Teller or Dreyfus of Today?" *London Times*, August 28, 1988, p. 1; Michael Rogin, "Allegories of Alger," *Nation*, September 26, 1988, 242–246; George Sirgiovanni, "One More Denial," *New Leader*, June 13, 1988, 18–19; Dennis Wrong, "The Rest of Him," *The New York Times Book Review*, August 7, 1988, p. G18.

27. See, for example, Christy, "The Man Behind the Symbol," O'Brien, "Truth-Teller," and Rogin, "Allegories of Alger."

28. This response to *Recollections of a Life* can be found in O'Brien, "Truth-Teller," and Rogin, "Allegories of Alger," who were sympathetic to Hiss, and Sirgiovanni, "One More Denial," and Wrong, "The Rest of Him," who were not.

29. Notably Kazin, "Alger Hiss's Unreflective Look Back," and Sirgiovanni, "One More Denial."

30. See MacMillan, "Alger Hiss's Wry Look Back," and O'Brien, "Truth-Teller."

31. Notably O'Brien, "Truth-Teller," and Rogin, "Allegories of Alger."

32. My account, in the next several pages, of Hiss's temporary "exoneration" by Russian general Dmitri Volkogonov is drawn from the following sources: David Margolick, "After 40 Years, A Postscript on Hiss," *The New York Times*, October 29, 1992, p. B14; Jeffrey A. Frank, "Stalin Biographer Offers Latest Twist in Hiss Case," *Washington Post*, October 31, 1992, p. A3; Allen Weinstein, "Reopening a Cold War Mystery," *Washington Post*, November 4, 1992, p. A19; Serge Schmemann, "Russian General Retreats on Hiss," *The New York Times*, December 17, 1992, p. A17; Bill Gertz, "Russian General Denies He's Able to Clear Hiss," *Washington Times*, December 18, 1992, p. A4; George F. Will, 'Exoneration' of Alger Hiss," *Newsweek*, January 11, 1993, p. 66; Jacob Cohen, "Innocent After All?" *National Review*, January 18, 1993, pp. 26–33; and Amos Perlmutter, "Soviet Historiography, Western Journalism," *National Review*, January 18, 1993, pp. 30–31. Additional sources are quoted in subsequent endnotes.

33. Lowenthal's meeting with Volkogonov and Volkogonov's memorandum are quoted in "After 40 Years," B14.

34. Lowenthal's videotape is quoted in "Russian General Denies," A4. The videotape was shown at Hiss and Lowenthal's October 29, 1992, news conference, which was held at the Algonquin Hotel in New York and broadcast on CNN. See Tony Hiss, "My Father's Honor," *New Yorker*, November 16, 1992, 100.

35. Hiss's comments to *The Times* are quoted in "After 40 Years," p. B14. Hiss's comments to the *Post* are quoted in "Stalin Biographer," p. A3.

36. Lowenthal's comment to *The Times* was quoted in "After 40 Years," p. B14 and his comment to the *Post* was quoted in "Stalin Biographer," p. A3. He made the comments about Chambers being a "total fantasist" and the Volkogonov statement's "pull[ing] the rug from under" his account of the Hiss case to Michael Wines for an article, "Hiss Case's Bogeymen Are Still Not at Rest," *The New York Times*, December 13, 1992, sect. 4, p. 6.

37. Quoted in "Stalin Biographer," p. A3.

38. See "'Exoneration' of Alger Hiss," p. 66.

39. *Newsweek* article: Tom Post, " 'He Was Never a Soviet Spy,'" *Newsweek*, November 9, 1992, p. 31, quoting Hiss. Tony Hiss's comments: "My Father's Honor," 100.

40. Buckley was quoted in "After 40 Years," p. B14 and "Stalin Biographer," p. A3. Dallin, Pipes, and Tucker were quoted in "After 40 Years," p. B14.

41. See Allen Weinstein and Alexander Vassiliev, *The Haunted Wood*, xi–xii (1999).

42. Weinstein's comments to *The Times* are quoted in "After 40 Years," p. B14. Weinstein's comments to the *Post* are quoted in "Stalin Biographer," p. A3.

43. "Reopening a Cold War Mystery," pp. A19–A21.

44. Weinstein's comments: id., A20. Volkogonov's letter to the *Independent Gazette* was quoted in "Russian General Retreats on Hiss," p. A17.

45. No report of Volkogonov's letter to the Gazette appearing in American newspapers until December 17: see "'Exoneration' of Alger Hiss," 66; "Soviet Historiography, Western Journalism," 30. Broadcast of the contents of the letter by the Federal Broadcast Information Service: "Hiss Case's Bogeyman," 6. Television networks failing to cover Volkogonov's letter to the *Gazette:* "'Exoneration' of Alger Hiss," 66.

46. Quoted in "Russian General Retreats on Hiss," p. A17.

47. Hiss's comments to *The Times* were quoted in "Russian General Retreats on Hiss," p. A17. The *Washington Times'* use of the photograph of Hiss and Johnson: see "Russian General Denies," p. A4.

48. "The 'Exoneration' of Alger Hiss," 66.

49. Hiss's claim is quoted in "After 40 Years," p. B14.

50. See Harvey Klehr, John Earl Haynes, and Fridrikh Igorevich Firsov, *The Secret World of American Communism*, v, xvii–xviii (1995).

51. Klehr, Haynes, and Firsov, *The Secret World of American Communism*, 73–83, 106–110.

52. Id., 301–302, 304–308, 309–321.

53. See John Earl Haynes and Harvey Klehr, *Venona: Decoding Soviet Espionage in America*, 2–4 (1999).

54. Id., 4–7, 47–56.

55. Id., 9.

56. *Venona*, 1579 GRU, New York to Moscow, September 28, 1943, quoted in id., 170.

57. Schwartz, Moosen, and Gorchoff as GRU agents controlled by Mikhailov: *Venona*, 177, 351, 359, 364. NKVD's authority to demand information from the GRU: see David J. Dallin, *Soviet Espionage in America*, 403–405 (1955).

58. *Venona*, 1822, KGB [NKVD] Washington to KGB Moscow, March 30, 1945, quoted in *Venona*, 171. "Gromov" was the alias of Anatoli Borisovich Gorsky, the controller of Washington-based NKVD agents at the time.

59. *Venona*, 340.

60. Akhmerov had been the resident handler of Guy Burgess, Anthony Blunt, Donald Maclean, and Kim Philby, the celebrated British Soviet spies, and had been transferred to Washington a year after Maclean was given a sensitive position in the British Embassy in Washington in 1944. For a brief biography of Gromov, see id., 392.

61. See Yuri Modin, *My Five Cambridge Friends*, 85–89, 99–101 (1994), a memoir by one of the Soviet controllers of Blunt, Burgess, Cairncross, Maclean, and Philby. Modin worked closely with Gromov in the handling of the "Cambridge Five."

62. See Christopher Andrew and Vasili Mitrokhin, *The Sword and the Shield*, 559 (1999) for the statement that Ales resembles a contraction of "Alger Hiss" in Cyrillic, and Christopher Andrew and Oleg Gordievsky, *KGB*, 285 (1999), for the statement by former NKVD official Oleg Gordievsky that Hiss's code name was Ales.

63. *Venona*, 172.

64. Id., 365.

65. In the second edition of *Perjury*, Allen Weinstein, in discussing the 1945 Gromov cable, stated, at 511, that "[m]ost likely" the Pol in the cable referred to Silvermaster. But there is no evidence that Hiss worked with Silvermaster or any of the participants in his network, which was affiliated with the NKVD. See *The Haunted Wood*, 157–166.

66. Fitin to Merkulov, April 25, 1945, File 43072, Vol. 1, pp. 96–97, NKVD (KGB) Archives, Moscow, quoted in *The Haunted Wood*, 269.

67. Harold Glasser as Ruble: *Venona*, 350. Gromov as Vadim: *The Haunted Wood*, 401. Weinstein and Vassiliev did not identify *Venona* as the source of Gromov's code name, nor indicated where they had located it.

68. Bentley made this statement to the FBI on November 30, 1945. See *The Secret World of American Communism*, 320.

69. Whittaker Chambers, *Witness*, 429–430 (1952).

70. *The Secret World of American Communism*, 321.

71. For Massing's original story, which she gave to the FBI in December 1948, see Weinstein, *Perjury*, 2d ed., 176–177; for the rebuttal of it at Hiss's second trial, see id., 425.

72. File 36857, Vol. 1, p. 23, NKVD Archives, quoted in *The Haunted Wood*, 5–6.

73. Moscow's cable to Bazarov: File 36857, Vol. 1, p. 24, NKVD Archives, quoted in id., 7. Akhmerov's cable to Moscow: File 36857, Vol. 1, p. 25, NKVD Archives, quoted in id., 8.

74. For more detail on Straight, see *Venona*, 152–157. Akhmerov's cable to Moscow: File 58380, Vol. 1, pp. 73–74, NKVD Archives, quoted in *The Haunted Wood*, 75–76.

75. The quoted passage is from File 58380, Vol. 1, p. 83, NKVD Archives, quoted in id., 80.

76. Tony Hiss, *The View from Alger's Window*, 240 (1999). After Alger's death Tony had written a eulogy, "Going Gently," in the December 2, 1996, *New Yorker*, at 46, in which he said that it was "only in his very last year, his ninety-second, that frailty actually kept him close to home . . . it was almost impossible to even to think about going outdoors." Hiss was admitted to Lenox Hill Hospital in mid-October with "acute bronchitis," Tony added, and remained there until he died. Id.

77. Hiss's claim that he had only visited the Moscow subway when he stopped there after Yalta: Michael Dobbs, "New Documents Name American As Soviet Spy," *Washington Post*, March 6, 1996, p. A1. Cable as "the smoking gun in the Hiss case": Eric Breindel, "New Evidence in Hiss Case," *Wall Street Journal*, March 14, 1996, p. A18.

78. Transcript #6229–1, *ABC World News Tonight*, November 15, 1996.

79. Bart Barnes, "Alger His Convicted in Celebrate Spy Case, Dies at 92," *Washington Post*, November 16, 1996, p. A1.

80. Robert D. Novack, "Alger Hiss: Traitor or Fall Guy," *Chicago Sun-Times*, November 21, 1996, p. 35.

81. Evan Thomas, "An American Melodrama," *Newsweek*, November 25, 1996, 35.

82. George Will, "Emblem of the Governing Class," *Washington Post*, November 21, 1996, p. A25.

83. Victor Navasky, Editorial, *Nation*, December 9, 1996, 6–7.

84. Janny Scott, "Alger Hiss, Divisive Icon of the Cold War, Dies at 92," *The New York Times*, November 16, 1996, p. 1, 31.

85. See Sam Tanenhaus, "Hiss Case 'Smoking Gun?' " *The New York Times*, October 15, 1993, p. A35; Jeffrey A. Frank, "Unending Trial of Alger Hiss," *Washington Post*, October 29, 1993, pp. B1, B4. See also Maria Schmidt, "The Hiss Dossier: A Historian's Report," *New Republic*, November 8, 1993, 17–18, 20.

86. See Ethan Klingsberg, "Case Closed on Alger Hiss?" *Nation*, November 8, 1993, 528–532.

87. Quoted in "Alger Hiss, Divisive Icon of the Cold War," 31.

88. Thomas Powers, "The Plot Thickens," *The New York Review of Books*, May 11, 2000, p. 53, 54. Not everyone agreed with Powers. John Lowenthal, in an impassioned essay, "Venona and Alger Hiss," 15, *Intelligence and National Security*, 98–130 (2000), said that Powers's claim that "no serious scholar" would now maintain that Hiss was innocent was incorrect, citing "twelve serious scholars who currently do not believe Chambers's claims against Hiss." Id., 129. Lowenthal's essay was a remarkable summary of the case for Hiss's innocence, containing attacks on virtually all of the evidence of Hiss's complicity that had surfaced since Chambers's first accusation. It also included an effort to buttress Volkogonov's 1992 "exoneration" of Hiss. Id., 128–129.

89. "The Plot Thickens," 55.

90. Id., 60.

91. Id.

CHAPTER EIGHT

1. For the full quotation from Chambers, see chapter four, endnote 13, p. 271.

2. For the Timothy Hobson story, as told by Tony Hiss, see *The View from Alger's Window*, 52–54 (1999). The dustjacket comment on that book was from Lawrence Wechsler, a staff writer for the *New Yorker*, who a year earlier had published *Calamities of Exile*, a collection of three extended essays on political exiles and their opposition to totalitarian regimes.

3. The most authoritative and accessible summary of the psychological concept of integration is Roy F. Bannister, "The Self," in Daniel T. Gilbert, Susan T. Fiske, and Gardner Lindzey, eds., *The Handbook of Social Psychology*, Vol. 1, 680–727 (4th ed., 2 vols., 1998). Particularly useful for me, in thinking about Alger Hiss, have been the sections on "self-deception processes," pp. 690–691, and "maintaining consistency," pp. 691–692. See also S. E. Taylor, "Adjustment to Threatening Events: A Theory of Cognitive Adaptation," 38, *American Psychologist*, 1161–1173 (1983).

Edward L. Deci and Richard M. Ryan, "A Motivational Approach to Self: Integration in Personality," in Richard A. Diensthier, ed., *Perspectives in Motivation*, 237–289 (1991) give a working definition of the concept of integration that I find applicable to Hiss. Deci and Ryan define integration as

> [T]he most basic developmental strivings of the self that can be considered at two levels of analysis. First, there is the tendency towards unity in one's "self," that is, toward coherence in one's regulatory activity and experience. . . . Second, there is the tendency toward interacting in a coherent and meaningful way with others so as to experience satisfying personal relationships with individuals and a harmonious relation to the larger social order.

Personal "development," Deci and Ryan maintain,

> involves the integrative tendency of the self as it meets the forces and events that arise internally . . . and externally. . . . Integration, and thus development, results when the person is able to make contact with and assimilate events.

Id., 243–244.

4. See Pavel Sudoplatov and Anatoli Sudoplatov, *Special Tasks*, 229 (1994); Yuri Modin, the Soviet controller of the "Cambridge Five," *My Five Cambridge Friends*, 238–242 (1994). For

more detail on the "Cambridge Five"'s connections to Soviet espionage in America, see Verne W. Newton, *The Cambridge Spies* (1991).

5. *Recollections of a Life*, 226.

6. Fuchs to William J. Skardon (an intelligence offer for MI5, the British domestic intelligence agency at the time), January 27, 1950, quoted in Robert Chadwell Williams, *Klaus Fuchs, Atom Spy*, 184 (1987).

7. *Klaus Fuchs, Atom Spy*, 184.

AFTERWORD

1. See HUAC Hearing, Vol. 10, pp. 921–925, in which John Davis had an exchange with Karl E. Mundt, Robert Stripling, and Richard Nixon about Hiss's difficulty in obtaining access to records he wanted to consult.

INDEX